Minerva's Message
Stabilizing the French Revolution

The French National Institute, including the Class of Moral and Political Sciences (CMPS), was established during the French Revolution to replace the abolished Ancien Régime academies. In *Minerva's Message* Martin Staum explores how what began as the institutionalization of critical Enlightenment social science culture became a tool to end revolutionary turmoil and establish social order.

In theory the CMPS was set up to enshrine the human and social studies that were at the heart of Enlightenment culture. Staum illustrates, however, that the Institute helped transform key ideas of the Enlightenment to maintain civil rights while upholding social stability, and that the social and political assumptions on which it was based affected notions of social science. He traces the careers of individual members and the factions within the Institute, arguing that discord within it reflected the unravelling of Enlightenment culture.

Minerva's Message presents a valuable overview of the intellectual life of the period and brings together new evidence about the social sciences in their nascent period.

MARTIN S. STAUM is professor of history, University of Calgary.

Minerva's Message

Stabilizing the French Revolution

MARTIN S. STAUM

McGill-Queen's University Press
Montreal & Kingston • London • Buffalo

Legal deposit fourth quarter 1996
Bibliothèque nationale du Québec

Printed in the United States on acid-free paper

This book has been published with the help of a grant
from the Humanities and Social Science Federation of
Canada, using funds provided by the Social Sciences and
Humanities Research Council of Canada. Publication has
also been made possible, in part, by a grant from the
Endowment Fund of the University of Calgary.

Canadian Cataloguing in Publication Data

Staum, Martin S., 1943–
  Minerva's message: stabilizing the French Revolution
  Includes bibliographical references and index.
  ISBN 0-7735-1442-2
  1. France – Intellectual life – 18th century – Political
  aspects. 2. France – Intellectual life – 19th century –
  Political aspects. 3. France – Intellectual life – 18th
  century. 4. France – Intellectual life – 19th century.
  5. France – History – Revolution, 1789–1799. I. Title.
  AS162.P27S82 1996   001.1'0944'09033   C96–900548–2

Typeset in Sabon 10/12
by Caractéra inc., Quebec City

To Sarah and Nina

Contents

Tables   ix

Preface   xi

1   Intellectuals, Revolution, and the Social Sciences / 3

2   Enlightenment Social Science Models / 19

3   The Institute Intellectuals: Change and Continuity / 33

4   Advice to Government and Prize Contests / 56

5   The Public Image of the Institute and the Decline of Encyclopedism / 78

6   Indelible Temperament and Condillac's Uncertain Legacy / 95

7   A Science of Morality / 118

8   Philosophical History and Political Discord / 136

9   Human Geography: Correlating Climate, Culture, and Civilization / 154

10   Rights, Utility, and Political Institutions / 172

11   Towards the Political Economy of Commercial Society / 191

12   Suppression and Resurrection of an Academy / 211

Appendix 1   Joseph Lakanal's List of Nominees for the Class of Moral and Political Sciences / 231

Appendix 2   Members and Associates of the Class of Moral and Political Sciences / 232

Appendix 3   The National Institute after the Reorganization of 1803 / 236

Appendix 4   Members of the Class of Moral and Political Sciences in the Academy of Moral and Political Sciences in 1832 / 238

Appendix 5   Number of Memoirs Read before the Class of Moral and Political Sciences and Published in Its Collection / 240

Appendix 6   Prize Contests of the Class of Moral and Political Sciences / 244

Notes / 251

Bibliography / 301

Index / 333

Tables

1 Plans for the Institute / 34

2 Provincial Academies and the Class of Moral and Political Sciences: Recruitment by Order and Noble Status / 43

3 Paris Academies in the Period 1700–89 and the Class of Moral and Political Sciences: Recruitment by Order and Noble Status / 44

4 Careers of Members of the Class of Moral and Political Sciences, 1795–1803, in percentages / 45

5 Career Patterns and Membership in the Institute / 46

6 The Publication of Memoirs by Members of the Class of Moral and Political Sciences and by Idéologues / 50

7 Memoirs Published in the Collection of the Class by Subject Areas / 50

8 Attendance at Meetings of the Class of Moral and Political Sciences by Members in the Four-Year Period from An VII (1798–99) to An X (1801–2), in percentages / 51

9 Prize Contestants and Members of the Class of Moral and Political Sciences / 66

Preface

For inspiration to pursue a study of the Class of Moral and Political Sciences of the French National Institute, I am grateful to my first teacher in the history of science, Charles C. Gillispie, as well as to one of the foremost historians of Revolutionary discourse, Keith Baker. At various stages of the project I have received moral support and encouragement from historians of science, of Revolutionary culture, and of the Idéologues, including Roger Hahn and Ken Margerison. I am especially indebted to Emmet Kennedy and Margaret Jacob for their useful comments on a complete draft of the manuscript. Both Sergio Moravia and Georges Gusdorf have cleared the path to meaningful discussion of the Idéologues. On my visits to France, I have very much appreciated the hospitality and intellectual stimulation provided by François Azouvi, Daniel Teysseire, Sylvain Auroux, Anne-Marie Chouillet, and the late and much regretted Jacques Chouillet and Roselyne Rey. Among many helpful librarians and archivists I have encountered, I should particularly acknowledge the cheerful and accurate assistance of Mme Laffitte-Larnaudie of the Archives de l'Institut and the help of Mme Lamarque of the Archives de l'Académie française in locating portraits. Any error of fact or interpretation is solely my own responsibility. I am especially grateful for the encouragement of Peter Blaney, editor at McGill-Queen's University Press, and for the indefatigable labours of my copy-editor, Henri Pilon.

Generous research grants from the Social Sciences and Humanities Research Council of Canada made several extended stays in France feasible. The Killam Fellowship Committee of the University of Calgary

.

provided for a term without teaching to enable me to continue work on the manuscript. The Aid to Scholarly Publications Programme of the Canadian Federation of Humanities and the Canadian Federation of the Social Sciences as well as a grant from the Endowment Fund of the University of Calgary made publication possible. Finally, my wife Sarah and daughter Nina have had to endure many hours without my attention because of the solitary nature of writing. This book is dedicated to them not as compensation but in recognition of their fortitude and support.

I should like to acknowledge permission to use for chapter 2 materials from tables that were published in "The Class of Moral and Political Sciences, 1795–1803," in *French Historical Studies*, 11 (1980):371–97. Some portions of chapters 3 and 9 appeared in different form in "The Enlightenment Transformed: The Institute Prize Contests," *Eighteenth-Century Studies*, 19 (1985–86):153–79, and in "Images of Paternal Power: Intellectuals and Social Change in the French National Institute," *Canadian Journal of History*, 17 (1982):425–45. The same periodical has published materials in chapter 5 as "'Analysis of Sensations and Ideas' in the French National Institute, 1795–1803" (December 1991). Portions of chapters 4, 5, and 7 are derived from conference papers in the *Proceedings of the Western Society for French History*: "The Institute Historians: Enlightenment and Conservatism," 13 (1986):122–30; "The Public Relations of the Second Class of the Institute in the Revolutionary Era, 1795–1803," 16 (1989):212–22; and "The Legacy of Condillac in the Revolutionary Era," 18 (1991): 207–17. Some materials published in "Human Geography in the French Institute: New Discipline or Missed Opportunity?" in the *Journal of the History of the Behavioral Sciences*, 23 (1987):332–40 (Clinical Psychology Publishing Co.) appear in chapter 8 in a completely different argument. An earlier, substantially different version of chapter 9 was "Individual Rights and Social Control: Political Science in the French Institute," in the *Journal of the History of Ideas*, 48 (1987):411–30. Similarly, *History of Political Economy* published materials in chapter 10 in an earlier conceptual framework as "The Institute Economists: From Physiocracy to Entrepreneurial Capitalism," 19 (1987):525–50.

Inaugural public session of the Institut national, 4 April 1796.
©cliché Bibliothèque Nationale de France, Paris, Département des
Estampes, Collection de Vinck, n° 6674, Photo: 78B80071

Minerva's Head: Seal of the Institut de
France. From *Célébration du deuxième
centenaire de la naissance de Napoléon*,
Publications de l'Institut pour l'année
1969, n° 15

Emmanuel-Joseph Sieyès, political theorist of
the Idéologues. Archives de l'Académie
française, 1G 77AF

Pierre-Louis Roederer, Idéologue and opportunist. Archives de l'Académie française, IAP 190

Constantin-François Chassebeuf de Volney, Idéologue author on ethics, history, and geography.
Archives de l'Académie française, IG 85AF

Jean-Jacques-Régis de Cambacérès, antimaterialist, second Consul, and opportunist.
Archives de l'Académie française, IG 15AF

Jacques-Henri Bernardin de Saint-Pierre, opponent of the
Idéologues. Archives de l'Académie française, IG 8AF

Minerva's Message

1 Intellectuals, Revolution, and the Social Sciences

> In meditating on the nature of the moral sciences, one cannot indeed help seeing that, based like the physical sciences upon the observation of facts, they must follow the same methods, acquire an equally exact and precise language, attain the same degree of certainty.
>
> Condorcet, 1782

The whirlwind of revolution in France had not yet subsided in the fall of 1795. After the high idealism of 1789 and the failed experiment in constitutional monarchy, the promise of uncorrupted popular sovereignty inspired republicans in September 1792. Nonetheless the Republic nearly expired because of foreign and civil war, while the ruling Committee of Public Safety attempted to stave off disaster with policies of Terror from the summer of 1793 to the summer of 1794. An atrocious civil war in the west of France killed even more people than the guillotine and firing squads of the Terror. In October 1795, fifteen months after the fall of Robespierre, the republican government still sought the difficult middle path between radical Revolution and a restored, possibly reactionary, monarchy. The moderate majority of the governing parliamentary assembly, the National Convention, in the spring of 1795 repressed the last uprising of Revolutionary Parisian sans-culottes. Early in October the moderates crushed a revolt in conservative sections of Paris against a constitution that seemed to perpetuate the power of two-thirds of the hated Convention. Just before yielding to the new regime of the Directory, in power from 1795 to 1799, the Convention passed on 25 October 1795 a comprehensive public education law establishing the National Institute of Sciences and Arts (Institut national des Sciences et Arts). This body replaced the separate Ancien Régime academies that had been abolished in August 1793. Its mission was to conduct research, publish discoveries, correspond with other learned societies, and advise the Directory about "scientific and literary works of general utility and promoting the glory of the Republic."[1] The second of the three classes of the Institute, that for Moral and Political Sciences (the Classe des Sciences morales et politiques), enshrined, for the first time in a government-sponsored academy, the human and social studies at the heart of Enlightenment culture. In March 1797 the Institute took as its seal the bust of a helmeted Minerva with a serpent, an image inspired by a statue at the Louvre known as the Pallas of Velletri.[2]

A principal argument of this study is that for both the Class of Moral and Political Sciences and governments the message emanating from Minerva's head was the need for stabilizing Revolutionary turmoil. For the vocal minority of influential thinkers in the Second Class known as the Idéologue philosophers (taken from the royalists' derogatory term for students of a science of ideas), an ambitious vision of social science led to social harmony. As physician Pierre-Jean-Georges Cabanis asserted at an early session of the class, "Only habits of reason can render [the republican government] stable and peaceful ... [T]he stronger temper given to its citizens demands of them a greater dose of common sense, so that their passions do not always tend to replace public utility."[3] The five executive Directors expected the "moral and political sciences" to "give new guarantees for domestic happiness by purifying morals, to direct the zeal of the administrator, to enlighten the conscience of the judge, and to unveil to the prudence of the legislator the future destiny of people in the tableau of their past virtues and even their past errors."[4]

There was an important technocratic tendency in the social theory of members of the Second Class, which was particularly visible when they were close to the levers of power in the friendly government of the Directory, and it aimed for the taming of passions by reason or the rechannelling of passions to socially acceptable goals. The new sciences held out the hope that the refinement of language might eliminate controversy, that climate and habits could refashion individual temperament, and that the lessons of history could instruct citizens in the most delicate art of government. But an equally significant cornerstone of the politics of the Idéologues, especially when they were in opposition during Bonaparte's Consulate (1799–1804), was their commitment to individual rights or guarantees. Hence, the foundations of liberalism tempered technocracy.

The Idéologue circle has already attracted considerable scholarly attention.[5] But the majority of the Class were not Idéologues and were indifferent or hostile to the construction of human sciences on the model of the natural sciences. In fact, opponents to the Idéologues had competing strategies for stabilizing society based on traditional moral discourse and on religious imperatives that were sometimes independent of the Catholic Church. Some of these opponents had been enthusiastic Enlightenment philosophes, advocates of reform in the Ancien Régime. But the Revolution, in their view, had already gone beyond such well-tempered change. Moreover, Bonaparte's government shared with still another faction of more conservative Institute members the objective of using religion for social control, and it also disdained the relatively undeveloped expertise of the human sciences. Bonaparte's route to stability included employing natural scientists and lawyers for pragmatic technical assistance in formulating law codes and assuring administrative efficiency. Hence, there were at least three or even four routes to stability – the path of the Idéologues, the route of the chastened ex-philosophes, the reactionary nostalgia of royalist conservatives, and the practices of Bonapartist pragmatists.

The objective of stabilizing the Revolution was itself twofold. As a positive project, it meant the intellectual legitimation of political regimes and of a social order, whether the Idéologue, Bonapartist, or reactionary ideal. As a repressive imperative, it also meant removal of sources of opposition by the Directory and Consulate governments through the direct control of clubs, the press, and political expression, or through using the new human sciences to silence controversy.

Only by moving beyond the previous studies of Sergio Moravia and Georges Gusdorf can we appreciate the intellectual and institutional obstacles to Idéologue goals within the Institute itself. Gusdorf has labelled the Second Class a "fief reserved for members of the Ideological school."[6] When we probe the manuscript minutes and the prize commissions we see how disparate were the views of the Class membership and how limited was Idéologue control. Exploring press reaction to the Institute reveals that the encyclopedic and Idéologue ideal of unifying the arts and sciences could be threatened by a seemingly trivial matter – the practical problem of organizing public sessions.

A second major aim of this study is to relate diverse aspects of Enlightenment and Revolutionary culture. Moravia long ago labelled the era of the Idéologues the "sunset of the Enlightenment," while Gusdorf has argued that they represented the "revolutionary consciousness ... the axis of the moderate Revolution."[7] A balanced view must consider both the Revolutionary context and the links to Enlightenment discourse and to Ancien Régime cultural practices. Keith Baker has convincingly argued that the "rupture" envisaged by Revolutionary political theorists masked relationships to Ancien Régime techniques of protest.[8] Although the self-image of the Revolutionaries was that they were creating a new political and cultural world, there were many continuities, both in discourse and in practice, between Ancien Régime academies and the Institute.

Nevertheless, continuity in vocabulary must not obscure changes in political culture. Enlightenment theories that were subversive in a world of corporate privilege may appear coldly conservative amid the egalitarian demands of the sans-culottes. Indeed, there were deep cleavages among surviving Enlightenment philosophes because of the Revolution itself, and in some cases they began even before the trauma of the Terror. Enthusiasm for the human sciences depended partly on a commitment to the political goals of at least moderate Revolutionaries.

A brief survey of the crowded historiographical landscape on Enlightenment–Revolution relationships will clarify preconceptions in this work. From the viewpoint of some literary theorists adopted by historians, all events are emplotted as texts, and all texts are events.[9] Such approaches enrich interpretations of a crowd scene, a revolutionary symbol, or the concealed ideology of a text. But, while this study repeatedly stresses hidden purposes of texts, the effort to construct or combat the principles of a social science in a text had none of the psychological charge of living through the experiences of the Terror. Although linguistic symbols were often at issue, the events of the Revolution were more than linguistic. Consequently it is not an obsolete question to ask how Revolutionary *events* in a (non-textual) context inflected *ideas* in texts about human nature.[10]

Such a discussion runs parallel to, and need not conflict with, Roger Chartier's brilliant synthetic essay on the cultural origins of the French Revolution. Yet, when Chartier refers to the Enlightenment as an invention of the Revolutionaries, who were searching for intellectual forerunners, he implies that the Enlightenment as a cultural movement is entirely an after-the-fact construction. This view ignores the sense that was in place well before the Revolution of a common reformist cause despite individual differences, the famous "party of humanity," so evident in the correspondence of such authors as Diderot and Voltaire.[11] The Enlightenment existed in the minds of its representatives before the Revolutionaries used its texts as self-justification. Moreover, in charting the path of ideas, no one at this late date is arguing that ideas or books "cause" revolutions. One may fully acknowledge the cultural significance of Jansenism, Freemasonry, and Grub Street resentments in desacralizing Church and monarchy and at the same time maintain the importance of Enlightenment authors for the Revolutionary construction of the social sciences. In short, ideas do not make revolutions, but revolutions take their programs from purveyors of ideas. Of course, participants in efforts to de-Christianize "wild" festivals responded to a different kind of anticlericalism than heirs of Enlightenment secularizers. If, as Michel Vovelle reports, a de-Christianizing sans-culotte in the Lyon region drank from a sacred chalice while daring God to strike him dead, one can hardly believe it was due to his reading of Voltaire or to rational arguments against superstition. Yet, if members of Revolutionary assemblies adopted anticlerical measures, the diatribes of eighteenth-century authors gave them significant prompting.[12]

Finally, Chartier's effort to subsume the Enlightenment and the Revolution in a more global phenomenon of secularization evades the question of where their intellectual ideals originated. In short, without engaging in an endless hunt for "influences," there is continued pertinence in enquiring into how specific Enlightenment authors helped shape particular philosophical viewpoints of the Revolutionary era.[13] Nor is our reference to Enlightenment models intended to idealize them or express nostalgia for eighteenth-century human science.

A peripheral issue in our discussion will also be the much debated question of whether the political vocabulary of 1789 anticipated and led to the psychology and practice of the Terror. In this view, the Manichean syndrome of plots and the unlimited sovereignty transferred to the nation from absolutism created an inevitable impetus to Terror. This interpretation does not fit well with the political theory of such Class members as Emmanuel-Joseph Sieyès. Though the Terror may have sharpened his denunciation of unlimited sovereignty or undivided legislative power in 1795, already in 1789 he sought complicated institutional mechanisms to rein in popular activism. One need not take the good intentions of the actors at face value to doubt their opposition to the perversion of the concept of the general will. Baker himself argues that the choice of the National Assembly in the constitution debates in 1789 partially set aside the supremacy of representation, the cardinal principle of Sieyès. To that extent, he would agree that Sieyès never intended the whole people to exercise ultimate, effective sovereignty and was not himself prefiguring the theory of the Terror.[14]

INTELLECTUALS AND POWER

Aside from the themes of social stabilization, of individual guarantees, and of Enlightenment–Revolution continuity and change, we shall explore the relationship between intellectuals claiming expertise and governments seeking friendly advice and image-enhancing prestige. The subject of intellectuals and power has generated a literature applicable to many periods in modern European history which gives greater resonance to French Revolutionary situations.

No doubt the term intellectual is an anachronism for the eighteenth century, but the reality existed before the term. The noun intellectual

originated in French, often in derogatory usage, from the signed man-
ifestos of certain authors and scholars protesting in 1898 the perceived
military and judicial injustice in the espionage conviction of Captain
Alfred Dreyfus.[15] The most famous of the protesters, Émile Zola
himself, noted an eighteenth-century parallel to his own accusations
against civil and military authority. Voltaire's pamphlet campaign of
1762 had represented individual conscience against reason of state in
the rehabilitation of the family of Jean Calas, a Protestant clothier who
was executed for allegedly murdering his son to prevent the young
man's conversion to Catholicism. In short, the concept of the intellectual became linked to an engagement against government policy. Perhaps for the first time in the eighteenth century, authors such as
Voltaire could appeal to a significantly large reading audience, far
beyond the limited circles associated with the sixteenth-century notion
of a European cosmopolitan and critical Republic of Letters.[16]

The attraction of defining the intellectual as an autonomous, prophetic voice clamouring against established authority appears even
now in the most recent work of the sociologist Pierre Bourdieu and of
the literary critic Edward Said. Contrary to postmodern notions that
all authors are inextricably "grounded" in their own culture, race,
class, and gender, and that there are no universal ideals to defend,
Bourdieu has strongly argued that men and women of letters must
retain the autonomy of a Zola or a Voltaire by controlling their own
cultural products independently of large bureaucratic organizations
and media. Said has called for resistance to the "lures of money and
power" on the part of intellectuals who must maintain universal
standards of truth and behaviour and who bear witness to injustice at
whatever cost to themselves, as did the Afro-Americans James Baldwin
and Malcolm X.[17]

Still other twentieth-century sociologists define intellectuals more
inclusively as anyone who frequently uses "symbols of general extent
and abstract reference" about humanity, society, nature, and the cos-
mos, including those acting as professionals. In this view, intellectuals
are not only critics or prophets, but consolers and legitimizers, as well
as active engineers and sophisticated managers.[18] The same analyses
also point out that advising or administering governments threatens
intellectual autonomy and leads either to a loss of critical perspective
or to employment as an expert who does not select goals but only the
most efficient means of achieving them.

Lipset and Basu agree that intellectuals are not necessarily innovative
but have often conservatively promoted values shared by regimes in
power. In their fourfold typology of intellectuals, only "gatekeepers"
and "moralists" have been true critics of authority. The gatekeepers,

not at all the inspectors of credentials the image suggests, are the sceptical, creative spirits who seek universal meanings and fundamental values. In China during the 1950s the short-lived Hundred Flowers campaign briefly permitted dissenting gatekeeping intellectuals to challenge the regime. The second and similar type, the "moralist," acts as a keeper of cultural conscience. In recent U.S. history the moralists were the egalitarian, antibusiness adherents of the New Deal or of the socialist left in the 1930s, the defenders of civil liberties against Senator Joseph McCarthy in the 1950s, and the opponents of the Vietnam war and the would-be guardians of the environment in the 1960s and 1970s. Evidently the moralist category could easily encompass the crusading philosophe and authors such as Voltaire and Zola.[19]

The other two categories identified by Lipset and Basu include the better integrated "protectors," conservatives who wish to explain to the public the traditions and national heritage of their society. The authors' illustration is the British old-boy network of graduates of recognized schools and members of prestigious clubs who rationalize and justify government policy. In the Eastern European environment of the post-1945 Soviet era, even Marxist intellectuals could fit the portrait of protectors justifying their regimes. The fourth category of the "conservative" is the "new monk" who has actually succumbed to the blandishments of government to become an administrator or expert – former professors like Henry Kissinger, for example, who acted as a Cabinet-level administration functionary.[20]

While this model is too rudimentary to be an infallible guide to intellectual roles, the typology suggests the need to question the automatic equation of the intellectual role with that of criticism. Indeed, if one looks more closely at the social position of the Enlightenment philosophe, is the moralistic perspective so pure? Eighteenth-century intellectuals embodied a constant tension between patronage and autonomy. Voltaire himself received Court appointments in France in the 1740s, and then in the 1750s he cheerfully accepted the patronage of Frederick II of Prussia and Catherine II of Russia. Ultimately, he was under no one's sway because his successful business investments assured him private wealth. Perhaps only a Rousseau could make a career of trying to avoid all ties of pensions or patronage. The more interesting phenomenon is how any critical work could appear in a world where writers were commonly indebted to private or state patrons.[21]

Robert Darnton and Alan Kors have already developed the paradox of "High Enlightenment" authors who would be unlikely to undermine the foundations of an Ancien Régime society which rewarded them well. In the typical case, Jean-Baptiste-Antoine Suard insinuated

himself into élite Paris salons and then edited the *Gazette de France*
of the Foreign Affairs ministry, received various pensions and gifts
from government ministers, worked as a royal censor, and edited the
Journal de Paris at government request, and thus obtained an
enormous income of 20,000 *livres*. Similarly, André Morellet, a key
figure in the history of the Académie française and in undermining
support for the Class of Moral and Political Sciences, was a veritable
artist in the game of eliciting Church and state patronage, so that by
1788 he was earning the magnificent sum of 28,000 *livres*. Diderot
called him a mercenary for his sale of his pen to the Controllers
General of the Ancien Régime and for his subservience to the Bureau
de Commerce. Morellet lost almost all his income and pensions in the
nationalization of Church property and the abolition of Ancien Régime
pensions. Enthusiastic Revolutionaries would more likely come from
the hack writers of Grub Street – the likes of Jacques-Pierre Brissot
or Jean-Paul Marat.[22] Similarly, Kors has commented that the coterie
of the notorious atheist Baron d'Holbach whose members, while less
radical (with the exception of Diderot) on religious issues than its
leader, "vied for formal positions and dignities ... served willingly as
agents of the authorities in their respective fields ... accepted the
legitimacy of the institutions of privilege into which they rose." These
personalities were comfortably ensconced in the literary world of the
Ancien Régime. In short, the Enlightenment philosophes cannot be
understood as an autonomous, free-floating group of intellectuals.

The complexity of categorizing intellectuals and of defining them as
inherently critical is illustrated by consideration of the philosophes as
well as the strange saga of the Idéologues. Idéologues and other
Institute members may have begun their careers as philosophe-
moralists. As soon as the Directory represented a new Revolutionary
order, the same group aspired to become the protectors stabilizing the
new regime or to play an administrative role. Lewis Coser has labelled
them exemplary legitimizers of power. After all, they gave moral and
political support to Bonaparte in the 1799 coup establishing him as
First Consul. Yet the Idéologues, far removed as they were from Grub
Street, cannot be passed off as perpetual functionaries of power. After
the end of 1800 the Idéologue circle mistrusted Bonaparte's religious
and educational policy and his repression of civil and political liberty.
Only the more pragmatic and opportunistic Institute members could
remain successfully integrated within the new bureaucracy. The Idéologues continued to hold well-paid, sometimes honorific government
positions, but real power eluded them, and in their writings they were
tempted to return to a moralist, prophetic stance. The short-lived
infatuation of the Idéologues with Bonaparte illustrates Robert Merton's

dictum that in the great majority of cases, the "union of policy-makers and intellectuals tends to be nasty, brutish, and short."[23]

Moreover, the very idea of a royal or state academy, as represented by the Institute in 1795 in its latest incarnation, qualifies the concept of intellectual autonomy. Recent scholarship on the Habermasian notion of the "public sphere" in the eighteenth century has shifted the focus from the idea of Enlightenment to the institutions. Habermas conceived the public sphere as an arena for free and open communication and for discussion of ideas on their merits, as occurred in the cafés, salons, Masonic lodges, and reading rooms of the Ancien Régime. Ever since the early seventeenth century, however, the French state was a major patron of the arts and sciences. The Crown funded academies as rewards for cultural and intellectual achievement but also enhance its own prestige and to encourage public display of learning.[24] Cardinal Richelieu created the Académie française in 1635 to solicit poetic praise for the monarchy. Jean-Baptiste Colbert, Louis XIV's faithful minister and masterful bureaucrat, increased the number of state-sponsored academies in order to solicit scientific advice and artistic commemoration. Members of the academies could be consultants on weaponry or on the hydraulics of Versailles fountains, or authors of inscriptions for royal monuments. The academies became part of the arsenal of state propaganda involved in the "fabrication" of the image of Louis XIV, and, as the poet Jean Chapelain wrote, in preserving "the splendour of the king's enterprises." As early as 1666, Charles Perrault, the transcriber of folk tales, proposed an anticipation of the Institute – a general academy of sciences and letters. Colbert favoured the plan, but the fledgling academies resisted any encroachment on their unique corporate identities.[25] Before the Revolution, there was a Masonic impetus to unify the teaching of the arts and sciences in one private academic society. The Société apollonienne, founded in 1780 as an offshoot of the Masonic Loge des Neuf Sœurs, was responsible, through the circle of the polymath linguist Court de Gébelin, for an educationally oriented lecture society, the Musée de Paris, in 1781. The Musée projected three program committees on "sciences, literature, and useful and pleasing arts," but could never realize its ambitious plans.[26]

Academies were state creations but they remained permeable to reformist Enlightenment influences. By the late eighteenth century, moral and political issues were so important in Enlightenment culture that even the literary Académie française awarded prizes to "useful" historical works and sponsored contests on education.[27] The Paris Académie des Sciences became concerned with demography and agricultural productivity. In thirty-two provincial cities, academies of sciences or belles-lettres modelled themselves on the Parisian institutions. There provincial nobles, wealthy state office-holders, lawyers, physicians, and other members of the well-to-do bourgeoisie discussed many acute social problems. Especially after 1770 there were prize contests for essays on economic or legal subjects such as hygiene, urban improvement, the elimination of begging, how best to educate the people, criminal code reform, the status of illegitimate children, and ending compulsory labour service (corvée).[28]

Though one may portray the provincial academies as preparing the spirit of Revolutionary reforms and manifesting independent judgment, academic culture was "innovation within tradition."[29] Most commonly these academies solicited royal charters, observed ceremonial occasions involving the royal family, read eulogies to illustrious rulers of France, and admitted as honorary members local nobles who were considered patrons of letters, the arts, and the sciences. Even in Paris the culture of academies, which stressed merit and equal intellectual opportunity, clashed with a world of precedence and privilege that penetrated the sanctum of the intellect.

Hence, eighteenth-century intellectuals were at once critics – moralists in the terminology of Lipset – and protectors, who were deeply implicated in tradition. This unstable equilibrium collapsed under the pressures of the Revolution.

After 1789 the academies could not escape the taint of royal patronage and corporate identity. The Paris academies continued their increasingly incongruous litanies for the King and eulogies for patrons such as Richelieu. The King still had a nominal final voice and veto power over the choice of academicians for new members from their presentation list of candidates. Though merit was the rationale for academies, the Académie des Sciences and the Académie des Inscriptions had internal hierarchies, including honorary members (mostly noble patrons) with precedence rights, senior active "pensioner" members, and unsalaried junior members. Thus, the academies tended to mimic the ranking of Ancien Régime society. Their privileges could also inhibit competing free societies or could include sometimes meddlesome rights to judge inventions. Malcontented intellectuals, such as Nicolas Chamfort in the Académie française and the painter Jacques-Louis David in the Académie de Peinture et de Sculpture, as well as the vitriolic journalists Brissot and Marat, would find oppressive the pretentiousness and alleged frivolity of academicians. Branding the academies contrary to the Revolutionary spirit, they called for their reform or suppression.[30]

The legislatures never acknowledged the abortive efforts of Paris literary, historical, and scientific academies in 1790 to reform their regulations, so the old rituals continued. The Académie française in 1790 even promised "moral and political instruction," while Morellet defended its philosophic spirit against Chamfort's attacks. By 1793, with the advent of Terror, the National Convention saw the academies as corporate and aristocratic anachronisms, despite their past usefulness. Increasingly, artisan organizations resented the pretentious judgment and approval by academicians of new processes and inventions. In the year of Terror a Convention deputy could praise the need for "free men" rather than "savants," and celebrate the fact that loyal sans-culottes were not scholars. On 8 August 1793, after a critical intervention by the painter David, the Convention abolished all Parisian academies, and during the year of Terror the governing committees would not contemplate their revival.[31]

The inauguration of the Institute in 1795 opened a new stage in the ambivalent relationship between the French state and institutions of higher learning. In addition to the Second Class of Moral and Political Sciences, the Institute included a First Class of Mathematical and Physical Sciences (Sciences mathématiques et physiques), as well as a Third Class of Literature and Fine Arts (Littérature et Beaux-Arts). The first public session on 4 April 1796 was a glittering ceremony in the newly refurbished Salle des Cariatides (or Antiques) of the Musée national des Arts, formerly a festival hall in the medieval Vieux-Louvre. Surrounded by twenty-two statues of French soldiers, preachers, and legal scholars, the audience included the five Directors heading the government, members of the foreign diplomatic corps, and over 1,500 citizens.[32]

In 1795 the Directory expected not only assistance in stabilizing society from the Second Class but tangible benefits from the Institute for Revolutionary war efforts, for improving agricultural productivity, and for promoting commerce. The propagandistic slogans of 1795 claimed that that the new republican government enjoyed a privileged relationship to learning. In our terminology, the intellectuals would be truly free under a free government. At the inaugural ceremony, the Director Letourneur expressed his happiness, in a conspicuous reference to the first *Discourse* of Jean-Jacques Rousseau, that the arts would no longer "cover their chains with flowers."[33] No longer would despots command praise, since now the philosophers, who called forth the Revolution by their attacks on superstition and tyranny, would be free. Learning would strengthen the Republic. The speaker for the Institute, Pierre-Claude-François Daunou, a former Oratorian philosophy teacher, defended the independence of opinion in the Institute against government orders.[34] Cabanis had stressed that a republic "fortifies itself by public enlightenment" and "does not fear to see its constituent principles and the power it exercises in the name of the people ... submitted to the most severe discussion."[35] Yet we shall see how the search for stability impelled the Directory to trample upon the vaunted independence of the intellectual élite. Bonaparte would celebrate the scientific prowess of Institute members but reject the idea of it as a forum for critical thinking. In the end it was difficult for members to be both prophets and priests. The Second Class of the Institute further illustrates how the imperative to end the Revolution and the interference of governments could tame and subordinate intellectual autonomy and audacity.

WHITHER THE SOCIAL SCIENCES?

Another goal of this study is to examine the development of the social sciences. A striking difference between the eighteenth century and our own era is in the feeling of emancipation that was attached then to the formulation of the human sciences. Now, these studies are vulnerable to attack for inflated ambitions and deceptive claims to truth. Yet there is no shortage of current prestige for contemporary social scientists in both academic and popular milieux. Psychologists issue respected advice on how to rear children or enhance family life, while managerial consultants earn high salaries for suggesting how to market products or elicit more productive labour or services. Political scientists advise legislators how to test and react to expressions of public opinion, while economists offer remedies for inflation, trade deficits, and the business cycle. Thousands of economists are directly employed by the U.S. federal government.[36] At least some of the social sciences have become sources for policy decisions, and in that sense the philosophers of the Institute have triumphed. Before discussing Enlightenment models for social science, an examination of twentieth-century debates will enhance the significance of the subject.

Some recent critics who maintain a respect for the natural sciences admonish that the social sciences have never achieved comparable reliability. Alasdair MacIntyre sees no justification to any claim for managerial expertise by social scientists because of a lack of a "stock of law-like generalizations with strong predictive power."[37] Dorothy Ross's fascinating study of American political science, economics, and sociology lambastes the ineffectiveness of social science techniques because of their "determined reliance on quantitative measurement and abstract bodies of theory far removed from the institutional and cultural contexts in which they must work." She suggests that the very notion of universal social scientific laws is a time-bound and culture-bound positivist relic.[38]

Indeed, the problematic character of Institute projects frequently stemmed from universal moral and economic claims based on human nature. Particularly where deductive methods with inflexible assumptions were used, there could only be one correct answer. However, we shall also find less universalistic aspirations in some empirical studies of psychology, geography, and political science, while laws of probability and tendency might of course have been inadequate for the prediction of any particular event.

The founders of the modern "critical theory" of the Frankfurt Institute of Social Research similarly attacked the scientific presuppositions of the Enlightenment because they believed the task of obtaining mastery of nature leads "to how to use it in order wholly to dominate it and other men." In their view, scientific abstraction in the eighteenth century led to more and more repression of the individual. Reason itself thus became totalitarian. Moreover, instrumental reason, unable to discriminate among ends, created a situation without moral foundations, and so it could be indifferent or apathetic about the will to destroy and torture, as represented in the Marquis de Sade.[39]

The Frankfurt critique may be justified in the sense that views of human nature can become pretexts for domination. Yet labelling all reason totalitarian would ignore, among other things, the aspects of the emerging political sciences which stressed individual rights, with the possibility of dissent. The second Frankfurt charge, about the lack of ethical standards, seems justified only in the sense of the practical difficulties of unassailably founding a naturalistic ethic. Almost all the Institute members, even those most philosophically inclined to materialism, were determined to defend an ethic and would have been horrified at an identification with Sade.

From a more radical anthropological or hermeneutic position, Peter Winch has argued that the purpose of understanding human behaviour is not control. Rather than attempting to formulate laws, the social scientist should understand meaning, purpose, and the rules guiding social activity from the agent's viewpoint alone. Extending the critique of the natural sciences model from J.G. Herder in the late eighteenth century through to Wilhelm Dilthey and Max Weber in the late nineteenth and early twentieth centuries, Winch saw empathetic understanding as the critical degree of immersion in the culture observed; modifying one's actions is irrelevant. Dorothy Ross also recently argued that "instrumental rationality" destroys the "qualitative human world," and she holds out hope for some kind of Weberian interpretive social science conscious of its historical context.[40] A completely hermeneutic approach may be ideally suited to certain anthropological or sociological studies. "Understanding" is especially important in avoiding a culturally conditioned assumption of European normality. Indeed, the bane of eighteenth-century human geography was just such a portrait of a progressive Europe with a mission to civilize "savage" peoples. But there is a crucial problem with exclusive concern with "understanding," especially when applied to one's own society rather than interaction with others. It implies maximum tolerance and minimal control. Most eighteenth-century thinkers were firmly convinced that either the abuses of the Ancien Régime or the dynamic of Revolution had to be controlled. They would have been unlikely to accept the admonitions of Herder. Similar dilemmas would beset anyone concerned with rational policy formation today.

An even more profound attack on the social sciences is a consequence of the collapse of an empiricist and positivist philosophy of science. After the questioning of theory formulation by Norwood Hanson, as well as the historical model for theory preservation and change by Thomas Kuhn and the anarchistic salvos by Paul Feyerabend against scientific method, there is widespread doubt that any competing set of scientific theories can be tested empirically by neutral factual language.[41] In this view objective knowledge is impossible, even in the natural sciences. The very terms of discussion may be shaped by a chosen theoretical framework. Choices between theories may be affected by the social interests of groups of scientists or even by broader questions of value. If the natural sciences are vulnerable to attacks by sociologists of knowledge, a fortiori the social sciences, bound up with questions of value and group interests, can have no objective character. The choice of theory might reflect either psychological or social needs.

Certainly this critique poses the greatest challenge to the assumptions of Institute members. They placed boundless confidence in the natural sciences. Our study will show how social and political assumptions affected their notions of social science. Establishing secular psychology and moral science as disciplines was very much influenced by the need to counteract the authority of the clergy. Moral assumptions about pleasure-pain motivation and about the desirability of the consumption of luxuries permeated both psychological and economic theories, while political scientists retained natural-law normative arguments concerning slavery and the practices of monarchy. Historians frankly avowed their search for lessons of morality, while economists, historians, and geographers all believed in European cultural superiority. It remains an open question whether the intertwining of social science theory and social values leads necessarily to a self-refuting relativism about all scientific theory.

One of the most trenchant variants of this critical view has come from Michel Foucault's study of eighteenth and nineteenth-century social sciences. Foucault's neo-Nietzschean claim is that the social sciences, like other knowledge, arose together with the disciplinary power structures controlling modern social and political life. At a more profound level than that of the relationship of the "general" intellectual to state power, Foucault argues that all knowledge about human beings is inextricably bound up with the exertion of the will to dominate others. Whether in the form of a hospital, asylum, therapeutic relationship, factory, or prison, disciplinary power structures are invariably conducive to the "hierarchical gaze." Social scientists, in Foucault's view, are members of a new secular priesthood who have assumed the right to label and classify normal as opposed to abnormal behaviour. With the monopolies they claim to specialized knowledge, they may in fact exert professional monopolies of power with a tendency to persecute all those who deviate from their definition of the normal, whether the label is insane, sick, or criminal.[42] As with MacIntyre's view, for Foucault the experts have feet of clay.

There is no doubt that some Institute academicians of the era around 1800 were insensitive to the problem of the sinister aspects of expertise, particularly its tendency for moralizing the people. Their assumption that there could be a single scientific natural morality left them open to condoning the abuses of clinicians and asylum directors who assumed that scientific knowledge gave them allegedly irrefutable conclusions on moral soundness and health. When Foucault depicts Jeremy Bentham's Panopticon prison guard (or factory foreman) at the hub of a spoke-like structure, the most repellent feature of the apparatus of expertise is the presumption of infallibility and the impossibility of dialogue. Moreover, there has been no shortage of occasions in the nineteenth and twentieth centuries when scientists of society have justified the manipulation of the weak, be they trusting, defenceless patients or presumed racial, sexual, or social inferiors. Even child psychologists have become aware of the detrimental effects of labelling a slow learner or maladjusted child as a failure.

To the extent that physicians and social scientists of all kinds are unable to establish "knowledge" at all, their assertion of power is illegitimate. Or, if there are no universally valid laws, the justification of their authority is significantly weakened. Foucault's perspective has been immensely stimulating in puncturing the mythology of expertise. The credibility of much of his critique therefore rests on the evaluation of the aforementioned arguments about whether there are any observable regularities that constitute knowledge in the social sciences.

If such knowledge exists, it would be obtainable only at the cost of deploying some expertise. To assume that the very act of filing information harms some essential element of humanity leads to a surrender in making any effort to attain systematic knowledge. A utopian perspective of a society without files, surveillance, or hierarchy surely raises other questions. How one educates children in norms, traditions, and ways of thinking without altering or gently controlling their behaviour is one problem. While each child demands a unique developmental path, there would be no transmission of any culture without some concept of norm. How one assists recovery from illness or enhances learning situations without files and examinations is another question. Even in non-totalitarian societies, the entire capitalist business community, not to mention schools of public administration, worships at the altar of effective management. If management goals ought to consist of more than profit and efficiency, then gathering essential information is still unavoidable. Governing without clarifying the potential recommendation of norms would indeed be difficult in a pluralistic society.

Let us grant Foucault's assumption that the generation of knowledge is inseparable from exercising power. The issue then becomes the cost of the refusal to exercise power even while committed to assuring maximum opportunities for individual fulfilment. As long as there are questions concerning what degree of intervention (to prevent abuse of the weak, for example) or indeed about what degree of surveillance (of drug dealers, let us say) are necessary to maintain the public interest, disdaining knowledge because it requires the exercise of power seems a doubtful prescription.

Thus our study will take full cognizance of Foucault's reappraisal of the potential for misguided expertise. Yet we shall not necessarily agree that any effort at constructing a social science is *ipso facto* an unjustified or sinister power grab. The current interest in Institute thinkers in any case is in their willingness to grapple with social dilemmas that are still unsolved. Tainted by the power-bound implications of all knowledge and tempted by the political power to which some felt so close, they vacillated between maintaining critical autonomy and giving advice to governments, between being technocrats and being defenders of individual freedom.

2 Enlightenment Social Science Models

Enlightenment thinkers were no doubt dazzled by the scientific successes of Newtonian physics and later by the revolution in chemistry of Lavoisier. There were innumerable aspirants to the title of "Newton of the mind" and "Newton of the moral sciences."[1] Each project hoped to enhance learning, understand, tame human passions, or promote a more satisfying social existence. Many were more speculative, less precise, and laced with more normative assumptions than the would-be Newtons would admit. Six of the models most influential to Institute authors were: (1) Montesquieu's formulation of a science of government, including both normative natural law assumptions and an at least partly empirical political sociology of physical and cultural influences on the principles of government; (2) the effort of medical and hygienic practitioners in the ancient Hippocratic tradition to relate physical and mental aspects of human temperament, with implications for individual psychology, for physical and political parallels in human geography and statistics, and for inviting empirical case studies and differentiating individuals; (3) the establishment of laws of circulation and exchange of goods based, in the Physiocratic case, on physical natural law, and, in the apparently more empirical case of Adam Smith, on the role of human labour and capital stock in creating wealth; (4) a model of stages of historical progress, endorsed by the economists, geographers, and historians, explaining the changes in modes of subsistence, and, when blended with theories of cultural evolution, conducive not only to historical optimism but also to Eurocentrism and social hierarchy; (5) the analytic "decomposition" of the mind by

Condillac, based on the "observed" fundamental faculty of sensation and the deductive derivation of all higher mental operations from sensation, with an emphasis on constructing a "well-made language" to fortify reasoning; and (6) the statistical "social mathematics" of Condorcet, partly an application of mathematical theory to political and economic problems, and partly the development of empirical demographic data to deal with problems of the government Treasury and ultimately all variables affecting mind and character.

THE SCIENCE OF GOVERNMENT AND THE ENVIRONMENTAL IMPERATIVE

The most important principle expressed in Montesquieu's *De l'esprit des lois* (1748) was his definition of law in human affairs as similar to laws of nature: "the necessary relations deriving from the nature of things." But Montesquieu also allowed a non-determinist flexibility in his system when he remarked that "the world of intelligence does not follow [invariable laws] as constantly as the physical world does." Montesquieu set out to chart the variations under different conditions of universal natural laws. His object was to relate the existing laws in any state to the "constitution of each government, customs, climate, religion, commerce, etc."[2] He would examine how the physical and cultural environment affected man-made laws, and then proceed to further deductions about social and economic life. He defined three ideal types of government, albeit in a form different from Aristotle: republican (democratic or aristocratic), monarchical, and despotic, which functioned respectively on the guiding principles of virtue, honour, and fear. All subsequent conclusions followed from these first principles, derived in reality from highly selective testimony and observation.[3]

Even more characteristically for eighteenth-century political science, Montesquieu furnished ambiguous definitions of the term natural law based on descriptive behaviour such as self-preservation, but also on rationally desirable norms such as peaceable conduct.[4] The ambiguous usage of natural law provided a precedent for Institute political theory – the use of allegedly descriptive natural laws as moral imperatives.

In the pre-Revolutionary situation, Montesquieu's preference for moderate, limited governments, such as the English monarchy, and for intermediate bodies, such as the courts in France, was clearly directed against the corruption of the French monarchy into despotism. During the Revolution his preferences could become mechanisms for social stability. Particularly important for such Institute theorists as Sieyès and Daunou was the principle of separation of powers, which was the basis of the Revolutionary constitutions of 1795 and 1799. The pro-Revolutionary priest Henri Grégoire identified separation of powers and representative government (which Montesquieu praised in the English House of Commons) as the greatest discoveries of modern political science.[5] Even such authors as Philippe-Antoine Grouvelle, who condemned Montesquieu's tolerance for pure monarchy and his aristocratic prejudices, valued the principle of separation of powers.[6]

A controversial critique of monarchy in 1748 could, however, seem conservative and counter-Revolutionary in the 1790s. As Olson has recently argued, Burkean conservatives could later take comfort from Montesquieu because they could find in him their own means of social stabilization – justification of any historically developed institution in its appropriate situation.[7] Revolutionary authors did, however, question Montesquieu's relativism. Cabanis's discussion of climate always remained secondary to that on the immutable principles of natural rights. Similarly, Condorcet reproved Montesquieu for seeking to understand the laws rather than clarify the nature of justice. Condorcet saw no reason to adjust laws to differences in climate. "A good law," he wrote, "must be good for all men, as a true proposition, is true for all ... Truth, reason, justice, the rights of man, the interests of property, liberty, security, are everywhere the same; one doesn't see why all the provinces of a state, or even all states, would not have the same criminal law, civil law, commercial law, etc."[8]

For Condorcet and for most other pro-Revolutionary authors in the Institute, the belief in natural and civil rights, based on the heritage of Locke and Rousseau, took precedence over any relativistic applications of a political science. Not all of them subscribed to a state of nature or social contract, but the belief in liberty and property as rights of man in society was sacrosanct.[9]

During the Empire, Idéologue leader Antoine-Louis-Claude Destutt de Tracy similarly disdained Montesquieu for being partial to monarchy and aristocracy. He could think of no better way of introducing the subject of political science, however, than by writing a commentary on *De l'esprit des lois*. Though he, too, went through the motions of describing the functioning of "special" governments, responsive to the privileged few, his main concern was refining the operation of "national" governments that followed the popular will.[10]

Montesquieu's most extensive influence stemmed from his more specific efforts to define the "general spirit" of a people by assessing the interaction of "climate, religion, laws, maxims of government, examples from the past, customs, and manners."[11] The emphasis on climate in the broad sense of physical geography provided an essential theme for Cabanis and for human geographer Constantin-François Volney. While Cabanis developed Montesquieu's views in line with the hygienic tradition, Volney believed climate was of less importance, even if Montesquieu himself had pointed out that a good legislator could counteract the "vices of the climate."[12]

Montesquieu was apparently acquainted with the ancient Hippocratic treatise *Airs, Waters, Places*, and so his discussion of climate intersects the tradition of hygienists and physicians. In addition, Montesquieu was undoubtedly aware of the political theory of climate in the sixteenth-century works of Jean Bodin.[13] During the Revolutionary era, hygienists, such as Jean-Noël Hallé and Cabanis, would try to assess the effects on inherent temperament for each age and sex of travel to different climates, changes in diet, exercise, occupation, and physical and emotional habits. Stemming from an ancient theory on temperament, this enterprise looked forward to a more sophisticated physiological psychology. It demanded individualized case studies with, if possible, statistical clinical tables for prescriptions for improving mental faculties and moral character.[14]

As Norman Hampson has noted, aside from the debate on climate and the concurrent influence of the hygienists, political thinkers found in Montesquieu a great quarry of materials for assessing the consequences of each form of government. Antirepublicans could argue that Montesquieu questioned the suitability of a republic for a large country and an allegedly corrupted people incapable of simplicity and virtue. Other authors might attempt to evaluate a suitable educational system, paternal power, or a trial jury for a society based on republican virtue.[15] When the public secondary schools (central schools) of the Directory established a legislation course, two-thirds of the instructors referred to Montesquieu's works, slightly more than the number who used Rousseau, the next most popular author.[16]

To label the science of government, one encompassing not only axioms such as natural rights but also descriptive regularities in the fashion of Montesquieu, Sieyès in the first edition of his *Qu'est-ce que le tiers état?* in 1789, Pierre-Louis Lacretelle in the *Encyclopédie méthodique* in 1791, Dominique-Joseph Garat in correspondence in 1791, and Condorcet in his education plan of 1792 all initiated the usage of the term *science sociale*, or social science.[17] Pierre-Louis Roederer, in his 1793 lectures, and J.-J. Régis de Cambacérès, in an Institute discourse of 1798, expanded that term's meaning to denote a unified science comprising ethics, legislation, and political economy. But in the Institute section designation of *science sociale et législation* in 1795, Condorcet's more restricted sense applied.[18]

POLITICAL ECONOMY

Political economy was no doubt the most systematically developed branch of the science of government, with British and French writers having explored issues of trade and production from the early seventeenth century. The mercantilist concern for prosperous treasuries through the protectionist promotion of a favourable trade balance and through promoting the welfare of the poor had metamorphosed into a doctrine of limited government intervention to benefit landed proprietors.[19] Institute members included one surviving member of the Physiocratic school of economists, and the works of Anne-Robert-Jacques Turgot and Adam Smith inspired the majority of authors. The supremely self-confident Physiocratic circle supplied a coherent intellectual system which claimed a basis in natural physical law. Once again, it highlighted the ambivalence of natural law terminology as both descriptive and prescriptive.

Court surgeon François Quesnay, long acquainted with the system for the circulation of the blood, refined his ideas of an economic circulatory system after a fateful meeting with provincial landowner and population theorist Victor Riqueti, the Marquis de Mirabeau, at Versailles in 1757.[20] In 1758 he proposed a lengthy statistical questionnaire to collect information from all French regions on climate, physical geography, agriculture, population, and commerce.[21] Quesnay carefully gathered evidence, but the exposition of his classic work initiated a quite different tradition in economics – a deductive theoretical model with carefully defined initial premises and tight reasoning, and in this case with definite policy implications.

In Quesnay's fascinating *Tableau économique* (1758), wealth, rather than blood, circulated among the three classes of society, the proprietors, the cultivators, and the "sterile" merchants and craftsmen. His incontrovertible axiom was that only land, through the proprietor's revenue, produced new wealth. Commerce merely transferred goods without increasing their value, while craft and industrial production transformed raw materials without producing a net surplus because labour and equipment costs consumed the additional value. Therefore, the volume of circulating wealth in the economy depended on increasing the proprietor's net product (his total revenue minus costs of production). Crop prices had to be appropriately high, while prices of other goods and all labour costs needed to be kept low. Maximum agricultural output would occur in an environment of internal and external free trade and competition. Quesnay showed how the consumption of each class helped replenish the advances available to the productive farmer and furnish income to the proprietor. As Mirabeau stated, "Each man works for others, while believing that he is working for himself." The proprietor was a good citizen, who enabled the enjoyment of abundance by all. These descriptive laws of the self-regulating market were also normative ideals to be followed.[22]

The Physiocrats insisted that nature demonstrated their universal economic laws. Quesnay and Mirabeau co-authored *Philosophie rurale* (1763), subtitled "general and political economy of agriculture, the immutable order of physical and moral laws which assure the prosperity of empires," while their colleague Le Mercier de la Rivière in 1767 outlined the "natural and essential order of political society."[23] The Abbé Baudeau baptized the doctrine *Physiocratie* (rule by nature) in 1767, and the same year Pierre-Samuel Du Pont de Nemours introduced an edition of Quesnay's new economic science as a "physical science, exact, evident, and complete." Du Pont was proud that the Physiocrats moved beyond Montesquieu's relativism, given that Montesquieu was ignorant of the "physical laws as well as the social conditions of reproduction of subsistence."[24] The subtitle of Baudeau's Physiocratic periodical, *Éphémérides du Citoyen*, became from 1767 to 1772 *Bibliothèque raisonnée des sciences morales et politiques*, the phrase inspiring Condorcet's name for the Second Class of the Institute.[25] Du Pont himself illustrated the attachment of the Physiocrats to what they called the "despotism of [self]-evidence." Criticizing Cesare Beccaria's lectures in 1769, Du Pont wrote that "gathering particular facts" was unnecessary for the "moral and political sciences," where principles "become evident on a little reflection."[26]

But the policy conclusions of the Physiocrats alienated many of their chosen clientele. The Physiocrats asked for a single direct tax on the proprietor's net product. They calculated that proprietors bore the burden of all indirect taxes with an effective hidden surcharge above the nominal amount. The single tax would be applied to all land, whether or not it was owned by the privileged orders of nobles and clergy. Du Pont still steadfastly defended the single land tax in his comments to the Institute in 1797.[27]

During the Revolution, the end of privilege and the sentiments of injustice at arbitrary indirect taxes convinced the Constituent Assembly to shift a much higher proportion of the tax burden to land. Certain conservative thinkers might still have wished to stabilize society by stressing the productive role of the landed proprietor. Other Institute thinkers, however, would find more appealing economic doctrines that were prepared to acknowledge the social importance of the merchant and industrialist. In both cases, the science of economics would justify the dominance of proprietors and countenance a hierarchy of wealth.

The Physiocrats also joined the chorus of natural law theorists favouring natural rights. An article by Quesnay in the *Journal de l'agriculture* (1765) defined natural right as the "right which man has to things suitable for his use ... self-evidently recognized by the light of reason."[28] Extending Locke's doctrine of property in one's own person, the Physiocrats anticipated the derivation of rights (by Institute authors Sieyès, Volney, and Destutt de Tracy) from the needs of a sensitive being.

Critics displeased with Physiocratic dogmatism were more favourable to the modified, but basically sympathetic outlook of Controller-General Turgot who in 1770 published anonymously in the Physiocratic journal his *Réflexions sur la formation et la distribution des richesses*. While he agreed on the agricultural origins of wealth, he legitimized commercial and industrial profit as a surplus after necessary advances.[29] Another less forward-looking author who was influential on Institute members Sieyès and Germain Garnier was the philosopher Étienne Bonnot de Condillac. In *Le Commerce et le gouvernement* (1776) Condillac agreed that land originated wealth, but he also maintained that commerce and industry added value to products and that all classes accumulated wealth. Both Turgot and Condillac therefore appealed to the proponents of greater prestige for commerce and industry.[30]

The most noted economic model competing with that of the Physiocrats, given in the *Wealth of Nations* (1776) of Adam Smith, proved attractive for three primary reasons. First, he appealed to antimercantilist opponents of tariffs and monopolies by supporting the principal Physiocratic conclusion, which was the "system of natural liberty," or self-adjusting market model of free trade and competition. Secondly, he acknowledged in full the contributions of commercial and industrial wealth. A lawyer like Institute member Roederer, who was also a glass manufacturer, approved this shift of perspective on sources of wealth.[31] Thirdly, Smith deplored the dogmatic "man of system," such as a Physiocrat, and relied on ostensibly observational premises for his economic reasoning.

The premises of *Wealth of Nations* were based on allegedly empirical accounts of the fundamentally self-interested propensity to "truck, barter, exchange" and the beneficial consequences of these activities in establishing the division of labour, key to economic growth.[32] The pursuit of wealth and status had unintended outcomes that assured the appropriate supply of goods and services to all. Yet the exposition in *Wealth of Nations* consisted mostly of the working-out of accepted premises. This practice may have corresponded to Smith's own definition of the Newtonian method, but the image of Smith as an empiricist was somewhat sharper than the reality.

Like the Physiocrats, he perceived political economy not as a narrow science of commerce, but as a branch of the "science of a statesman or legislator," with links to ethics and jurisprudence. In the Revolutionary era, Destutt de Tracy would attempt to separate political concern from economic doctrines, but his own passionate commitments against luxury and slavery made this task formidable.[33]

Interpreters of Smith have already suggested that his historical schema in Book III was intended less as critical scholarship than as support for the general economic theory. Yet his four-stages framework of economic development, already promoted in modified form by Quesnay, Du Pont, and Turgot, proved a provocative influence on Institute geographers and historians. The model gave a Eurocentric view of development of modes of subsistence, and it expressed, except in Rousseau, Enlightenment confidence in material and cultural progress of the human species. The dynamic of the four stages arose from both the need for self-preservation and the need for more refined conveniences in life after meeting basic needs requirements. First, hunter-gatherers lived in small groups, with hardly any property, in a situation of equality based on poverty, few amenities, and hardly any government. In the second stage, the former hunters discovered the benefits of pastoral life. Nomadic tribes could accumulate more wealth, so that greater social distinctions appeared and chieftains became more despotic. Only the third stage, a settled agricultural society, produced a true civilization with the emergence of luxuries, a flourishing of the arts, and distinctions of rank based on land ownership and personal service. While the Physiocrats generally ended the schema here, though they did allow for greater development of commerce and industry, Smith added a fourth stage, commercial society. In European history, the great demand of landowners for luxuries stimulated the growth of trade and manufacturing in towns and cities. New wealth in self-governing cities shifted the balance of political power by enabling the "middling ranks" to ally with the Crown against the nobles. In commercial society, free labour replaced personal servitude, the free exchange of goods and services prevailed, and culture reached new heights of civility and refinement.[34]

The four-stage schema imposed upon human geographers the prejudice that primitive peoples could not possibly achieve greatness in the fine arts because they required settlement and leisure. The mission of Europeans was therefore to benefit these peoples with their unquestionably superior civilization. Historians absorbed from this picture the guiding assumption that a modern society, with landed property, social distinctions, and complex government, was an improvement over simpler forms of social organization. The assumption of universal economic laws for a static nature was of course qualified by this notion of the historicity of human behaviour. As a practical matter, however, because the epoch was one of advanced agricultural or commercial society, current economic theory could ignore earlier propensities. Before the Revolution, Smith's model justified greater political power for the "middling ranks." However, in Revolutionary circumstances his model could justify a degree of social hierarchy as a mark of a civilized society.[35]

DECOMPOSING THE MIND AND PERFECTING LANGUAGE

In the deepest sense, historical progress rests on the ability to acquire knowledge. As epistemologist, psychologist, and logician, the Abbé de Condillac had an all-pervasive influence. In the Revolutionary era, editions of Condillac's major works proliferated, and in the Directory's central (secondary) schools, 82 per cent of teachers of general grammar used some works by Condillac.[36] The leaders of the Idéologue circle, Cabanis and Destutt de Tracy, aspired to be his critical disciples. The very name of the first section of the Institute's Second Class, analysis of sensations and ideas (*analyse des sensations et des idées*), was a phrase taken by Condorcet from Condillac's philosophy.

Condillac's first important message was the Encyclopedist imperative to unify the sciences by a common method of "analysis" – the "decomposition" of complex ideas into their simplest elements, and their "recomposition" into a complex whole showing the origin and generation of the elements. Condillac, somewhat like Descartes, transformed a "first well-constituted fact" into a generative idea for deducing an entire system.[37]

Condillac's second important contribution to Institute thinkers was his application of the analytic method to the faculties of the mind, or metaphysics in the restricted sense of psychology and epistemology. Subsequent chapters will refer to his "transformed sensations" model. The primary, temporally and logically, prior irrefutable fact of mental operations was sensation. In the *Traité des sensations* (1754), Condillac genetically and deductively transformed the primitive fact of sensation into all faculties of the understanding (attention, memory, imagination, comparison, and judgment). There was no autonomous faculty of reflection, as in Locke's psychology. In addition, each primary sensation, through its affective component of pleasure or pain, generated human passions and the faculties of the will.[38] The paradox of Condillac was that his deductive reasoning served the cause of empiricism.

By the Revolutionary generation, locating the origin of knowledge in sense experience and of motivation in pleasure and pain (as with Hobbes and Locke) had become commonplaces. Disciples of Condillac could freely engage in their favourite pastime of introspective decomposition of the faculty of thought.

In more practical matters, Condillac set the agenda for theories of pedagogy and for political rhetoric. Salutary habits acquired through striking sensations and the "liaison of ideas" were the most effective means both of learning and of moral education. Thus, the use of pageantry and festivals was an effective means of enhancing loyalty to country. The power of habit became a leitmotif for the theory of both individual and collective psychology and also for the art of social stability.[39]

To Condillac's irreverent followers and to more religious nineteenth-century observers, empiricist philosophy denied the unobservable, hence it would deny God and a spiritual soul. A philosopher like Claude-Adrien Helvétius based his psychology on physical sensitivity and his moral theory on manipulation of self-interest by education and legislation. Cabanis saw no reason to distinguish physical nervous sensitivity from sensation before following Condillac on the transformation of sensation into thought.[40] Yet Condillac himself strongly denied any materialist implications in his theory. To him, "sensation, although produced on the occasion of movement, is not that movement itself." Therefore, "sensations are not in the organs," and a self is necessary to integrate sense-data. In short, the "soul is a different substance from the body." An important characteristic of many thinkers in the Revolutionary generation was the acceptance of Condillac's empiricism and dualism as compatible and not contradictory. However, Idéologues like Pierre Laromiguière and Joseph-Marie Degérando began gradually to move away from empiricism itself.[41] Hence, one of the leading causes of disarray among the Idéologues was disagreement over the relationship between empiricism and materialism.

Condillac's third model for the Revolutionary era stemmed from his contention in *Logique* (1780) that the "art of reasoning is reduced to a well-made language."[42] In the first *Essai sur l'origine des connaissances humaines* (1746), he stressed the importance of linguistic signs for generating complex ideas.[43] To work well, the analytic method required clarity in each decomposed element. Since artificial signs helped arrange ideas in appropriate relationships, one had to perfect language to improve the sciences. In his posthumous *Langue des calculs* (1798), Condillac explored the idea that all scientific language could be as well defined as algebraic symbols. All sciences could conceivably achieve the clarity of mathematical demonstration.[44]

Condillac's heirs shared his fascination with the power of words, definitions, and symbols. In 1787 chemist Antoine-Laurent Lavoisier and three colleagues appealed to Condillac's principles to reform the names of chemical compounds so that the form of each name helped reveal the actual chemical structure.[45] Names thus disclosed the order of things. This striking success stimulated the imagination of other authors who hoped for a universal symbolic language or who sought an etymological dictionary on a basis for reordering knowledge.[46] The partisans of the analytic method, even in clinical medicine, thus became technicians of language as well as anatomists of mental faculties.

SOCIAL MATHEMATICS AND STATISTICS

A final model for aspiring social scientists of the Revolutionary era emerged from the Institute's godfather, the Marquis de Condorcet. Inspired by Turgot to believe that the moral and political sciences would achieve the same "degree of certainty" as the physical sciences, Condorcet thought that only a "small number of facts is necessary to establish the first foundation of ethics, of political, civil, or criminal legislation, or of administration."[47]

While the political abuses of the Ancien Régime helped motivate Condorcet to his axiomatic belief in natural rights, the fiscal and social problems of the time helped interest him in the mathematical analysis of social questions. His *Essai sur l'application de l'analyse à la probabilité des décisions rendues à la pluralité des voix* (1785) was partly a reaction to Turgot's interest in consultative assemblies to supplement the provincial Estates in France and to the interest of legal reformers in juries. Turgot and Condorcet both believed that the will of a jury or an assembly should not merely represent a consensus of opinion, but should have assured grounds for belief (giving it an intellectual imperative analogous to the moral imperative of Rousseau's general will). Condorcet therefore analysed questions of truth and rational choice, not merely opinion. In fact, in a lecture of 1787 in the private adult education centre of the Lycée, he explored the question of probable guilt of an accused, given a jury decision. In other words, given the adoption of a resolution by a simple majority, what is the probability of a "decision conformable to the truth"?[48] Benefiting from Pierre-Simon Laplace's discussions in the Académie des Sciences, Condorcet assumed that the probability of rational choice would be greater than 50 per cent in an enlightened assembly and less than 50 per cent in an unenlightened assembly.[49] By arithmetic calculation the larger a numerous, unenlightened assembly, the less likely were correct decisions. Condorcet produced a fruitful discussion of the merits of preferential rank-order voting and run-off balloting. However, he could never avoid a somewhat tautological element, the proposition that enlightened voters yield enlightened decisions. Thus, even a probabilistic approach to political sciences reinforced the need for an informed public.

At the instigation of mathematician J.-C. de Borda, the Académie des Sciences adopted a rank-order voting system in the 1780s, and Revolutionary legislators later discussed appropriate balloting and majorities for juries and electors. Early in the Revolution, in 1790 Sieyès and Condorcet founded the politically moderate Société de 1789, in which, with thirteen of the future members of the Class of Moral and Political Sciences (including club secretary Grouvelle, Cabanis, Roederer, Du Pont, Charles-Maurice Talleyrand, and L.-F.-É. Ramond), Condorcet discussed a "social art" devoted to agronomy, economics, public finance, government, and law reform.[50] By 1793 he had broadened his concern with decision theory to a comprehensive "social mathematics." In this category, he placed virtually all mathematical theory or analysis concerned with such economic issues as agricultural production, taxation, interest, and banking. Mathematical techniques were critical for calculating the retirement of government debt and the relative advantage of interest rates on categories of French Treasury loans – perpetual loans, life annuities, lottery loans. To make these calculations accurate, social mathematics also required a reliable empirical base – demographic surveys of "particular facts" leading to "discoveries of general facts" about life expectancy and mortality.[51] Ever since the Académie des Sciences had become interested in estimates of the population of Paris in 1780, mathematicians assisted the government bureaucracy in seeking a general law of mortality. The government also needed such information for social assistance, because a viable pension fund might rest on the life expectancy of small investors in an interest-bearing fund.[52]

Ultimately, Condorcet hoped to collect data through world-wide research teams of census-takers or through sampling techniques on physical and psychological characteristics of populations. Seeking influences on life expectancy, marriage rates, fertility, mortality from disease, body build, physical strength, intelligence, and character, he would correlate the factors of climate, soil, diet, habits of life, customs, occupations, medical and hygienic practices, laws, governments, and other social institutions. These mathematical techniques would make more sophisticated the environmental imperative of Montesquieu and the hygienists. The famous *Esquisse d'un tableau historique*, posthumously published in 1795, foretold the critical influences of malnutrition for the life expectancy of the poor, of dietary abuse by the rich, and of sanitation and hygiene for the community at large. Condorcet foresaw that a proper statistical data base could enable physicians to help make organs perfect and to give prescriptions for strength, dexterity, and more acute sense perception.[53]

This ambitious research program blended with both varieties of established eighteenth-century information-gathering. On the one hand, the German founders of *Statistik*, and after them the French regional geographers, stressed the qualitative correlation of the physical geography of a region with its culture. In the Institute statistics became a subdivision of geography. On the other hand, social mathematics was even more akin to the British tradition of "political arithmetic."[54] Institute economists would take up the mission of calculating mortality and life expectancy by strictly quantitative techniques.

To modern critics of the social sciences, the most chilling aspect of social mathematics was the opinion that agreement on social policy could end Revolutionary disorder. Condorcet hoped that mathematical precision would "impose silence on prejudices and bad faith." One could destroy the "empire that talk has usurped over reason, the passions over truth, active ignorance over enlightenment." Yet several qualifying reminders are in order. The most careful recent study of Condorcet reminds us that, despite his élitist and technocratic side, he was also a political liberal committed to natural rights. In his vision of human society in the future, there would indeed be social harmony, but also one where "any action violating another's right will be physically impossible, as cold-blooded barbarism is to most men today."[55] The statisticians would be independent scientists, not government policy-makers. Hence, Condorcet thought the social sciences would contribute vast new powers to improve health, intelligence, and character. At the same time, he saw no great dilemma in reconciling science and freedom.

For the Institute, the inheritance of Enlightenment culture included an empirical and possibly statistical environmental study intended for human geographers, physicians and hygienists, and statisticians. The more tailored to individual cases such studies were, the more flexible the policy recommendations. Though the eighteenth century was a self-proclaimed age of loyalty to the Newtonian method and to proper observational technique, a surprisingly significant component in the models for all social sciences rested on postulates that were followed by deductive reasoning. The subtle regularities in Montesquieu's thought could be challenged as too relativist. Montesquieu and the economists themselves rested their views partly on supposedly descriptive natural laws that could be invoked as moral imperatives. Even a more empirical economist like Adam Smith reasoned from a few fundamental, virtually self-evident assumptions about human nature. Even greater impetus to the gap between the empiricist ideal and deductive practice came from the Condillacian paradox. One could reason geometrically about the transformation of sense-data or manipulate signs to perfect language. Such deductive reasoning could introduce rigidity, allowing less room for empirical refutation and resulting in more of an unchecked tendency to use science for control.

The doctrines of Montesquieu could be used in the republican context to try to forestall any unwelcome deviations from republican virtue. Physiocratic and Smithian economic doctrines could stress the importance of defending proprietors. Geographers and historians could too easily revert to a four-stages justification of European superiority and of social inequality. However, the belief in individual rights and guarantees meant that political theory offered some counterbalance to social control. Subsequent chapters will explore more closely the themes of the conversion of doctrines that threatened the Ancien Régime into tools for stabilizing the Revolution and maintaining critical individual faculties in the face of a newly strengthened government. Given the development of the moral and political sciences at the heart of Enlightenment culture, Revolutionaries would take advantage of the atmosphere of reconciliation and reconstruction after the Terror to place these studies at the summit of new cultural institutions. After consideration of the planning of the Institute, we shall explore just how much of a break with the past the membership and practices of the Class of Moral and Political Sciences represented.

3 The Institute Intellectuals: Change and Continuity

THE ENCYCLOPEDIST SPIRIT

The Encyclopedist spirit that was so prevalent in the late Enlightenment promoted the underlying unity of knowledge and the reciprocal benefit of interaction among the arts and sciences. Encyclopedism was the rationale for the existence of the Class of Moral and Political Sciences because it assumed that moral and political subjects could become scientific, according to Enlightenment social science models. This embodiment of Enlightenment aspirations was the most striking innovation in the founding of the Institute.

Yet Institute members manifested surprising continuity in social origins and political opinions with Ancien Régime academic élites. The republican Directors nominated the first third of their number but clandestine royalist political opinions persisted. The nostalgia for old-style history and literature academies among apolitical scholars and politically reactionary writers also worked against Encyclopedism to hasten the abolition of the Institute's Second Class.

The first of three Revolutionary incarnations of Encyclopedism appeared in the comprehensive reform plan for academies of 1791. Before his death that April, the great orator Honoré-Gabriel-Riqueti de Mirabeau included a discourse on academies in his public education project, published several months later by Cabanis, his physician and collaborator. In September 1791 Talleyrand, speaking for the Constitution Committee, proposed a much more ambitious education plan, but the adjournment of the Constituent Assembly prevented any

Table 1
Plans for the Institute

Mirabeau Plan	Talleyrand Plan	Condorcet Plan
National Academy	National Institute	National Society of Arts and Sciences
CLASSES	CLASSES	CLASSES
1 Sciences	1 Mathematical and	1 Mathematical and
2 Literature	Physical Sciences and	Physical Sciences
3 Philosophy	Mechanical Arts	2 Moral and Political
	2 Philosophy	Sciences
		3 Applications of Sciences to the Arts
Arts Academy		4 Literature and Fine Arts

discussion. Talleyrand had carefully read Condorcet's memoirs on public education in the *Bibliothèque de l'homme public* (1790–91). Finally, the hubbub of the French declaration of war on Austria and Prussia in April 1792 in the Legislative Assembly sidetracked Condorcet's own education plan until December, when the National Convention considered it in a more anti-élitist atmosphere.

The first impressive feature of each of these three proposals was the topos of mutually reinforcing Revolutionary liberty and learning. Long before the Terror, Mirabeau stated: "Let us not make a revolution of Goths and Vandals."[1] He would eliminate the objectionable royal veto in academy elections, as well as aristocratic honorary members. But "public opinion" would be represented by the Assembly education committee and a committee of the Paris Department which would both present nomination lists to academicians.[2]

Encyclopedism itself was a second major theme in each report. For the first time since the ill-fated Perrault proposal, philosophy was included by Mirabeau as one of three sections of a new National Academy. He endorsed the universal applicability of Condillac's "analytic" method, and recommended chairs of higher education in an "encyclopedic school," the National Lycée, in universal history, public economy, and ethics.[3]

Talleyrand, who invented the name National Institute, spoke of a "studying and teaching encyclopedia." The various classes of the Institute would hold common public sessions. He envisioned not just a forum for research and discussion, but also a teaching corps that would include all existing chairs in Paris at the Collège royal and the Jardin des Plantes. Talleyrand's encyclopedic unity differed somewhat from Condillac's and also from Condorcet's. His First Class (see Table 1), dedicated to "physical man," would be composed of sciences of empirical observation. The Second Class, for "moral man," lumped rational philosophy with literature and the arts. This separation of human studies from the empirical and natural sciences did nothing to promote their scientific status, but may have reflected the actual deductive and literary practice of many eighteenth-century models of the social sciences.

Academic divisions could help define emergent sciences and direct academy members to areas of study. Talleyrand anticipated some of Condorcet's categories. In the first section, for ethics, of the Second Class, Talleyrand included logic and metaphysics, the latter encompassing a "science of the soul, or psychology." The second section, science of government, included public law or law of nations, political economy, and political arithmetic. The third and fourth sections would replace the Académie des Inscriptions and comprise ancient history and antiquities, and modern history and languages. A fifth section of grammar and rhetoric and a sixth of eloquence and poetry would replace the Académie française.[4] Thus, the first two sections anticipated four in the Institute's Second Class, while the third and fourth history sections would be redivided in 1795 between the Class of Moral and Political Sciences and the Class of Literature and Fine Arts.

Condorcet's National Society would have supervised the *lycées* for higher education without being accountable to a ministry, but it would not itself teach. Encyclopedism in the context of 1792 included Diderot's desire to give new dignity to the mechanical arts. Hence, seventy-two applied scientists would outnumber the forty-eight pure scientists. Condorcet stressed the "natural relations" of the all sciences amid the benefits of mutual communication and cross-fertilization of knowledge.[5]

Condorcet divided his Second Class of Moral and Political Sciences into five sections: (1) metaphysics and the theory of moral sentiments (from Adam Smith), though Condorcet's higher-education plan employed the more Condillacian "analysis of sensations and ideas"; (2) natural law, law of nations, and *science sociale* (the theoretical science of government); (3) political economy; (4) public law and legislation (the applied science of government); (5) history, separate from the antiquities and monuments section of the Fourth Class of Literature and Fine Arts. Geography appeared only in the hydraulics and navigation section of the applied sciences class.[6]

Condorcet thus provided the essential blueprint for the Institute as founded in 1795, while Talleyrand furnished the name. Even in 1792 Condorcet called attention to differences from the existing academies. The King would have no voice, there would be no internal hierarchy of members, and all members would work for "public utility" and the "glory of the *patrie*." With half the membership from the departments, Paris could not dominate national cultural life.[7]

By the end of 1792 the accumulated resentments against the academies resulted in the rejection of the National Society by the Convention. Revered moralists such as J.-H. Bernardin de Saint-Pierre had warned that folk wisdom was superior to that of academies. The Convention's abolition of academies on 8 August 1793 was the culmination of anti-aristocratic and antiroyalist fervour, rather than an attack on science or on learning itself.[8]

After the sobering interlude of the Terror and in the final months of the more moderate Thermidorian (post-Robespierre) Convention, the draftsmen of the new constitution of 1795 judged the moment opportune to resurrect the academies. The papers of education commissioner Pierre-Louis Ginguené indicate some private fears, which he never publicly voiced, that a new caste of intellectuals would hamper a more democratic policy of awarding government pensions. To the older themes of the correlation between learning and freedom and the Encyclopedist imperative to unify learning, the Convention Constitution Commission of Eleven added new obligations to atone for the "vandalism" of the Terror and to achieve national reconciliation. On 24 June 1795 the commissioner, Daunou, ignored suggestions for a teaching body and proposed instead that the new academies occupy themselves only with "extending the progress of the sciences and arts" (later amended to include both publication and research) and advising the government.[9]

In the commission's official proposal, Daunou largely followed Condorcet's divisions, but the first section of the Class of Moral and Political Sciences became analysis of sensations and ideas, while the second section gave ethics prominence as an independent science. Daunou conflated the theoretical and practical sciences of government in the single section of social science (*science sociale*) and legislation. History and political economy rounded out the subject-matter of the Second Class, while antiquities and monuments remained in the Class of Literature and Fine Arts.[10]

On 24 August and 6 September, in a conference with Daunou, two delegates of the Convention's Public Instruction Committee, Joseph Lakanal and chemist Antoine-François Fourcroy, eliminated the applied sciences class. Possibly Fourcroy feared competition with his own related proposals for establishing or consolidating the civil, military, and naval engineering schools. He therefore incorporated physicians, agronomists, and mechanical engineers in a much larger Class of Mathematical and Physical Sciences. Specialists in the defunct hydraulics and navigation section would occupy a sixth, geography section in the Class of Moral and Political Sciences.[11] Indeed, this section would soon become a strange amalgam of scholars, diplomats, and practical navigators.

In reporting on the public education law to the Convention on 15 October, Daunou, despite tributes to Talleyrand and Condorcet, expressed aversion for any "academic church" that would supervise the educational system. The Institute would be independent only if it did not rival a government ministry. Nor would the Institute be a new corporation threatening the formation of other learned societies. Daunou claimed that in an atmosphere of both liberty and order the Institute would be the "epitome of the learned world, the representative body of the republic of letters." The independent men of learning in the Institute would inhabit a "national temple whose doors would always be closed to intrigue, and would open only to the impact of a justified renown."[12] At the first glittering public session on 4 April 1796, Daunou reiterated the theme: "Those who have the right to ask work of the Institute would not have the power of commanding its opinions; and since it has no means of building itself into a rival of authority, it will also not become the slave or instrument of tyranny." The image of the autonomous intellectual, heir to the philosophes, was all-powerful. In what would become the enduring mythology of the Institute, in which knowledge and freedom are linked, Daunou repeated that the "moral and political sciences ... prepared, during this century, the imposing revolution which finishes it and which calls twenty-five million men to exercise their rights and to study their interests and duties." Conversely, only a Republic would permit the free development of the human sciences.[13]

In the Revolutionary atmosphere, the reality of political considerations intruded upon Daunou's image of "doors closed to intrigue." The myth of the break with the past would supposedly mean the exclusion from the Institute not only of overt royalists but also of overt partisans of Terror or of Jacobinism (neo-Jacobins). Indeed, Joseph Lakanal's report on the Institute in 1796 to the legislative Council of 500 celebrated a republican gallery of talents purged of aristocracy and royalism.[14] Yet the collective biography of the Class of Moral and Political Sciences reveals a surprisingly broad political spectrum, despite firm government control. A significant number of members and associates were from the former privileged orders or had made their reputation under the Ancien Régime. Some manifested little interest in Revolutionary politics or were evidently opposed to further revolutionary action. These could not share the Idéologues' concepts of political stability. For some members, Enlightenment philosophical interests coincided with a conservative view of the Revolution, while others had never shared the critical spirit of the Enlightenment toward religious institutions. Both these groups were right-wing moralists – protectors in Lipset's sense of purveyors of tradition, but hostile to an anticlerical regime. In addition to its initial control of nominations, the Directors excluded a few persons with dubious political opinions in the critical period after the antiroyalist coup of Fructidor in September 1797, when they purged a Class member, C.-E.-J.-P. Pastoret, and an associate, the Director F. Barthélemy.[15]

Moreover, the accepted historical image of the Class is as a "privileged bastion of the Idéologues."[16] The seven members and four associates known as Idéologues (see Appendix 2 for an annotated list of the Second Class) were a group of physicians and philosophers who advocated empiricist epistemology, anticlericalism, and sometimes monist metaphysics. The antipathy of their leaders to religion, even of the deist variety, was the chief reason for anti-Idéologue hostility and for their weakness as a cohesive movement. The élan of the Idéologues gave them disproportionate influence in the Class. Yet this minority could not impose its choices for new members or entirely control the Class agenda. Reflecting on the achievements of the Idéologues and on their weaknesses will show that they in fact accomplished little to justify the abolition of the Class in 1803, but they could be provocative enough to provoke the anger of the First Consul.

NOMINATIONS AND PATRONAGE: THE DEPENDENCE OF THE MEN OF LETTERS

Even the initial nomination in November 1795 of the forty-eight members in the "electing third," who would choose their other ninety-six colleagues, involved last-minute intrigue to remove the politically unacceptable. The Directory revised Lakanal's list for the Convention by rejecting twenty-five of his forty-eight choices for the Institute, and five of his twelve for the Second Class, including the moderately royalist economist Du Pont and conservative historians Garnier and Anquetil (see Appendix 2).[17] As a political ploy, the move failed, since the electing third chose most of the removed candidates, and one of the Directory nominations for history, Jean-Baptiste-Claude Delisle de Sales, would prove to be a notorious opponent of antiroyalist policies in 1797.[18]

The individual friendships that influenced the election of members in December 1795 and the election of associates in February 1796 spanned all three classes.[19] The election system of the Institute allowed the entire electing third to choose members and all members to choose associates. In subsequent elections after February 1796, each class presented a list of three to the general assemblies of the Institute, which could overturn the first choice of any class. We can locate at least two foci of patronage, however, and one other less coherent, but internally related group: (1) the Idéologues (defined in Appendix 1) and the Auteuil salon circle; (2) a military-naval-diplomatic service élite; and (3) the Académie des Inscriptions group. In the famous distinction made by twentieth-century neo-Marxist philosopher Antonio Gramsci between "traditional" apolitical intellectuals and "organic" articulators of aspirations of a particular social class, the third group could be labelled traditional, while, without oversimplifying to make them out to be bourgeois puppets, the Idéologues fit more closely a portrait of defenders of the new Revolutionary élites.[20] Only the Idéologues of the Auteuil circle were self-conscious and clearly oriented toward Enlightenment social science models. They met unofficially at the salons of Madame Helvétius until 1800, and later at those of Destutt de Tracy and Madame de Condorcet in the Paris suburb of Auteuil. Only a few in the military-naval-diplomatic group shared the interests of geographers in determining physical-political relationships, while the third group, composed of historians, was indifferent or hostile to the social sciences. The last two groups were moderate to reactionary in their politics when they expressed political preferences.

In Volney's absence, the most likely providers of patronage for the Auteuil circle were Sieyès, its veritable patriarch, and the politically active Daunou and Garat, with assistance from two dramatists in the Third Class, Marie-Joseph Chénier and, later, F.-J.-S. Andrieux.[21] Ginguené, director-general of public instruction in the Interior ministry, probably chose his employee Le Breton, also a fellow journalist on the *Décade philosophique*, a periodical linked to the Idéologues.[22] Garat probably recommended Cabanis for his writings on medicine, and Sieyès was a friend of Roederer, a former colleague in the Société de 1789 and in the Department of Paris administration.

In electing associates, the Auteuil circle managed to place A.-L.-C. Destutt de Tracy, the most philosophically sophisticated *habitué* of Madame Helvétius's salon, in the analysis of sensations and ideas section. Ginguené probably named another Interior ministry employee, Jacquemont, and a journalistic colleague, Grouvelle; Garat had also employed Grouvelle in the Justice ministry, and he knew the outstanding École normale student Laromiguière. Cabanis could have recommended Montpellier medical graduates de Sèze and Roussel, who both appeared at Madame Helvétius's salons.

Links among the Auteuil circle went back to the pre-Revolutionary Masonic lodges. Helvétius's discussions with astronomer Jérôme

Lalande had helped found the philosophers' Loge des Sciences in 1766, which ultimately became the Neuf Sœurs in 1776. Lodge members included Garat (an apprentice in 1783–84), Cabanis (an apprentice in 1778 and 1783), Ginguené (a journeyman in 1783 and an officer in 1784), Volney, and Sieyès. Destutt de Tracy was a member of a different lodge, La Candeur, in 1776–77, and he appears in the military Bellone lodge of the Penthièvre infantry regiment in 1788. Despite the precedent of the Musée de Paris, however, there is no evidence that either the Neuf Sœurs lodge or its successor, the Société nationale of 1790–92, somehow shaped the Institute agenda.[23]

The Auteuil circle subscribed to Ancien Régime academic culture, in which successful prizewinners might become candidates to the academy. In this way, Degérando, who won the influence of signs on ideas contest in 1799 (the commissioners were Ginguené, Volney, and Roederer) and Prévost, the runner-up in the contest, each in turn became analysis of sensations and ideas section associates in 1800–1.[24]

The sixteen members of the Auteuil circle were a youthful generation (the average age at election was 40.3, and for the eleven Idéologues, it was 41.1). Because seven of the sixteen had no striking accomplishments to their credit before election, patronage played a considerable role. The Institute had special significance for their careers because they had no previous claim to celebrity. The impressive network of the Auteuil circle certainly created a powerful nucleus for shapers of opinion within the Class. But other partly independent networks existed as well.

The second major grouping, the military-naval-diplomatic service élite, existed, among other reasons, because naval officers and diplomats were prominent among available candidates for the geography section. There were as yet no professional geographers, but diplomats were expected to know the population, resources, and military strength of other countries, which was precisely the definition of "statistical" geography.[25] Practical navigators also often became scientific researchers, and the Brest Royal Navy Academy had affiliated with the Paris Académie des Sciences in 1771.[26]

At an organizational meeting of the Institute in December 1795, a member proposed an additional fourth class, for the military and naval arts, thus resurrecting the applied arts class of the Public Instruction Committee.[27] While the suggestion foundered, the election of retired officers to the Second Class effectively achieved a similar objective. The curator of the Dépôt des Cartes et Plans de la Marine, J.-N. Buache, and his former patron and the minister of the Navy, C.-P. Claret de Fleurieu, launched this military-scientific network.[28] There were probably also allies in the First Class, like astronomer Jérôme Lalande, mathematician J.-C. Borda, and geographer G.-R. de Prony. In addition, Buache and Fleurieu selected two former admirals (Liberge and Verdun), a nautical terminology specialist (Romme), and a colonial administrator (Lescallier) as associates. A mining specialist (Coquebert) and a fortifications engineer (Le Michaud) were protégés respectively of the chemist Fourcroy and the military engineer Lazare Carnot in the First Class.[29] Aside from the Navy network, Sieyès and Talleyrand helped designate two diplomats, Reinhard and Barthélemy, both without significant scholarly works and later inactive in the Institute.

In sections other than geography, Carnot and the naturalist Lacepède, both of the First Class, would have supported the candidacy of the military administrator and free-trade advocate Lacuée for the political economy section. The geometer Monge probably recommended the reputed philosopher-officer Caffarelli du Falga to the analysis of sensations and ideas section, and the editor Roederer knew journalist and retired officer Villeterque, an ethics correspondent. Dupont and Lacuée even outwitted the Auteuil circle in electing another retired cavalry officer and journalist, Toulongeon, to an analysis of sensations and ideas vacancy in 1797 on the strength of the memoir he submitted on diet and politics. In this electoral process, the Class as a whole presented Toulongeon, and Tracy tied for second; however, the Institute general assembly ignored the preferences of the Idéologues and section members. Hence, the military-scientific patronage group could sometimes prevent the Idéologues from winning elections.[30] While Idéologues like Sieyès and Roederer may have nominated some of the military and naval members, the non-scholars resembled a de facto, though not necessarily socially élite, "honorific" group, whose members read few memoirs to the Class.[31] Only Fleurieu was an innovative thinker.

While Lakanal trumpeted the republican character of the Institute, its members failed to eliminate the pension distinctions of the style familiar in the Ancien Régime. In the former Académie des Sciences and Académie des Inscriptions, seniority most often determined rank and eligibility for the places of royal pensioners. For the Institute, the Councils had legislated a fixed stipend of 1,500 *livres*, but in August 1796 the Institute limited new members to 900 *livres* as part of a long-term plan to create three tiers of seniority, with stipends respectively at 900, 1,500, and 2,100 *livres*. While that specific plan apparently never came into effect, budgetary records show that from at least 1798 until the reorganization of 1803, new members received only 900 *livres* (including 300 *livres* that were withdrawn from the total fund, for attending meetings), while the remainder of the stipend was distributed equally to all founding members. The only members not receiving the latter windfall occupied remunerative public offices, which required suspension of the entire indemnity. The Institute, in turn, reassigned these suspended indemnities in equal portions to members over age sixty.[32] Hence, continuity of academic practice took precedence over republican simplicity.

In another way the more specifically "honorific" service élite represented continuity with the Ancien Régime. Ten were former nobles, while three members (Fleurieu, Bougainville, and Toulongeon) and three associates (Verdun de la Crenne, Liberge de Granchain, and Barthélemy) had royalist inclinations. Certainly they gave the Second Class a different tone from that of the majority of the republican Idéologues, though only the full members would have been consistently present for Institute meetings in Paris.

The third group, the former members of the Académie des Inscriptions, did not have well-defined patronage networks, but there was an apparent bias towards electing former members of academies, as in the case of Académie des Sciences member Bougainville for the geography section.[33] What, after all, could have been more appropriate for a message of reconciliation and stability than to give these new chairs to former academicians? The Directory had nominated former Académie des Inscriptions members Lévesque for the Second Class history section, and J. Dussaulx, P.-J. Bitaubé, C. Dupuis, and A. Mongez for the Third Class sections of ancient languages and of antiquities and monuments. Since the history section was not large enough, the Institute members chose legal historians formerly in the Académie des Inscriptions for vacancies in the legislation section. Pastoret was a historian of ancient Near Eastern, Roman, and criminal law, while Houard, an associate, studied Norman customary law. The other seven former Académie des Inscriptions members and one correspondent (Anquetil) were in the history section. The politically conservative Anquetil wrote popular works on sixteenth- and seventeenth-century France. Dacier, a renowned medievalist who lost precious manuscripts in the closure of the Académie des Inscriptions in 1793, had been its permanent secretary and would work consistently for the re-establishment of a separate history academy. He found a willing colleague in Delisle de Sales, who had not been in the academy but was inimical to Idéologue concerns. The associate and former refractory cleric J.-J. Garnier, author of the most recent portions of a multi-volumed history of France, declined to participate in the Second Class but read memoirs to the reorganized Class of History and Ancient Literature after 1803.[34]

Table 2
Provincial Academies and the Class of Moral and Political Sciences:
Recruitment by Order and Noble Status

	% of members of provincial academies, 1700–89 (average for 33 societies)	% of members in the Class of Moral and Political Sciences, 1795–1803
Clergy	20	20
Nobility	37	26
Third Estate	43	54
Noble status	43	27
Roturier status	57	73

Source: For information on the provincial academies, Daniel Roche, *Le Siècle des lumières en province: Académies et académiciens provinciaux, 1680–1789* (Paris, 1978), 2:381–4, 387. The author gratefully acknowledges permission granted by Mouton Éditeur and the École des Hautes Études en Sciences sociales to use data appearing in this volume for Tables 2, 3, and 9.

SOCIAL ORIGINS AND CAREERS

The differences among the patronage groups and friendship networks in the Second Class suggest both political divergences and philosophical differences on Enlightenment social science ideals. We may be able to evaluate better how much change and how much continuity there was in the Institute by investigating social origins, occupational distribution, and patterns in the careers of members. In one respect, the Class of Moral and Political Sciences continued a long-term trend towards a diminished role for the clergy. In principle, this development could have favoured the secular social sciences, although their most bitter opponents were as likely to be deists as Christian. Tables 2 and 3 show that seventeen members were clergymen (20 per cent of total membership), as was the case in the provincial academies in 1789, a lower percentage than in the Paris-based Académie française or Académie des Inscriptions. Almost all seventeen were from the lower clergy, with Talleyrand the only one of noble ancestry. The members of the group were more analogous to the *curés*, who were "ordinary members" and "associates" in the provincial academies, than to the aristocratic bishops and eminent abbots in the Paris academies.[35] By 1795 only four clergy were still active in the Class, constitutional bishops Grégoire and Talleyrand, deacon J. Gaudin, and Protestant minister J. Senebier, while seven former clergy were secularized in status as well as in outlook, some with antagonism to clerical interests (Sieyès, Daunou, Lakanal, Le Breton, Laromiguière, Jacquemont, and Champagne). Four others retained religious values but had adapted to the new order by taking teaching or library positions.

Table 3
Paris Academies in the Period 1700–89 and the Class of Moral and Political Sciences:
Recruitment by Order and Noble Status

	% Académie française	% Académie des Inscriptions	% Académie des Sciences	% Class of Moral and Political Sciences, 1795–1803
Clergy	42	32	13	20
Nobility	38	38	27	26
Third Estate	20	30	60	54
Noble status	75	51	(est. 30)	27
Roturier status	25	49	(est. 70)	73

Source: For information on the Paris academies, a summation of figures in Daniel Roche, *Le Siècle*, 1:287; 2:437, Table 45B; McClellan's figure in "The Académie Royale des Sciences, 1699–1793," for clergy in the Académie des Sciences is 15.6 per cent for nobility, 26.2 per cent, and for the Third Estate, 58.2 per cent.

The Revolution itself was responsible for the scarcity of clergy in academies, but the secularizing trend was also the culmination of a longer process. Daniel Roche's study shows the reduced rate of recruitment of clergy to the Académie française after 1750 (48 per cent from 1700 to 1750, but 29 per cent from 1750 to 1790), as well as the low average in the eighteenth century (13 per cent) in the Académie des Sciences.[36] A recent study of the nineteenth-century Académie des Sciences morales et politiques failed to find a single clergyman active in it from 1832 to 1852, while the recruitment of clergy in the Académie française in the first half of the nineteenth century declined to 7 per cent.[37]

After all the Revolutionary denunciations of noble status during the Terror and the genuine threats made as late as November 1797 to noble citizenship rights, one might expect former nobles to be in an analogous decline in the Second Class. But the figure of twenty-two nobles (26 per cent of membership) is about the same as the century-long average for the Académie des Sciences and includes men from seven *noblesse d'épée* families and seven *noblesse de robe* families, as well as four members who were personally ennobled and four of unspecified noble ancestry.[38] With the exception of Destutt de Tracy and the rather slippery Talleyrand, they formed a covert royalist contingent. While the Directory purged suspected royalist opponents of the coup of Fructidor in 1797, the Institute never considered action against ex-noble members, not even Liberge de Granchain who was erroneously on the émigré list in 1797–98.[39]

In addition to this measure of continuity in the Class with Ancien Régime élites, the composition of the former Third Estate members

Table 4
Careers of Members of the Class of Moral and Political Sciences,
1795–1803, in percentages

LEGAL AND MEDICAL CAREERS	
Judges, high legal officials	6
Lawyers, legal historians	6
Physicians	5
SCHOLARS AND MEN OF LETTERS	
Active clergy	5
Faculty professors	7
Teachers, school administrators	6
Librarians, archivists	10
Writers, scholars, journalists	16
CIVILIAN GOVERNMENT SERVICE	
Diplomacy or navy and colonial administration	8
Other high government administration	11
Government officials	7
ACTIVE AND RETIRED MILITARY OFFICERS	11
PROPRIETORS	1
UNKNOWN	1

resembled the non-entrepreneurial bourgeoisie of Ancien Régime academies (see Table 4).[40] Many non-noble sons of merchants or financiers opted for letters and public service, while sons of professionals, officials, and proprietors chose intellectual careers, such as teaching, archival work, journalism, and writing.[41] As in the Ancien Régime literary academies, scholars and men of letters predominated in the Second Class. Professional and official notables also leavened the contingent who were in intellectual careers.[42]

A look at the social origins of the Second Class shows the near disappearance of active clergy and the relatively better opportunities for former *roturiers*. Yet there is continuity as well as mutation – a formerly aristocratic group persisted.[43] While honorary membership disappeared, a military-naval-diplomatic service élite achieved election in an effectively "honorific" category. A hierarchy among members even reappeared with the differential adjustment of stipends. The choice of careers among academicians was surprisingly similar before and after the Revolution. This is not to minimize, however, the changed meaning of being a teacher or an author after 1789. In the post-Revolutionary era there was an increase in employment opportunities for journalists and secular teachers, and, in an age of pamphleteering,

Table 5
Career Patterns and Membership in the Institute

%	Pattern
14	Institute aided political and cultural prominence
21	Election was a reward for prominence and aided career advancement
19	Election was a reward for prominence but advancement was unrelated to Institute
36	Election was a reward for prominence; career remained stable
10	Relationship of Institute and career not determinable

Prominence defined as eminent government service or authorship of successful work
Advancement defined as movement to greater literary or scholarly success after election to the Institute or promotion to a more prestigious or powerful position after election to the Institute

men of letters found a wider market and possibly higher pay for their skills.[44]

A study of the patterns in the careers of members and associates (Table 5 defines career advancement) further differentiates the "new men" of the Revolution from the persistent élite of the Ancien Régime. For our purposes we have necessarily been subjective in defining prominence for all those who held high legal, administrative, or military positions. Thirty-six per cent of the Class achieved renown *before* 1789 and their careers remained, relatively speaking, on a plateau after their election to the Institute. Twenty-six of them made up a group of apolitical or moderate conservative scholars and military officers, somewhat like Gramsci's traditional intellectuals. The Institute sanctioned existing prestige for these men of the Ancien Régime. Nineteen of them were from the traditional fields of ethics, history, and geography, and only three were from the Auteuil circle.

POLITICAL OPINIONS

A true picture of the commitment of the Second Class to the Revolution must include consideration of the political élite of twenty-eight men who served in Revolutionary assemblies before election to the Institute. Not one was a geographer, and only one was a historian. Despite the constraints of Directory republicanism, there was not a monolithic political attitude among this active élite. The most common inclinations of the entire Class membership were to be patriotic in 1789, cautious and ambivalent in August 1792, persecuted or frightened in 1793–94, relieved after Thermidor, and supportive of political moderates after 1795. For thirty-four members and associates of the Second Class (39 per cent of the total), the Terror was indeed terrifying. Fifteen were imprisoned for periods of as long as fourteen months,

while eight took refuge from denunciation or proscription. Five emigrated from France, while six others prudently hid out from any
possible investigation. The effects were as serious for scholars as were
the tragic circumstances for scientists in the Académie des Sciences.[45]

Little wonder that the trauma of the Terror reinforced the quest for
stability, or that "popular furies" haunted Class members. One may
arrive at a tentative, if crude, index of revolutionary fervour that is based
on known "progressive" or "conservative" reactions to: (1) the 1789
crisis; (2) issues in the Constituent Assembly; (3) republican or monarchist opinions in 1792; (4) the roll-call of votes in the Convention; (5) the
Girondin crisis of 1793; (6) the Terror (as manifested by emigration,
imprisonment, and refuge); (7) the coup of Fructidor; (8) Bonaparte's
actions in 1800–2; and (9) the restoration of Louis XVIII.[46]

The results are inevitably skewed because there are numerous
recorded opinions for some members but hardly any for others. By
these flawed criteria, the most radical in the Second Class were members of the Convention – the regicide Garat, the moderate Mountain
faction members Deleyre and Merlin, the regicides Sieyès, Grégoire,
and Lakanal of the Plain, the pro-Fructidor Director La Revellière-
Lépeaux, the even more moderate Convention member Cambacérès,
and the Council of 500 member Cabanis. Other Idéologues, such as
Volney, Tracy, and Daunou, as well as Baudin and Girondin allies
Garran-Coulon and Creuzé-Latouche, all three members of the Convention, were close to the centre of the political spectrum within the
Class. Roederer was distinctly to the right, while at the other extreme
were Pastoret, a moderate royalist, and royalist sympathizers Degérando, Delisle de Sales, the future consul Lebrun, the historian Papon,
and the conservative retired admirals Bougainville, Verdun de la
Crenne, and de Liberge de Granchain. Almost all of the known expressions of opinion in the history section are conservative or reactionary.
Royalists were easier to find in the Class than extremists of the left or
neo-Jacobins.

Politically sensitive events, such as the purge of the Institute after
the 1797 coup of Fructidor, pitted a triumphant republican Director
La Revellière-Lépeaux against the suspected royalist Director Barthélemy and his scientific colleague Carnot. In short, the moderate
republican faction of the political-scholarly élite acted against the much
smaller clandestine royalist faction. The coup accentuated divisions
between republican heirs of the Enlightenment and royalist Enlightenment conservatives such as Toulongeon, Delisle de Sales, and the
naturalist and legislation associate Ramond de Carbonnières.

Members of the newer disciplines may have been more politically
active because of their youth. Though there is no linear relationship,

the younger men were more sympathetic to the Revolution, and the older historians and geographers the least.[47] Only one historian, Koch, sat in any assembly before 1802, when the Senate chose him and Dacier for the already purged Tribunate. Fleurieu, later a senator under Napoleon, was the only geographer in an earlier Revolutionary assembly, and the Directory purged him after the coup of Fructidor.

For the historians, the Revolution not only brought little promise of increased social or intellectual ascendancy, but in a few cases it wreaked great havoc on their incomes. Anquetil surrendered his parish and left the constitutional clergy for a temporary position as archivist with the ministry of External Relations. Dacier lost precious Froissard manuscripts in the government confiscation of papers of the Académie des Inscriptions, as well as his salary as permanent secretary of the academy. Papon, historian of Provence, lost three pensions from the defunct Estates of Provence (8,000 *livres*), from the King's brother, the Comte de Provence, and from the royal Treasury. Garnier retired to an obscure collège in the Vendée after refusing the constitutional oath at the Collège royal. At least four historians, Anquetil, Koch, Garnier, and Papon, and possibly as many as three others, Delisle de Sales, Dacier, and Gudin, were *sub rosa* royalists. Garnier destroyed the portions of his history of France that could be construed as antiroyalist, while Koch wrote an open letter to his department expressing horror at the overthrow of the monarchy. During the Terror, four historians, Dacier, Garnier, Papon, and Gaillard, voluntarily retired to country hiding-places; one, Gudin, was outlawed, and three, Anquetil, Koch, and de Sales, endured prison terms.[48]

The geographers were more evenly split on loyalty to the Revolution, but four were decidedly royalist. Fleurieu had been governor of the Dauphin in 1792, Bougainville resigned his Navy commission early that year, and both were devoted to the royal family. The Navy struck Verdun de la Crenne from its list in May 1791 for failure to report, and he emigrated to Spain in 1794. Liberge de Granchain was an ex-noble suspect in 1793, and proscribed again after the coup of Fructidor. Fourcroy managed to save from arrest ex-noble geography associate Coquebert de Montbret. The deported Director Barthélemy was, of course, one of the prime targets of the Fructidor coup.

The collective biography shows, then, that the Second Class continued the decline in the role of the clergy and the numerical preponderance of the bourgeois, already evident in pre-Revolutionary cultural élites. Yet there was no definitive break with the past. Rather, the Class was a short-lived union of older, more established, more conservative, or apolitical men in traditional disciplines such as history and geography, with more youthful, pro-Revolutionary (though far from politically radical) men in the innovative social sciences. With a substantial contingent of former nobles, its body of illustrious Ancien Régime men of letters, including the group from the Académie des Inscriptions, the Class was more than a purely republican meritocracy.

IDÉOLOGUES AND ANTI-IDÉOLOGUES

The Idéologue circle had the most coherent intellectual program within the Second Class. Its members were important enough to induce Bonaparte to reorganize the Institute, but this action was mostly due to his irritability at political opposition outside the Institute. The Idéologues did little in the Class to anger Bonaparte, and non-Idéologues also heavily participated in meetings and in the publication of memoirs.

The influence of the Idéologues enabled them to retain, in violation of the rules, Destutt de Tracy, Laromiguière, and Degérando as non-Parisian associates even though Tracy lived in the nearby Auteuil suburb and the others had nominally disqualifying (effective after a year of residence) *de facto* Paris residence. Three of nine Class secretaries, Daunou, Ginguené, and Le Breton, were from the Auteuil circle. Secretaries' reports for public sessions or to legislatures were normally not politicized, though the First Consul might have been displeased that two of his political enemies, Ginguené and Daunou, were secretaries in 1802. However, the reorganization of the Institute failed in any conceivable way to remove their influence: after 1803, while the harmless Dacier was permanent secretary of the new Class of History and Ancient Literature, Ginguené and Daunou still wrote notices of Class activity.[49]

The Idéologues, who comprised about one-sixth of the Second Class, excluding associates, were disproportionately active in Institute committee work, especially on prize-contest commissions. Eighteen of twenty-three commissions had at least one Idéologue member, and 28 per cent of commissioners were Idéologues. Roederer, Ginguené, and Daunou were especially prominent. Even more remarkably, the Idéologues wrote thirteen of twenty surviving prize-commission reports, though Roederer's preparation of five reports in political economy distorts the figures. The Class generally adopted the commissioners' recommendations. In this context, Roederer and Daunou in particular had unusual influence in shaping the public image of the Class.[50] This preponderant influence did not extend, however, to Class public sessions, where Idéologues delivered only 19 per cent of the readings.

A more impressive indicator of the influence of the Idéologues appears in the tabulation of memoirs published in the Class collection.[51]

Table 6
The Publication of Memoirs by Members of the Class of Moral and Political Sciences and by Idéologues

	Memoirs Written	Memoirs Published in the Collection of the Class	Total Pages Published in the Collection of the Class
SECTION			
Analysis of sensations			708
and ideas	31	17 (incl. 2 abridged)	56
Ethics	35	3 (incl. 1 abridged)	235
Social sciences and			68
legislation	23	7	1739
Political economy	61	5	273
History	118	42 (incl. 12 abridged)	
Geography	50	12	
Idéologues	46	16	764

Table 7
Memoirs Published in the Collection of the Class by Subject Areas

	SUBJECT AREAS						
SECTION OF THE MEMBERS	Analysis of sensations and ideas	Ethics	Social science and legislation	Political economy	History	Geography	Total
Analysis of sensations and ideas	15			2			17
Ethics		2			1		3
Social science and legislation		1	5		1		7
Political economy			1	4			5
History	2	5			35		42
Geography						12	12
Total	17	8	6	6	37	12	86

The analysis of sensations and ideas section had a more successful rate of publication (55 per cent) than its nearest competitor, the history section (36 per cent) (see tables 6, 7). The seven Idéologue authors published only 35 per cent of their memoirs, chiefly because of Roederer's preference for his own promptly published newspapers, the *Journal de Paris* and the more specialized *Journal d'économie publique*, with their higher circulations than the published series of memoirs.

Table 8
Attendance at Meetings of the Class of Moral and Political Sciences by Members
in the Four-year Period (except as indicated) from An VII (1798–99) to An X (1801–2),
in percentages

Idéologues		Others			
Daunou	70	Delisle de Sales	95	Le Breton	55
Ginguené	44 (3 yrs)	Naigeon	95	Champagne	54
Volney	26	Saint-Pierre	94 (2 yrs)	Bigot	53 (2 yrs)
Sieyès	18	Mentelle	93 (3 yrs)	Bougainville	52
Roederer	18	Buache	91 (3 yrs)	Lacuée	48 (2 yrs)
Cabanis	4	Legrand d'Aussy	91 (3 yrs)	La Revellière-	
Garat	3	Gossellin	88	Lépeaux	43
		Poirier	88 (1 yr)	Creuzé-	
		Lévesque	85	Latouche	34 (1 yr)
		Anquetil	85	Fleurieu	29
		Baudin	83 (2 yrs)	Toulongeon	16
		Mercier	78	Lakanal	15
		Grégoire	74 (3 yrs)	Cambacérès	8
		Du Pont	68	Reinhard	6
		Garran-Coulon	67	Merlin	3
		Bouchaud	67 (3 yrs)	Talleyrand	3
		Dacier	57	Lebrun	1 (2 yrs)

Average attendance for Idéologues: 26%
Average attendance for non-Idéologues: 58%
Average attendance for all members: 52%

Source: AI, Registres de dépouillement des feuilles de présence, 1D, 13–14, ans IV–XI.

Nevertheless, one should not underestimate the reading time consumed in ordinary sessions of the Class by the prodigious number of
geography and history memoirs. The history section easily ranked first
in number of memoirs read, as did the subject of history as a field of
interest. The Idéologues, in their signal success in publication, could
not completely overshadow their colleagues.

In addition, the attendance rolls, compiled for members only, show
a conspicuously poor Idéologue record (see Table 8). Cabanis was
either ill or busy with the Council of 500 and the Senate. Sieyès was
a diplomat in Berlin in 1798 and a Director in 1799, Ginguené was
ambassador in Turin in 1797 and editor of the *Décade*, while Garat,
ambassador in Naples in 1797, seemed preoccupied with journalism
and his history lectures at the Lycée. Roederer was a true workhorse
until he joined the Council of State in 1800, when in any case he broke
with the goals of the Idéologues. Daunou, despite his political career,
was the only consistently assiduous Idéologue. By contrast, Idéologue
critics Bernardin de Saint-Pierre, Mercier, and Delisle de Sales attended

from 78 to 96 per cent of the meetings in the period from 1799 to 1802.

Certainly the intellectual strengths of the Idéologues in the Class included the permeation among non-Idéologues of the empiricism of Locke, Helvétius, and Condillac. Lévesque, the prolific historian and former protégé of Diderot, wrote four philosophical memoirs, including a study of "obstacles of ancient philosophers [Pythagoras, Plato, and Aristotle] to sound philosophy" (12 Prairial v). Here, Lévesque condemned the ancients for their acceptance of authority and for opposing, at least by their practice, the crucial principle that "man knows only by the senses" which "correct each other's errors." Even Aristotelian physics was guilty of this transgression. In another "ideological memoir" (presented on 22 Fructidor v), Lévesque insisted that natural law was relative to circumstances and that nature included the "savage" and the atheist as well as the civilized and the religious person.[52]

Similarly, the principal of the Prytanée (formerly Louis-le-Grand) school, Jean-François Champagne, a social science and legislation section member, could recommend Aristotle, though only apologetically, because Helvétius cited him and because Aristotelian metaphysics allegedly anticipated the principle described by Locke and Condillac that knowledge comes from sensations.[53] In a memoir on the Stoic ethics of Epictetus in late 1802, legal historian Bouchaud chided both Epictetus and Descartes for calling the soul a portion of "Divinity" and for believing in innate ideas of the sacred and the just. The Class secretary, Daunou, abstracted Bouchaud's memoir with the approving reflection that the hypothesis of innate ideas retarded progress in the theory of knowledge, interrupted useful inquiries about experience, and enshrined unsupported systems.[54]

Yet, for all the measurable intellectual and institutional influence of the Idéologues, they did not have the floor to themselves. Opponents of the Idéologues also sought their own routes to stabilizing the Revolution. They may be divided into two groups: deist partisans of the Enlightenment who were frightened by materialism and the less vocal conservatives who had never been sympathetic to the Enlightenment critical spirit. To the Idéologues, morality was more firmly supported on a natural basis than through religious scaffolding. To their critics, ignorance of morality engraved divinely in the human heart was profoundly threatening to social stability. By the spring of 1797 there was an anti-atheist, antimaterialist counter-current, even among the moderate politicians in the Directorial camp which was otherwise sympathetic to the establishment of moral or social science. In 1797 Director La Revellière-Lépeaux advocated a cult to promote public morality.[55] Less than a year later, in February 1798, Cambacérès, a lawyer and a future Bonapartist opportunist, defined social science as a union of ethics, legislation, and political economy. At the same time he appealed to the legislative experience gained over centuries in the struggle against the "fanaticism of idolatry, the scepticism of the Academy, the man-machine of La Mettrie, the absurd man of the materialists," all of which weaken and destroy the foundations of society.[56] Cambacérès was probably warning against the leading Idéologues, Cabanis and Destutt de Tracy, who by now had both finished a major series of memoirs that were often interpreted as "materialist." One must also recall that after 1800 the Idéologues themselves were divided on the issue of materialism. Later chapters will show how Degérando and Laromiguière drifted away from the doctrines of Cabanis and Destutt de Tracy.

The most vocal opponents of the Idéologues did not constitute a definable patronage group. They were three men of letters who were already famous under the Ancien Régime, but did not become obscure during the Revolution: two eccentric writers and ethics section members, Bernardin de Saint-Pierre and Mercier, and historian Delisle de Sales. Former engineer, botanist, Rousseauist, and ethics lecturer at the École normale, Saint-Pierre had long opposed such conventional science as the Newtonian theory of the tides. On 3 July 1798 he was supposed to report on the ethics section prize contest on institutions suitable to establish public morality. The Class had, however, apparently voted to prevent Saint-Pierre from reading the report, which misrepresented the memoirs as tending toward atheism. Instead, he published a brochure on the nature of ethics which condemned moral relativism. A particular target was Cabanis's study of the influence of age, sex, and temperament on ideas and passions.[57] In Saint-Pierre's autobiographical manuscripts, he charged that Cabanis, in response to the report on the contest presented in private session, shouted, "There is no God and one should renounce speaking of this chimera." The line seems uncharacteristically dogmatic for Cabanis, who later speculated about the existence of a First Cause. Saint-Pierre also ascribed to the Christian Grégoire the unlikely warning that the mention of God's name would bring catcalls, and to Morellet, who was not even a member of the Class, a warning that one must march in step with the century. Since the record is obviously inaccurate, the incident involving Cabanis remains apocryphal.[58] Nevertheless, Saint-Pierre was clearly opposed to the Idéologue project of a moral science based on natural morality.

Saint-Pierre may have felt that a cabal denied him access to the printed memoirs of the Institute. But, aside from a memoir with instructions on diet and musical entertainment for the expedition of Captain Nicolas Baudin to Australia, which was prepared for a public session, Saint-Pierre wrote only five memoirs – a deliberately provocative critique of prize contests, a complaint on pirated editions, two proposals for studying tides and ocean currents to prove their relation to the melting of polar ice, and a dialogue on the death of Socrates. True enough, Saint-Pierre rarely served on Institute committees. His pre-Revolutionary attack on academies and his querulous temperament might have ruffled any such élite group.[59] His brooding dissent is a fine example of the sentimental Rousseauist Enlightenment at odds with the sceptical, scientific Voltairean spirit.

Mercier, a journalist, dramatist, and utopian author, polished his reputation for originality with an anti-Newtonian flat earth theory and with a critique of the genius of French classical dramatists. His personal mission in the Institute from 1799 to 1802 was to launch diatribes against the Idéologues, particularly by defending Kant's philosophy. Kantian morality was thus another avenue towards moral and social stability. A third opponent of the Idéologues within the Class was historian Delisle de Sales, who claimed in the *Mémoire en faveur de Dieu* (1802) that he was surrounded by atheists in the Institute. He stressed that great philosophers could be religious and that civil and moral laws needed divine sanction.[60]

Within the Second Class, then, the fear of irreligion and of the subversion of moral philosophy produced opposition to the methods and goals of the Idéologues. After our study of the functioning and intellectual accomplishments of the Second Class in succeeding chapters, we shall return in the conclusion to the account of its demise at the behest of the First Consul and his advisers, with the acquiescence of historians such as Dacier and Delisle de Sales.

Thus far, we have seen that the Idéologues played an important and disproportionate role in organizing the Second Class, in judging prize contests, and in publishing memoirs in the Institute collection if they so desired. They also interested their colleagues in the merits of Condillacian empiricist philosophy. By no means, however, did the Idéologues dominate the Class to the exclusion of competing viewpoints. While geography and history figured importantly in the Idéologue agenda for the sciences of man, we must not assume that the prolific historians and geographers of the Institute necessarily shared the philosophy or politics of Idéologues. Indeed, Lévesque was an exception in the history section, and the geographers often neglected the study of human beings.

If one ignores the contentious points of religious doctrine and the foundation of moral philosophy, then the more politically conservative Institute members were as much interested as the Idéologues in stabilizing the Revolution, though by a different, non-scientific route. And, when the opportunity came in 1799 to rally to a strong man, both the Idéologues and their scholarly colleagues seized it with alacrity and harboured similar illusions. The Idéologue problem in the Consulate was whether stabilizing the Revolution would allow the human sciences to retain a vocation for political criticism. By 1801 they diverged from such opportunists as Cambacérès and Roederer, who both became enthusiastic agents of Bonapartist policy.

The Second Class was not the totally republicanized academy promoted in the official literature of 1795, nor was it solely dedicated to an innovative intellectual program. Aside from the diminished influence of clergy, the social origins and occupational identity of members demonstrate considerable continuity with the past.

Another assured way of maintaining continuity for the sake of reconciliation and social stability was to follow the traditional practices of academic culture in advising the government and in running prize contests. Class members wished to maintain their independence, given the already existing ideal of the autonomous philosophe, but they also wished to stress their public utility. How, then, could they as pensioned academicians influence the government, respond to requests for government advice, and guide public opinion to a harmonious resolution of problems made more acute by the Revolution? A perennial problem of the relationship between intellectuals and power is the intensity of the demand by the public and government for experts and the need to sift among their sometimes contradictory recommendations. For intellectuals the problem is how to advise governments without becoming inextricably entangled in merely expedient policies.

4 Advice to Government and Prize Contests

The Convention's requirement that the Institute advise the government on scientific and literary matters renewed the eighteenth-century commitment of academies to public utility. At the same time, the autonomy of the Institute's members, which was so much celebrated in the speeches of Daunou, was imperilled by attaching them to government objectives. Aside from the obligation to publish memoirs and the decision to hold quarterly public sessions, a second legal stipulation, following Ancien Régime precedent, was to stimulate literary, artistic, and scientific talent through prize-contest memoirs. Throughout its brief existence, the Second Class would attempt to act in both the consultative and the pedagogical modes. The responses by the government to the Class's initiatives at that time reflect similar difficulties social scientists have had ever since then. Governments listen to advice they want to hear or, alternatively, they have little money to carry out ideal prescriptions. Instructions for military or naval expeditions of high strategic priority were far more palatable than costly plans for teaching the human sciences. Nor was a critical role on education the kind of public utility envisaged by Bonaparte. The group achievements of the Class of Moral and Political Sciences lacked overwhelming prestige, and Bonaparte's government could tap politically reliable individual talents, often trusted scientists, for technical expertise, or opportunistic lawyers such as Roederer for educational advice.

The success of the prize contests depended on the willingness of the potential contestants to discuss sometimes abstruse issues. The Class could use its prize contests, though, to frame questions potentially significant for public policy. If in the first round the commissions refused to award a prize, they often guided competitors' responses with new instructions. Though the prize questions often reflected debates already proceeding in the late Enlightenment, they illustrated a major objective of the Class that was shared by governments – ending Revolutionary turmoil.

An incident during the final organization of the Institute in the spring of 1796 illustrates the fragile legislative support for the services of the Institute. The lyrical speeches of 1795 had suggested that learning had made the Revolution possible and would continue to be necessary to preserve it. Yet, when the Directory proposed an annual stipend of 2,000 *livres* for Institute members, the legislative Councils almost rejected it. Villers, the expenditures committee reporter, suggested that writers and scholars should learn to "control desires and regulate needs," since wealth was "difficult to reconcile with the love of literature and philosophy."[1] Only the intervention in the Council of Five Hundred of Institute members Cambacérès, Pastoret, and Boissy d'Anglas assured passage of a 1,500 *livres* payment.[2]

Certainly, the consultations of the Second Class could not hope to rival the scientists' invention of the metric system.[3] Yet the Directory Councils and the Directory Interior ministry, spurred by Institute members within them, involved the Class of Moral and Political Sciences in planning education. In a conscious effort to aid the government, the Class explored the moral and economic issues of public assistance, which helped result in a reallocation of aid to foster parents. Class member Talleyrand helped outline the objectives of a colonial expedition, and the Directory asked for research questions for Egypt. Even Bonaparte's regime used the Institute as a body for geographic and "anthropological" advice for a scientific expedition to Australia.[4]

The Second Class undoubtedly aspired to assist policy-making in education. In July 1796 Grégoire and Roederer joined an Institute-wide committee on higher education, or "special schools."[5] This group met with the public instruction committee of the Council of Five Hundred, which also included three Class members, Daunou, Pastoret, and Sieyès. Daunou's final report of June 1797 insisted that the public secondary-level "central" schools fulfil Idéologue goals by including "analysis of sensations and ideas" and "method of the sciences" in the existing course for "general grammar." He also advocated a preliminary "theory of the social state" for the legislation course. Even more ambitious was a plan for nine higher-education lycées, each divided into three sections like the Institute. These schools would testify to the Encyclopedist principle of the "reciprocal influence of the branches of human knowledge." The moral and political sciences section in the *lycées* would include: (1) logic and general grammar; (2) private morality, legislation, and diplomacy; (3) political or public economy; and (4) history, geography, and statistics.[6]

The Councils rejected such an enormous outlay for higher education. Idéologue Destutt de Tracy would continue to dream of an advanced school in 1801 (or at least of a chair in political economy at the Collège de France) to create a community of savants in the moral and political sciences. Yet Bonaparte did not value the human sciences sufficiently to invest in professionalized expertise. The education law of 1802 provided for a school in "public economy, geography, and history," but this was never implemented, and it also projected ten law schools, which, when formed in 1804, omitted any theoretical courses on legislation or natural law.[7] Thus, higher education in the moral and political sciences remained a beckoning mirage that was dissipated by financial difficulties in the Directory and by Bonaparte's suspicion of Idéologue ambitions in the Consulate. Traditional metaphysics, ethics, history, and geography would eventually find their way into the secondary-level *lycées* and the Université impériale, though not as part of a unified plan to create human sciences.[8] The Interior ministry, with its staff which included, in 1802, Institute chemists J.-A. Chaptal, A.-F. Fourcroy, and the now opportunistic Roederer, would be the architects of these changes rather than committees or assemblies of the Institute.

The Directory Interior minister, François de Neufchâteau did, however, draft individual Class members as advisers to reform the central school curriculum. This Council of Public Instruction, appointed in November 1798, included Destutt de Tracy, Garat, Daunou (who was replaced by Ginguené), Le Breton, and Jacquemont. The members examined the course notes of the professors of the central schools, conducted inquiries about courses and enrolments, recommended textbooks, and prepared curriculum circulars. Destutt de Tracy originally intended his major philosophical series, *Éléments d'idéologie*, to be primers for the central schools. As author of several Council of Public Instruction circulars, he tirelessly sought to ensure that general grammar courses teach Condillacian "ideology" and discuss truly universal grammar, not merely French grammar. He hoped legislation courses would educate citizens in morality and natural law with texts from Enlightenment naturalistic moralists d'Holbach and Saint-Lambert rather than merely provide professional training for law students in civil law. History was to be a truly philosophical lesson in the "march of mind," relating cultural advancement to prosperity. We have else-where shown that central school teachers largely adopted Condillac's empiricism, aroused interest in public law and comparative govern-ment, and taught history with a didactic moral purpose. However, Destutt de Tracy failed to achieve his highly valued goal of a secular-ized curriculum or to enforce the adoption of recommended textbooks. Most disappointing of all to him, Bonaparte's government ignored the final report of the council in October 1800 which recommended a comprehensive reform of the central schools, and it replaced them with a revised *lycée* curriculum of Latin, mathematics, and the sciences, supplemented by more traditional philosophy and history.[9]

In this contest of two programs for stabilizing society, reconciliation with the Church triumphed over an educational system that aimed at institutionalizing the human sciences and creating a new class of experts. Members of the Class of Moral and Political Sciences thus occupied reasonably important advisory positions in the Directory's educational bureaucracy, but after Bonaparte's coup in November 1799 advice from anticlerical and politically hostile critics was dispensable.

Cabanis probably spurred a second series of Class initiatives on public assistance – a subject of moral and economic concern absolutely vital for social stabilization. The severe winter of 1795 and the run-away inflation of the currency aggravated the disastrous loss of tax revenue and seigneurial dues for hospitals and other public relief institutions. State pledges to care for the poor and sick rang hollow with the Treasury teetering into bankruptcy. While the Legislative Councils debated public assistance reform in 1796, a Class committee composed of Cabanis, Lacuée, and Baudin surveyed the subject. In late September and early October 1796 the Class heard invited papers by the dean of the École de Médecine in Paris, Michel-Augustin Thouret, on prisons and public assistance, and by an Interior ministry official, Charles-Antoine Leclerc de Montlinot, on hospitals for foundlings.[10]

Montlinot noted the shocking increase in the number of abandoned babies, even among legitimate children, since 1789. Inflation had completely eroded the modest public stipends for wet-nurses. He there-fore recommended a measure, adopted by the government in December 1796, to control costs by restricting public payments to wet-nurses of children that were illegitimate or of unknown parentage. There is no record of whether the Institute endorsed recommendations which com-bined genuine humanitarian sentiment with a stern fiscally conservative concept of discouraging married parents from abandoning children. Certainly no amelioration of the disastrous fate of abandoned children had occurred by the early Consulate years.[11]

On the more comprehensive issue of public assistance, Thouret, like Cabanis later, strongly voiced his opposition to a legislative transfer of responsibility for hospital assistance to disparate municipalities from a more equitable centralized national system. He thought the English Poor Law amply demonstrated the flaws of a local administration – it led to the attraction of the poor to wealthier regions, to resentments among local ratepayers, and legal restrictions on the movement of "burdens" to the parish. The majorities in the Councils, however, asserted that local government could best determine local needs. In the Council of Elders in October 1796 Lacuée was more concerned with free trade in hospital property than with higher hospital revenues. Under Bonaparte, the restored local indirect tax (*octroi*) consolidated municipal jurisdiction over hospitals in 1800.[12] The Second Class apparently did not press its inquiry further once the Directory Councils had voted. On public assistance, advice to reduce national Treasury expenditures was more politically acceptable than criticism of municipal poor-rates. The government listened to intellectuals most eagerly when they eased its budgetary problems.

THE HUMAN SCIENCES AND COLONIAL EXPEDITIONS

Aside from education and public assistance, the greatest advisory role of the Second Class concerned the conduct of French military and scientific expeditions. During the Directory, the Institute played a catalytic role in justifying the expedition to Egypt as a salutary colonial venture. Institute geographers characteristically believed that European civilization was at the most refined and advanced stage in human development. French colonial enterprises were therefore not construed as vehicles for conquest or pillage, but rather as heroic efforts to diffuse European civilization.

Talleyrand, in July 1797, several weeks before his appointment as Directory foreign minister, became the intellectual godfather of the expedition to Egypt with a widely acclaimed Institute memoir calling for new French colonies in the Mediterranean or in Africa. He appealed to Institute geographers Bougainville and Fleurieu to find sources of tropical crops and areas for settlement to create a profitable market for French goods. Even more important, colonial ventures would help stabilize France at home, for Talleyrand thought that colonization could cure "the unfortunate victims of political diseases" and "regulate agitation for public happiness." The "science of government" would promote harmony within France by finding work and "new perspectives" for the frustrated. In 1768 Choiseul had already sought Egypt as compensation for Canada and losses in India.[13] A diverse press sampling of reactions to Talleyrand reveals the pro-government newspaper *Clef du cabinet des souverains*, the moderate *Journal de Paris*, and the royalist *Nouvelles politiques* all praising the work ethic and the safety-valve of imperialism.[14] Talleyrand also stressed the mission of France to "bring enlightenment and work" to a fertile country.[15] As foreign minister in February 1798 he recommended the expedition to the Directory in order to "lift [Egypt] from the hands of the most appalling [Mameluke military] tyranny" and to "bring it prosperity." There was no doubt of the perceived superiority of French civilization, though for tactical reasons Bonaparte attempted, unsuccessfully, to conciliate local élites by tolerating Islam and Egyptian customs. For their part, French scientists were genuinely curious about Egypt, the fabled birthplace of the sciences.[16]

Bonaparte's expedition to intercept British routes to India was part of a long French tradition of seeking trade supremacy in the eastern Mediterranean. It was also a great scientific venture intent on developing the Egyptian economy by European technology. The 167 sciences and arts commissioners (General Caffarelli du Falga, an associate of the analysis of sensations and ideas section and director of the Engineering Corps, was first military president) carried out a breathtaking panorama of projects in less than three years, under harsh conditions of isolation, food and equipment shortages, and native rebellion.[17] The commander himself organized thirty-six of the most distinguished savants (Monge, Fourier, Berthollet, and Geoffroy Saint-Hilaire among others) into an Institut des Sciences et des Arts d'Égypte, with four classes for mathematical sciences, physical sciences, political economy, and literature and arts. Political economy was the poor relation, and only a few Cairo Institute memoirs (dealing with the customs and lifestyle of modern Egypt) concerned the human sciences.[18]

Each Class of the Paris Institute prepared additional questions for their Egyptian disciples in December 1798. The Class of Moral and Political Sciences commission included Volney, renowned for his explorations in Egypt, Fleurieu, and Grégoire, a leading advocate of international scholarly contacts. Already in 1793 Volney had prepared statistical questions for travellers on behalf of the Interior ministry, and then again for the External Relations Commission.[19] The Class instructed the Cairo Institute to explore Egyptian demography (population, life expectancy, and health), to examine ethnic stock, language families, and Arabic vocabulary, to provide geographical information on climate and natural resources, and to explore the local regimen, occupations, and family law. For Idéologues like Cabanis a primary assumption was that the physical environment, climate, and regimen helped determine physical constitution and character. Volney's own work had stressed that religion and government were more crucial than climate and soil. He probably inspired the question sent from Paris about the interaction of religion with character, government, and knowledge.[20]

In addition to the Cairo Institute there were other more extensive inquiries in the human sciences by the commissioners for the sciences and arts. Late in 1798 engineer P.-S. Girard had already conducted a thorough examination of agriculture, commerce, industry, natural history, and antiquities in each region of upper Egypt. The chief topographical engineer, Pierre Jacotin, prepared questions late in 1799 on the descriptive physical, social, and economic situations of each region. A team surveying a route for a possible Suez canal described trade and navigation on the Red Sea. Eventually, in 1799, after Bonaparte's departure, the arts and sciences commission section for modern Egypt (separate from those for ancient Egypt and for natural history) outlined a research program to include religious and civil law, property and fiscal policy, the "policing" of markets, games, and festivals, government and history, military affairs, commerce and industry, agriculture, the medical history of the people, monuments, and costumes. The engineers gathered much information on modern Egypt in the final period of French occupation in 1800–1. While their achievements were uneven, the government ultimately published the memoirs and plates in the massive but carefully sifted ten-folio volume, *Description de l'Égypte* (1809–28).[21] The general editor, Edme Jomard, a specialist of Oriental languages, topographical engineer, and a future founder of the Société de Géographie of Paris, discussed the Egyptian population, civil engineer M.-A. Lancret wrote on Egyptian taxation and administration, while civil engineering student Gaspard-Antoine Chabrol de Volvic sketched Egyptian customs. The cartography prepared by the expedition was its most impressive geographic accomplishment, but it doubtless stimulated the development of geography as a social science.[22] More important, it trumpeted the role of French science and technology in rescuing modern Egyptians from their benighted government. Institute geographers, such as Mentelle and his disciple Conrad Malte-Brun, celebrated in 1803 the uniform administration and new concept of private property the French had brought to Egypt.[23]

The Paris Institute was certainly an inspiration and benevolent patron for scientific achievements in Egypt. There was little difference in cultural attitudes or in tolerance for cultural diversity between the armchair geographers of the Institute and the government engineers. Yet the Cairo engineers and scholars probably would have carried out their specific projects whether or not they had received questions from the Paris Institute. Regardless of the assistance it received from Paris, Bonaparte's expedition founded Egyptology in France, with its exaltation of the country's ancient splendour and its relative disdain for a modern Egypt awaiting European civilizing influence.[24]

Even as Consul Bonaparte did not hesitate to turn to competent Institute advisers with naval experience. In March 1800 Captain Nicolas Baudin presented a new plan for circumnavigating the globe to all three Classes of the Institute. Fleurieu, former Navy minister and soon to be president of the Navy section of the Council of State, and Bougainville, an experienced navigator, had both recommended Baudin to the Navy and the Colonies ministry. They now served on an Institute commission which limited Baudin's objectives to Australia and the East Indies, wrote the strategic and scientific instructions for the expedition, and chose the scientists to accompany it. France was still seeking a possible colonial claim in southern or western Australia or an opportunity to forestall the British from settling Tasmania. Buache, curator of the Dépôt des Cartes et Plans de la Marine, prepared a series of geographical questions concerning northern Australia, New Guinea, and ancient historical navigation by the Malays.[25] As we shall see in Chapter 9, the Institute requested instructions for Baudin from the private Société des Observateurs de l'Homme. This group produced the most interesting anthropological documents he was to receive, the memoirs on observation of "savage peoples" by Cuvier and Degérando. The government also sought guidance from members of the Second Class, though their official positions often made them the logical choices regardless of their Institute affiliation. Nevertheless, from beginning to end the Institute promoted this voyage by Baudin. Fleurieu accepted responsibility for classifying its records in 1804 (except the natural history collections received by the Muséum national d'Histoire naturelle), and Degérando, as secretary-general of the Interior ministry, assisted with their eventual publication. Bonaparte here gratefully accepted the Institute consultative role, which also stimulated his interest in the private societies. He found more acceptable a project for national prestige and scientific achievement like this one than an Idéologue-style plan to reshape French culture. Indeed, a final irony was that when the surviving naturalist and "observer of man" in the expedition, François Péron, returned in 1804, the Second Class no longer existed. Thus, in addition to his memoirs for the museum and the Société de Médecine, he presented both commercial and human geography papers to the Class of Physical and Mathematical Sciences in the Institute.[26]

The Class of Moral and Political Sciences provided a reservoir of technically knowledgable talent for the planning and conduct of

military, naval, and scientific expeditions, as well as on certain boundary and diplomatic problems.[27] Aside from the indirect influence of
Volney and the direct suggestion of Talleyrand for the Egypt expedition,
the members of the Second Class and their Institute colleagues defined
the objectives for the Baudin expedition to Australia and East Indies.
The spread of French national prestige and European cultural values
united both intellectuals and power. Yet, on more sensitive social issues
such as education and a national system of public assistance, the Second
Class could not overcome the handicaps of the fiscal problems in the
Directory or, later, Bonaparte's suspicion of higher education in the
human sciences. Even Roederer's plans for the human sciences in the
Council of Public Instruction were unceremoniously brushed aside by
Bonaparte's trusted chemists Chaptal and Fourcroy.

THE PRIZE CONTEST CULTURE

In addition to solicited and unsolicited consultations with government
ministries, the Institute adopted a pedagogical mode in running prize
contests. In many respects the prize contests represented the best effort
of academies to create a "public space" for the communication of ideas
by free citizens, though their conventions frequently encouraged rhetorical excess. Academic culture had long employed the prize contest,
which was so predominant in Ancien Régime education, to focus
public interest and stimulate young talents. The Académie française
had regularly awarded gold medals in poetry and eloquence since
1671, while the Paris Académie des Sciences had held prize competitions since 1711. In the late eighteenth century thousands of prize
contestants submitted memoirs to over thirty provincial academies.
After 1760 these were not just ritual eulogies of monarchs and statesmen but also discussions of crucial social, economic, and political
issues. The academy in Châlons-sur-Marne received one hundred
essays in 1776–77 on the elimination of begging, and it later ran a
contest on commuting the *corvée* labour services. From 1783 to 1788
the Metz academy elicited discussion of criminal law reform, treatment
of illegitimate children, and the condition of Jews. From 1788 to 1791
there were discussions of openly political subjects like patriotism in
the Third Estate and the vital problem of easing famine conditions.[28]
    Competitors always sought sensational successes, such as Rousseau
in his two discourses for the Dijon academy in 1749 and 1755. In 1780,
before the Revolution, Jacques-Pierre Brissot entered the Châlons penal
law reform contest, while Jean-Paul Marat offered criminal code
reforms to the Société économique de Berne in 1778 and to the Châlons
academy in 1780. Robespierre himself entered the Metz contest on

judicial penalties involving loss of civil status in 1784, and read a memoir to the Arras academy on the Metz contest subject of illegitimate children in 1786. The audience for prize contests resembled the Grub Street of hack writers who were portrayed in the studies of Robert Darnton.[29]

As with academy membership, the prize contestants illustrate the diminished cultural role of the clergy (see Table 9). The competitors were an urban bourgeois élite, with occupations similar to those of their Institute judges. The professionals in law and medicine seemed to be self-appointed commentators on philosophical and public issues. The new "academic" public now included only a handful of former nobles, but had a few representatives of the dynamic bourgeoisie of bankers, merchants, and skilled craftsmen, and even a few students and women. This new public would fill the local societies of commerce, of industry, and of applied science in the nineteenth century, while lawyers continued to dominate the new provincial academies.[30] As is logical in appeals for public recognition, the contestants were also clearly younger (their average age was 40.8) than members of the Class of Moral and Political Sciences (average age of 50.6).

Seventeen, or at least one-fifth, of Class members and associates had entered prize contests in the eighteenth century as the first stage in their career along the traditional route to fame in the French world of letters. Eight became members of either the Académie des Inscriptions or the Académie française.[31] In the Class of Moral and Political Sciences prize contests, five of seven winners became Institute associates, correspondents, or, after 1816, members at large.[32] Entering a contest gave reasonably favourable chances for recognition. Close to 20 per cent of 204 memoirs received either a prize or an honourable mention, and almost half of the 36 given honourable mention subsequently appeared in print.[33] The prize medal was half a kilogram of gold worth about 1,667 francs (roughly $5,000 today), the equivalent to the annual income of a minor official or schoolteacher.

Despite this earnest search for recognition, some correspondents of the Institute mocked the entire process. An anonymous author suggested in the summer of 1796 that the Second Class should ask, "Who should be saved first by the father of a drowning family – his wife, mother, or ten-year-old child?"; the discussion would include the value of filial gratitude, parental responsibility, humanity, and service to the fatherland. The next year, an antiroyalist author proposed, "Which is more absurd, deciding civil suits by lot, or attributing political powers by heredity? Will the first procedure be more likely to achieve justice than the second, good government?" Given the seriousness of some Revolutionary contemporaries, one can never be sure that the satire was intentional.[34]

Table 9
Prize Contestants and Participants in the Contests of the Class of Moral
and Political Sciences

	Participants in the Contests of the Provincial Academies of the Eighteenth Century	Participants in the Contests of the Class of Moral and Political Sciences	Members and Associates of the Class of Moral and Political Sciences (n=83)
Unspecified noble	10		
LEGAL-MEDICAL			
Judges, high legal officials		9	6
Lawyers, legal historians	17	12	6
Physicians, health professions	11	10	5
Subtotal	28	31	17
SCHOLARS, MEN OF LETTERS			
Active clergy		8	5
Faculty professors	29	4	7
Teachers		19	6
Librarians, archivists	10	3	10
Writers, scholars, others		15 (including 2% students and 2% women)	16
Subtotal	39	49	44
CIVILIAN GOVERNMENT SERVICE			
Diplomats, navy, and colonies			8
High administration			11
Officials		10	7
Subtotal		10	26
Active, retired military officers, engineers		6	11
Commerce, banking		2	
Engraving		2	
Agriculture			1
Unknown	23		1

Source: For column one, Daniel Roche, *Le Siècle des lumières en province* (Paris: École des Hautes
Études en Sciences sociales et Mouton éditeur, 1978), 1:336–9, 2:135–6. Different versions of this
table have appeared in the *Canadian Journal of History*, 17 (1982):426 and in *Histoire, épistémologie,
langage*, 4 (1982):116.

Three of the sixteen prize subjects (see Appendix 6) demonstrated direct continuity with Ancien Régime prize contests, though in the changed Revolutionary circumstances. For example, Daunou had been the runner-up in a 1787–88 Berlin Academy contest on paternal authority. The radical revisions in Revolutionary family law stimulated an even greater worry about the disappearance of hierarchy within marriage and the family. The 1798–1802 contest of the social science and legislation section on paternal power thus responded to a continuing debate, as well as to Cambacérès's urgent immediate concern with formulating a definitive Civil Code and with fathers' rights to dispose of their property.[35] Turgot had sponsored in the years from 1765 to 1767 for the Société royale d'agriculture de Limoges a prize competition, closely followed by one sponsored by Du Pont, on the incidence of taxation. In 1799 Du Pont and Roederer persuaded the political economy section to set the same question.[36] The debate about the Physiocratic theory of the single land tax levied on the proprietor's net product had gained intensity when Revolutionaries shifted more than half the tax burden to direct land and personal taxes. A third subject, for the contest of 1797–1800, on establishing morality of the people, had indirect roots in previous competitions, such as that at Amiens in 1790–91 on the topic of educating the people.[37] The new Revolutionary concept of citizenship heightened the urgency of moralizing the people to end the Revolution. Assignment of the same or similar prize subjects was a literal expression of a persistent culture of academies.[38]

While the Class of Moral and Political Sciences never reached the interest level obtained by the poetry prize contests in the Class of French Language and Literature, where there were 55 and 110 memoirs in 1804 and 1805 respectively, the audience seemed most fascinated by ethical, linguistic, and psychological subjects (see the table at the end of Appendix 6). The ethics subjects, with their focus on control of individual passions, the cultivation of natural sympathy, and the transmutation of self-interest into virtue, elicited the highest average response.[39] The topic of cruelty to animals meshed well with the concern of hygienists to develop the "sensitive" temperament and with the general political goal of the Class in moralizing the people. The analysis of sensations contests also had ethical implications for moral education and the existence of the soul. By contrast, difficult historical or geographic subjects requiring extensive research or previous knowledge usually elicited few responses.

The most politically sensitive legislation subjects were less attractive than the moral issues, perhaps because they seemed more intractable. Yet the Class persisted in running these contests because of the importance it assigned to the issues.

PUBLIC MORALITY

The most impressive feature of the prize contests was the effort of the Class to shape the responses as potentially useful resources for government policy. The most popular prize subjects often directly challenged religious and moral values. In one case, Interior Minister Lucien Bonaparte set the contest question for judgment by the entire Institute. With forty valid responses, this contest of 1800, on suitable public regulations for funerals and burials, was more successful than any of the subjects chosen by the Class of Moral and Political Sciences alone. The collapse of Church authority amid the bloodshed of the Terror had left no real consensus on the rituals accompanying death. There had been months, if not years, of profanation of royalist tombs and of neglect of the corpses of enemies. By 1795 there was full, if temporary, separation of church and state.

Already in July 1796 Roederer read a memoir on republican funeral institutions which anticipated many themes of the contest replies. He deployed the strategy of secular moralization, a veritable leitmotif of the Class contests. He argued that morality outside a religious framework would guarantee social harmony. While assuring religious tolerance, Roederer thought that the management of the emotions of the bereaved was a public obligation. Ceremonies would calm the fears of families, enrich their memories, and turn profound feelings of grief towards the "happiness of humanity." Funerals, for example, might be occasions for public rewards of esteem for the departed.[40]

In November 1798 Baudin des Ardennes, along with Naigeon and Fleurieu, reported on a way of placing "ethics in action," and of providing a public example to the "laborious multitude" who were unaware of Institute meetings or memoirs. The entire Institute would form a cortège proceeding to the burial of any deceased colleague. This spectacle of crêpe-bearing savants would "excite public attention" and help in itself to re-establish public morality.[41]

In fact, the Institute prize judges of the forty memoirs submitted agreed with Roederer that appropriate pomp would inspire funeral participants to virtue. Funerals would deeply affect spectators at their most vulnerable moments of contemplation of their own mortality. The judges recommended annual municipal festivals of the dead with prizes and eulogies for recently deceased worthy citizens. Praise for sober lives might inspire others to try to control their own passions.[42]

The government adopted many of the recommendations of the Institute commission chaired by the physician J.-N. Hallé that were most relevant to public health. However, in 1800 no civic ritual for virtue was acceptable to the government. Although authorities provided public funeral escorts, families had entire freedom of religious ritual. Despite Interior ministry sponsorship of the contest, religious and moral policies, so vital to the Class, were untouchable while Napoleon Bonaparte planned a reconciliation with the Church.[43] The secularized intellectuals finally had to admit defeat.

The establishment of public morality during the Directory was, by contrast, a continual effort to find a secular or non-denominational morality to serve the stabilizing function of religion. Not only were funerals neglected, but the National Convention established a civic cult with patriotic speeches, often delivered in churches, on every tenth day of the ten-day week of the Revolutionary Calendar instituted in 1793 to sever ties with a perceived counter-Revolutionary Church. These ceremonies seemed to provide little incentive to the practice of virtue.

Yet those who managed this ethics prize program, the second most popular after public funerals, sought to avoid bitter "political or religious arguments." After the antiroyalist coup of Fructidor in 1797, the ubiquitous Roederer ruled out any questioning of the Republic and took for granted that consensus was in place since 1789 on rights of "liberty and property" as well as on equality of rights. Nor could religion be an issue when the state promoted no particular religion but tolerated all. Hence, the official Institute program eschewed all the questions of repressive legislation and efficient punishment which Destutt de Tracy saw as central to public morality in his 1798 essay on the margins of the contest.[44] Roederer's memoir of 1799 portrayed the ideal "moral catechism" as one that, like the work of the secular Enlightenment moralists d'Holbach and Saint-Lambert, would need no "religious basis" and would stress rational control of vicious passions or the manipulation of one passion by another. Patriotism and enlightened self-interest would transform the common passions for wealth and glory.[45] In the prize program, Roederer directed the contestants to discuss family law, education, and moralizing institutions such as the press, clubs, the theatre, monuments, and festivals. His own favoured instrument of moralization was the work ethic, which "attaches the poor to society more by the hope of well-being than the degrading fear of extreme need," and which makes the rich ashamed of idleness.[46]

After the incident of Bernardin de Saint-Pierre's stifled critique of the first round of the contest, Roederer, with Daunou and Du Pont, submitted a new report and new prize program which demanded a comprehensive dissertation on moral habits.[47] In line with the fashionable Condillacian theory of learning and motivation, the acquisition of habits would be the key to happiness. Contestants were asked therefore to discuss "how habits are contracted and conserved," as well as the "regulation of habits of memory and imagination for [the] association and representation of ideas and sentiments, reflection and reasoning for the formation of judgments, [and] those of movement and physical action for independence of moral wills," in short, all those "habits [that] are capable of making men happy."[48]

The judge in the second round, Ginguené, wondered if such elaborate Class instructions had "frozen the genius" of contestants. Contrary to Roederer, he thought that a discussion of religion as the basis, though an unnecessary one, for ethics, or the nature of republican government, as distinct from a "pure democracy," might have been more fruitful. Moreover, the Class denied a prize to journalist Louis-Germain Petitain who advocated an overly rigid social hierarchy.[49]

A judgment against Petitain is an object lesson in the management of a prize contest and in the defence of an open society. Petitain had proposed a rigid division of labour between an "intelligent, active directing class ... and enlightened oligarchy," and a "working class ... its passive instrument." A society would be virtuous if workers avoided the temptation of overeducation.[50] This view caricatured Idéologue leader Destutt de Tracy's portrait of an unquestioning general public absorbing moral science from the experts. Yet fellow Idéologues Ginguené and Roederer found the memoir repugnant. Ginguené castigated Petitain's explicit attack on Condorcet and Cabanis as a "poor understanding of the doctrine of perfectibility."[51] Roederer's manuscript critique of Petitain's memoir disavowed an inflexible social structure: "The Class cannot admit these opinions ... [that] citizens obliged to work and feed themselves can leave ignorance only to fall into error, and leave their professions only to fall into the most insane torments, and corrupting condition." Restlessness and depravity came from poverty, not overeducation. Roederer therefore hoped for improved education of the "working classes" with better teaching methods, at a time "when a little well-being permits artisans to exercise their reason a little beyond their workshops."[52] His ideal was hard work in a competitive and mobile, albeit stratified society. Public virtue did not mean sullen resignation. Too frozen a class structure meant all social order and no progress. In short, the Idéologues were not for social stability at the price of stifling individual mobility and opportunity. They continually sought secular moralizing institutions which, if overly intrusive, could have carried the menace of technocracy.

PATERNAL POWER AND JURIES

The directly political contests in legislation and economics subjects allowed the Class to foster realistic options for the government. Members wished legislation contestants to discuss the same issues as Civil Code or Criminal Code reformers. The paternal power question, on the "extent and limits of the power of the father," had a built-in bias towards moderating the extremes of unlimited paternal power and the alleged laxness of Revolutionary family law.[53]

Even before the Revolution, Daunou had rejected an unlimited natural right to paternal authority. Beyond the age of majority, the father's surveillance was less necessary and his freedom in making a will only assured a penalty for disrespect.[54] But the modest reforms in 1788 assumed a different character after Revolutionary legislation which diluted the father's power to arbitrarily imprison children, to disinherit them, or to block an unwelcome marriage.[55]

A manuscript note by Cambacérès to Baudin des Ardennes suggested an Institute prize contest on the testamentary freedom of fathers.[56] During the Convention and Directory Cambacérès drafted a Civil Code that promised to "overthrow entirely the system of paternal power" and eliminate the "prejudice of primogeniture and accumulation of fortunes so contrary to republican equality."[57]

By the time of the Institute prize contests of 1798–1802, there was a strong social reaction for reaffirming paternal power, a reaction reflected by eleven of the twelve contestants.[58] Petitain, the only advocate of an egalitarian family, argued that society must abolish the father's coercive power and testamentary freedom. Misinterpreting Montesquieu, he claimed that republican virtue, without any other laws, itself guaranteed moral behaviour in families.[59] At the other extreme, judge A.-J.-S. Nougarède's more convincing reading of Montesquieu led him to defend the hierarchical family for promoting a "spirit of subordination necessary to all civil society." Nougarède saw no obligation by society to care for abandoned children of doubtful paternity, and recommended a rather aristocratic freedom for fathers to will half of the value of an estate, even if one son were favoured.[60]

The first-prize reporter, J.-F. Champagne, shared Nougarède's view that the family was auxiliary to the state in controlling public morality. Otherwise, women would dominate marriages, children would become disobedient, and youthful passions would rage uncontrolled.[61] He repudiated the ideal of the egalitarian family but still approved an honourable mention for Petitain. The Class then took the exceptional step of overruling its own prize commission's designation because the members "disapproved of the general system." If egalitarianism got short shrift, so did the patriarchy of Roman law. In the second round, Daunou rejected a prize for Nougarède because the Class opposed his sympathy for primogeniture and found horrifying his disapproval of laws against abandoning children. Daunou wrote, "If the Class is not stopped by this reflection, it would have little difficulty with the others."[62] On the whole, the commissioners praised memoirs advocating greater paternal power, with hardly a good word for the mother's role, but not patriarchal despotism.

By March 1800 Bonaparte's government had eliminated equality of inheritance and it soon initiated discussion of a new Civil Code.[63] The rhetoric of utility, or social good, was interchanged freely with that of natural rights. Bigot de Préameneu, the conservative prize commissioner and drafter of the Civil Code, argued in the Council of State that primogeniture was dangerous and that one must strike a balance between "property rights and social interests."[64] Too much fragmentation of property might be economically detrimental to society, but too much concentration of property would be too aristocratic. On this basis alone the Institute commissions agreed that society could limit individual property rights.

Bigot and Cambacérès were both directly involved in the Institute contests and in the Council of State debates. It is difficult to prove that the Institute contest had a major influence on the outcome of the Civil Code since private citizens and the various courts had ample opportunity to state their own equally significant views. The consensus rested on the utilitarian benefits of paternal power to provide social control in the family and to stop overly rapid social change. In general, the Civil Code provided for increased functions of surveillance, overturned the hesitant steps toward equal rights made by women during the Revolution, gave a greater power to fathers to imprison wayward youth, and allowed fathers a testamentary freedom of one-fourth to one-half their estates depending on the number of children. It did not advocate absolute paternal power that would stem from natural conditions at the birth of the child. But there was also a retreat from the ideals of a more egalitarian family that were prevalent in 1793. Cambacérès, under Bonaparte, contributed to the restoration, not the overthrow, of paternal power.[65] The authors of the prize contests, as well as the Institute intellectuals judging them, apparently reflected genuine social revulsion at the perceived pace of Revolutionary change in the family.

The contest on juries of 1801–2 also occurred at Cambacérès's suggestion, without any intention on his part to oppose Bonaparte. The Class adopted his suggestion of the topic, however, just after Bonaparte proposed special criminal courts without juries to hear cases of vagabondage and seditious assembly, and of certain violent crimes, such as armed robbery by brigands. In the Tribunate the Idéologues Daunou, Ginguené, Marie-Joseph Chénier, and their ally Benjamin Constant had pleaded for reforming, not abolishing, the jury.[66] Indeed, the Class framed the question so as to bolster the jury: "By what means may the institution of the jury be improved in France?"[67]

The fears of most Institute members now were of the tendencies of jurors to overindulgence or intimidation because of the all too widespread brigands. The defence of property was the significant issue.[68] Daunou's draft constitution of 1799 limited eligible jurors to an élite of the most highly taxed and of government appointees. The law of March 1800 required jurors of accusation (indictment) to come from the 10 per cent of citizens on the "communal list" and trial jurors to be from the 1 per cent (perhaps 60,000 citizens in all) on the "department list."[69] Many appeals courts were hostile to the jury system, and criminal court judges were deeply divided. Yet, defence of the jury system was not solely an opposition view. Bonaparte pursued discussion in the Council of State of trial jury reform, and the Council of State until 1808 repeatedly voted to retain both kinds of juries in *regular* courts.[70]

Almost all the authors, including the two prizewinners, went along with the prevailing antidemocratic sentiment to place property or being on a "list of notables" as qualifications for jury membership. Only one of eight contestants opposed the special courts, but his alternative juries would include government officials.[71] Most used Montesquieu's relativist principle that juries must be compatible with the French form of government. Hence, as the prizewinner, Judge C.-S. Bourguignon, wrote, the appropriate jury for France would have modest income qualifications since France, like Britain, was intermediate between democracy and aristocracy. In a later memoir on juries after the contest had closed, Bourguignon added: "Political liberty is sometimes stormy, accompanied by civil troubles, popular agitation which can harm the operation of government, but it's not the same with civil liberty, which imposes on individuals only the restraint of the law, and which protects from the disconcerting effects of the arbitrary."[72]

In fact, Bourguignon's ultimate recommendations differed little from the conditions for trial jurors imposed in 1808 by the Council of State – a high taxation level, higher education, or a respectable occupation.[73] Once again, direct influence from the Institute to the Council of State may be difficult to prove. But the Institute had succeeded in eliciting responses that could plausibly be used as guides to policymaking.

Bigot and Cambacérès represented the now conservative Bonapartist opportunists who were willing to approve secret written indictment procedures and to risk eliminating a workable jury system.[74] In both the legislation prize contests, on paternal power and the jury, there was an overriding concern with social stability. Propertied jurors would better defend all property. The testamentary freedom of the father would allow more discretion in solidifying family fortunes. But the social utility of discouraging aristocratic landowning did qualify the absolute right in making a will.

Prize contestants as well as Institute judges shared the government objective of moderation in the use of paternal power, though the vocal Idéologue minority was more attached to the jury than were Bonaparte or his opportunistic lawyers.

PRIZE CONTESTS AS PROVOCATION?

The motivation of the Class to enter into public debate also dictated the choice of questions in the political economy section. The first draft question, – "Are public loans essentially contrary to the interest of the nation?" – reflected the hostility of prominent Enlightenment thinkers, such as Hume and Smith in Britain and the Physiocrats, Montesquieu, and d'Holbach in France, to public loans.[75] This utopian formulation ill-suited a nation beset with internal economic crises and continuing expenditures for war. Once again Roederer masterminded the political economy contests from 1796 to 1801 on the revised question: "For what objects and under what conditions is it suitable for a republic to open public loans? Should credit be given citizens in savings banks or should the government borrow to give public assistance? Consider political, economic, and ethical aspects."[76] As in the morality contest, Roederer himself attempted to guide competitors with a 1797 memoir advocating a moderate degree of borrowing.[77] Indeed he worried that there would be a scarcity of responses, since it seemed probably "useless and perhaps ridiculous to be concerned with a theory of public loans [that would be] impossible to realize."[78] His best efforts could not elicit a realistic compromise approach to public borrowing in any of the fifteen memoirs.

In the end the Class rejected a prize for the most promising memoir which might have received an honorable mention since the author took an unconventionally positive view of public credit. Government spending, he argued, created new wealth, interest payments benefited deserving small creditors, and economic growth would assure payment of the debt by future generations.[79] Unrecorded disagreements about the memoir among the Institute prize commission composed of Roederer, Sieyès, Lacuée, Duvillard, and Ginguené led to the refusal to award a prize.[80] This action was an especially good tactical move in view of Bonaparte's strong suspicion of financiers and his aversion to open government borrowing.

The related issue of the burden of taxation on proprietors assumed new significance in the contest of 1800–1 because Bonaparte was in fact continuing the trend begun by the Directory to draw the preponderance of revenue from indirect taxation. Nicolas Canard's prizewinning memoir approved this trend as equitable.[81] In the political economy contests, the Class seemed to reward contestants who followed prevailing government policies on loans and taxation and to reject unconventional alternatives. Whether from timidity or from an essential agreement with the government, here the Institute intellectuals charted no bold initiatives.

Finally, we should ask whether any prize contest was so provocative to Bonaparte that it helped seal the fate of the Class. The jury contest could have been the most sensitive. It interfered in a realm where the Idéologues had directly opposed Bonaparte, yet it produced no memoir challenging the government. Despite the new Concordat with the Roman Catholic Church, the second history subject was the "influence of Luther's Reformation on the political situation of the different European states and on the progress of enlightenment." Bonaparte, if he had wished, could have suspended the offending contests. Perhaps he was satisfied merely to ensure that no similar contests would be launched in the distant future. In 1803 the successor Class of History and Ancient Literature assumed without any government interference all responsibility for continuing the prize contests of the Class of Moral and Political Sciences.

Early in April 1802 the Class launched the Reformation contest on the same day Councillor of State J.-E.-M. Portalis presented a speech to the Legislative Body on applying the Concordat. Did the very selection of that topic insult the government?[82] A close reading of Portalis's speech even suggests that official government policy on Church-State relations would look sympathetically on a discussion of the Reformation. He attacked the medieval doctrine of the temporal power of the Church and alluded to the "false doctrine of pretended infallibility" of popes. Though a strong defender of religious beliefs, Portalis saw tolerance as a "duty," and he believed "intolerance offended reason." The Spanish government was so appalled by these favourable views of religious toleration that it banned distribution of Portalis's speech.[83]

Aware of this official view, the contestants used Portalis's arguments to attack Catholic fanaticism. The moderate prizewinner, Charles Villers, devoted considerable attention to abuses by the medieval Church and to the disappearance, after the Reformation, of papal absolutism and pretended infallibility. The contestants also asserted the economic benefits of toleration and Protestantism in England and Holland. In addition, they argued that religious disputes increased the study of languages, biblical interpretation, and archaeology.[84]

The conservative Catholic press wrote veritable diatribes against Villers's essay. To Charles Delalot, the *Mercure* reviewer, Luther planted the seeds of eighteenth-century attacks on religion, which in turn inspired the bloody Revolution.[85] But conservative displeasure with Villers in 1804 did not come from the Council of State. A discussion of Reformation influence would not necessarily attack the Concordat.

The Second Class thus certainly formulated prize questions from Enlightenment perspectives of perfectibility, tolerance, and secular moralization of society. The members wished to define the limits of acceptable discourse in the emerging moral and political sciences. Again and again Roederer, often viewed as the *éminence grise* of the prize contests, and other Class reporters intervened to try to revise the topics, write related memoirs themselves, or refuse the award of a prize or an honourable mention. Their purpose was to guide discussion into channels useful for policy makers. In practice, the Class ultimately had insufficient influence to play a primary policymaking role through its prize contests any more than it could through its direct government consultations. Yet, in some cases, such as that on the trial jury, the solutions presented by prizewinning memoirs resembled the final choice of the Council of State.

Each theme could also serve a function of stabilizing the political and social atmosphere after the Revolutionary upheaval. In the public morality contest, the Class focused on theory and techniques of inculcating salutary habits. Acquired moral habits would tame individual passions. By 1802 the relaxation of paternal power during the Revolution seemed dangerous to the family. The Class as a whole shared a repugnance for the egalitarian family, but it had somewhat more liberal opinions about paternal power than the two opportunistic members, Bigot and Cambacérès, who helped draft the Civil Code. Paternal power would be reaffirmed, but not made tyrannical. The trial jury would be retained, but jurors would be members of a propertied élite. The prize commissioners for the most part shared, for want of a better term, a liberal socioeconomic consensus resting on individual rights, equality of rights, and a hierarchical, if unprivileged society. Except on unlimited testamentary freedom, they wished to defend civil liberty without granting democratic political liberty. Taxation theory would help justify a new series of indirect taxes and oppose the Physiocratic view of the supremacy of landowners. On public loans, the rejection of an overconfident use of state credit followed many theorists' warnings and Bonaparte's own preferences. Indeed on issues of taxation, loans, and property the Class had few differences with Bonaparte, though its members would later be uncomfortable with the new nobility and with trade protectionism. Both the government and the Class majority shared the goals of a stable society open to the advancement of talented individuals. The post-Revolutionary ideology enshrined the principles of property, an end to noble privilege, the work ethic, productivity, self-help, and the prospect of social mobility.

Greater divergences occurred on political, religious, and moral issues. For that reason, the contests on such civil liberty issues as the jury and the Reformation, which presumably affected religious policy, have usually appeared to have been provocative. But the government itself was not averse to a continued exploration of the value of the jury and to a firm defence of religious tolerance and of state supremacy over the Church. Yet, even the possibility of public criticism of policy was unpalatable to Bonaparte. And, so, aside from a select public of devotees, the search for useful knowledge through the prize contests did not convincingly demonstrate to Bonaparte the public utility of the Class. The poignant irony was that neither the direct advice of the Class for naval expeditions (as contrasted to contributions of officials or talented individuals) nor the public forum of prize contests was considered valuable enough to assure the survival of the Class or to encourage research in the human sciences.

Besides the prize contests, the second pedagogical mode of the Class of Moral and Political Sciences was the reading of memoirs at quarterly public sessions. The most popular readings reflected similar themes as the prize contests. But the practical difficulties of convoking a hetero-geneous Institute before a diverse audience in a large hall helped play an important role in undermining that spirit of Encyclopedism upon which the existence of the Class rested. The direct purge of the Institute in the Fructidor coup of 1797 also threatened the vaunted indepen-dence of men of letters. Hence, after the fall of the Directory there was much attention in the press about how to maintain the reputation of the Institute and to assure pre-eminence of French literary culture in a scientific age.

5 The Public Image
of the Institute and
the Decline of Encyclopedism

The choice of memoirs for quarterly public sessions and the corresponding press reviews illustrate the goals of the Class majority in supporting moderate Revolutionaries and in magnifying projects bringing national prestige. Yet the demands of a large audience and the unwieldy format of these sessions weakened the Institute's commitment to the Encyclopedist spirit. In addition, two controversies about elections to the Institute and its organization demonstrated the real political divisions within the Class. The solution of governing political moderates to stabilizing the Revolution was to remove the threat of royalism. They envisaged violating the constitution for a moment in order to safeguard it against all conspirators. A detachment of Bonaparte's Army of Italy returned to Paris to ensure the success of the Directorial majority. Hence, after this antiroyalist bloodless coup of Fructidor in September 1797 the ministry purged from the Institute one Director and other politically active royalists who had been expelled from France for alleged counter-Revolutionary behaviour or treason. Political passions in the Institute tarnished the myth of its intellectual independence and scientific neutrality. Moreover, the ideal promoted by one-time Enlightenment philosophes who had now turned into counter-Revolutionary royalists, such as Delisle de Sales and André Morellet, and the Ancien Régime literary culture of eloquence, proved detrimental to Encyclopedism. Literary eloquence and unity of knowledge were now in conflict for social and political reasons linked to assessments of Revolutionary events and institutions.

These microcosmic issues enable us to classify the critics of Ency-clopedism and those of the Class itself on a larger grid of Enlightenment-Revolution relationships. The program of the Idéologues, the most self-conscious group in the Class, depended on linking the natural and social sciences, and on diffusing ideas through literature and art. Only the validity of the Encyclopedist ideal secured the moral and political sciences within the Institute. The first crack in this façade was the Rousseauist attack on science as futile and even detrimental to moral virtue. For Mercier and Bernardin de Saint-Pierre, such suspicions predated the Revolution and the Institute. The religious Romantics, like Chateaubriand, would reinforce the attitudes of the critics. Now they would be joined by such aging philosophes as Morellet, formerly in the *coterie holbachique* and other illustrious salons, who feared that the Revolutionary distortion of philosophic aims threatened the once pre-eminent polite and decorous literary culture of France. Even some Idéologues worried about the decline of poetry and eloquence, while the right-wing press condemned the Institute for alleged literary deca-dence. The deist historian Delisle de Sales would attack from within the organization of the Institute. Hence, for cultural and political reasons, there was an unravelling of the literary and Encyclopedist strands of Enlightenment culture. One-time opponents of Ancien Régime despotism were now frightened defenders of a literary élitism amid allegedly tasteless Revolutionary language. In the Ancien Régime Académie française, discourses demonstrating eloquence had been a vehicle for protest against clerical restrictions and political abuses. Now eloquence was a code for social and political conservatism.[1]

PUBLIC SESSIONS

The most comprehensive "public" of the Institute included all the readers of contest announcements and meeting summaries in the rele-vant portion of the periodical press, which had an estimated circulation of 30–35,000. A multiple of ten readers for each issue printed would place the estimated readership at somewhere around 350,000 out of a French newspaper audience of about three million.[2] The audience at the joint public sessions in Paris of all three Institute classes consisted of throngs of up to 1,500 in the Salle des Antiques of the Louvre, designed to hold 1,200 spectators at most. Even a few artisans attended, according to a report of a dyer who grudgingly admired the chemist Guyton's extensive knowledge of vegetable dyes.[3]

An obstacle to the serious communication of erudite or difficult sub-jects was the ornamental and generally socially prestigious character of these sessions, especially in the presence of Directors or of General Bonaparte. The greatest excitement and most elegant audience appeared in April 1800 when the First Consul presided over the meeting in his capacity as President of the Class of Physical and Mathematical Sciences, while Josephine sat in the gallery.[4] The element of display in a large, overcrowded hall also worked directly against effective communication. The press continually complained about poor acoustics for soft-spoken readers, the lack of a recess during four-hour marathon sessions, and, at the outset, even the lack of a program.[5] The format of the public sessions also suffered because of the secretaries' academic rituals. The time required for summaries of that quarter's work, eulogies of deceased members, prize-contest programs, and announcements of results forced presiding officers to omit sixteen of forty-two Class readings. In 1801, when the secretaries distributed printed quarterly reports, the *Décade* exulted at the long-sought change.[6] The practical problems were material incentives for requiring each Institute Class to hold separate public sessions between 1803 and 1816.

The need for a cavalry squadron to control crowds amid the hubbub at the first session convinced Institute members not to seek too much public attention. The Institute hastily repealed an amendment to regulations permitting public attendance at regular working sessions on the grounds that it would destroy the "silence, calm, and meditation" befitting such an august body.[7]

The need to provide entertainment handicapped the Second Class, which lacked the option of Class of Literature and Fine Arts to cater to the popular taste for poetry. Press commentary hesitated between clamour to "avoid ennui," and a recognition that the Institute "must be erudite, not just seek to please."[8] Most readings made no concessions to frivolity. Yet audiences generally seemed to appreciate the moralistic anecdotes of the noted economist Du Pont. Early in 1797 he regaled the public with amateurish talk in natural history on the sociability and morality of the wolf, fox, and wild dog. "Let's not speak ill of wolves," he warned, after years of Revolutionary turmoil. They, after all, keep contracts to share their prey. Rousseau would have condemned the domesticated dog for losing his freedom and moral fibre. In a second reading, Du Pont commended the intelligence of ants with the remark, "We are superior to ants, but I say this as a man. If I were in an academy of a flourishing anthill, I would reach a different conclusion."[9]

This desire to hold the attention of the audience certainly inhibited a greater number of public readings concerning Physiological or Rational Ideology. The memoirs on mental faculties by the non-Idéologue Toulongeon were "moments of relaxation from the writing of his history." But Cabanis read only one memoir in public on physical-mental relations in man, for, as Roederer pointed out, "too many circumstances distract attention in a great assembly for a numerous audience to give him as much applause as readers would give esteem." The Class chose no readings at all by the associate Destutt de Tracy, while a *Clef* reporter found Pierre Laromiguière's memoir on ideas less satisfying than Condillac's work; the latter, in defining the word idea, "knew where to stop ... [M]ay he also be imitated." Degérando's commentary on Dr J.-M.-G. Itard's methods of educating the wild child from Aveyron would have been captivating, but the *Décade* reported that an "indisposition" prevented Degérando's attendance.[10]

The messages conveyed in the very first public session included a paean by Daunou to Encyclopedic unity of knowledge. "The interest of letters," he claimed, "as well as political interest requires the association of all forms of knowledge." The solemn alliance of "taste and reason," that is, of literature and science, was, after all, an underlying rationale for the creation of the Institute. Only the "enthusiasm" aroused by the arts would compel acceptance of "moral truths."[11] This spirit would soon run afoul of public indifference and fears of literary decadence.

Another common theme of the public readings praised by the press was the correlation between science and freedom and, during the Directory, pointed, politically motivated warnings against unruly factional clubs.[12] Stabilizing the Revolution was as much a theme of public sessions as it was of prize contests. Even the right-wing press praised Du Pont's plea in 1799 for an increased number of primary schools. His case for literacy coincided with the goal of social control – education to preserve respect for property. The *Publiciste* chose to highlight Du Pont's attack on Spartan-style boarding schools, the kind of educational establishment most congenial to the Mountain.[13]

In the period of the Consulate, some Class members feared that dissent would be stifled, rather than the government threatened by the clubs. Once, in October 1801, a Class selection of a reading on "public spirit" by the moderate royalist Toulongeon could have come closest to a political challenge to any government. While he attacked the *esprit de coterie* of private society, he also maintained that a "well-regulated spirit of opposition" did not violate public spirit. Toulongeon may have originally written the memoir in 1797 as an adjunct to a periodical of the same name, *De l'esprit public*, that he edited. But in 1801 opponents of Bonaparte would have welcomed such a warning, and the *Décade* reported that it "did not know why this reading did not occur."[14] Toulongeon later had no difficulty in publishing the memoir or, for that matter, his history of the Revolution which was sympathetic to Louis XVI.

The most popular category of public session readings concerned internal politics given, as we have already argued, that colonialism could be a safety-valve for agitated Frenchmen. Especially from 1797 to 1800, constantly recurrent themes were the worldwide mission of Revolutionary France and the Franco-British competition for empire. The audiences and the press praised Talleyrand's memoirs on Anglo-American trade and his subsequent plea for new colonies. He attributed the loss of French commercial opportunities in the United States to old trading habits, to the British ability to supply merchandise and credit, and to linguistic and cultural affinities that condemned France to a secondary role.[15] We have already discussed the enthusiasm over his hope for a new colonial expedition before the Egyptian adventure and its reputed diversion of agitated spirits. Perhaps the most sophisticated geography memoir was Fleurieu's ethnographic description of the American northwest coast. The press appreciated Fleurieu's resolute statement of a civilizing mission for France.[16]

Even readings that appeared to be merely erudite or picturesque could relate to French imperial objectives. Papon's 1801 report on Genoese medieval trade in the Near East originated as a request from Talleyrand for information relevant to the Egypt expedition.[17] Bougainville's inspiring portrait of the courage of Arctic navigators reflected his interest since 1773 in finding the Northwest Passage. He now realized the route would be unprofitable for commerce, but he still thought that France should challenge the English for fishing, whaling, and prestige.[18] Buache in January 1799 used the discoveries of J.-F. Lapérouse, d'Entrecasteaux, and James Cook to chart new routes for the vocation of the French in the Pacific. Bernardin de Saint-Pierre prepared, but could not read for lack of time, an entertaining instruction for Baudin's Australia expedition by suggesting the launching of bottles to study ocean currents. He also appealed to ship captains to assure fresh water and a supply of salt beef and to boost crew morale by providing a daily bagpipe concert and dancing.[19]

Early in 1798 the geography associate Daniel Lescallier planned to read an exotic description of the Hindu pagoda at Chalembron. There were vivid accounts of dagger dances, the clinking bracelets of the *baladères*, and the spectacle of walkers on hot coals near the ceremonial ablutions in the Ganges. Around the same time, Lescallier, an official of the Colonial Office, submitted a memoir to the Directory that called for a naval expedition against English possessions in India. Lescallier timed his memoir to heighten public fascination with India when it might become a theatre of war.[20] However, at two successive sessions the usual scheduling problems scuttled the reading.

The public sessions won remarkable press approval when they appealed to Revolutionary patriotism, to victory in the imperial contest with Britain, and to the concept of a French mission in the world. The decline in the predominance of public geography readings after 1800 was due primarily to the British interception of French adventures in the Pacific and Indian oceans.

THE FRUCTIDOR EXILES

At the inaugural public session of the Institute, the members of the Directory had remained standing while the acting president of the Institute, Jean Dussaulx, delivered introductory comments. Roederer, both a member of the Class of Moral and Political Sciences and editor of the *Journal de Paris,* lauded this obeisance of power to "knowledge, which should be first in the sanctuary of the sciences."[21] This vignette masked the harsh reality that political expediency would soon wither intellectual independence. True enough, there was no longer the toadying for position among noble benefactors and government ministers that had characterized the Ancien Régime quest for patronage. But two incidents in 1800 manifested the incontestable Revolutionary politicization of pensioned intellectuals. The first *cause célèbre* was the reintegration of Institute members purged in the Fructidor coup of September 1797.

This coup was a pre-emptive strike by the Directory majority, including ethics section member La Revellière-Lépeaux, against their two suspected royalist colleagues, Carnot, an engineer in the mechanics section of the First Class, and geography associate Barthélemy, as well as the annulment of elections in 49 departments and the expulsion of 53 Council deputies from France. Its motivation was the fear of a royalist counter-Revolutionary conspiracy that was encouraged by the success in the 1797 elections of moderate or even secretly pro-royalist candidates. Ostensibly the coup manoeuvred for that ever-elusive political stability that also motivated the majority of the Second Class. Its unintended outcome was to create more instability than ever.

Less than a year later, royalism was no longer rampant, but in the annual legislative elections the neo-Jacobin left gained new strength. In the coup of 22 Floréal (11 May 1798), the Councils, with Directory prodding, selectively annulled the proceedings of electoral assemblies to exclude 127 candidates, of whom 86 were thought to be neo-Jacobin. Despite this politics of the see-saw, neo-Jacobin candidates still gained some victories in the March 1799 elections. Amid charges of corruption and military defeat, the Councils now elected Sieyès a

Director, and in the coup of Prairial forced the resignation of two Directors who were also members of the Second Class, Merlin de Douai and La Revellière-Lépeaux. They were now accused of undemocratic practices in the coup of Floréal. Violating the constitution in the coup of Fructidor in order to save it had produced a dangerous, uncontrollable precedent of government by *coup d'état*.[22]

The Fructidor coup was the only one that left scars within the Institute itself, though Institute members were heavily involved in all three coups. Merlin de Douai moved after the Fructidor coup from the Justice portfolio to a Director's position. Among the post-Fructidor Institute exiles were social science and legislation section member Pastoret, for the opinions he expressed in the Council of Five Hundred, and, for their journalism, Louis Fontanes, poetry section member and contributor to *Le Mémorial*, and R.-A. Sicard, grammarian and contributor to *Annales catholiques*.[23] Within a few weeks of the coup the Interior minister ordered the Institute to fill the vacancies of the deportees, who automatically lost French citizenship. The muzzled press voiced no protests. Daunou had even boasted to the governing Councils shortly before this order that the Institute was "scrupulously faithful to contain itself in the prescribed limits for its political influence."[24]

An isolated private protest came from historian and moderate royalist Delisle de Sales.[25] He wrote to a Director that a "political crime could not imply a literary penalty," so that the expulsions from the Institute were illegal. Indeed, even in rare expulsions by the monarchy, there had also been approval by an academicians' vote, though the King had sometimes refused to approve those presented first in elections, and royal ministers had intrigued to prevent undesirable candidacies.[26]

In the spring of 1800 the issue of the integrity of the Institute resurfaced after the readmission into France of all the deportees (some to government office) by Bonaparte's new Consulate government, itself a product of the coup of Brumaire (November 1799). At the March 1800 private general assembly, the Institute re-elected Carnot to a vacancy in the mechanical arts section, over de Sales's protests that an illegal expulsion did not require a new election. De Sales then launched a pamphlet campaign to persuade successive Institute assemblies to reintegrate Fontanes, Sicard, Pastoret, and Barthélemy, even though the latter was ineligible for an associate's position since he was now a senator, resident in Paris. Denied the floor, de Sales wrote that the Institute, "now under a protective government," should not hesitate to "annul past oppressive action." The coup of Fructidor had been a *journée à la Robespierre*. Both the moderate Roederer and the right-wing Joseph Fiévée gave de Sales ample and sympathetic publicity.[27]

By late April 1800 Roederer warned more soberly that the Institute could not legally exceed its statutory membership total of 144. While he praised resistance by individuals to political oppression, he ominously condemned any position taken by the Institute "as a corps."[28] "The Institute," he thought, "should not interfere in political affairs," lest it destroy public power. The Republic of Letters should be "present by its enlightenment, not its actions."[29] The Institute adopted his compromise of inviting the four returnees to meetings but without voting or stipend rights. The right-wing *Gazette de France* now condemned the "petty considerations, not justice," that were influencing all large assemblies, and praised de Sales's new memoir about the "cowardly fear of upsetting a no longer existing government." The equally conservative *Journal des Débats* lamented the "influence of Revolutionary passions, too much felt in this learned society." The four returned exiles, meanwhile, politely but unctuously declined to attend meetings while the Institute regarded them as "foreign."[30] Roederer's compromise was anything but a neutral, apolitical solution.

At the May 1800 general meeting Delisle de Sales moved the invalidity of any political expulsion from the Institute. The *Ami des Lois*, edited by a moderate, now leaked a detailed account of how de Sales's supporters, poets and dramatists G.-M.-J.-B. Legouvé and J.-F. Collin d'Harleville and physician J.-N. Hallé, proposed that new elections be required for successors of the deportees. The surgeon R.-B. Sabatier and the naturalists B.-G.-E. Lacepède and Georges Cuvier diplomatically favoured government arbitration, perhaps to raise temporarily the membership quota. However, the opportunistic scientists closest to the government, P.-S. Laplace, A.-F. Fourcroy, and Roederer, warned that the Legislative Body would be out of session for months. To vindicate the "freedom and regulations of the Institute," the Class rejected de Sales's motion.[31] In its view, validating political expulsions proved Institute independence. In fact, it merely refused to give comfort to royalists. In a reaction that even Napoleon thought excessive, Roederer, as press monitor, now suppressed the *Ami des Lois* for heaping "ridicule and sarcasm on meetings of men who honour the Republic by their enlightenment and each day extend the circle of human knowledge."[32]

The entire affair exposed the dependent position of Institute intellectuals both in the Fructidor coup itself and during the attempt to reinstate the exiles. The underlying issue might seem obscure. The Consulate, after all, had no quarrel with the four, the Institute re-elected Sicard in 1801, and the general Interior ministry reorganization of January 1803 quietly reassigned Fontanes to the new Class of French Language and Literature and Pastoret to the new History Class.

But in the spring of 1800 Napoleon had not yet consolidated his personal power and he had to avoid too many apparent concessions to royalists. More important, Bonaparte, who himself highly valued his Institute membership, could not possibly condone an implicit invalidation of his own election in December 1797. The vacancy at that time in the mechanical arts section had only existed because of the post-Fructidor purge of Lazare Carnot.[33]

THE ACADÉMIE FRANÇAISE

Already, during these discussions, the *Journal des Débats* regretted the absence in the Institute of "men who were the glory" of the Académie française. Indeed, even the *Décade* in late 1799 thought that unforeseen political circumstances and petty rivalries had conspired to bar such accomplished poets and authors (all now royalists or counter-Revolutionaries) as J.-F. Saint-Lambert, J.-F. Laharpe, J.-F. Marmontel, and Jacques Delille from the Institute.[34] As a first step, several groups now launched a movement to revive the Académie française. Interior Minister Lucien Bonaparte, a self-styled patron of literature, encouraged the plans of former Académie française members, only one of whom was in the Institute. In addition, the former academicians worried about the alleged usurpation of their corporate proprietary rights over the academy's Dictionary. Thirdly, a wide circle of enthusiasts for poetry and eloquence disliked the restricted place of literature in the Third Class of the Institute, particularly in its public sessions. Now might be an opportunity to reassert the authority of Ancien Régime standards of taste, in some cases with covert royalist designs.[35] To partisans of the culture of the Ancien Régime, rhetoric, Latin, and dabbling in verse were essential marks of the socially acceptable individual. The movement to restore the *collège* curriculum to secondary schools manifested the same social insecurity.[36] The entire right-wing press, including the *Mercure*, the *Gazette de France*, and Suard's *Publiciste*, shared this worship of the purity of language and of authoritative principles of poetry, rhetoric, and grammar.[37] Moreover, without advocating the restoration of an academy, with its overtones of privilege and royalism, some Idéologues and members of the Literature Class also worried about the decadence of French literary genius.

The first incentive for change was the typically heterogeneous program at Institute public sessions. At the first meeting in April 1796, Fourcroy conducted a demonstration on the explosion of chemical mixtures and then Grégoire presented his piece on the political sciences, while the meeting concluded with poet P.-D. Lebrun's ode on enthusiasm. The next year, Fourcroy's paper on the composition of horse urine preceded Talleyrand on Anglo-American commerce. The difficulty of maintaining attention during the science memoirs was obvious to press correspondents (who were sometimes Institute members themselves). As early as July 1796 the *Décade* proposed that "each class should have its own public sessions."[38] Late in 1800 the editor Ginguené thought that "poetry makes the principal ornament of public sessions, because it produces the best effect on men assembled."[39]

Meanwhile, the private publication in 1798 of the 1793 manuscript of the Académie française Dictionary rankled surviving former members of the academy, such as Morellet and J.-B.-A. Suard.[40] Lucien Bonaparte encouraged these disgruntled royalist intellectuals to petition him for the revival of the academy in June 1800. The *Journal des Débats* hoped that the "lack of place for literature" in the Institute would permit a new academy to emerge as the authority for "good principles in every type of eloquence and poetry."[41] In subsequent days seven former members of the Académie française, Suard, Morellet, G.-J.-B. Target, S.-J. Boufflers, Saint-Lambert, H.-C.-J.-B. d'Aguesseau, and Institute member J.-F. Ducis, drew up a list of proposed colleagues. They chose all seventeen survivors, with places reserved even for the seven émigrés in case they returned, including the notorious royalist cardinals Rohan and Maury. To ensure government support, they also tapped highly placed administrators: Napoleon and Lucien Bonaparte, Third Consul C.-F. Lebrun, Roederer, Talleyrand, Councillor of State Jean Devaisnes, and J.-É.-M. Portalis. To defuse opposition from the Institute, they drafted Volney, Garat, A.-V. Arnault, Collin d'Harleville, Dacier (the ex-secretary of the Académie des Inscriptions), and Bernardin de Saint-Pierre.[42]

The First Consul's return from the Marengo campaign on 2 July 1800 quickly ended any immediate plan to restore the Académie française. Bonaparte hesitated to deflate the prestige of the Institute, which in his eyes replaced all the former academies. He thought the name Académie française "would tend to resurrect suppressed institutions," no doubt alluding to the notorious royalism of its proponents.[43] A *Décade* reviewer the next year pointedly commented: "God knows how a revived Académie française would have been honoured by enemies of every new institution, by partisans of a 'regime of our fathers'! ... They would call every Institute member a 'Jacobin,' a wild revolutionary."[44] Government members, including Lucien Bonaparte, hastily refused their nominations, while Morellet then rebuffed a face-saving effort to establish a private literary society of working members which would have had neither government funds nor eminent public figures.[45]

At this juncture, late in July the intrepid Delisle de Sales took up another lost cause with a defence of the Académie française. He noted the urgent need for a literature academy separate from fine arts. He commented on the bizarre barriers between some Institute sections (antiquities and history in different classes, for example), the heterogeneity of the public readings, and the unjust exclusion of the academicians of 1793. Removing four fine arts sections from the Institute Class of Literature and Fine Arts would leave room for four sections of eloquence, medieval languages, modern foreign languages, and inscriptions and medals. This reorganized Institute could then reintegrate the ten resident former Académie française members, ten more Académie des Inscriptions survivors, and, of course, the four Fructidor exiles. The proposals in many respects anticipated the government reform of 1803. Yet de Sales could hardly be the source of these reforms, since the Consulate police seized his royalist pamphlets in 1800 and 1803, while Bonaparte also envisaged expelling him from the Institute.[46]

With the cause of the Académie française lost, a memoir, written possibly by Morellet himself, appeared in both the *Mercure* and the *Journal de Paris*. The author regretted the "abandonment of conventions and confusion of all social nuances" in the Republic, as well as the "barbarous neologisms ... a revolting argot which should not have reappeared after the 18 Brumaire." This vulgarity "undermines the characteristically French [features of] politeness and graces."[47] These sentiments cast new light on the entire movement to reform the Institute. For, in addition to government suspicion of Idéologue secular materialism, there was a desire to conciliate the members of the conservative intelligentsia and their nostalgia for traditional literary culture. In November 1800 the first draft proposal for the reform of the Institute by the new Interior Minister J.-A. Chaptal planned an eloquence section in the Literature and Fine Arts Class. Further, the proposal noted that "all the distinguished talents of the Académie française could not find a place in the Institute in the narrow framework offered by the law."[48]

To forestall further intrigue, the government assigned to the Institute the task of carrying on the Dictionary of the Académie française. Even the Idéologue Andrieux, the Dictionary commission reporter for the Institute, in 1801 shared Morellet's concern about the decline of poetry and eloquence. He was no less disgusted that during the Revolution "uneducated or poorly educated men" had used "barbarous words" and "audacity of language suited to their audacious conduct." Now, in a time of peace and political stability, the Institute should "restore order in the French language." But Andrieux remained dedicated to Institute Encyclopedism since members from all classes in the commission could remain sensitive to the evolution of language on the frontiers of various fields of knowledge.[49]

Morellet's pamphlet response to Andrieux's report, which was favourably reviewed in the *Journal des Débats*, castigated the "obscure grammarians" (perhaps Urbain Domergue) and "young littérateurs without fame and consequently without authority" (Ginguené and Andrieux?) who would dare continue the academy's Dictionary project. Moreover, some "savants" on the commission were "not the most familiar with the language spoken by citizens of rank, fortune, and education and whose occupations have kept them in a distinct category." Even if such learned societies as the Institute had the same members as they did in the Ancien Régime, the "situation and totality of circumstances were different then." No longer was there that "decency, that tone of politeness, measure, feeling for the conventions, that delicate taste that preserved in language and conversation what one properly called *bon ton*, the tone of good company."[50]

Morellet had himself been the son of a modest paper merchant, though he acquired an immense fortune by the 1780s through tireless intrigue for clerical sinecures and royal pensions. If anyone was a "hired pen," it was certainly Morellet working for the Bureau de Commerce in the 1760s and 1770s as an antimonopolist and pro-Physiocratic economist. The Revolution deprived him of the property he had purchased, of his clerical seigneury, and of almost all of his state-funded pension income. Having lost his magnificent Paris dwelling, he also lost his temporary lodging with Madame Helvétius in 1790: the catalyst was a political quarrel he had with two of her other guests, Cabanis and La Roche, in 1790 over the issue of sympathy for peasant violence in the southwest. Before the Revolution, Morellet had defended the philosophes against the satire, published after 1760, of Charles Palissot and he had supported Turgot's free-trade initiatives. In fact, he was not an enemy of the moral and political sciences as such, since he himself prepared a lengthy plan for a dictionary of commerce and political economy. No purely sociological explanation, nor animus to the human sciences, would explain Morellet's diatribe.[51] Perhaps he was thinking of the public session fiasco of the summer of 1799. At that time an eccentric author, L.-S. Mercier fatigued the audience with a forty-five minute memoir on the death of Cato of Utica, though he had been assigned a ten-minute time slot. When the exasperated president implored him to stop, Mercier intoned, "I will not leave before I have finished Cato." Indeed, the session had to be adjourned.[52]

Morellet's real objection to the Dictionary commission was not only its alleged gaucherie but also its political convictions. His battle was in microcosm historian François Furet's depiction of the entire Revolutionary struggle over symbols, for Morellet found repulsive a supplementary volume to the academy Dictionary which defined new Revolutionary terminology. There, an aristocrat was not only someone noble and privileged, but "generally an enemy of the government." An émigré was someone who "left illegally and failed to return before the date specified by law." Morellet was shocked by the inclusion of argot such as *enragé*, *sans-culottes*, and *révolutionner*. The Institute commission members, according to Andrieux, were also concerned about barbarous Revolutionary language, but they were undoubtedly more committed republicans than the survivors of the academy. The re-establishment of the Académie française was still therefore an exercise in resuming political control of language.[53]

The most surprising document in the protracted battle was Director-General of Public Education Roederer's own manuscript plan, prepared in 1802 for the Council of State, to "establish in the Institute itself a class which represents the former Académie française and like it [is] instituted for the decent, measured praise of the government." Authors would respond to prize contests encouraged for the latter purpose. Roederer continued: "Louis XIV knew very well what he was doing in protecting the Académie française. It struck more medals for him in a century than he could have earned from all the merits of the kingdom."[54] Roederer thus came to see an academy as much as a government propaganda auxiliary as a haven for autonomous thinkers.

With combined moderate and right-wing support, Interior Minister Chaptal's proposal of January 1803 abandoned the Encyclopedist ideal by abolishing the Class of Moral and Political Sciences and converting the Institute into a federation of the three classes resembling the Ancien Régime academies of sciences, inscriptions (history), and literature, with the addition of a fourth academy for fine arts. As was universally desired, public sessions and elections would henceforth be independent for each class. In 1816, however, the Restoration government, which was without any sympathy for Encyclopedism, re-established a single session as an annual showcase for the four "academies."

In 1803 Chaptal fully accepted the pleas of Morellet and the *Journal des Débats* about the need to foster eloquence.[55] Morellet triumphantly returned as chairman of a Class Dictionary commission of French Language and Literature with exclusive jurisdiction, while the counter-Revolutionary Suard was made permanent Class secretary. The Idéologue Garat, always quick to praise Bonaparte, certainly provided a sample of Roederer's desired eloquence in his capacity as president of the Institute in 1809: the Institute, he said to the Emperor, was a "kind of spiritual militia at the head of which you march to the conquest of all truths which most perfect human destiny."[56]

Morellet later chided Bonaparte for fearing discussion of all the basic principles of government.[57] But the logical consequence of the abandonment of a stricter Encyclopedist ideal and the elevation of literature was a firm separation between the culture of letters and of the sciences. Morellet represented the counter-Revolutionary Enlightenment, which was now politically opposed to the partisans of perfectibility through the human sciences and through social mobility. In his memoirs he attempted completely to dissociate the relatively harmless philosophical discussions of the *coterie holbachique* from the excesses of the Revolution.

The cast of characters in these highly instructive sagas on the Fructidor exiles played roles illustrative of post-Revolutionary fragmentation of the Enlightenment and the decline of Encyclopedism. Delisle de Sales's position resembled Morellet's – a minor philosophe turned counter-Revolutionary. Like Morellet, de Sales had exercised freedom of expression at the price of imprisonment, and he had received the accolades of Voltaire. In 1777 the Châtelet court briefly imprisoned de Sales on charges of Spinozism, a deism which left God undefined, and for risqué passages in his *De la philosophie de la nature* (1770). Both Morellet and de Sales had favoured modest reforms in 1789, but by the October march on Versailles de Sales was as disillusioned with Revolutionary violence as Morellet had been when he watched the "horrible agitation" of the 14th of July crowd. From 1789 on, both of them considered that the Revolution had, in François Furet's phrase, "skidded off track." De Sales endured nearly five months in prison in 1794 for royalist sympathies, and Morellet barely avoided arrest as a suspect academician who had never cheered the crowds overthrowing the monarchy. Despite a commitment by both of them to Enlightenment freethinking, and despite Morellet's economic interests, the foundation of the Institute had disrupted the old historical and literary cultural communities. Now Morellet, the self-appointed guardian of the Dictionary of the Académie française, and de Sales, the lobbyist for discomfited royalists, could find common cause in the desire to restore a literary élite. The unity of the sciences meant little to them. Chaptal would ultimately heed their pleas to restore a literary academy.[58]

The activity of these two Enlightenment counter-Revolutionaries may be compared to the other internal opposition in the Second Class – the Enlightenment Rousseauists who were opposed to mathematical science and Voltairean scepticism. Bernardin de Saint-Pierre, the highly successful author of *Études de la nature* (1784) and of the sentimental novel *Paul et Virginie* (1788), was not a counter-Revolutionary, though he was moderate enough to favour a royal veto in 1789. An Interior

ministry pension of 1795 and a post at the École normale had compensated him for the loss of his intendancy at the Jardin des Plantes
two years earlier. His sensitivity to alleged Institute atheism stemmed
from pre-Revolutionary antagonism to savants. The unaided, non-
experimental study of a nature suffused with Providence (in short, to
paraphrase Wordsworth, not murdering to dissect) and folk wisdom
were his supreme values. The "moral laws of nature," arranged by
God's Providence, imbued human beings through final causes with a
sentiment of Divinity. For years he defended his anti-Newtonian theories that the tides were caused by the melting of the ice-cap and by
the elongated shape of the earth. And he bitterly warned that one
risked becoming an imbecile if one consulted savants. Saint-Pierre's
concepts of science and morality could hardly countenance Idéologue
models of a human science.[59]

His colleague Mercier, an erstwhile utopian prophet of far-reaching
social change (author of *L'An 2440*: editions of 1770 and 1786), had
been a more ardent Revolutionary. Like the Idéologue majority, he
favoured the Girondins, suffered imprisonment under the Terror, and
feared royalist counter-Revolution in the Directory. But like Saint-
Pierre, his anticlericalism was tempered by sentimental deism and an
overriding desire for moral orthodoxy.

Mercier, too, became a bitter satirist against Newtonian mathematical science and an opponent of the epistemology of Locke. A tell-tale
verse of 1799 noted that "All of algebra at work in great bravado/
Never made a lettuce grow in our fields." In 1806 he published a work
claiming the sun moved around the flattened disk of the earth.[60] For
him, as for Saint-Pierre, the human science of the Idéologues would
have all the futile jargon of moral geometry.

In the early years of the Consulate, the context of this antigeometric
Rousseauism changed with the Catholic revival and the early Romantic
movement. Now there was a host of royalist or pro-Catholic writers
who also warned against the futility of science. The Dhombres' comprehensive survey of attitudes toward natural science uses exemplary
texts to reveal a new quarrel of literature and science. Louis Fontanes's
review of Madame de Staël's *De la littérature* in 1800 warned: "One
especially must not exalt the sciences at the expense of the fine arts
... [P]oets, not geometers and chemists, made the earth fall on its knees
to the graces and to glory, virtue, and beauty." François-René Chateaubriand in his 1802 *Génie du christianisme* saw no hope for
progress from the sciences, much less anything new in the moral
sciences. Science "desiccated the heart, disenchanted nature, led weak
minds to atheism, from atheism to crime." The fine arts might lead to
virtue through eternally unchanging religious truths.[61]

To these examples we may juxtapose the tirades of the anti-Enlightenment, counter-Revolutionary right-wing press, which sought a greater barrier around the polite culture of letters. To it any human science, especially one with materialist implications, was in itself dangerous. In 1800 Joseph Fiévée warned in the *Gazette de France* against Degérando's memoir on the observation of savages that the "knowledge of man could go too far … [W]hen metaphysicians wrote fiction on savages, they broke the man of society."[62] In 1803 the same newspaper gloated over the reorganization of the Institute: "no more declamation class and especially none of political economy, to excite people to reason or rather mis-reason in all the most important questions of legislation, politics, and administration."[63] Thus, the advocates of art and literary eloquence inflected in a Catholic and anti-Enlightenment direction the antimathematical Rousseauism within the Institute.

The public sessions of the Class had wide appeal when they highlighted patriotism and presented, partly as a diversion from Revolutionary strife, glorifications of the mission of French explorers and colonizers. The necessity of entertainment gave the Idéologues little reading time in public sessions except as prize reporters. Cabanis was not an effective orator, Destutt de Tracy made no appearances, and Degérando did not carry out his projected reading.

Contrary to the science-freedom topos, the ideal of the independence and scientific neutrality of intellectuals was no easier to maintain under a republican government. Hostility to royalism motivated the Directory purge of the Institute and the refusal of the Consuls to atone for it in 1800. Both the reintegration incident and the unsuccessful effort to revive the Académie française displayed persistent political passions rather than prevailing harmony.

Finally, the Ancien Régime culture of eloquence and poetry proved useful to a government in search of odes to its own immortality. As the Encyclopedist ideal foundered, so did the human sciences as intermediate links between literary or artistic insights into the human condition and scientific method. Varied opposition voices perceived the Class for Moral and Political Sciences as a hindrance to the desired re-emergence of an older literary culture and thus hastened its disappearance.

Both the distinct achievements of each human science and the intellectual and institutional obstacles to their development require closer investigation. The next six chapters will ask how the scientific stabilization of the Revolution and defending the rights of dissent motivated the work of the Class in each area of study. Revolutionary circumstances will also help explain changes from Enlightenment models of the human sciences.

Just as Morellet and Andrieux had wished to reassert control over vocabulary, within the Class there was a marked concern with perfecting language that led to such dangerous Revolutionary misunderstanding. Revolutionary passions also influenced attitudes toward education. Indeed, learning and motivation, by modifying temperaments, sharpening sensations, and correcting judgments, were at the heart of the enterprise the Institute called analysis of sensations and ideas.

6 Indelible Temperament and Condillac's Uncertain Legacy

When Destutt de Tracy defined Ideology (a new science of the formation, expression, and deduction of ideas), he differentiated between his own deductive study of Rational Ideology and the more difficult empirical science of Physiological Ideology.[1] In Cabanis's terminology, the comprehensive "science of man" comprised three fields of physiology, the analysis of ideas, and ethics. These critical disciples of Condillac sought to enrich the understanding of the operations of the mind by a rigorously naturalistic relation of physical and mental. The overtones of materialism (a label they denied) that came from seeing "physical and mental confounded at their source" alienated their most promising disciples and handicapped the development of a common approach among Idéologues towards a modern psychology.[2]

The secular commitment highlighted a fundamental disagreement between the Idéologues and religious believers about strategies to attain social stability. In the religious view the Church was an essential mediator and guardian of social order. Even in the deist view, whether of a Voltaire or a Robespierre, the threat of damnation of an immortal soul by an all-powerful God reinforced the notions of active human minds with free will and moral responsibility. The Idéologues saw all spiritual beings as ghostly metaphysical scaffolding. Moral conduct which stabilized society rested on knowledge of firm natural laws of self-interest and sociability and of physical laws of temperament. Therefore, physicians and other "scientific" experts who mastered the techniques of hygienic regimen, education, or linguistic reform would replace priests and unskilled propagandists. The improvement of character would thereby harmonize public and private interests and cultivate natural sympathy. The socioprofessional consequences would be the emergence of a new élite, one that did not necessarily exclude genuine representation of the people.

Regardless of materialism, the relevant medical tradition was to influence the body in order to affect the mind, or the converse, according to the ancient Hippocratic doctrine of temperament. The balance of humours, the solid-fluid equilibrium, or, as it was expressed later, the equilibrium of muscular energy and nervous sensitivity, formed an initial constitution of intelligence and character as much as an inherent constellation of strength and weakness in the body. By the eighteenth century the guiding assumption was that a physician, by careful dosage of food, drink, and medicine or a change in the physical environment, could modify temperament.

Our long previous study of Cabanis will make necessary here only a sketch of his important contributions. Secondly, a study of the theory of gender held by ethics associate Pierre Roussel will show how unalterable he thought the temperamental difference was between men and women. The natural organic dispositions of women were, in his opinion, almost a secular equivalent of original sin. Empiricist optimism about the perfectibility of temperament gave way to the complacent assignment of women to a separate, politically and culturally, inferior role. The post-Revolutionary society, confronted with a momentary prospect of rights for women, perpetuated the defence of domestic and social rigidity. Thirdly while briefly considering Destutt de Tracy, who has been the subject of three full-length studies, the main focus here will be the fate of Condillac's agenda of the "well-made language," the "transformation of sensations," and the power of habit in the analysis of sensations and ideas section of the Second Class.

The "well-made language" was a fascinating eighteenth-century enterprise to remove ambiguity and potential misunderstanding from scientific nomenclature. Condillac's dream was that all sciences could emulate the example of mathematics in achieving precision and could strive for the high predictive probability of the natural sciences. In the Revolutionary context, it seemed a way of assuring that ignorant protest could be overwhelmed by precisely defined moral and political terms. As interpreted by some Institute members and prize contestants, the subordination of the uninformed or of "savage" peoples could be at least temporarily justified by their imprecise language. Language was also important because artificial linguistic signs facilitated thinking, or were necessary for it. Garat, Cabanis, and philosophy teacher Laromiguière all magnified the influence of language. Destutt de Tracy and the analysis of sensations and ideas section associate Degérando rejected the notion of a perfect language as utopian, though not the necessity of highly developed language.

Critics of materialism considered the transformed sensations model of Condillac dangerous because it apparently precluded an active mind or will. They believed that the monist reading of Condillac by Cabanis and Destutt de Tracy made human beings into passive creatures. They therefore deliberately attacked the Encyclopedist assumption of the unity of knowledge – a single scientific method for both natural and human subjects. They also doubted the unity of nature itself, preferring to believe in separate material and spiritual worlds. Degérando, Laromiguière, François-Pierre Gontier Maine de Biran, and the Idéologue patron, Sieyès himself, all rejected the transformed sensations model. The resulting disunity led to a nearly natural progression of metaphysically dualist Idéologues to its polar opposite – the introspective psychological method of eclectic spiritualism which triumphed in the late Empire and Restoration. Moreover, the anti-Idéologue Mercier introduced Kant's philosophy into the Second Class as a new weapon against alleged materialism and moral decline.

Condillac's empiricism also lent itself especially well to a theory of learning and motivation through a "liaison of ideas," linguistic signs, and the power of habit. Certainly, even a believer in innate ideas might concede the power of habit. But for Condillac and the Idéologues, crucial intellectual development occurred by fortifying memory, using imagination, and training good judgment.[3] Some prize contestants tended to marginalize those with "inferior" experience – primitive peoples or the uneducated. Inexperienced sensations handicapped these as much as unrefined language. Until they were properly educated, their undesirable habits blocked their access to equal political rights. The pedagogical mission of Revolutionary leaders coincided with this imperative to uproot the corrupt or ignorant habits of Ancien Régime subjects and to promote virtuous republican habits, often by visual symbols, pageantry, and festivals.[4] Finally, Maine de Biran, prizewinner in the habit contest, warned about the ambivalence of habit if it substituted rote learning for creative thinking.

TECHNICIANS OF TEMPERAMENT

Cabanis's seven Institute memoirs he prepared from 1796 to 1800 relating *physique* to *moral* merged the modernized theory of medical temperament with Condillac's philosophy. In Cabanis's hands, the age-old medical body-mind parallels rested on the primacy of physical nervous sensitivity. While not a believer in mechanistic materialism,

Cabanis excluded a spiritual soul and substituted a single substance, however defined, in living matter. Among his objections to Condillac was the latter's failure to appreciate the significance of internal impressions from partial centres of sensitivity, such as the stomach, diaphragm, or reproductive system, on organic dispositions, and even on the brain itself. Since these internal impressions might have as yet uncharted effects on ideas and passions, changing organic dispositions might affect mental or emotional phenomena. In addition to a catalogue of the uncontrollable factors of age, sex, and illness, Cabanis detailed how climate, regimen, diet, and occupation all might affect organic dispositions and temperament. The objective was to help make the physician an auxiliary to the legislator or moralist – to develop a science of individual improvement providing a balanced temperament that was possibly more sanguine, sensitive, and sociable.[5] Individuals would bind themselves to society by enlightening their self-interest or cultivating their sympathy through hygiene and physical habits as well as pedagogy and logic.[6]

Cabanis conceived the medical profession as a "kind of priesthood, and in other respects a true magistracy." The physician could estimate the effect of "moral impressions" on patients and learn the "art of exciting and moderating the passions." He would sweep away prejudices to exercise "an apostolate of common sense and virtue." Physicians would be "superintendents of morals [in the context of their fight against quacks] as well as of public health."[7]

As a technician of temperament in an already established medical profession, Cabanis raised all the issues of normalizing judgment and of a hierarchical gaze so aptly defined by Foucault. Certainly, Cabanis had a hierarchical approach towards the patient and towards unlicensed practitioners. In view of the innumerable abuses committed in the name of authority and of the hasty, culturally induced creation of disease entities such as monomania and hysteria in hospitals and psychiatric asylums in the nineteenth century, Foucault wisely saw the inexorable intertwining of knowledge with power. We cannot resolve here whether physicians like Cabanis actually "cured" their patients and thereby exercised legitimate authority.[8] However, some caveats are in order before a rush to judge the "science of man" exploitive in all respects or intolerant to the unconventional and the poor.

The utility of a science for manipulating climate and regimen was undoubtedly limited by the inability of the impoverished majority to travel, to change diets, or to change occupations. Nevertheless, Cabanis included in his analysis of the far-reaching effects of climate the need to adjust medical dosage and the importance of soil conservation, land reclamation, and other public projects that might change surroundings for the poor, even without travel. The entire impulse towards perfectibility of temperament also gained confidence from Cabanis's belief that climatically induced alterations of temperament might be inherited. Moreover, no matter how poor, everyone could improve their health by knowing the effects not just of exotic, expensive foods, but also of stimulants, beverages, drugs, vegetarianism, sleep, and exercise.[9]

Foucault's view of normalization implies conformity to predetermined standards of health, but the temperament theory in its very essence made allowances for individual variations of age, inherent constitution, medical history, and existing climate and regimen. No matter how much the goal was for a "well-tempered" individual, there would always be individual eccentricities and the emergence of new needs for new surroundings. With no single correct temperament, the Hippocratic science of temperament lacked the rigidity of the deductive method. Cabanis's goal was in the long term to eliminate temperamental obstacles to good citizenship as a complement to more conventional educational techniques. In the short term he was far from democratic in his political theory. But, as a believer in perfectibility, Cabanis genuinely envisaged the improvement of individual temperaments as the "physical education of the species," which might ever more closely "approach a perfect type."[10]

INDELIBLE FEMININITY

In one respect the theory of temperament made no concessions to variability. No amount of habit could counteract the indelible impression of sex (the term is used advisedly, because a natural, not a cultural concept, was intended). Thomas Laqueur's recent analysis of gender and sex places eighteenth-century physicians in the context of a transition from the ancient Aristotelian model of women as "lesser males" to a new image of "incommensurable difference" between the sexes. Whether or not these two images are so chronologically distinct, late eighteenth-century physicians stressed the pervasive, distinctive influence of the female reproductive system. Laqueur plausibly attributes the change to the perceived social threat of women in the public sphere during the Enlightenment and Revolution (though the model of a predominant reproductive system certainly predated the Revolution). His statement that "all but the most circumstantial statements about sex are, from their inception, burdened with the cultural work done by those positions" will be more controversial. But cultural presumptions, reflected in Rousseau's highly restricted social role for women as pleasant helpmates for their husbands, undeniably affected physicians. They articulated a vision of a natural female temperament irreversibly fixing this cultural role.[11]

Pierre Roussel was a medical disciple of famed Court physician Théophile de Bordeu, a modest *habitué* of Madame Helvétius's salon and a journalist for the *Décade* and the *Mercure de France*. Elected ethics associate of the Class, he sent no memoirs to the Institute. But his *Système physique et moral des femmes* (1775) went through five editions by 1809 and was highly touted by *Décade* reviewers in 1802 and 1805 as a "brilliant success ... one of the best products of philosophy, literature, and ethics."[12] Doubtless Roussel was a decisive influence on Cabanis's conventional portrait of feminine character.[13]

Roussel's major premise was that behavioural differences between the sexes were caused not by "education or manner of life" but by "organization," that is "innate radical differences, in all countries and peoples." In women's bodies, according to Roussel, there was a final cause that adapted all women to the destiny of bearing children and caring for them. They had a more constant temperament, therefore, in all climates and generally pursued a few customary occupations.[14] They conserved longer the original softness and suppleness of children's bodies. This flexibility enabled them to withstand the continual shocks of menstruation and childbirth, which otherwise would destroy rigid organs.

Yet organic flexibility did not translate into more adaptable intelligence. Women had briefer, finer sensations, giving them an "imagination too mobile and inconstant for the arts" and a faculty of thought "less capable of lofty conceptions." The "weakness of organs" prohibited the "efforts of that contention of mind necessary to the study of the abstract sciences, even to be mistaken." Women were more intuitive than rational. Reflecting obvious cultural prejudice, Roussel thought that their destination was to "please by the natural graces of the body" and that "pursuing reputation by study would detract from them."

While this image would ban women from politics, its positive aspect was the raising anew of the pedestal of moral sensitivity. Women had distinct virtues, rather than appearing merely as imperfect men. Women's muscular weakness developed a "sense of natural pity ... sweet, affectionate feelings," which constituted their principal charm and made them more inclined than even male moral theorists to show sympathy to their companions and neighbours. The reviewer Imbert thought women would be particularly pleased by this observation. Though this behaviour could be altered by education and circumstances, such exquisite sensitivity was the natural condition of women.[15]

Roussel's work displayed the conversion of the cultural gender stereotype, associated with the élite male image of the submissive, pleasant, non-threatening woman to a physiologically determined natural state. Whatever their powers of habit, typical women could not become typically active, intelligent men. Because they had weak fibres and sensitive temperaments, the physiology of women was indeed destiny, or to paraphrase Laqueur, destiny became physiology.

In Cabanis's work the genital subcentre of sensitivity had a strong sympathy with the brain, which affected the sex drive and also the feelings of "benevolence, tender and gentle sensibility." While in Cabanis there was a more uninhibited repudiation of the taboos on the expression of sexuality than was the case with Roussel, he preserved the radical male-female differences. Weaker cerebral pulp in women's brains produced livelier sensitivity and an easily exhausted nervous system. Female physiological weakness led to the desire for a strong protector and for charming the male: "man must be strong, defiant, enterprising; woman must be weak, timid, dissimulating." Women were unsuited for long meditation but excelled in their proper sphere of expressing sympathy and consoling suffering. They entertained literary and political aspirations only at the price of losing their charms.[16] Physiologically determined moral sensitivity in women contributed to the nineteenth-century image of the separate domestic sphere of women and their suitability for such helping professions as nursing.[17]

The proclamation by a few Revolutionary women of their rights and the enthusiastic actions of republican women's clubs in 1793, which so scandalized the Convention, had little apparent effect on either Cabanis or Roussel. The naturalized image of women's cultural role, already a powerful weapon in the 1760s, persisted during the debates on political rights and social roles in post-Revolutionary society. The Institute paternal power contest seems to reveal a reaction towards male dominance within the family, but in the work of Roussel in 1775 and of Cabanis in 1797 the ideal woman, condemned (or in their view exalted) by her temperament, is the same Rousseauist Sophie.

Only Destutt de Tracy, in a late work published in Italian, rejected a distinct female sensitivity. He claimed that though women had a different constitution, they "did not have a different nature." He actually praised the mixing of women in society and favoured the emancipation of young women for marriages of love rather than of interest. He accepted without scandal unwed mothers and easier divorces, but he still judged women unfit for political rights and most occupations. Hence, Tracy's effort testifies to his antipathy for restrictive families and his belief in sexual liberation, but not to a new political or occupational role for women.[18] Political and social rigidity on gender issues remained a hallmark of the drive for stabilizing society in an era of revolutionary change.

Before the founding of the Second Class, the most sanguine acceptance of Condillac's well-made language model occurred in Garat's highly successful École normale lectures of 1795 on "analysis of the understanding." Garat compared Condillac, whom he had met at the salon of Mme Helvétius, to Kepler and Newton and claimed that the "science of understanding was as certain as the physical sciences." Garat, like Cabanis, also thought language preceded distinct sensations and the very first ideas. Lavoisier's chemical nomenclature was a remarkable precedent for new signs reforming every science. Garat dreamed of a perfect language, or at least of a European republic using a universal language.[19]

The other great proponent of Condillac's well-made language was Laromiguière, the ex-Doctrinaire college philosophy teacher, friend of Lakanal, and author of an elementary metaphysics text in 1794. A protégé of Garat and Sieyès after 1795, he lectured as philosophy professor at the Faculté des Lettres in the Université impériale for two years (1811–13), until he was disabled by a chronic bladder infection. His published lectures remained a classic philosophy text for *lycée* instructors as late as 1844 and ran through seven editions by 1858.[20]

Laromiguière's *Paradoxes de Condillac* (1805) discussed sympathetically a work he had helped publish posthumously, Condillac's *Langue des calculs* (1798).[21] Laromiguière maintained that a complete science was a series of identical dependent propositions derived from a single basic proposition expressing a sensible idea. Consequently, all reasoning was like calculation, and "there is only one method for all the sciences."[22] Moreover, obscurity in the moral and political sciences was due to "the vices of their language," the lack of simplicity, analogy, and indeterminacy of the signs. In principle, all sciences could achieve demonstration, but reforming the language of metaphysics and ethics was a daunting task. One day a "well-made language" would prevail. The art of reasoning was an art of speaking well.[23] From Condillac he preserved the idea that languages were analytic methods and that the well-made language was the key to scientific precision.

This mirage of a language of precise signs haunted many eighteenth-century scientists who were without political motives. The anatomist Vicq d'Azyr in 1786 had contemplated a rational anatomy involving the renaming of all the bones and muscles. The Abbé Roch-Ambroise Sicard at the Institut national des Sourds-Muets taught a gestural language based on certain root-signs. The semaphore signal device, or "telegraph," for military communications was a breakthrough for relaying messages from the Channel ports to Paris. English authors had worked out a shorthand system for the rapid transcription of speech.[24] But, most notably, the chemist Antoine-Laurent Lavoisier had directly credited Condillac's *Logique* as his inspiration for reconstructing the language of chemistry so that each true element had a distinctive name: the chemical structure of compounds could then be deduced from a new nomenclature of elements with special suffixes denoting how much of an element, such as the "acidifying principle" or oxygen, had combined with other elements. The nomenclature enabled compounds to be related to each other clearly in a quantitative way. Such impressive success similarly inspired the physician Philippe Pinel in 1798 to 1802 to reformulate a nosology – that is, a systematic classification – of families of diseases and types of insanity.[25]

In Condillac's framework, the degree of precision in universal analytic method would determine whether each science supplied incontrovertible answers. The underlying political agenda, muted in Garat and Laromiguière, was the hope for the settlement of issues in the moral and political sciences after long years of Revolutionary agitation. These reflections inspired the analysis of sensations and ideas section to choose for its prize contest of 1796 to 1799 the "influence of signs on the formation of ideas." The corollary questions were whether all sciences were equally capable of demonstration and whether the perfection of signs was the means to that end.[26]

A minority of contestants believed that signs precede ideas and aspired to construct an ideal language from a new system of algebraic roots.[27] Naval engineer Pierre-François Lancelin projected the ethical equivalent of Lavoisier's nomenclature: universal definitions of virtue (including love of work) and vice (including fanaticism). Synoptic tables and abstracts would replace the charlatanism of ill-defined signs and the traditional pedagogical distortions of rhetoric and theology. Lancelin also unveiled the potentially élitist implications of a philosophical language. He pointedly contrasted the talk in "popular societies ... the central office of ignorance," with discussion in learned academies. Markedly less democratic even than Cabanis and Destutt de Tracy, Lancelin recommended contentment with one's lot.[28] Hence, the well-made language might stifle dissent of the unfortunate.

CRITIQUE OF THE WELL-MADE LANGUAGE

Joseph de Maimieux, a former officer in a German infantry regiment, published in 1797 a symbolic universal language, *Pasigraphie.*[29] A special chart (a spreadsheet of its day) interpreted twelve symbolic characters. For example, the first of three symbols in a word appeared at the head of a column, the second at the head of a row, and one of six possible third characters then specified the meaning.[30]

Destutt de Tracy's evaluation of Maimieux's efforts in the spring of 1800 for a Class commission owed much to Degérando.[31] Tracy condemned pasigraphy as a "vicious project in principle," since a spoken language was superior to all merely symbolic systems.[32] An ex-"federalist" (anti-National Convention) rebel from Lyon in 1793 and an exile after the 1797 coup of Fructidor, Degérando was more politically conservative and also more religious than most Idéologues. His own 1799 prize memoir on the influence of signs began to demote the importance of language in itself. Despite political differences, Tracy fully accepted Degérando's systematic attack on philosophical languages. Degérando, in his four-volume elaboration of his ideas published in 1800, had doubted a prospective philosophical language could meet all its necessary conditions – simplicity and distinctness of the signs, sufficiency of signs for nuanced meaning, and analogy among signs and to ideas.[33] Tracy and Degérando both argued that before a language could be perfect, ideas needed to be perfect, an obvious impossibility. Even as early as 1796 Tracy thought that the quest for *perfect* signs was a "chimera," and in 1803 he wrote that their imperfection stemmed from a "radical vice of the human mind."[34] An imposed universal language would suffer local corruption, while a universal scholarly language would be "undesirable for the progress of the enlightenment" to ordinary people.[35] Hence, for all his élitism, Tracy never believed in handicapping communication between the "experts" and the general public. In 1804 he even condemned Condillac's fundamental suggestion in the *Langue des calculs* to manipulate verbal language as if it were algebra.[36]

Condillac may not in fact have believed a "well-made" language would be perfect.[37] In any case, Tracy's critiques show a loss of enthusiasm for the demonstrability of all sciences. He continued to hope for the piecemeal language reform of alphabets, spelling, and syntax, and for the elimination of ambiguity and exaggerated rhetoric.[38] Degérando agreed that a philosophical and etymological dictionary would be more feasible than a universal language. Most Idéologues were content to encourage analytic scientific classification.

Degérando's prizewinning memoir further argued that the importance of signs in abstract mathematics was not equivalent to their role in experimental chemistry. Lavoisier's experiments enabled nomenclature reform, while the new names did not guarantee experimental success.[39] In the partly abstract, partly factual human sciences, inadequate or incomplete observation was often more damaging than sterile nomenclature. In the human sciences of ethics and politics, there was disagreement on how to apply such generally accepted maxims as doing one's duty or moderation in government. From Degérando's own, but unspoken, religious perspective, philosophers would do better leading virtuous lives than to try to solve human problems by perfect signs.[40]

Among Degérando's most interesting remarks is one on the relationship of language and power. Revolutionary circumstances had taken much of the lustre from Condillac's brilliant vision. In the Revolution, liberty was the label for acts of despotism and equality for those of iniquitous proscription. All tyrants corrupt language when proclaiming a reign of liberty. Somewhat anticipating Marx's concept of the ideology of the ruling class and Foucault's knowledge/power axis, Degérando added: "The language of politics is the only one where definitions are almost never made by philosophers, but are in a way an attribute of power, or rather a prerogative that belongs to the strongest."[41]

While the mythology of the well-made language declined, Degérando, like Destutt de Tracy, worried that primitive or uneducated people lacked sophisticated linguistic tools to interpret sensations. Fanatics might use emotive symbols or poetry to "mislead youth and women."[42] Similarly, artisans and labourers, "even of higher conditions ... could not understand abstract ideas."[43]

Revolutionary circumstances had at first given a democratic slant to Condillac's analytic method. A report by Joseph Lakanal on the École normale that was, however, probably written by Garat, said in 1794: "Analysis applied to all kinds of ideas in all schools will destroy the inequality of enlightenment ... which will easily penetrate everywhere."[44] Yet this democratic connotation could now be undercut by the belief (also found in Condillac) that primitive languages could not be abstract and that the savant had more analytic experience than the ignorant.[45] Already, Condillac foreshadowed the stages theory of history from hunters to commercial civilization so prominent in the work of the cultural geographers.

CONDILLAC'S TRANSFORMED SENSATIONS

Garat's École normale lectures vigorously rejected the concept of innate ideas and endorsed completely that of the "never-changing nature of sensation" as it metamorphosed into other mental faculties.[46] Roederer, a lawyer and a member of the political economy section, was a peripheral Idéologue before 1801–2 when he gave his pragmatic support of Bonaparte's Concordat and education laws. In his Lycée lectures of 1793 he aspired, like Garat, to "reduce politics and ethics to rules as certain and evident as those of geometry" and to have "demonstrations as simple, sure, and at bottom of the same kind as the so-called natural sciences."[47] Roederer also accepted the transformed sensations model and encouraged the study of anatomy and physiology in order to understand sensitivity and human passions.[48]

Undoubtedly the most important proponent of the transformed sensations model was Destutt de Tracy himself. Given the abundant study of Tracy that has been published, there will only be a brief sketch here of his philosophy of Ideology.[49] Tracy, who had meditated on Condillac's works while in prison during the Terror, emerged in 1796 a convinced, if reserved, disciple. He first introduced the concept of Ideology as a "science of ideas" to replace "psychology," which implied a soul, or "metaphysics," as if humans were beyond the physical world. While claiming that Ideology, properly speaking, was a "branch of zoology," and while denying the spiritual soul, Tracy spent most of his time discussing the faculties of sensitivity and motility, the existence of external reality, the faculties of the understanding and will, the use of signs for the improvement of the individual, and the effect of habit. He originally hoped that this new science would find its Newton and have the same "degree of certainty" as the mathematical sciences.[50] There were corrections to Condillac's scheme – a faculty of motility encountering resistance, not just touch, was necessary to contact the external world, and the deduction of one faculty from another was not just an equation of identities but an opening up of "Chinese boxes" of smaller scope contained in larger faculties of remembering, judging, and willing. But, though Tracy doubted the idea of the well-made language, he largely accepted the transformed sensations model. In fact, Tracy tightened his arguments to claim that even judging was a sensing of relationships.[51]

Laromiguière's two published Institute memoirs of 1796 had already showed uneasiness with the proximity of sensation to physical sensitivity. At all costs, there had to be a barrier between thought and physical movements. He shared Condillac's basic principle of sensations as the origin of ideas. But in his search for "principles or generative elements of the mind" he found the faculty of attention a direct aspect of the "activity of the soul." This notion of the activity of attention, in contrast with passive sensation, was the crucial break with the transformed sensations model. Already Laromiguière spoke of the "sublime idea of Divinity" evident as the source of virtue within the human heart.[52]

Degérando demonstrated a similar, though more pronounced philosophical evolution.[53] In 1800 he sharpened Laromiguière's focus on the faculty of attention, a faculty "which transforms sensation and judgment into perception." Late in 1801, while he was still an empiricist, in a lecture at the Lycée on moral philosophy, Degérando condemned authors who "degrade man, and by baseness of mind, misanthropy, or materialism, even assimilate him to brutes." By 1802, in a Berlin Academy prize memoir on the origin of knowledge, he spoke of attention as an independent mental principle of activity, and the soul as a "thinking and willing principle."[54] In his history of philosophy in 1804, he condemned Condillac's "sterile theory" of transformed sensations and particularly Garat's materialist reading of Condillac.[55] In 1808 Degérando's official Institute report on recent progress in philosophy stipulated an "essential distinction between the thinking principle and material organs." Moreover, he affirmed that philosophy should have the "august mission of announcing the Being of Beings to human reason."[56] Degérando had become committed to "reconciling and mediating" divergent philosophical systems, such as Lockeanism and Kantianism, an act embodying eclecticism.[57]

In 1811, when Laromiguière completed his first year of philosophy lectures at the Paris Faculté des Lettres, Pierre-Paul Royer-Collard was frontally attacking Condillac's doctrine with the aid of Thomas Reid's "philosophy of common sense." Four years later Royer-Collard's alternate at the faculty, Victor Cousin, condemned Laromiguière for conceding too much to sensation. Laromiguière assured his audience that Condillac believed in the soul, though he had also unintentionally aided materialists. According to Laromiguière sensation was necessary for knowledge, but no more than other sentiments of relationships, of the internal active faculties of the soul, and of morality. Thus, inherent intellectual and moral capacities produced intellectual and moral ideas. By the time the lectures were published in 1818 Laromiguière's empiricism was tenuous. From the outset, then, Laromiguière's insistence on the existence of God, the soul, and free will had distinguished him from Cabanis and Destutt de Tracy. His students would not absorb materialism from the lectures.[58] The *grand-maître* of the Université impériale (Napoleon's national teaching corps), Louis Fontanes, sympathetic to reconciliation with the Church, could safely recommend Laromiguière for the new École normale and for the Paris Faculté des Lettres in 1810.[59]

SIEYÈS, CRITIC OF CONDILLAC

Aside from Laromiguière and Degérando, a third critic of the transformed sensations model was the political theorist and patron of the

Idéologue leaders, Emmanuel-Joseph Sieyès. Sieyès had met Cabanis and Destutt de Tracy at Mme Helvétius's salon, and had corresponded with Cabanis as early as 1792. In 1773, when he was a rather unorthodox priest and canon in Brittany, he read Condillac's *Traité des sensations* and found that the arbitrary statue metaphor (senses awakening one at a time) distorted the multiplicity of simultaneous sensations. He wrote: "sensation is passive, [and] attention and judgment [are] active," so that "it is false that with only one sense the soul has the germ of all its faculties."[60] In a manuscript notebook dating from the period of the Consulate or the Empire, Sieyès even mocked Condillac's whole enterprise of "decomposing the understanding and will":

What does it matter that seeing, comparing, judging, recalling, reflecting, etc. are always *sensing*? A futile, arbitrary decision! You make sensation the generic word and you conclude that the mind, in all its operations, does nothing other than sense. That is not well done. Someone else prefers "attention" or some other generic word, and he has just as much right to say that all can be reduced to attention, etc. These general expressions are our invention, with no counterpart in nature, and remote from reality. There is nothing real but our particular intellectual acts.

Commenting on these passages, Murray Forsyth too hastily classified Sieyès with idealist advocates such as Fichte of a "self-determining man," not of a man as a "prolongation of nature."[61] True enough, Sieyès proposed Kant as an Institute foreign associate to "clear a path for Kant's philosophy in France."[62]

In his comments on the brain and instinct, however, Sieyès displayed a greater interest than most idealists in a physiological human science. In a 1795 note on the "social art," he insisted that "intellectual truths are the result of a mental digestion, which modifies, elaborates, and appropriates a true nutrition to the brain."[63] In his notebook he even boasted that "instinct arises from impressions received by internal organs, [according to] Cabanis, who owes me this idea as well as the one of comparing the brain (I had added the senses) *digesting* the sensations to the stomach *digesting* the food it receives."[64]

Despite the work on physiology by the renowned X.-F. Bichat, Sieyès confounded involuntary instinct with will. Instincts may also be educated, he wrote, "organs do improve, and improvements are transmitted to the races by propagation." Educating physical temperament was therefore a legitimate enterprise. "Whipping a schoolboy or hanging an accomplice of a criminal ... stimulate directly instincts and by their consequences change the direction of character."[65] Sieyès therefore had sympathy for a thoroughly physiological "science of man," though he disclaimed materialism. For, he wrote, "moral or physical observation at least reveals a certain dependence between two things." And so, while Sieyès rejected both transformed sensations and materialism, he was unlike the German idealists when he insisted on direct body-mind relationships. He remained an advocate of the Hippocratic temperament tradition if not of Condillac's analytic decomposition of thought.

THE DECOMPOSITION OF THOUGHT

The final analysis of sensations and ideas prize contest, announced in October 1802, returned to the basic exercise of the "decomposition of the faculty of thought and recognition of its elementary faculties."[66] Only four of eighteen sampled memoirs still supported the transformed sensations model, while four others expressed horror at any physiological decomposition of the mind. For example, philosophy teacher J.-B. Maugras satirized Cabanis's stomach-brain metaphor and found the indivisible substance of the soul "as real as liberty, virtue, eloquence, and piety." Coffee, he gibed, would not be the key to improving the mind, nor sugar, to sweetening customs.[67] The majority of contestants willingly related physical to mental, but firmly rejected materialism or transformed sensations.[68]

The prize went to Maine de Biran, a political conservative who was engaged in a tormented spiritual odyssey. He was seriously committed to traditional morality and wary of materialism. Both an unfinished note on signs in 1798 and a letter to Degérando in 1802 display his discomfort with Cabanis's monistic metaphors and language.[69] By 1802 he had endured the death of his first wife and experienced a conversion which took him closer to the religious orthodoxy he would attain only after 1815.

Maine de Biran provides the finest example of the conflict between the two aforementioned intellectual strategies for achieving social stability. In his own person he sought to combine a fascination with physical-mental correspondences with a deep conviction in the activity of the mind. He praised Cabanis's plan for seeking organic states corresponding to happy or virtuous feelings, but he also sought to restrain Physiological Ideology from encroaching on the *moi*, or self. There needed to be a "subjective Ideology" that was concerned with the "intimate relations which the thinking subject has with himself in the free exercise of his intellectual acts."[70] The sensations founded on effort were of a different order from those of the organs, and resulted from a movement produced by a "hyper-organic force named *will*." Consequently, the observation of consciousness "individualizes and simplifies," unlike physiological observation, which is designed to "generalize." Thus began a long intellectual tradition culminating with Henri Bergson in the late nineteenth century that sought the "immediate data of consciousness" beyond the determinations of science. This declaration of independence for psychology prefigured Biran's later warnings that the two different categories of sciences should not be confused.[71] Biran now rejected Condillac's "decomposition" of a truly indivisible soul. The activity of the self could not be identified with passive modifications.[72] Passive affectability, the sphere of material organization, was necessary, but it was not sufficient for the science of moral and intellectual man. The motive force of the will beyond sensitivity introduced a new active order.[73] Such would be the basis for Biran's ultimate break with the Idéologues, after expressing the hesitant hybrid views of the memoir on habit.

THE AMBIVALENCE OF THE POWER OF HABIT

Besides language and the faculty of thought, the third great question explored by the heirs of Condillac was the power of physical, mental, and moral habits. Roederer's Lycée lectures of 1793 had already called attention to the practical uses of Condillac's liaison of ideas, long before the public morality contest of 1798. Habit was the master educational tool to enlighten judgment, to "prevent false association of ideas," and to "assure recall of good reasoning." Habit was also the means of directing passions to "moralize public opinion" and to strengthen a weak temperament. One could transmute "love of wealth" into "industry," and "love of power" into "social virtue."[74]

As Mona Ozouf has argued, the belief in institutions such as Revolutionary festivals was independent of particular political opinions. Jacobin painter Jacques-Louis David was far from the only advocate of public festivals to mobilize opinion. As much as any Jacobin, the moderately conservative Roederer recommended spectacles, festivals, and dances to arouse republican sentiment. New sculpture, painting, and public monuments could arouse virtuous emotions and make vice odious.[75] But Roederer also thought that the most difficult habits to change were political and social customs. One must change politics and ethics to enable leading "men without bayonets, to reach agreement without courts of law, to become happy without disappointment."[76] Thus, Roederer's principal interest was the political art of inculcating habits – a combination, as he so astutely observed, of Condillac and Machiavelli. The undeniably necessary educative function of habit had a sinister, manipulative correlative, not surprising perhaps in a thinker who opportunistically hitched his destiny to Bonaparte after 1800.

While Roederer, in his praise for public festivals, typified many Revolutionary enthusiasts, the Idéologue leaders Cabanis and Destutt de Tracy had become sceptical on the issue by 1798–99. Despite his collaboration with Mirabeau in 1791 in a discourse on festivals to inspire "sensitive beings," Cabanis warned by 1799 that compulsory attendance and a "mechanical and vulgar power, displayed with pomp," would never match the moral influence of the ancients, nor would a "political effect" be easy in modern times. Tracy in 1798 had rejected sermonizing and festivals as means for improving adult moral behaviour in favour of efficient and appropriately punitive legislation.[77]

In 1798 Tracy's memoir on the "frequent return of the same intellectual operations" discussed how repeated sense-impressions leave durable traces in the brain or nervous system. Hence, memory becomes easier with repetition, as do mental operations, such as mathematics, and muscular movements for musicians or dancers.[78] Vehement desires could become passions with repetition, but repeated, successive, and similar judgments might become imperceptible. The chief goal of education, however, was to "make good judgments habitual."[79]

Like the contestants in the signs contest, Destutt de Tracy worried about "slower, more difficult operations of the mind" among "savages" and "analogous phenomena among the class which has the least extended and varied communications."[80] Despite having excellent faculties, isolated peasants or inexperienced individuals might be incapable of modifying or extending their ideas. Untouched as yet by good habits, their passions and prejudices could be impediments to the science of the understanding.[81]

The ambivalence of habit could foster liberating education of physical powers and mental faculties but also a stifling indoctrination. Roederer's habit formation through arts and festivals sounded like an exercise in scientifically managed Revolutionary propaganda. Élitist exclusion of the ignorant and the isolated from the polity could be a social repercussion of the theory of habit. Thus, the experiences of the Revolutionary era had sharpened the edges of empiricist learning theory, which was as necessary for perfectibility as for repression.

The Second Class found the subject so scintillating that from 1799 to 1802 it ran two rounds of a contest on the "influence of habit on the faculty of thought" and the "effect of frequent repetition of the same operations on each of our intellectual faculties."[82] A perennial Institute competitor, Nicolas-François Canard, a mathematics teacher from Moulins, received an honourable mention in the second contest for a sophisticated essay on the probable value of testimony. He also saw habit as the fundamental principle of knowledge and a substitute for attention, but a danger if it reinforced fears and prejudices.[83]

A local official from the Gironde, Charles Mullot, vigorously endorsed the work ethic to "coordinate habits" in modern society. His notion of social hierarchy recalled Petitain's public morality memoir. Among the "many illiterate in the lower classes" were some people who were "closer to some apes than to the most enlightened men." They needed the guidance of village proprietors and small merchants for moral values. Government rewards for inventions or improvements would help tie artisans to the public interest. To accept the "inequality of enjoyments," however, the "prejudices of sentiment" would have to serve since it was hopeless to "enlighten the minds" of these unfortunate people. Here was a bald, albeit unheralded, statement of the political use of habit as propaganda for social quietism and élitism. [84]

The Institute commission, which included Destutt de Tracy, the reporter, and Cabanis, was no doubt enthralled with prizewinner Maine de Biran for his seriousness of purpose in dissecting each mental faculty and his fascination with physical-mental relations.[85] By the second contest of 1802 he had distinguished "passive habits" of sensation, perception, and imagination from the "active habits" founded on the will and on the use of voluntary signs.[86]

Despite his long correspondence with Cabanis and Destutt de Tracy, Maine de Biran broke with Cabanis (and, unwittingly, with Sieyès) in distinguishing acts of free will from the passive role of the brain in internal impressions and sensitivity.[87] By 1802 he insisted that habit could not improve internal or purely instinctive impressions. Hence, he closed Cabanis's direct physiological path to affecting the will.[88] He also argued that habit strengthened the passions when they were products of passive imagination, akin to Cabanis's hallucinations produced by special cerebral sensitivity. Hence, imaginary fears or even effects of erotic stimuli could be purely physical, not the mental acting on the physical.[89] Certain "phantoms ... beyond the experience of the senses" were "powerful engines of fear or hope," but entirely internal or instinctive. Believers in miracles, or devout persons who imagined themselves as saints, were displaying a kind of delirium. Biran warned against the effects procured by "signs of archetypical ideas" that helped "the power of seducers ... certain heads of sects, of parties" to acquire "such monstrous control, so disastrous to the perfectibility of individuals and of the species."[90]

Biran thus seemed to be pleading for reason against the siren songs of both political and religious enthusiasm. He had seen enough of Revolutionary propaganda to make him wary. He also perceived the danger in the rote learning of catechisms and multiplication tables, which discouraged analysis and could stifle intelligence. In a rare social comment, he shared Adam Smith's misgivings that the division of labour could make habit hinder intellectual and moral development so that "mechanical work" created "blind automata, true machines."[91]

The cultivated use of language and the philosophical analysis of signs were the indispensable safeguards against an overheated imagination and rote learning. One could disdain signs without meaning or illusory images. Biran and the Idéologues shared a distaste for enthusiasm and the false eloquence of rhetorical devices. Biran also held out no hope for the clarity of a universal language or for the demonstrability of ethics. Metaphysical questions were not like mathematics, since unanalysed signs would bring the worst perils of habitual, unperceived judgments. The philosopher had to prevent the "most complicated operations from losing the strength of analysis because of inaction while thought sleeps."[92]

So, while Maine de Biran remained a student of physical-mental relations, he would remove Cabanis's tool of organic sympathies from the arsenal of influences on the self. Habit could perfect perception and voluntary movements, but it could also promote prejudices and delusions. In the end he discarded both the transformed sensations and the ideal language models before making his complete break with Condillac in the decomposition of thought memoir.[93]

KANT VERSUS CONDILLAC

With the gradual defection by Laromiguière, Degérando, and Maine de Biran from belief in transformed sensations, the Idéologue circle was losing its potential disciples. The disarray was no less real for being only partly visible when the Class of Moral and Political Sciences was dissolved in 1803. At the same time, those who were opposed within the Class to the Idéologues openly attacked empiricist views of the mind.

Early in 1799 Mercier's ethics memoir assailed the "incorrect doctrine of Locke and Condillac," which he inaccurately claimed classified sensations, ideas, and sentiments as physical sensitivity. The Institute, he said, was the only place in Europe that still supported Locke. Innate ideas were spiritual visions of beings, a tableau of celestial truths. Thinking preceded sensing. The "false and insignificant doctrines of these bold Idéologues" have "annihilated the human soul ... [T]hey want to drag us by force into the obscure cavern of their terminology so they can there trumpet their victory." Free will subordinated sensuality to reason, and the performance of duty was not automatic, but a triumph over the opposition to virtue.[94]

With this outlook, Mercier especially appreciated the moral philosophy of Kant. From the time Sieyès and others considered Kant a suitable Institute associate, Kant now became in the eyes of Grégoire, the émigré Charles Villers, and other French-speaking disciples a rampart against atheism and materialism. From 1800 to 1802 Mercier read four memoirs on innate ideas, the philosophies of Kant and Fichte, and the acts of the self. He compared the Idéologues' doctrine once again to the "mechanical metaphysics ... of pulleys, springs, levers ... a thinking automaton" of the materialist La Mettrie of Berlin. Kant, by contrast, was able to show the real existence of the invisible categories of space and time and the moral imperative of duty. The cognitive self was an active force, the will was "innate, powerful, and creative."[95] Mercier himself summarized his philosophy in the Institute quarterly report: "as pure, sublime, consoling, and quite opposed in every respect to the dark monstrosities of atheism." Moreover, "nature's laws are our own cognitive laws ... space is our way of seeing, time is ours ... the knowledge of God is even more visible in ourselves than in the order and majesty of the universe."[96] One wonders if Kant might have been pleased to be called "supremely religious." In 1802 the conservative *Journal des Débats* welcomed Mercier's critique of the "sensualism" of Helvétius and the "doll" (statue) of Condillac as "desolating systems."[97]

Degérando's manuscript prize memoir of 1799 (his public memoir of 1801 is available only in summary) had criticized Kant for an "abundance of sophisms," such as the belief that time and space were in ourselves, not in perceived relationships among objects. Degérando found Kant too sceptical of the existence of God, a God derived from our ideas of moral perfection, intelligence, and power. Kant also needlessly separated feelings from the essence of the *moi*. At the same time, practical reason was an almost "magical power" to restore morality after denying knowledge of God. Rather than protecting religion, Kant aided sceptics who would gladly consider only "pure reason."[98] By 1804 Degérando's comparative history of philosophy sought to reconcile empiricism with transcendentalism. He praised Kant for believing in the freedom and activity of understanding and reason.[99] On the other hand, he still considered Kant's a priori truths "complicated and obscure."[100]

The controversy heated up in August 1801 when Charles Villers, the counter-Revolutionary ex-military officer living in Hamburg, dedicated a summary in French of Kant to the Institute. Destutt de Tracy mocked Villers's superficiality, and in the spring of 1802 formulated his own commentary on Kant, which was filtered through a French translation of a Dutch exposition.[101] Tracy noted that the French proudly followed

Condillac's method but not all his conclusions. Kant, on the other hand, was an obscure systematizer. For Tracy, "sensing a perception after an impression is active … sensing is therefore manifestly acting." Kant was a poor physiologist if he declared sensing passive. Even internal impressions came from active internal organs. Nor did activity postulate free will. Reason was not an independent faculty, only a series of judgments.[102]

Thus, Kant re-entered French philosophical controversy over the issues of the moral consequences of mental passivity and activity. French Catholic conservatives even allied themselves with Mercier to attack "sensualism." Degérando and Maine de Biran would soon form the core of a set of eclectic philosophers who would inspire the next generation.[103] In 1814 Biran's diary spoke of a Société de Philosophie which included Pierre-Paul Royer-Collard, Ampère, Cousin, and François Thurot. Even residual disciples of Condillac, like Laromiguière, were unacceptable to Biran and Cousin in the period from 1817 to 1821. But Laromiguière's revisions to Condillac, expressed in immensely popular lectures, the personal influence of Biran, and Degérando's historical approach helped launch the eclectics' movement. From 1825 to 1827 Théodore Jouffroy proclaimed in the *Globe* the death of Condillac's empiricism, while Jean-Philibert Damiron hailed eclectic spiritualism. Cousin's 1828 Sorbonne lectures condemned empiricism for fostering social instability. The philosophies of Kant (taught by Cousin in 1820), Hegel, and the Scots Thomas Reid and Dugald Stewart could dissipate the spectres of atheism and materialism, and ultimately they would create for the intellectual élite a philosophical supplement to religious faith for the masses.[104]

Cabanis's thought, with its relation of physical to mental and detachment from Condillac's empiricism, endured to challenge the eclectics. For a new generation of physicians, including such phrenologist disciples of Franz-Joseph Gall and Johann-Caspar Spurzheim as François-Joseph-Victor Broussais, inherent intellectual and moral faculties would derive from the development of regions of the brain.[105] In the new Academy of Moral and Political Sciences, Broussais would conduct a debate with Jouffroy on the legitimacy of physiological psychology against Cousin's introspective psychological method.[106] Moreover, while discarding the Idéologues' materialism and Condillac's well-made language, philosophers in the tradition of positivism embodied by Saint-Simon and Comte would return to the hope of a universal scientific method precisely because they also sought social stability. Their organic society repudiated individual rights, and rested partly on a spiritual power of experts in a social science that could determine suitable roles for individuals amid the imperatives of order and progress.

CONCLUSION

Had Cabanis and the medical Idéologues constructed an effective physiological science, they might have acquired formidable powers as technicians of temperament. They aspired not only to enhance the physical health of individuals, but also to improve their intelligence and character. Yet the need to tailor each treatment to individual eccentricity militated against the creation of uniform or docile temperaments. Like most instructions in hygiene, theirs would have been more feasible as self-help than as mandatory prescriptions. The great paradox is that the most genuinely repressive of all consequences of the temperament theory was an irreversible attribute: the perceived natural sexual traits were disabling to women who sought enriched cultural and political status. Not all the Revolutionary rhetoric of rights changed the late eighteenth-century Rousseauist image.

Condillac's legacies of the well-made language, transformed sensations, and even the power of habit all had to endure searching analysis, despite their apparent dominance in the philosophical discourse in the Institute and in the central schools. Divergent interpretations of Condillac highlighted increasing disunity in the Idéologue circle. Revolutionary turmoil seemed to make even more urgent the optimistic effort to eliminate linguistic ambiguity. The more sinister corollary was that an unambiguous political language could stifle incorrect answers to political and social problems. Yet, despite the visions of Garat, Laromiguière, and Lancelin, Degérando and Destutt de Tracy himself recognized that the power of signs was limited. Improving linguistic clarity might still be desirable. Revolutionary experience had, however, apparently shown that language was not a reliable tool for stability. Degérando saw that the moral and political sciences could not be as certain as mathematics partly because the powerful turned language to their own advantage.

While Sieyès rejected the search for generative principles of the mind, Garat, Cabanis, and Destutt de Tracy remained adherents of Condillac's transformed sensations model. Their colleagues and critics worried that if sensation itself produced thought, physical sensitivity might be assumed to produce sensation, with unwelcome materialist consequences. Hence, Laromiguière and Degérando insisted that attention was not transformed sensation but an active generative faculty. Such activity was more reconcilable with the existence of an immortal soul, and with the eternal punishment considered necessary for social stability. Idéologue leaders also hoped to achieve stability, but with natural enlightenment of self-interest or cultivation of sympathy.

The power of habit was double-edged, even in Condillac, who warned that it permitted the persistence of prejudices. Learning by experience was open to all, but the civilized and educated, as opposed to the primitive and the unenlightened, already had more varied experiences. The people at large needed guidance to correct their "bad habits" and erroneous judgments. Maine de Biran was astute enough to warn against the phantasms generated not only by the clergy but also by secular messiahs. Thus, the alleged means of perfectibility that was not subjected to sophisticated philosophical analysis could become demagogic indoctrination.

Yet the Idéologues, like the Robespierrists before them, insisted that the power of habit applied not only to learning but to motivation, through the channelling of desires, aversions, and natural sympathies. Having analysed the origins and expression of sensations and ideas, then, the next challenging project was to define a secular science of natural morality. This goal would arouse vigorous opposition within the Class of Moral and Political Sciences.

7 A Science of Morality

No question was as crucial to the stability of post-Revolutionary society as appropriate moral education. The majority of the population undoubtedly hoped for the reopening of churches in 1795 and may have been quite content with a revealed morality of divine commandment taught by the *curé*.[1] For most members of the Class of Moral and Political Sciences, both the Enlightenment philosophical critique of "fanaticism and superstition" and the dramatic Revolutionary break with the orthodox Catholic Church made such reconciliation unpalatable, at least at that juncture. While there was not a predominant Enlightenment "moral science" model, the project of either a secular or a deist natural morality was virtually a defining characteristic of French Enlightenment thought. Within the Class, the major issues centred first around whether a metaphysics of divine sanction supported or handicapped moral behaviour. A second question was whether removing corrupt institutions would liberate natural "goodness" or sympathy, or whether education and the laws faced a more onerous task in enlightening prudential self-interest. A critical variant of this latter question was whether external legislation to direct passions could succeed without the sense of internal struggle of conscience against inclination. The Idéologue leaders unhesitatingly chose a secular moral science, but contended with views in the ethics section that ranged from friendly but ineffectual atheism to hostile deism and to a Christianity nominally different from secular morality but similar to it in practical moral commands.

The Newtonian model of scientific explanation fascinated eighteenth-century moralists as well as psychologists. The Idéologues read two secular moralists in particular, Claude-Adrien Helvétius and Paul Thiry, Baron d'Holbach, who both searched for a psychological law of gravity in the single, all-encompassing principle of self-interest. As with Hobbes and Locke, they sought their allegedly observable natural law in the pursuit of self-preservation, which would stem from the physical sensitivity of pleasure-seeking and pain-avoiding human beings. Helvétius expected this "science of morality which is finally that of legislation" to harness natural inclinations to the goal of public utility.[2]

In his discourses *De l'esprit* (1758) and treatise *De l'homme* (1772) Helvétius aspired to find the "happiness of the greatest number" by harmonizing "personal and general interest." Human nature had no "original goodness," so moral science would have to use education and legislation with appropriate rewards and punishments. Once enlightened, self-love would guarantee love of others.[3] This morality was rigorously secular since he saw Christian morality as manifestly ineffective in preventing crimes and moral transgressions. To Helvétius, bishops lived in hypocritical luxury and drained tithes from the populace. Most important, priests found their own self-interest in "ridiculous observances and ceremonies" which suited neither the "public interest" nor the "interests of justice."[4]

Similarly, the militant atheist d'Holbach hoped to find moral distinctions in secular scientific laws, which are the "eternal and invariable relations subsisting between human beings living in society," resting on knowledge of diverse human temperaments and the universal motive of self-interest. He, too, would see happiness being achieved by directing self-interested passions toward the social good.[5] The teaching of honesty, temperance, and generosity would rest on sound calculation of interest rather than on unprovable divine command.

Other "natural moralities" of the Enlightenment were equally anticlerical but, as in Rousseau, they rested on a sentimental deism and suspected the moral efficacy of self-interest. To the adherents of this view natural goodness would triumph when corrupting social institutions were removed. Mercier's utopian dream of a reformed France (*L'An 2440*, published in 1770) seven hundred years in the future condemned the scourge of theologians who debated the attributes of God. But he was confident that once the society was freed from despotism, luxury, and arbitrary penal codes, it would be possible to teach a "universal morality," one that was already "in all hearts," of "courage, sacrifice of egotism, and generosity."[6] Some social institutions might still be required for gentle enforcement. For the recalcitrant idle, there would be Roman-style "censors" assigning work. Most important, morality needed the sanction of a "palpable, consoling, and salutary truth," a Supreme Being worshipped in a temple of God. In a kingdom where many frivolous books had been burned, the citizens preserved Rousseau's deist educational treatise *Émile* and moralistic novel *Nouvelle Héloïse*.[7]

Around the same time, Delisle de Sales's *De la philosophie de la nature*, first published in 1770, showed "happiness and self-love" as the "great mainspring of our actions." However, the "motive of virtue" was also "in our hearts." Remorse levied a harsh penalty on vice, and only virtue gave peace of mind. Self-love achieves happiness "only when we are beneficent and recognize the common good" otherwise it risks degeneration into egotism. Such a morality based on happiness could not be consistent with Christian original sin, nor did it need the extra support of Revelation. The design in the universe and the reality of moral action, however, led to belief in God. Like virtue, God's image was in every heart. Explicitly attacking Diderot, La Mettrie, and d'Holbach, de Sales called atheism a social crime which destroyed the possibility of heroism. The "basis of universal morality" assuring fear of eternal punishment was belief in the immortality of the soul. De Sales's work actually had a remarkable success, going through seven editions. Never lacking confidence, de Sales engraved a motto on his own bust, "Dieu, la nature, l'homme, il a tout expliqué." The dramatist F.-G.-J.-S. Andrieux maliciously retorted, "Mais personne avant lui ne l'aurait remarqué." ("He has explained everything – God, nature, and man." "But no one, apart from himself, would have noticed.")[8]

Enlightenment efforts to construct a natural morality seemed more urgent in the Revolutionary circumstances of a complete break between the French government and the orthodox Roman Catholic Church. In 1790–91 half the clergy who refused to take the loyalty oath to the nation became "refractory" and subject to increasing harassment and, ultimately in 1792, to compulsory deportation. When the Pope excommunicated the "constitutional," or oath-taking, clergy, many devout Catholics, especially in western France, more readily chose their faith instead of loyalty to the state. Covert or open refractory involvement in counter-Revolution led patriots to suspect any association with Christianity. During the Terror representatives on mission for the National Convention executed thousands of refractories.

Even at the level of the élite, secular republican moral catechisms became the order of the day. The dramatic result in many regions of France was a popular de-Christianization campaign late in 1793 with abjurations by many constitutional priests, some of whom married, wild bonfires of clerical vestments, and charivaris with bishops' mitres paraded on donkeys. The Commune of Paris encouraged the rededication of Notre Dame as the Temple of Reason in November 1793, and it effectively closed Paris churches for eighteen months. The thoroughgoing cultural Revolution included the purging of saints' names and the adoption in October 1793 of a non-Christian calendar with the proclamation of the Republic in September 1792 as the beginning of year 1.

Robespierre's Committee of Public Safety eventually controlled de-Christianization, warned against atheism, and replaced it with deist worship of the Supreme Being amid the moralistic republic of virtue (meaning the supreme ideal of sacrifice to the aims of the *patrie*) in the spring of 1794. Robespierre idealized Rousseau's ethic of good citizenship and criticized Helvétius's "egotism," though none of the Institute Rousseauists would have supported his efforts. After Robespierre's fall, in an effort to pacify western France the Convention completely separated church and state in February 1795. But throughout the Directory there was a cultural struggle between the majority of the population, which sought return to Christian worship, and the governing élite, which urgently wished secular catechisms to replace politically unacceptable Christian doctrine. The Idéologues were opposed to Robespierre and would have been scandalized at the wild abandon of de-Christianizing crowds. But the Directory's fear of clerical royalism and disdain for "fanaticism and superstition" favoured the rise of such civic or deist cults as Theophilanthropy rather than the constitutional Church.[9]

VOLNEY'S CATECHISM

In this atmosphere after 1795, Idéologues such as Roederer and Cabanis especially praised a quasi-official moral catechism, *La Loi naturelle, ou catéchisme du citoyen français,* that had been published by Volney in September 1793.[10] Interior Minister Garat had commissioned the text in the spring, and Cabanis himself had supervised its printing. Though Volney was away from the Institute and in the United States from 1795 to 1798, this pamphlet represented a significant incarnation of Idéologue moral philosophy.

Morality now would be a scientific subject. In his second edition of the catechism, Volney referred to ethics as a "physical and geometric science."[11] Destutt de Tracy's essay of 1798 called ethics a "science that we construct, like all others, from results of experience and reflection."[12] Although claiming that ethics was based on observation to illustrate its "scientific" character, Volney used language making it almost a deductive discipline. Of course, none of the Idéologue moralists conducted psychological survey research on the origin of the passions, and only the physician Cabanis referred to case histories. Yet, to the Idéologues the pleasure-pain principle was empirically based common sense, and from this psychological observation a host of important deductions followed. The supposed discomfort of the clergy with the pleasure motivation proved to the Idéologues their lack of realism about human character.

Strictly speaking, Volney's manual was deist because God was the acknowledged source of natural law. Given the more naturalistic texts he had written two years earlier, some interpreters of Volney see these references as concessions to the deism of Robespierre's Committee of Public Safety. To be sure, Cabanis did not praise Volney for his deism but rather for his refusal to acknowledge Christian original sin and eternal punishment.[13] The anticlerical Volney denigrated monkish virtues, mortification of the flesh, and absolute chastity. Natural law did not demand such practices.

Volney took advantage of the fundamental ambiguity of the term natural law to slide from a "constant and regular order of facts" to the same natural law as a "guide to perfection and happiness."[14] The facts considered universal for all times and places were the overriding need for self-preservation, with pleasure and pain as indicators of the beneficial and harmful. The moral standard furnished by nature was the fulfilment of natural needs essential to life and health. Volney assumed that there could be no controversy that these goals were preferable to illness and death. Moreover, nature did not prohibit, by making it a sin, the moderate use of pleasures.

In Spinozist psychology there was also the principle that the exercise of reason itself was a pleasure.[15] Similarly, Volney saw human life as more than survival. Nature provided human beings with faculties of reason and imagination, and Volney assumed that the full employment of these faculties was necessary for a richer life and better health. The natural criterion for beneficial actions therefore included the "development of human faculties." Every person would have an interest in education, in sharpening the mind, in strengthening the body, and in gaining the courage to use natural capacities.[16] An ideal society would promote the exercise of reason. The goal of morality was not just stabilizing society into docile submission, but the development of uniquely human capacities.

Like Delisle de Sales, Volney thought natural law assists the enlightenment of self-interest. Overindulgence of the appetites of the senses would "tend to destroy life and health." For the individual, therefore, natural law was virtually self-enforcing. There were also similar checks on abuses of natural law in families. Natural attraction between the sexes established families and fostered domestic virtues. But Volney thought that physical, psychic, and economic well-being could only be maintained in the monogamous family. Libertines who did not moderate their search for pleasures destroyed their physical health, tormented themselves with remorse, and squandered their finances.[17]

Like Helvétius and d'Holbach, Volney also assumed a natural need for sociability and for obtaining the favourable dispositions of others. True happiness required sympathy for others. Even if this view made others instruments of our own happiness, Volney saw no danger of the deliberate deprivation of others' needs, given his postulate that everyone had similar basic needs. Thus, Volney could not have comprehended the existence in a regenerated society of Sadean characters, who wilfully enjoyed the suffering of others.

Like all Revolutionary moralists, Volney had to admit that the facile equivalence of happiness and virtue could not be observed under existing conditions. Given the obvious corruption induced by "ignorance and passions," the power of habit through education was a primary solution. Everyone needed to learn "habits of action useful to the individual and to society." These habits would lead not only to self-preservation and education, but also to the secular golden rule of "Live for your fellow beings, so that they may live for you," thus anticipating Auguste Comte's "Live for others!"[18] Paradoxically, for all his denigration of Christian virtues of self-abnegation, the core moral precept was still Biblical.

Volney thus unwittingly posed an unresolved dilemma between rights and social utility that was characteristic of the Idéologue position. The individual needs of an independent, sensitive being demanded liberty, equality of opportunity, and rights to property.[19] Yet individual desires might conflict with social harmony. Utilitarian virtue, inculcated as an acceptable habit, might threaten individual rights or independence, just as Rousseauist virtue would soon threaten enemies of the Republic with the Terror. Our discussion of political science will show that the Idéologues refused to choose consistently between rights and utility. They oscillated towards utility in the era of the Directory when they were intellectuals close to power, and towards rights in the Napoleonic era, when they formed a disorganized political opposition. This oscillation reflected competing values of social stability and individual freedom.

As a theorist of geography, Volney was also aware that climate, topography, and culture affected human behaviour. Yet he had no hesitation in proclaiming his natural laws universal. Not surprisingly, they strike us today as the context-bound, almost stereotypical ideal of the nineteenth-century European middle class, with their disdain for aristocratic luxury and libertinage, modesty, sobriety, work, marital fidelity, and a rather harsher view of poverty than Jacobins such as Robespierre had.[20] Servants were to obey masters and women their husbands, and the poor were to work hard to better themselves rather than overindulge their dangerous passions.[21]

SECULAR MORALITY OR GOD'S LAW

Cabanis, Destutt de Tracy, and Roederer, before his Bonapartist conversion of 1800, welcomed Volney's ethic precisely because it remained free of Christian metaphysics. In an era of post-Revolutionary enlightenment, they saw an opportunity to apply the principles of Helvétius and d'Holbach. Cabanis feared the loss of a "solid base" for morality if it were derived from invisible powers that were doubted by the educated. Ethics therefore should be based on "needs and faculties" and on the "necessary relationships of men in society," prior to the variations dictated by age, sex, temperament, climate, and regimen.[22] Similarly, Destutt de Tracy refused to postulate a soul as the cause of our desires and warned against the "antique prejudice" of eternal punishment.[23]

The only potentially strong ally of the Idéologues in the ethics section was the aging *érudit* and committed atheist Jacques-André Naigeon, formerly of the Diderot–d'Holbach circle. In 1789 Naigeon had opposed reference to a Supreme Being in the Declaration of Rights of Man, and he later spoke against the provision made by the Constituent Assembly for a state-salaried constitutional clergy. Like Cabanis, he thought moral rules, based on the "nature of man, physiological needs, and well-known relationships," would be a greater brake on passions than a religion granting absolution or expiation of sins. The purpose of moral behaviour was to "obtain the esteem and benevolence of men ... to live happily on earth ... to feel good about oneself." In utilitarian calculation, being good and just was therefore the best policy.[24]

The memoirs of his colleague Henri Grégoire offered a possible explanation for Naigeon's failure to contribute to the Class of Moral and Political Sciences despite frequent attendance. At an early Institute general assembly, Naigeon called for a resolution to direct "chemists and geometers to show that God does not exist." Pierre-Samuel Du Pont defended Naigeon's freedom of speech, but responded: "I agree to tolerate the atheism of Naigeon, on condition that he tolerate my theism, because I believe in God." After the motion was rejected, Naigeon lapsed into sullen silence.[25]

At the other extreme from secular morality was the staunch Catholic democrat and crusader for human rights, the constitutional priest Grégoire, who was steadfastly loyal to the Church through all the Revolutionary vicissitudes. He was himself enthralled with the liberating potential of the human sciences. But he believed morality would collapse "where the discretion of egotism teaches the respective interests of all individuals and society." For Grégoire, "without religion there is no guarantee of faithfulness of wives, obedience of children, and honesty of servants." Moral principles must be attached to a divine being; otherwise atheists would treat "men as only machines whom one can break without scruple."[26] Hence, one needed Christianity both to stabilize society and to safeguard individual dignity.

The paradox was that a commitment to human brotherhood and educational perfectibility could be shared by Christians and Idéologues. As an architect of Jewish emancipation and a zealous advocate of black and mulatto rights for forty years, Grégoire stressed the responsibility of persecution and of the social environment for the apparent degradation of the disadvantaged groups.[27] While maintaining European superiority over Africans, Grégoire repudiated any concept of inherent, irreversible racial hierarchy.

In 1799 Grégoire read an early draft of a work on the "intellectual and moral qualities of the blacks and mulattos." The finished 1808 publication predicted a brilliant future for blacks if only Europeans would spread their civilization instead of tormenting and murdering blacks. Grégoire defended the monogenetic theory of racial origins, propounded by Buffon, Cuvier, Lacepède, and Gall. He argued that slavery had stifled the talents of blacks and robbed them of their self-respect. He enumerated all the instances he could find of their "industry, courage, and generosity." Blacks were not a species apart, but, as the geographers would say of native Americans and Pacific islanders, educable and susceptible of civilization. Grégoire thought the polygenetic theory of human races was fashioned either to protect colonial interests or to attack the story of biblical creation.[28]

Yet Grégoire's concept of human brotherhood was based on Christianity, not moral science. A memoir on the Spanish bishop Bartolomé de Las Casas, an ardent defender of indigenous Americans, illustrated this view. Grégoire claimed that Las Casas was not responsible for the idea of substituting African slave labour for that of native Americans. In fact, modern historians agree that the African slave importation into Spanish America long preceded Las Casas's letters, but they think that the chronicler Herrera found in Las Casas's papers a genuine proposal (which he later regretted having made) to introduce an African work force. Grégoire's main contention was that the Church itself, judged by its most enlightened representatives, was not guilty of oppressing either Africans or native Americans.[29] Hence, stereotypes in the Enlightenment on Catholic intolerance needed re-evaluation, and human brotherhood did not have to be based on the equality of sensing outlined in the psychology of Condillac.

Apart from the lone atheist and the single vocal Catholic, the deist Class members who were politically akin to the Idéologues feared that without a Supreme Being, the threat of eternal punishment of an immaterial soul, or a cult, morality would be pallid and ineffectual. Ritual was necessary for social solidarity. Although he was a scornful anticlerical, the Director La Revellière-Lépeaux argued that the people "need a religious cult ... not the pedantry of a subtle metaphysics." Any philosophical "cold calculus" would "chill us against the good we must do." Consequently, as Director he most likely gave financial aid to the deist circle of Theophilanthropists, who were authorized to use eighteen nationalized churches in Paris from 1797 to 1801.[30] He was acutely conscious of the need to "displace the sense of the sacred" from Church ritual. Condillac's psychology had stressed the impact of sense-knowledge and spectacle. Rousseau's prescriptions for Poland included rituals of fraternity to promote public virtue. La Revellière-Lépeaux hoped for civic ceremonies at family occasions of birth, marriage, and death. He also hoped that national festivals, legislated by the Convention, would "kindle the imagination and elevate the soul to the most sublime ideas" of "love of liberty, conservation of the laws," and "readiness to sacrifice for the glory of the Republic."[31] Here was a dramatic example of conflict between values of individual self-preservation and community survival. Managing moral passions meant inspiring patriotic consciousness and even willing individual sacrifice for the Republic.

The pre-Revolutionary *moralistes* were more deliberately hostile to the Idéologue project. In the atmosphere of Napoleon's 1802 Concordat with the Church, de Sales condemned the "very dangerous void of Ideology." Nor could he approve the "derisive and sacrilegious parody" of Theophilanthropy. For social order, he now advocated a kind of providential theism or purified Christianity. Its typical representatives were quite a diverse group – the Anglican Locke, the not very orthodox Lutheran Leibniz, the quietist Catholic bishop Fénelon, and the Jansenist Catholic Pascal.[32] If all were more committed to churches than they were deists, de Sales never specified an institutional religious framework. He also never gave up the idea that happiness and virtue were easily compatible.

SELF-INTEREST AND SYMPATHY:
RECONCILING HAPPINESS AND VIRTUE

The Idéologue leaders Cabanis and Destutt de Tracy repudiated Delisle de Sales's theism but shared with him and Volney the principle that virtue would easily triumph. Their two moral alternatives were utilitarian prudential self-interest moderated by the common good and the morality of feeling or natural sympathy. No matter which motive prevailed, the outcome would be morally desirable. Education and legislation would enlighten natural self-interest and cultivate natural sympathy.

Cabanis was more optimistic that Destutt de Tracy about social harmony. He refined suggestions made by the physician and analysis of sensations and ideas section associate Paul-Victor de Sèze and used them to postulate an organic sympathy at the summit of a hierarchy of universal forces of affinity, from gravitational attraction to nervous sensitivity.[33] Culturally conditioned moral sympathy thus had an instinctive and subconscious basis, as, for example, did sexual attraction, the maternal instinct, and reactions to animal heat and to the modulated human voice. Cabanis was aware that sympathy might produce unwelcome results, as in movements of crowds and emotional oratory in a great legislative assembly. But on the whole he thought that the force of natural sympathy could generate acts of compassion for the poor and the sick. We could thus find "the principles of perfectibility of the human race in its very organization."[34] Yet Cabanis also knew that self-interest is the inevitable result of physical sensitivity. Private interest, he asserted, "never sleeps" and was therefore the most effective means for educators and legislators to "direct and perfect human nature."[35]

Natural sympathy and self-interest balanced each other. The mature moral philosophy of Destutt de Tracy as set out in his *Traité de la volonté* (1815) explicitly postulated two equally powerful forces of self-interest and sympathy. Here Tracy derived his physiological ideas less from Cabanis than from François-Xavier Bichat, who divided the body into organs of the internal "life of conservation" and of the external, animal "life of relation." Satisfying our internally and externally generated desires was indeed necessary for self-preservation. But the "sentiment of sympathy ... immediate source of benevolent passions ... softens the hard and repelling aspects of individuality." With Tracy, as with Helvétius, Naigeon, and Volney, only benevolent actions make us truly happy. In society, therefore, we judge the virtue of actions by their benevolent tendency to "promote the good of humanity."[36]

In reflecting on the 1798 Institute public morality prize contest, Tracy was far less sanguine than Cabanis about reconciling the "distinct and opposed interests" of individuals. During this élitist and technocratic phase of his development, Tracy would promote public morality chiefly by stern laws and efficient police action in order to make crimes contrary to the self-interest of the individuals concerned. Good laws scrupulously observed would elevate public morality. For example, civil equality and equality of inheritance among heirs would diminish crimes against property, while the legality of divorce would enhance family harmony.[37]

The entire Idéologue enterprise was intended to enlighten the judgment of citizens so that they could regulate their desires and make better moral choices. Given their aforementioned scepticism about public festivals by 1799, Cabanis and Tracy both seemed to assume that instruction alone would bring more sophisticated judgment, and that therefore a sharper mind would most likely bring a more reflective and therefore more sociable character.[38]

By contrast, the deist Bernardin de Saint-Pierre was unconvinced that either punitive laws or natural inclinations of self-love or sympathy could bring social peace. His highly successful novel, *Paul et Virginie* (1788), suggested that the important private virtue of modesty clashed with self-preservation itself. In the novel, discord shattered the utopian idyll on the island of Mauritius. The heroine refused the efforts of a sailor to save her from a sinking ship because she was too modest to disrobe and consign herself to the arms of a stranger. For Saint-Pierre, true virtue was a struggle, even against the imperative of survival.[39]

Saint-Pierre, in a memoir expressing discontent with the public morality contest of 1798, advocated a morality that is "celestial ... established by God."[40] Unlike the Idéologues he saw secular natural law as insufficient for morality, and unlike Delisle de Sales and the utilitarians he would never found an ethic on self-love. "A passion, even if reconciled to the general interest," could produce ambition, greed, and sensuality. After the events of the Terror, he thought the fallacy of the greatest happiness principle of Helvétius was evident. "Love of the social order," as advocated by utilitarians, could be a pretext for repression. Even Adam Smith's natural "sympathy" avoided the question of duties to oneself. There was, for Saint-Pierre, an "immutable Golden Rule in the heart of each" person but it depended on the rational conscience, not on feeling. Or, in the words of a character in *Paul et Virginie*, virtue is an "effort made upon ourselves for the good of others with an intention of pleasing God alone."[41] Morality in nature could only be tied to divine commandment. While

Saint-Pierre does not appear to have read Kant, he was here anticipating a proto-Kantian imperative that was tied to duty, not to inclination.

The Revolution had also affected Mercier's confidence in the utopian teaching of virtue. His previously discussed defence of Kant was explicitly intended to attack the "gross precept of self-love" and to preach "free submission to the categorical imperative." This variation of Volney's "live for others" stressed not the control of natural law but the self-discipline of the rational mind. The rational good would not rest on individual caprice. Self-interest as a principle would undermine all sense of moral obligation and weaken the bonds of society. Like Bernardin de Saint-Pierre, Mercier rooted ethics in a "celestial instinct … the Divine soul."[42] While still anticlerical, Mercier was now sympathetic to the deist cult of Theophilanthropy and unwilling to be guided by philosophers in an academy.[43]

Any morality resting on divine command could not share a foundation in merely natural law. Delisle de Sales was the only consistent theist to believe in the reconciliation of happiness and virtue. Though the practical consequences of Volney's "living for others" and of the Kantian categorical imperative might be a secularized golden rule, the theoretical justifications were quite different. For the Catholic Grégoire and for the Rousseauist deists Saint-Pierre and Mercier, a natural morality meant an unethical yielding to natural inclination at the expense of conscience. Hence, their strategy for a moralized population could not rest on an automatic or enforced equivalence of happiness and virtue. To be meaningful, practising virtue had to be an internal struggle against the self, not just obedience to external laws. Moral obligation, not happiness, was the essence of the moral act.

THE MORAL ART

The public morality prize contestants, on the contrary, responded enthusiastically to Roederer's call for moralizing civic institutions.[44] Their premise was not internal conscience but the duty of the Republic to promote a moral art of desirable habits. In his Utopian essay *Olbie* (1800) Jean-Baptiste Say, a future liberal economist, thought, like fifteen other contestants, that public festivals would promote family ties and fraternity. One author called for a re-creation of the Olympic Games (to be called the Franciade) to encourage physical fitness as well as patriotism.[45]

A less fraternal yet openly avowed purpose of public festivals was social control, as it had been with the Roman circus. Instilling public virtue in festivals would also stifle revolutionary impulses. One author hoped that diversions would "make inequality cease to be odious" and avert idleness at cabarets on rest days.[46]

Yet nearly half the contestants, including Say, resurrected Mercier's old idea of a morals inspection – an elected or appointed board of censors to honour the virtuous and openly embarrass the insolent or recalcitrant. They were clearly impressed with ancient Roman or Chinese precedents, or perhaps with Rousseau's reflections. Censors, they thought, could at least deny access to public festivals to the wayward. If necessary, there could be public lists of demerits and possible curtailment of access to public office. J.-B. Say recommended tax reductions for virtuous families.[47] The urban élite as represented by the prize contestants perceived rampant moral corruption remediable by prying into their neighbours' visibly undesirable behaviour. Even Say, a confirmed partisan of economic freedom, advocated such intrusiveness. In a curious way, their views anticipated the strange modern American combination of free-market enthusiasts who would nevertheless sternly regulate perceived transgressions of traditional Christian moral law.

The promotion of benevolence was also a leading theme in the prize contest of 1802–4 on the "barbarous treatment of animals." Most contestants defined cruelty as the imposition of gratuitous suffering in sports such as cock-fighting and dog fighting, or in village carnivals which permitted passers-by to stone the necks of geese. In several vital aspects, the topic had deep affinities with the most fundamental goals of the Class.

Pelosse's study has analysed the contestants' belief that they were a sensitive élite obligated to moralize the gross masses of cruel coachmen and butchers, as well as children who gleefully tormented cats.[48] Cultivation of the "sensitive" temperament was after all a primary goal of Cabanis's "science of man." Robert Darnton's *The Great Cat Massacre* (1984) explores the genuine difference in sensitivity between a vaporous bourgeois mistress who mourned her house-cat and ribald printers' apprentices who took exquisite pleasure in seizing a pretext to kill the pet along with a host of bothersome alley cats.[49] Indeed, Darnton suggests that the difference stemmed partly from the understandable desire of the apprentices to protest their conditions, which were far less pampered than those of the cat. The Institute contestants' most frequent concern was not with ending economic exploitation but rather with cultivating the natural sensitivity which would extend compassion to all animate creatures. The "habit of vulgarity and outrages," thought one author, would stifle all feelings of compassion, even for children or the aged. The "moral contagion" of cruelty to animals might legitimize any gratuitous violence or condone the most dangerous of all impulses towards Revolutionary disorder.[50] And so, the prize contests disclosed a social or cultural orientation of the urban élite to wish to punish corruption and moral deviance and to curtail tendencies that upset social stability.

VIRTUE, THE SOCIAL ORDER, AND THE ART OF CONTESTS

After Adam Smith there was always a privileged relationship between morality and political economy. Nowhere was this more evident than in the advocacy of the work ethic as the great moralizing mechanism. To Smith, political economy was just one branch of a wider "science of the legislator." J.-B. Say reversed the emphasis when he wrote, "The first book of ethics would be a good treatise of political economy." A code of work, frugality, self-help, and saving would assure both prosperity and virtue, while luxury, lotteries, and cabarets erode both industry and morality.[51] Other Idéologues were also enthusiastic proponents of the work ethic. Cabanis recommended work to prevent melancholic ennui and to correct "errors of imagination."[52] Roederer in 1793 found work the "true principle of domestic and social virtues," for it gave the rich "industry and frugality, the poor, dignity and satisfactions."[53] A sober lifestyle would tame the unruly passions associated with the subversive, Revolutionary impulse. Virtue in this sense meant work within the existing social order.

To the individualists Say and Roederer, however, work also meant an opportunity for social mobility. Delisle de Sales, the royalist advocate of Stoic serenity, provides a striking contrast. In his mature, post-Terror *De la philosophie du bonheur* (1796) de Sales praises self-control and the restraint of passions. The happiness of the sage, apparent to someone recently imprisoned, is serene contentment with one's lot.[54] The direct political and social consequence was an attack on equal rights. He maintained that the "classes composing the political hierarchy have a different right to happiness proportional to wealth, power, enlightenment, and the artificial prestige of opinion which is its instrument."[55] His fellow royalist historian Toulongeon also subscribed to a natural "hierarchy of talents, enlightenment, faculties, and wealth" in the belief that the rich or enlightened will "always form a habitually preponderant order."[56]

The previously discussed castigation by Ginguené and Roederer of Petitain's public morality prize memoir demonstrated their critique of a society that was rigidly divided between "intelligent" and "working" classes.[57] But perhaps the best illustration of the congruence between morality and liberal economics appeared in another ethics prize contest in 1800–1 on "emulation as a good means of education."[58] The concept of emulation rested on the theory of enlightened self-interest transmuted into virtue by the clever educational technique of the teacher. Diderot's *Encyclopédie* defined emulation as a "noble and generous sentiment which fills us with admiration for the great actions of others and strongly excites us to try to imitate and even surpass them if we can." Such individual achievement suited well a dynamic, competitive society.[59]

Since religious teaching orders almost universally employed emulation, the utility of contests as a contest subject had to be paradoxical. Perhaps the irrepressible Bernardin de Saint-Pierre helped select it, since, like Rousseau, he energetically condemned emulation as useless, immoral, and a "source of the most outrageous passions ... jealousy, hatred, intolerance, and cruelty."[60]

Daunou's prize commission report clearly supported the prizewinner's argument that emulation was educationally effective. The leitmotif of the drive of the Class of Moral and Political Sciences towards social harmony was the conversion of self-interest into a need for the esteem of others.[61] Finally, emulation suited an individualistic society of equal rights and unequal outcomes as idealized by the Class majority. The Napoleonic era certainly enshrined the triumph of "emulation" in the baccalaureate examination, the *grandes écoles* entrance *concours,* and the Legion of Honour.[62]

Opponents of emulation disapproved of an appeal to sinful self-interest and vilified the disruptive social ambitions of those who practised it. One teacher lamented that "every brat thinks he's called to be Cicero, Virgil, or Voltaire."[63] A worried rural proprietor found emulation a part of the "fatal philosophy" that created a "mutinous people" and an egotism capable of the iniquity of the Terror.[64] From a more radical viewpoint, one contestant thought emulation incompatible with civil equality.[65]

The prizewinning contestant, librarian L.-F. Feuillet, spoke of harnessing necessary passions to virtue, as a ship navigator had to learn to use the winds. Passions could "assure the happiness of men by making them contribute to the happiness of all members of society."[66] According to Feuillet a telling argument in favour of emulation was the model of the classroom as a microcosm of society. He explicitly referred to Adam Smith's demonstration of the benefits of competition for prosperity and the utility of competition as an antidote to idleness and prodigality. In the school, as in society, each contestant had an equal opportunity. But the outcomes would be unequal because of the necessary conditions of social and economic inequality.[67] Montesquieu had long before advocated adapting education to the "general spirit" of society. Feuillet also endorsed the suitability of emulation in a society which permitted the social mobility envisaged by Roederer, Destutt de Tracy, and Say. Feuillet thought that in a "free, rich, industrious society" no class of people would be perpetually assured of wealth or condemned to poverty. A wise legislator might even go so far as to "set limits to private fortunes to preserve the well-being of all, preventing and prohibiting all tendencies to accumulate and fix wealth in an overly small number of hands."[68] Thus, in the socio-economic realm as in educational practice, emulation was a fitting application of the moral art.

CONCLUSION

The secular moral science of prudential self-interest of the enlightenment and its transformation into virtue by education and legislation assumed critical importance when the Church was discredited as a fount of morality. In Enlightenment debates on morality, Rousseauists such as Mercier and Delisle de Sales already believed in the easy reconciliation between happiness and virtue, since God implanted goodness in the human heart. Volney's catechism of 1793 reiterated a largely secular, prudential, utilitarian view that happiness under natural law was impossible without living for others. Given the power of religious ritual, however, even anticlerical deists feared the consequences of detaching ethics from the compulsive force of divine command or from the socially useful and necessary threat of eternal punishment. The Director La Revellière-Lépeaux sought patriotism and social stability through the solidarity of a civic deist cult. Like Volney, he raised but did not resolve the potential conflict between individual self-preservation or individual fulfilment of reason and imagination with public utility or community norms.

Despite the traumas of revolution, the Idéologues Cabanis and Destutt de Tracy ended up blending physiologically based doctrines of natural sympathy with the self-interest of physical sensitivity in the confident assumption that virtue would triumph. Both the Idéologues and such hostile authors as Delisle de Sales assumed that the pursuit of health, self-preservation, and social harmony were easily within human reach. Since no one observed such infallible social cooperation, they all wished, like the Enlightenment utilitarians, to cultivate sympathy or harmonize individual interests by appropriate education and legislation. For Tracy, civil equality, equal inheritance, the possibility of divorce, frugal government, and free trade were almost enough to guarantee public morality. For the Christian Grégoire, the regenerate utopian Mercier, and the deist Bernardin de Saint-Pierre the horrors of the Revolution only accentuated the failure of natural morality. Virtuous behaviour demanded divine inspiration and an effort of rational conscience against the natural inclination to seek pleasure or self-preservation. In French moral philosophy outside the Church, the wave of the future was clearly this insistence on an innate conscience, which, in Kant's view, led to the postulation of God's existence. Victor Cousin derived from Kant the importance of duties in morality, although they were duties of a psychologically determined free being who could understand moral distinctions.[69]

While the Idéologue leaders Cabanis and Destutt de Tracy became sceptical of public festivals, Roederer and many prize contestants, including Say, hoped that moralizing civic institutions would promote public virtue and even censure the behaviour of individuals. All Revolutionary governments staged festivals and cults but none actually carried out a censorship plan. If realized, such a scheme might have highlighted the conflict between censorship and principles of individual rights. The urgent goal of social stability was always in a delicate balance with individual fulfilment, as was the development of critical faculties with submission to social norms. Under Bonaparte and in the Restoration the politically powerless Idéologues tended to return to a defence of individual rights for fear that the utilitarian common good would be defined by authoritarian or reactionary governments. But even economic liberals were not averse to inculcating public virtue so long as it promoted competitive success and did not arouse turbulent individual passions that threatened the market-place.

Bonaparte viewed religion as the most desirable form of social control. The Idéologues' political demise prevented them from realizing their vision of experts discerning the principles of universal natural morality. No one in this entire debate (though Bernardin de Saint-Pierre was closest) seems to have heeded the admonition of David Hume who argued the principle that natural facts cannot logically lead to moral judgments.[70] The objective of a secular moral science had won relatively little acclaim from the Class ethics section. The Concordat of 1802 meant that moral instruction in Bonaparte's *lycées* and later in the Université impériale would not contradict Catholic doctrine. During the Restoration, Cousin's efforts to teach a non-religious morality in 1819–20 would be partly responsible for the suppression of his university philosophy course. Later Auguste Comte claimed expertise in the moral science of reading the altruistic trend throughout history, just as the Idéologues had claimed to decode the underlying forces of human nature.[71] The notion of an objective moral science embedded in nature would remain in the evolutionary or social Darwinist ethics of the late nineteenth century. The real fruition of the project of a secular morality would come with the curriculum of the French public school system in 1882. Educators such as Ferdinand Buisson and Paul

Janet prepared a neo-Kantian ethics curriculum completely detached from the views of any religious denomination, albeit acknowledging God's existence. Émile Durkheim, the founder of modern sociology, argued in 1902 that a rational, or scientific, moral education was possible and used the term "science of morality" in his uncompleted final work.[72] However, few contemporary moral philosophers, not even those who claim that "ought" can be derived from "is," have the pretensions to objective expertise inherent in the idea of a natural science of morality.[73] The Idéologue project illustrates both the philosophical difficulties of assuming that the natural is fit for moral prescription and also the sinister potential of assuming that there is a universal morality for all times and places.

One consequence of Volney's natural morality was his devaluation of history as the field of error. He even whimsically suggested that a good novel might do more for morality than history because vice and prejudice too often triumphed in real life. He also worried about the accuracy of detail necessary for useful political deductions. But even Volney thought that biographical examples of virtuous lives would be useful for school children and that history offered the potential for arriving at the principles of government and political economy.[74] Indeed, Institute historians reiterated that the past would provide sound examples for moral and political practice. Where else was there an inexhaustible series of moral dilemmas ripe for meditation, or, if need be, exhortation? Hence, any aspiring moral science had to contemplate the full range of past human experience.

8 Philosophical History and Political Discord

PHILOSOPHICAL HISTORY

Along with the Idéologues, the aging, established scholars in the history section of the Class of Moral and Political Sciences were eager to explore the past as an inexhaustible source of moral and political lessons. The two groups disagreed markedly, though, on what history might teach the present. In the aftermath of Revolutionary turmoil, both hoped to calm political passions, but they had contradictory visions of a more stable future. Conservative historians lamented the sufferings of the Church and the disrespect for the monarchy. The Idéologues hoped to solidify a Republic without privilege or an established Church and to find guidance in directing cultural change. Even the more pro-Revolutionary historians used past disorders as a caution against excessive democracy or the illusion of social equality. They also employed a model of social development by stages to justify necessary social hierarchy and European superiority.

To draw meaningful lessons, however, all historians had first to assess the authenticity and accuracy of documents. All of them at least nominally valued the meticulous, critical assessment of evidence to attain the highest probability of historical truth. The history section members absorbed these values from the tradition of scholarship since 1701 in the Ancien Régime Académie des Inscriptions. For the Idéologues, Volney's remarkable series of École normale lectures on history in 1795 invoked all the scholars' canons discussed since the sixteenth century to assess the credibility of witnesses and documents.[1]

To be "philosophical" and instructive to the nation, historians also had to reflect on the diversity of human experience. As with Voltaire's implicit condemnation of Bossuet, universal history had to include all the people, not just biblical narratives. The increased scope of history meant diverting attention from warfare and royal courts to domestic policies, culture, and social customs.[2]

During the Revolutionary era the Voltairean program for philosophical history assumed that accuracy and wider scope would be necessary conditions for utility. But this program had two additional demands – a strictly secular history and the pursuit of causal explanations befitting an emerging science. The Marquis de Condorcet, in his famous *Esquisse* (1795), clearly expected philosophical history to demonstrate the progress of the human mind, that is, the superiority of science over superstition, and to function as a moral and political science, that is, to illustrate human motives and the operation of social institutions.[3] Like Condorcet, Destutt de Tracy in his circular to history teachers at central schools in 1799 recommended studying how cultural and philosophical progress affected economic advancement.[4]

Volney also outlined a new "analytical or philosophical" method for history as a "physiological science of governments" with exacting standards for "quite positive and well-verified" historical facts. He wished to purge myths and legends and to eliminate stories contravening natural law, which could only serve the purposes of despotism.[5] For Volney, the study of history, an "immense collection of moral and social experiments," could enlighten individuals on ethical conduct and direct informed legislators to suitable government policy. History was an inquiry revealing the "genealogical order of causes and effects" of great events. Volney envisaged both a static kind of human geography, a distant forerunner of the *Annales* school of history, that would relate physical and political circumstances of a people, and a dynamic "biographical history of a people" that would yield the reasons for its growth and decline. Freed from scriptural moralistic fables and from idealization of often unworthy Greeks and Romans, history, properly studied, could help formulate "fixed and determined principles of legislation, political economy, and government."[6]

The problem for the emerging science was that historical facts never yielded pure ethical and political principles untouched by the preconceptions of the interpreters. If anything, as Destutt de Tracy and Condorcet warned, the past provided a dangerous display of fruitless metaphysics, superstition, and servility to despots.[7] Volney's moral principles rested on a supposedly unchangeable human nature, and Tracy urged the clarification of the principles of legislation before approaching the study of confusing historical complexity. Volney assumed a pre-existing consensus on the ideals of 1789, that is, on natural rights, equality before the law, representative government, and the separation of powers.[8]

Yet there could be no consensus among the relatively conservative and often religious historians on the principles of 1789, much less a staunch republican commitment. Disagreements on the Revolution itself and on the relative merits of religious devotion and scepticism made the emergence of an Enlightenment model of philosophical history impossible. Only Delisle de Sales and Lévesque among the fourteen history section members and associates were kindred spirits to Enlightenment philosophes. Others, such as Papon and Anquetil, would repudiate even the Enlightenment ideal of religious tolerance.

A SCHOOL OF MORALITY

The conventional utilitarian aim of Institute historians was to contribute to an improved individual morality and political *savoir faire*. Delisle de Sales, always the committed moralist, wrote his universal history to show "ethics in action" in the hope of "making men better." Solon and Pericles would inspire modern lawgivers, while after the Revolution the sufferings of persecuted men of letters, like La Fontaine and Bailly, would inspire compassion.[9] De Sales used every opportunity to "denounce war and political crimes," first in his discussion on early Roman emperors, and later on the iniquities of the Revolution.[10] Papon's history of Provence warned readers about the "vices and weaknesses in human nature," while Garnier believed his history of France was a "treatise of ethics and politics" which showed the duties of the public man and the "rights and obligations of the simple citizen." François-Emmanuel Toulongeon, an analysis of sensations and ideas section member, asserted in his history of the French Revolution that the historian must be a moralist teaching how to avoid the disastrous madness of party spirit.[11]

The Institute historians were aware, at least in principle, that an overly moralistic stance would be counter-productive. Anquetil claimed that he intended to show the dangers of fanaticism in the civil wars of the sixteenth century, but he would impose no judgments upon the reader. Similarly, Garnier warned that the real task of the historian was to authenticate facts before judging "the living and the dead in a court without appeal." Toulongeon promised to follow a middle path between fanatic extremes.[12] Yet in their practical concern to instruct, these historians found overt condemnations unavoidable.

This rush to judgment never prevented the Institute historians from recognizing a modicum of relativism in the mutability of human nature. Indeed, the most widespread modes of subsistence theory of the progressive development of society encouraged the belief in inherent differences at each stage of development.[13] In the Institute Lévesque propounded in 1796 a three-stage theory, which he had revised from a 1784 work, of hunting, pastoral, and civilized peoples. In the first stage, men had few needs, little communication, and unrefined manners. Pastoral society strengthened social bonds, created movable property, and initiated the arts, commerce, and written language. War and slavery led to further differentiation of social ranks. The key to civilization was agricultural society, with its promotion of industry, great wealth, greater social inequality, permanent settlement, landed property, and a love of the fatherland. Unlike Condorcet but like some of the Idéologues, Lévesque thought social inequality was an inescapable sign of progress. He even argued that natural law itself evolved, since in the most recent era it required more sacrifices of individual liberty for social tranquillity. This model of development could thus be another tool to justify a post-Revolutionary hierarchical and strongly ruled society as well as a Eurocentric condemnation of more primitive peoples.[14]

The three developmental stages implied that human nature in an earlier stage could not be judged by later standards. Yet Lévesque still sternly reproved earlier customs and ideas. In a fine expression of what now would be called a Whiggish view, Lévesque maintained that historians should choose "what instructs and pleases posterity," not what was significant to the actors.[15] He did not spare the customs he found reprehensible – the savage domestic life of Homer's Greeks, or the mythology of Hesiod which demanded the "credulity of our countrywomen." The preliterate Romans were a rough, crude, warlike people, while nothing exalted could be expected from the "barbarous constitutions" of the early Franks.[16] Similarly, Delisle de Sales condemned the "ferocity of a savage people" in Solon's legislation decreeing death for adulterous women, while merely fining male kidnappers of women.[17] The medievalist Legrand d'Aussy found the burial customs in ancient Gaul "absurd and execrable", the Salic code of the Franks, which gave no equality before the law, a product of "barbarous times," and the twelfth- and thirteenth-century poetry of the northern French trouvères examples of "bad taste and a sordid ethic."[18]

CAUSAL EXPLANATION AND SCHOLARLY SCEPTICISM

Such facile moralizing could not in itself establish history as a moral and political science. Most Institute historians at least aspired to providing more complex causal explanations of great events like the decline of Rome or the Crusades. Thus, Papon attributed the decline of Rome to political tyranny, the corruptions of commerce and luxury (a kind of inversion of the three stages), a delight in spectacles, and enervating hot baths. Misguided human passions, such as greed and superstition, were explanations Lévesque and Papon gave for the Crusades.[19] Few of these explanations sought the universal laws Volney had envisaged.

However, out of twelve prospective, but not selected, history prize contest topics, four were causal questions (the causes of cultural progress in Greece, the effects of the Crusades, the effect on manners of the discovery of America, and the effect of the Reformation on politics and culture). In addition, the final topic chosen for the only contest completely administered by the Class of Moral and Political Sciences, in 1799–1800, asked: "By what causes has the spirit of liberty developed in France, from François I to the convocation of the Estates-General in 1789?"[20] The prizewinner, Nicolas Ponce, in many ways fulfilled Condorcet's program for relating cultural and political progress. He highlighted the intellectual stimulus to liberty provided by Renaissance letters, Reformation criticism of authority, Enlightenment philosophy, and classical republican ideals in French education. He also cited the long-term enervating struggle of the monarchy with the nobility and the Revolutionary precedents of the French civil wars and of the Dutch, English, and American revolutions. Though he was hardly innovative in his causal explanation, Ponce mollified the conservatives by warning against the political "chimera of equality" and the popular "exaggeration" of sound philosophical ideas of equality of rights.[21]

Toulongeon took most seriously the mandate of philosophical history. His essay on writing history claimed that "only causes and their results make past events interesting ... [K]nowledge of causes can teach us to avoid unhappy results and bring about prosperous results." If indeed historians were more concerned with teaching lessons, the "science of political economy would be much more advanced." He was one of the few conservatives to speak of the inevitability of revolutions because of a "ripeness of things" in the moral order, just as there were inevitable physical revolutions of the globe. On the other hand, Toulongeon noted that in revolutions "monstrous effects are often unforeseen results of indirect causes."[22]

The quest for accuracy was more scrupulously honoured than the search for laws stemming from causal explanation. Yet sometimes the ideals of scholarship conflicted with artistic ideals of eloquence. The associate Class member Gabriel-Henri Gaillard justified his fictional harangues because he based them on "substance from authentic mem-oirs," which he duly cited in his notes. Delisle de Sales purged such speeches from his memoirs in principle, but could not resist reprinting Thucydides's oration of Pericles. On the other hand, Toulongeon point-edly remarked that if ancient historians had possessed original docu-ments they would not have had to improvise speeches.[23] Except for Anquetil, who sought a larger popular audience, most Institute histo-rians scrupulously cited sources, balanced authorities, criticized inscriptions, and inserted primary documents.[24]

In 1803–4 Lévesque refought the sceptics' battles of the old Académie des Inscriptions in the 1720s. He rejected most traditional claims about the early centuries of Rome, including the Trojan foun-dation of Rome, the commonly accepted date of 753 BC, the laws of Numa, and the accounts of Livy and Plutarch of the early sack of Rome by the Gauls. Yet with no greater foundation, the same Lévesque placed the voyage of the Argonauts three centuries before the Trojan War.[25]

Delisle de Sales paid lip-service to reliable records, but treated Greek gods as if they were one-time heroes and named Moses, Hermes, and Zoroaster as historians.[26] His own elaborate speculation on the prim-itive Atlanteans could claim no severe critical standard. For de Sales, these people, the first to be civilized, were natives of the Caucasus, who appeared after a primitive flood in the Atlas mountains, hence their name Atlanteans. Plato's lost continent of Atlantis was only a Sardinian colony, as the Atlanteans gradually populated the emergent Eurasian land mass.[27] In the project of a scientific, reliable history, then, there was certainly genuine evaluation of ancient evidence but also a persistent temptation among the more popular authors to indulge in fascinating speculation and to insert a few imagined speeches to enliven their narratives.

THE SCOPE OF HISTORY

If accuracy was a common goal, so was widening the scope of histor-ical subjects to draw lessons for more varied aspects of human life. Even before the democratic impetus of the Revolution, conservative historians agreed that history should not be a litany of sieges and battles. In the 1780s Garnier and Papon urged the study of law, finance, commerce, arts, manners, and customs through the use of notarial records.[28] Papon also accepted Volney's assumption that a full study of the climate, topography, and natural history of a region was a prerequisite to understanding its human history. His history of Provence began with an encyclopedic geographic survey, and it ranged from the culture of medieval chivalry to a sixteenth-century excommunication of insects and a vivid, Thucydidean account of the plague at Marseille in 1720.[29]

At least four historians planned a cultural history, which would have been consistent with Condorcet's ideal. Delisle de Sales announced to the Institute an elaborate outline for a history of literature from Marcus Aurelius to the French Republic. At his premature death Legrand d'Aussy left manuscripts for a comprehensive history of French language and literature, the arts, and the sciences. Lévesque had already written in 1779 a short history of the progress of the human mind. Even Anquetil studied the unpublished prize memoirs of the Académie des Inscriptions in the period from 1735 to 1744 on science and letters in France from the age of Charlemagne to Charles VI.[30]

In the 1770s, under the tutelage of the renowned medievalist Lacurne de Sainte-Palaye, Legrand d'Aussy began studying the short verse and prose stories of the twelfth- and thirteenth-century trouvères, the northern counterparts to the troubadours. His perspective is reminiscent of that Vico or of Herder – in the poetry of an age we find its "spirit, sensitivity, imagination." Despite their gross language and their "vulgarity, ignorance, and superstition," the trouvères gave "astonishingly true portraits of the human heart," the morals of a different age.[31]

In 1782 Legrand also projected an extensive history of the private life of the French. He thought an effort to portray the "bourgeois in his city, the peasant in his hut, and the gentleman in his château" would be worthwhile.[32] The only section ever published was three volumes on food that detailed the use, storage, processing, and distribution of vegetable and animal foods as well as of beverages. Legrand excelled in the piquant detail. We learn from him that the Church permitted chicken for Lent until the ninth century and that the one-time Lenten prohibition of eggs played a role in the significance of the Easter egg. He gave recipes for English punch, commented on the unfashionability of cafés except for the idle, the young, and foreigners, and related the introduction of ice-cream by the Florentine Procope in the 1660s. Changes in social habits included the delay of dinner to mid-afternoon and of supper to late evening because of the elaborate *toilette* of eighteenth-century upper-class women.[33]

During the Directory, Legrand d'Aussy turned to the sombre subject of burial customs. Despite his anticlericalism, he focused on monuments as a reaction against the "vandalism" of Revolutionary crowds and the suspension of Church funerals, which often removed all ritual. He creatively classified ways of treating the dead, the materials of coffins, and tomb decoration.[34] In addition, he fully supported the goals of Alexandre Lenoir, the director of the Musée des Monuments français, to display a comprehensive collection of tomb architecture and sculpture to show the development of the arts and of social customs.[35]

In this long memoir, Legrand said little about *attitudes* toward death, unlike the recent study by Philippe Ariès, but studied the external practices: (1) menhirs or dolmens; (2) the later burial mounds near cremated remains in ancient Gaul; (3) genuine burial mounds; (4) Roman funeral pyres; (5) pagan masonry tombs; and (6) Christian sarcophagi of stone, terracotta, and lead. By the twelfth century eminent families had mausoleums of marble, bronze, or stone. Despite scarce evidence, Legrand thought he had sufficient archaeological samplings to risk making this theory of tomb periodization. He noted in the last period the gradual change from 1550 to 1650 in tomb statuary from reclining to kneeling effigies.[36]

This early anticipation of some of Ariès's schemes extended to a remarkable degree the historian's subject-matter. From nutrition to disease and death, cultural constructions with biological roots were already the province of the Institute historians. The pleas of Legrand and Lévesque for archaeological work in ancient sites and of Anquetil for folklore collections show a clear departure from complete dependence on the written text.[37]

SECULAR OR RELIGIOUS TEMPERAMENT?

Despite impressive forays into cultural, geographic, and social history, deep religious and political disagreements handicapped the secularizing scientific program of Condorcet, Volney, and Destutt de Tracy. Among anticlericals, the conservative but Lutheran public law professor C.-G. Koch condemned a depraved clergy for abetting the spread of venereal disease and for tolerating houses of prostitution in Strasbourg from 1495 to the triumph of the Reformation.[38] The associate member of the Second Class Edme Gautier de Sibert in 1765 had portrayed the wars of religion as the "defence of God by unenlightened zeal" and charged Christianity with responsibility for more ferocious wars than even paganism or biblical Judaism had fought.[39] Legrand d'Aussy, a former Jesuit but now an anticlerical, found the code of the Visigoths filled with the "superstitious ethic and intolerance of the clergy," especially in its provisions against Jews and heretics. Throughout his memoir on national burials, he stressed that studying tombs was valuable despite the "imprint of the religious prejudices of our fathers." Even in his pre-Revolutionary account of medieval short stories he took special delight in monastic narratives that were a "grotesque alliance of religion and gallantry."[40]

Enlightenment secularism had already undermined traditional accounts of Joan of Arc. Gautier de Sibert did not credit inspiration of the Holy Spirit, but believed Joan either an instrument of royalists or a clever manipulator who used her "voices" to sway followers. Lévesque's history of the Valois also offered a rationalized version of her life, in which Charles's adviser, Baudricourt, orchestrated Joan's identification with the King and her command of the armies.[41]

In a more summary, less documented account in 1805, the very religious Anquetil confessed he could not imagine Joan's "marvellous exploits" as natural phenomena. His *Précis d'histoire universelle* claimed to be secular, but it managed to introduce sacred history by discussing "opinions" on the Creation. The Fall of Adam, the Deluge, and the communication of the Jews with the Supreme Being were all significant in the narrative.[42] Delisle de Sales, although an anticlerical, had defused criticism before the Revolution by proclaiming his consistency with the books of Moses. Thus, universal history could not fulfil a Voltairean, anticlerical purpose despite the extensive discussion of non-biblical Oriental peoples.[43]

Committed Catholics like Papon also condemned religious fanaticism, such as the "drunken zeal of the Crusaders," who were motivated by superstition, debauchery, and debt evasion.[44] Yet Papon displayed an entirely different tone in asserting that the odious abuses of the Inquisition were "less harmful than civil wars." Anquetil in 1805 republished his apology of 1767 for the revocation of the Edict of Nantes on the grounds that two religions could not easily subsist in a kingdom such as seventeenth-century France. He even retained occasional references to Protestantism as the "pretended reformed religion."[45]

Anquetil and Papon, in contrast to Delisle de Sales, never shared the Enlightenment critical spirit towards religion. They refused to accept the Enlightenment program of religious toleration. Anquetil blamed only "false zeal" and human passions, not Christianity, for the horrible massacres of the civil wars, and noted that ancient Greece, which was neither Christian nor royalist, had its share of the evils of war. As for the philosophes, in 1805 he wrote that the "least flaw of the *Encyclopédie* was to have created a multitude of demi-savants." Papon was equally vocal in condemning the "frightful scepticism" that helped produce the Revolution. Earlier, in 1778, he had denied any "right to censure the faith of our fathers."[46] One could hardly imagine a viewpoint more distant from that of the Idéologues or of the deism of the Class majority.

THE SCHOOL OF POLITICS

The deep political divisions among the historians in the Second Class on the Revolution amplified their striking disparities in religious temperament. Together, these differences ended any possible consensus on a philosophical history. Hardly any Institute historian had a favourable view of the Revolution as a whole. Lévesque and Delisle de Sales wished to dissociate sound Enlightenment philosophy from Revolutionary violence. Anquetil and Papon wavered between acceptance of constitutional monarchy and nostalgia for absolutism.

Before the Revolution, authors such as Gautier de Sibert had glorified the establishment of the Estates-General and the extension of the political nation to municipal deputies in the Third Estate. Gautier de Sibert thought both Gauls and Franks had been part of a Third Estate, even at the early gatherings of the Champ de Mars.[47] But Lévesque, as early as 1788, had rejected history as a guide to the fate of the monarchy. A careful study of the early dynasties of France had convinced him that Mably's depiction of an ancient role of the Third Estate was untenable. For Lévesque, the early capitularies describing assemblies of the "people" on the Champ de Mars or the Champ de Mai referred only to the high nobility and the clergy. Without a true public opinion there could only be a pro forma ratification of the royal will by the most eminent Franks. Gudin's history of the Estates-General had independently reached a similar conclusion. There were no rights for the common people in the era of the Frankish war councils and no estates of society until the separation of the medieval clergy. Moreover, the Estates-General had never produced a national will. In line with the stages theory of development of civilized government, Lévesque did not seek good institutions in barbarous times. The rights of the nation would not be found, he concluded in 1788, "in the formless archives of barbarous centuries, but in the nature of man and society."[48] The rejection of historical precedent was in fact double-edged. A precedent over a long period, as invoked by Boulainvilliers, could not justify aristocratic rule. But also, the primitive equality among the Franks could not be the reason, as used by Mably, for reforming the Estates.

After the Terror, when ending the Revolution was the main goal, Lévesque also steadfastly refused to find political models in ancient Greek or Roman democracy or egalitarianism. Early in 1800 he argued that the vaunted economic equality among Spartian citizens masked the aristocratic domination of society. In the "warrior convent" of Sparta there was not true equality or true freedom, or even the "mild virtue making the charm and glory of humanity."[49] From 1799 to 1801 Lévesque was equally harsh on the Athenian constitution. Solon's apparent democracy was really a popular tyranny. The "indolent, passionate multitude" had too much power in popular assemblies, where "indigent citizens working at jobs that did not permit any education had preponderance over others." Later, he warned against the excessive number of Athenian judges drawn from the poor and from the "suspicious and fearful people." While he worried here more about popular cruelty than indulgence, the Class selected this memoir for public reading at the time of the debate about jury membership.[50]

Lévesque generalized his suspicion of popular deliberative assemblies to warn in 1802 that "moral sympathy" promoted enthusiasm and fury at their meetings. He praised the Consulate constitution that separated discussion in the Tribunate from approval of laws in the Legislative Body and that permitted only a few citizens to be eligible for public functions. He approved the election of officials by a "small number or even one alone." While Lévesque was perhaps the most pro-Revolutionary historian, his memoir of 1803 on the early French dynasties concluded with a ringing anti-Revolutionary statement: a "rising against any government means living for a time in anarchy ... the greatest of evils that can afflict humanity."[51]

This denigration of democracy was not a new post-Revolutionary conviction for Lévesque. Already in 1784 he had declared "absolute equality a chimera ... invented by the poor and weak" that would guarantee only inertia. Government should assure only equality before the law and the security of property. Merit, in his view, was most often found in the "middle class."[52] Both Lévesque's political views and his anticlericalism made him closest in the history section to the Idéologues. He even once dared say that atheism was a natural phenomenon of the human mind. Unlike some of his fellow historians, he also vigorously defended, when he was secretary, the industriousness of the Class of Moral and Political Sciences.[53]

THE REVOLUTION AS HISTORY

The other active members of the history section were even more alienated from the Revolution. More than ever they demonstrate why Georges Gusdorf's view of the Idéologues as the "axis of the moderate revolution" cannot simply be extended to the entire Class of Moral and Political Sciences. The most balanced view appears in Toulongeon's massive seven-volume work, which he supplemented by many original documents.[54] He attributed the "inevitable" Revolution to the "dogmatic philosophy" of Rousseau, Voltaire, and Montesquieu, the weak and inept leadership of Louis XVI, the frivolous Court, and the bankruptcy crisis. In a very modern insight, he appreciated the importance of symbolic, emotive language. The cry for "liberty," which appeared first in the Réveillon riot of April 1789, was a "vague idea ... which turned over the chariot of revolution."[55]

Otherwise, Toulongeon presented a constitutional monarchist view. Himself a titled noble deputy to the Estates-General, he had wished to preserve the orders in 1789. He hinted that the English bribed the French Guards who deserted during the attack on the Bastille, and that the English possibly provoked the grain shortage in July 1789.[56] He missed no opportunity to commiserate with Louis XVI. The King accepted the constitution of 1791 in good faith and was never crafty. His ride to Varennes in 1791 was never intended as a flight out of the country. The notorious *armoire de fer* of the Tuileries, with its documents apparently incriminating the King and Queen, contained only the "archives of a contested and tottering royal authority" trying to defend itself.[57] Like other royalists, Toulongeon regarded the Directory coup of Fructidor in September 1797 as a catastrophe since only General Pichegru was guilty of plotting against the government. In short, Toulongeon espoused royalist principles that were similar to those of his Institute colleagues Delisle de Sales, Du Pont, Ramond de Carbonnières, and Pastoret.[58]

Toulongeon astutely perceived the danger of the Declaration of Rights, which promoted equality of rights but could not change the "unequal distribution of physical and intellectual faculties." Some citizens were thus deceived into questioning the "inevitable inequality of properties which is the first basis of the social order which guarantees them."[59]

To Delisle de Sales natural rights did not exist, and in society there were differential rights to happiness. He ran afoul of the First Consul in 1800 with a pamphlet proposing a referendum on the return of the Bourbons. Following on his noisy defence of the Fructidor exiles in the Institute and his campaign to restore the Académie française, in his continuation in 1802 of Millot's history he found the Revolution immoral and antisocial.[60] Bonaparte's censors disapproved of the nostalgia for royalism and the mockery of a possible invasion of England. The First Consul himself was at the origin of orders to seize de Sales's edition of Millot's history in a letter to Cambacérès enquiring whether the government "could not exclude a man who writes against the state from the Institute."[61] In fact, the incorrigible troublemaker de Sales attracted more attention than Anquetil, who published his counter-Revolutionary history of France in 1805 with official tolerance. Possibly the controversy over the coup of Fructidor, which Bonaparte had supported, was an additional source of frustration for the First Consul.

Anquetil's history was still old-fashioned enough to highlight the monarchy as a component of French national identity. "Vive le roi!" was the "cry of joy" of all Frenchmen, it said.[62] Already in his history of the Ligue (1783), Anquetil had depicted the "populace as always the same; crude, ferocious, easily seduced, quickly aroused, showing no control once yielding to its passions" and exercising a "tyranny

more redoubtable than the *Grands*."[63] In both his universal history
and his history of France 14 July 1789 was a "day of anarchy," and
the sans-culottes were the "dregs of the populace who found honour
in rags of poverty and in this word of scorn ... and who hated all
beyond their knowledge and habits." Despite Anquetil's modest mercantile bourgeois background, he had no democratic inclinations. Nor
would he accept even the basic principles of 1789. The events of
4 August showed the "dangers of deliberative assemblies," and the
Declaration of the Rights of Man was the "seed of sacrilegious measures contrary to the degree of subordination necessary to government."[64] While Pastoret did not write a history of the Revolution, his
attack on ancient Egyptian despotism included the comment that the
lack of a hereditary dynasty raises "perfidious hopes in the heart of
people," so that factions can "use the support of the people also to
become tyrants."[65]

Sophisticated interpretation and refined causal explanation were not
characteristic of the discussions of the Revolution by the historians.
With the exception of Toulongeon, explanations rested often on individual shortcomings and external plots. We find in Delisle de Sales,
Anquetil, and Papon conspiracy theories of the Revolution of the kind
popularized by the Abbé Barruel. Another of de Sales's pamphlets,
published in 1800, expressed confidence that the new government
would unravel the manœuvres of the "intractable Jacobins," some of
whom were heirs of the communist Babouvist advocates of an "agrar-
ian law," while others were followers of the "mystics of Freemasonry
and the Illuminati."[66] Papon cited Monjoye's *Histoire de la Révolution*
and a *Vie de Cagliostro* to blame the antireligious, republican and
democratic Illuminati faction for provoking the Revolution. Both
Papon and Anquetil also saw an Orléanist conspiracy at work in July
1789, with the tricolour formed from Orléanist red and white.[67]

Papon's history of the Revolution was so extreme that it appeared
only posthumously in 1815 under the auspices of his younger brother.
In it Papon boasted that in 1788 he had already seen the first Assembly
of Notables as a "source of insubordination." The antisocial materialism of some philosophes had helped promote the worst excesses. The
equality of rights proclaimed in 1789 was only a pretext to attack the
King, the nobles, and the great proprietors.[68] The Revolutionary
assemblies had provoked the equivalent of a slave rebellion, heedless
of the fact that by necessity slaves have no rights. Papon advocated
royalty and religion as the bases of all government. Even the 1791
constitution was republican in principle, and the refractory clergy were
fully justified in refusing to give allegiance to it. Jacobin intolerance

and persecution were worse than any religious fanaticism, and the Committee of Public Safety had been the worst tyranny since the early Roman emperors. Besides the plot theory, Papon resorted to an explanation of the unbridled passions and egotism of the Revolutionary personality, determined to usurp positions of power and opposed to Christian humility.[69]

For the counter-Revolutionary historians, and even for the moderates horrified by the Terror, the Revolution became the most vivid source of *exempla* displaying the moral and political utility of history. Papon considered his history a tribunal for posterity. He could thus assess for the reader the "danger of opinions and manœuvres by which factions mislead the mind and corrupt the heart, and arouse the passions of the multitude against the institutions on which public tranquility rests."[70] For the more clerically inclined, religion was indeed the basis of social order. Men needed a brake on their more furious passions, and the secular morality of the Idéologues was pitifully ineffectual.

INSTITUTIONAL CHANGE AND SCHOLARLY CONTINUITY

The History section was obviously more conservative than the majority of the members of the Second Class, who reaffirmed the principles of 1789 and shared Enlightenment values, including its criticism of religious orthodoxy. Aside from Gudin's reformist work of 1789 and 1791, Lévesque's support of the National Assembly, and Dacier's participation in the moderate Paris Commune of 1790, there were hardly any expressions of sympathy among the historians for Revolutionary objectives. If intense political disputes, such as the discussion on Fructidor exiles, were not frequent, the reason was that traditions of academic life prohibited indecorous discord.[71]

After Bonaparte began planning a reorganization of the Institute, historians were especially eager to enhance their own intellectual prestige in a restored academy of historical studies. Papon, an Institute associate, did not live long enough to benefit from the reorganization of 1803, but he doubtless would have welcomed it. His history of the Revolution attacked the Institute for its membership of "little merit" and composed of "elements sympathetic to the spirit of the Revolution."[72] A second associate, Garnier, in effect voted with his pen against the Institute of 1795. Once an assiduous member of the Académie des Inscriptions, he ignored the Class of Moral and Political Sciences until after the reorganization of 1803, when he was reintegrated as a full member of the Class of History and Ancient Literature. He would submit two memoirs on ancient literature before his death.[73]

Two other historians may have played a more direct role in the Institute reorganization of 1803. Bon-Joseph Dacier, the prominent perpetual secretary of the Académie des Inscriptions, submitted no memoirs at all to the Class of Moral and Political Sciences; yet he accepted the honorific election as president of the Class for a six-month term in March 1802. In that capacity he may have met with the Interior minister on future developments. His biographer, Silvestre de Sacy, claims that he "advised the government on the reorganization of the Institute and had great influence on its determinations." He definitely was one of the Class representatives on the commission to redistribute members after the Institute reform decree. Regardless, within a few days of the reform the new Class of History and Ancient Literature elected Dacier as perpetual secretary in a conscious gesture of resurrecting former procedures and personalities.[74]

Finally, Delisle de Sales obviously had no influence at all with the government. Yet the Chaptal report of 1803 reflected ideas from de Sales's 1800 memoir on academies, though perhaps these were also advocated by others. In 1814 de Sales commented that the Institute reorganization was the "fulfilment of the wishes of the greater part of men of letters."[75]

In the new Class of History and Ancient Literature the moral and political sciences could be discussed "only in their relationship to history." The *élan* disappeared from the Idéologue venture to make history a moral and political science because more traditional scholars were now the majority. In fact, Daunou, Toulongeon, and the economist Germain Garnier, all originally outside the history section, more than ever focused their memoirs on history.[76]

Yet it would be a mistake to see a great rupture for historians in 1803 except in the fortunes of Idéologue philosophy. While Daunou preserved the impetus of Volney in his Collège de France lectures on history as late as the period from 1819 to 1830, the scholars of the Class of History and Ancient Literature continued during the Empire to present the same kinds of memoirs and practise the same techniques as had been the case in the Class of Moral and Political Sciences. In 1805 Anquetil prided himself at having the temperament of a provincial small-town scholar, so that the "charms of literature brightened for me days whose serenity was only weakly disturbed by the Revolutionary torment."[77] Despite the risks to their personal lives, scholarship for many Institute historians, especially in ancient and medieval history, remained unruffled, even while they pointed the finger of accusation at Revolutionary demagogues.

CONCLUSION

The historians in the Institute and the Idéologues all agreed on the moral and political utility of history, at least through *exempla*, if not usually full-fledged generalizations. In fact, faced with the new generation of Romantic historians who sought empathy with every epoch, Daunou in his Collège de France lectures in 1829 defended the concept of history as a moral and political science. The Romantic historians, he charged, believed that "history must teach nothing ... How indeed could it be foreign or useless to all philosophical study?"[78] Daunou was transmitting the eighteenth-century goal of learning from history, beyond mere contemplative appreciation.

It would be a mistake, though, to think that the utilitarian function of history, with its implied natural law model, prevented any genuine historical consciousness.[79] Even the stages view of social development promoted the notion of a unique spirit in each historical era. That historical consciousness was not the same, though, as nineteenth-century empathy. The Institute historians insisted upon judging barbarous eras by later standards. Legrand d'Aussy considered medieval poetry and tombstones eminently worth preserving and studying, but he had no particular reverence for them.

For a truly philosophical history, both accuracy and a widened scope were preconditions. Even before the Revolutionary era, the more traditional scholars had developed the concept of history as a critical, sceptical craft, although some authors curiously combined credulity in ancient myths and speculation about ancient peoples with a nominal scepticism. All agreed on the necessity of consulting primary documents and manuscripts critically. They anticipated the great age of nineteenth-century archival research. At the same time, religious commitments limited scepticism in cases of biblical accounts and allegedly supernatural inspiration. The vastly increased scope of such innovative scholars as Legrand d'Aussy looked forward to the work of Augustin Thierry in his early nineteenth-century search into the "depths of social history." This sensitivity to private life was the distant origin of a late twentieth-century historical interest. The movement away from the description of battles and royal courts also resulted in more attention to cultural history.

The Institute historians showed by their prize questions that they expected and valued causal explanations. However, they did not consciously attempt to realize the program of Condorcet, Volney, and Destutt de Tracy for a scientific history. Particularly when dealing with the Revolution, except for Toulongeon they let human passions and plots play a much greater role than did nineteenth-century writers, including François Guizot and Adolphe Thiers.

In the post-Revolutionary context, writers like Lévesque employed the stages model to suggest the necessity of social inequality and the obsolescence of democracy in a highly developed modern society. Conjectural history in the mode of Montesquieu could of course have a conservative slant, if it meant accepting whatever existed as justified by the "general spirit" or by a stage of social development. Burke and de Maistre, in fact, would counsel slowly developing traditions instead of destructive change.[80]

Nineteenth-century liberal historians, such as Guizot, François Mignet, and Adolphe Thiers, would recapture history for the purpose of justifying past Revolutionary change. They would find many precedents for the French Revolution in the struggle of conquered and conquerors and of feudal against antifeudal social classes. Thus, the "political use of history" in the Restoration era justified the rise of the bourgeoisie from the medieval era when liberties extended to municipalities. The new liberals departed from the disavowal in 1789 of a historical precedent for natural law. They would justify historically the political and economic consequences of the Revolutionary era – representative government and the ascendancy of a new commercial and professional élite.[81]

The sharp polarization of opinion on religion and Revolutionary politics made quite impractical the assumption of Volney and Destutt de Tracy that a consensus on moral and political principles would precede the study of history, which could then refine the application of accepted principles. Committed Revolutionaries in 1789 and beyond who wished to break with the past could hardly view history in the same light as those who valued the accumulated wisdom of the ages. As in the disputes over the nature of language and of the mind, and in the quarrel over a secular morality, both sides agreed that the post-Revolutionary world was in dire need of stabilization. The Idéologues sought scientifically verified regularities in the past as beacons to legislators committed to preserving the principles of 1789 in a calmer, post-Revolutionary society. The conservative historians wished for a return to Catholic doctrine, which Bonaparte provided in 1802, and a return to a form of monarchy, which came in 1804 when the Empire furnished a temporarily satisfying surrogate for those nostalgic for the Bourbons.

Volney in his history lectures had hoped for a dynamic understanding of the growth and decline of peoples. But an equally important component was in probing the simultaneous correlations among physical geography, national character, and government. On a larger scale, this program applied the hygienists' plan to relate the physical and mental in individual temperament. One could hope to find the collective temperament of a people (Montesquieu's general spirit) by examining its situation within a physical environment and a cultural environment of religion and government. The blueprint of the stages of development would help classify the peoples of the earth in their diverse habitats. What the annals of history revealed in time required a complementary analysis by explorers and geographers who roamed over vast, scarcely charted expanses of the earth.

9 Human Geography: Correlating Climate, Culture, and Civilization

The establishment of a geography section in the Class of Moral and Political Sciences confirmed the fundamental place of the physical environment in the human sciences. Scholars agreed that the influences of climate, situation, terrain, and soil on peoples were comparable on a large scale to the effects of the Hippocratic "airs, waters, places," and regimen on the individual.[1] If observers could separate physical, social, and cultural variables affecting intelligence and character, they might be able to suggest physical habits or changes in manner of life to counteract socially undesirable inclinations. Environmental constraints that are inevitable would also demand adaptation.

The few cartographers and explorers who were in the eighteenth-century Académie des Sciences had already helped issue instructions to French naval expeditions for observing the human species as well as for collecting natural history specimens.[2] The map makers, diplomats, officials in the Navy, and the Colonies ministry officials who filled the Second Class geography section were only mildly interested in *human* geography.[3] However, Volney's pre-Revolutionary observations in Egypt, his sojourn in the United States, and his interest in "statistical" questions for travellers had set a precedent for a new human science of geography that would estimate the relative weight of physical, political, and cultural environments. The new statistical approach of English and German scholars encouraged some members in the Second Class to correlate physical features and economic resources of a region or country. In addition, the seasoned Navy officers and explorers Bougainville and Fleurieu focused attention on the encounter of Europeans with remote, often "savage" peoples. The promotion by the Institute of the Baudin expedition to Australia heightened this ethnographic interest. In practice, this early anthropology promoted a sense of superiority, as European observers distributed peoples along a chain of historical development. The notion of a European civilizing mission served to heighten confidence in the need to diffuse European scientific methods and commercial products throughout the world.[4] The beginnings of a more open attitude toward the other, a sense of understanding of the diversity of world cultures, may also be glimpsed in certain passages of memoirs to the Class of Moral and Political Sciences by Degérando or, after the demise of the Class, in the works of the most illustrious human geographer in France, Alexander Humboldt.

THE NOBLE SAVAGE AND MODELS OF PROGRESS

Unlike other subjects, human geography produced no political polarization over issues of religion or form of government. If anything, royalists and conservatives, such as Bougainville, Fleurieu, and Degérando, demonstrated the greatest empathy with non-Europeans, while committed Revolutionaries, such as Volney and Mentelle, a staunch republican and the author of textbooks, wished to deflate the Rousseauist myth of the noble savage and to attack religion. Nor was there any great conflict between intellectuals and those in power. Almost all authors supported the Directory and Consulate governments by enthusiastically justifying the French civilizing mission. Geographers rarely, however, expressed Talleyrand's vision that this mission also promoted internal stability.

In another sense the goal of stabilizing society affected judgments that were made of exotic peoples, for the Institute authors used the four-stage model to pay tribute to settled agricultural and commercial societies and to criticize hunting societies. The competing Enlightenment approach to "savage" people was the glorification, as in Rousseau's two *Discourses*, of wise, uncorrupted, and happy "natural" human beings who were without property or social hierarchy.[5] The Revolutionary break with the past accentuated the Rousseauist criticism of privileged, over-refined aristocratic European societies. The idealization of people closer to nature meshed well with invocations of natural law and innate natural goodness. By 1800 a new generation of emerging Romantic writers, including François-René Chateaubriand, also praised the natural virtue of the American native, which was enhanced by Christianity.

The fear of Revolutionary disorder had also made attractive the four-stages model in which "savages" were "ignoble." Since the late 1750s such Scottish writers as Henry Home (Lord Kames), Adam Ferguson, Adam Smith, and William Robertson, and such French authors as Turgot, Helvétius, and Quesnay had presented European society, with its necessary social inequality, as the summit of civilization and progress.[6] Private property was thus superior to anarchic communal ownership. Moreover, bringing the advantages of civilization to less developed peoples opened the door to trade, which could open the door in turn to colonialism. A "discovered" people could be brought out of its hunting society childhood by commercial contact. The doctrine of the rights of man could be relativized to mean allowing each people to realize its potential.

RACE AND PHYSICAL AND CULTURAL ENVIRONMENT

Aside from the dilemma of the noble and ignoble savage, the other great debate in human geography was over the kind and degree of variation that was environmentally induced. The most rigid possible view was that inherent racial differences determined the intellectual and moral capacity of a people. In 1795 the French comparative anatomists Georges Cuvier and Étienne Geoffroy Saint-Hilaire attempted to base a racial hierarchy on anatomist Peter Camper's "facial angle" on the grounds that a protruding jaw distorts the shape of the head to leave less cranial capacity for the brain.[7] Earlier racial theories certainly influenced Bougainville, while more subtle versions of racial superiority, whether or not they included a belief in a single human species, would command overwhelming adherence later in the nineteenth century.

Most of the disputes within the Class of Moral and Political Sciences, however, were not about *whether* but *how* the environment influenced people. Helvétius had offered the extreme views that "education is capable of everything" and that neither climate nor individual temperament influences intelligence.[8] Thus, governments could re-form the character of a people. In the relatively optimistic Revolutionary era, there were more adherents of the concept of the educable, civilizable "savage" who was not trapped by race or climate.

The hygienists, Montesquieu, and Volney all allowed a considerable role for climate. In fact, to settle the question of physical versus cultural impact Condorcet dreamed of a gigantic research project that would include the study of the effect of temperature, climate, soil, occupations, and form of government on physical, intellectual, and moral characteristics.[9] Neo-Hippocratic temperament theorists, such as the hygienist Jean-Noël Hallé and Cabanis, generally believed in correlations between, for example, a hot climate on the one hand and a pleasure-loving, passionate temperament on the other, and between dry winds and docility, as well as in inverse relationships such as that between muscular vigour and nervous sensitivity.[10] Like "possibilist" geographers a hundred years later, the neo-Hippocratic authors were not rigid climatic determinists, but recognized a definite, limited impact on individuals of their physical surroundings.[11]

The same medical tradition had stimulated Montesquieu to develop his renowned theory relating climate, habits, and government. Montesquieu's widely echoed view was that "nature and climate rule almost alone over the savages," while civilization enhanced the importance of religion, law, customs, and social institutions. Although Montesquieu did not enumerate four chronological stages, he recognized that the complexity of codes varied with the level of subsistence – hunting peoples have the simplest codes, commercial societies the most complex.[12]

Despite unfairly criticizing Montesquieu for slighting political and cultural influences, Volney carefully assessed climate. In his learned treatise on physical and political conditions in the Turkish provinces of Egypt and Syria, published in 1787, Volney found that the Nile Valley and the fertile soil in Egypt bred indolence, while the Syrian and Egyptian deserts and the mountain region of Lebanon each in its own way fostered free-spirited temperaments. On the whole, however, Volney maintained that "social government and religion" (in this area the allegedly stifling influences were Islam and Turkish despotism), not soil and topography, were "the governors of the activity and inertia of individuals and nations." While Volney did not adhere to the four-stages model, he already in this work criticized Syrian society for its failure to guarantee property. Without true ownership and inheritance law, agriculture could not flourish.[13]

In a questionnaire, which he enlarged for the External Relations Commission in 1795, Volney proposed a thorough survey of both the physical and the cultural factors in a given region. After investigating the effects of the "physical state" – climate, soil, and natural resources – on the habits, customs, and character of a nation, and its government and kind of laws, then the physical appearance and health of the population, occupations, agricultural practices, industrial arts and methods, commerce, type of government and legal system, family authority, and education would be examined. In his École normale lectures the same year, Volney recommended a thorough study of changes in habits, diet, and lifestyle of migrant peoples in different regions, to assist the science of government.[14]

Volney himself, in the analysis of sensations and ideas section, was better prepared than any Institute geographer to fulfil his own program, yet he read no geography memoirs in the Class. After returning to France from the United States in 1798 he planned to publish a physical and political geography of that country. However, tense Franco-American diplomatic relations in 1803 inhibited him from publishing the political section. He included in his work only some provocative reflections on the American government and Canadian colonists and observations on native American Indians. The free, "mild" republican government of the United States promoted salutary individual proprietorship, as much as the Ottoman Empire induced indolence. Otherwise, Volney wished to expose American exceptionalism by stressing the corruptibility of this supposedly regenerated people. Like Helvétius, Volney thought governments could "change the character of nations." His reflections on French-speaking colonists in British North America, living in the same climate as the Anglo-Americans, confirmed the importance of "habits and national character ... domestic education and government." Accustomed to hunt and fish, largely illiterate, unwilling to prepare for the future, too sociable and talkative for industrious work, the settlers from what had been New France on the Mississippi and Erie frontiers could not make farms flourish.[15]

This work also contained his famous observations on American natives which Moravia has shown to be partly appropriated from William Robertson's *History of America* (1777). Volney condemned Cornelis de Pauw's racial interpretation, dating from 1768–69, of the native American as inferior, apathetic, and uneducable. But in a classic anti-Rousseauist statement on the ignoble savage, Volney depicted "cultivation of the earth and, by its immediate consequence, landed property" as the "essential basis of the social state." The realities of a hunting society that was without property or developed law, not an inauspicious climate, degraded the native American. The so-called natural man was warlike, ferocious, and prey to exalted passions. In an interview with the tribal chief Little Tortoise, Volney quoted him (perhaps more wishfully than accurately) as recognizing the doomed fate of a hunting people and as hoping to become a cultivator. Volney also targeted the mythological nature of Chateaubriand's depiction of virtuous natives in the "Natchez" series of novels, such as *Atala* (1801).[16] Volney held no brief for the allegedly "natural" man, when only a settled society could protect liberty and property. Climate and soil affected manner of life, but the customs of hunters precluded civilized behaviour. In Syria, in the French-speaking frontier outposts, and among American natives, only agriculture and property could realize human potential.

STATISTICS: THE CORRELATION OF
PHYSICAL AND POLITICAL FEATURES

As well as the explorers, the emerging statistical geographers followed Volney's lead in correlating physical and political features of regions or nations.[17] Indeed, the governments of the Directory and Consulate were engaged in a colossal effort to collect information about their own country as well as about their neighbours. Institute associate Coquebert de Montbret had little time after his election in 1802–3 to work for the Class of Moral and Political Sciences. Previously, however, he had shown some affinity to "what German professors call statistics," a descriptive, qualitative regional survey rather than the British quantitative isolation of variables, or "political arithmetic." Eventually he headed Napoleon's Bureau de Statistique (1806–12).[18] His outline for physical and economic geography lectures at the Lycée in 1798 to 1800 asked questions similar to Volney's for each region or province. In the 1790s he helped direct the first mineralogical survey of France, which classified regions within departments topographically, and included as well summary notes on ethnic composition, history, agriculture, and industry.[19] The purpose was less theoretical than practical – describing already exploited mines and future prospects for mineral extraction in a particular soil and terrain.[20]

A former École normale lecturer, Edme Mentelle, also called early in 1796 for a "statistical geography" archive in the Institute to consist of information collected from French ambassadors (no response is recorded). He thought the geography section particularly suited to tabulate the state of the population in each country (age distribution and sex, longevity, and the classes to which citizens belonged), estimates of military and naval forces, finances, commercial activity, and agricultural yields.[21] This highly saleable strategic information would evaluate the natural and human resources of a nation, whether friend or enemy. He thus reduced Volney's comprehensive vision to a narrower economic and military plan. In another memoir, Mentelle gave a schematic list of how much each of the three partitioning powers of Poland – Russia, Prussia, and Austria – gained in territory, population, and value of products.[22] Mentelle hoped to be useful to ministers, though he rarely reflected theoretically about human beings in their environment.

In rereading before the Class his École normale lectures on Russia, Mentelle compiled surveys of that nation's population, mortality rates, political divisions, military and economic strength, revenues, trade balances, and principal cities.[23] However, his rapid survey of the peoples of Russia revealed less about their customs and beliefs than about his own Voltairean anticlericalism. In his account, the nomadic Samoyeds of western Siberia practised polygamy, measured their wealth in cattle, lived in filthy, stinking tents, and were victims of "deceitful and ridiculous magicians." The Mongol Kalmuks of regions near Tibet were "so brutish that they undertook nothing without consulting their priests, or lamas."[24] Moravia remarked some years ago that a condition for the development of the human sciences was "openness to the other," that is, some degree of empathy for other cultures.[25] Mentelle's lecture on Russia reads like a gallery of current clichés about backward primitives. There is no trace of "openness to the other."

CLIMATE AND CULTURE:
NORTH AMERICA, TAHITI, AND
AUSTRALIA

The heavy baggage of two hundred years of discussion of "savage" peoples weighed down even the more subtle ethnographic descriptions in the works of two sophisticated officers, Bougainville and Charles-Pierre Claret de Fleurieu. The intrepid Bougainville at first vacillated between the "monstrous savage" image of such early explorers as Jacques Cartier and the *bon sauvage* of "robust natural virtue" propounded by the Jesuits long before Rousseau. The Institute memoir Bougainville wrote during the Revolution would arrive at the more nuanced view of an educable people.

Bougainville's private journal when he was an army officer in New France in 1756 shows that his first contact with non-Europeans generated uncomplimentary stereotypes. While he admired the "instinct superior to all reason" that the Iroquois displayed in interpreting wilderness tracks and ambushing the enemy, Bougainville lamented their self-love, pride, improvidence, and superstition. Most of all, he found repulsive the "cruelties and insolence of these barbarians which is horrible; their souls are as black as pitch. [Theirs] is an abominable way to make war." He patronizingly described how he sang in Iroquois cadence a war-song called "Trample the English underfoot."[26]

The captain of a voyage to the South Pacific from 1766 to 1769, he juxtaposed in his narrative, published in 1771, both ignoble and noble images. More simplistically than the hygienists or Montesquieu, he theorized that a harsh climate produces hideous, suspicious people, such as the Pécherais (Yahgan Indians) of Tierra del Fuego, but a mild, bountiful climate produces beautiful, friendly people, such as the Tahitians. Arrayed successively in the pages of Bougainville are miserable, virtuous, and villainous "savages."

After observing the Pécherais, Bougainville assured his readers that "one cannot prefer man in this state of nature to civilized man," who demonstrates quite distinctive virtues. The Fuegians became a byword for the lowest rung on the human chain of being.[27] Since Bougainville had to drive off Solomon Islanders and other Melanesians with gunfire, they too fulfilled the stereotype of ignoble villains. Before the more common environmentalism of the Revolutionary era, he casually offered a racial explanation – that the darker the colour of their skin, the more ferocious men are. This theory of inherent racial differences would assume far greater importance as cranial typology and facial angle measurement triumphed in nineteenth-century anthropology.[28]

In the same volume Bougainville included a rapturous depiction of the Tahitian landscape and a captivating description of Tahitian women. Whatever his intentions, the naming of Tahiti as "New Cythera" alone induced Rousseauist idealization. Amid the lush fruit trees of an interior valley, he wrote that "I believed myself transported to the garden of Eden."[29] All his first impressions seemed to indicate that this statuesque, intelligent, hospitable people was peaceable. As Joseph-Marie Degérando later remarked, explorers' assessments of peoples vary with their reception. While Samuel Wallis fought his way ashore in Tahiti and James Cook had to punish natives for serious thefts, in Tahiti Bougainville enjoyed an enchanting welcome. His readers could not help but pause at the scene of the Tahitian woman who clambered aboard his ship to reveal herself "like Venus to the Phrygian shepherd." These pages gave a licence to Denis Diderot, whether or not he always idealized the natural man, to portray a society emancipated from repressive European religion, sexual restraints, monogamy, and property. Unlike the four-stages theorists, Diderot saw there the absence of property as fostering natural happiness. The South Pacific could become the new utopia, with Europeans the unforgivable agents of corruption.[30]

The literary furore about the South Pacific, which was abetted by Philippe de Commerson, Bougainville's Rousseauist botanist, distracted attention from Bougainville's own sober second thoughts. The New Cythera portrayal certainly contributed to tendencies in later observers to slide precipitously in their descriptions from noble to ignoble savage. Yet, after his twelve-day idyll on Tahiti, Bougainville seriously questioned his native informant Aoutourou (Ahu-Toru), who had embarked with him for France. He discovered that Tahitians were "superstitious," that is, that they worshipped divinities and practised human sacrifice, and that they were brutal, executing prisoners in warfare. Their semi-feudal regime enshrined social inequality, with polygamy and a carnivorous diet reserved chiefly for the rich. This existence of a hierarchical society appealed to later stages theorists, who now found the Tahitians more civilized. Bougainville never presented Tahitians as paragons of ideal social behaviour.[31] His own personal reaction to the signs of liberated sexuality was simply less scandalized than were the accounts of Wallis or Cook. Then, too, Cook argued that the women greeting the ships were atypical and were like port city prostitutes in England.[32]

Bougainville presented a hierarchy of peoples that was based partly on race and partly on an undeveloped climatic theory of temperament. His first reaction to native Canadians and Americans was to see them as ignoble. A reliable Tahitian informant at least tempered his idealization of the Polynesians. The Revolutionary atmosphere affected his one memoir on human geography.

Bougainville's 1799 memoir returned not to the South Pacific but to his early fascination with North America. He related at length a native embassy to the French authorities, Philippe Vaudreuil and Louis-Joseph Montcalm in Montreal in 1756 (Bougainville was in Quebec City, but the incident was comparable to others he had witnessed) to discuss alliance or neutrality during war with the British. Though his account paternalistically portrays the native people as capricious in their demands for brandy and childlike in their wish to see a French New Year's Eve celebration, on the whole he abandoned the overt reproaches that were in his earlier private journal. He described thoroughly the elaborate wampum-belt communications that were necessary for an illiterate culture, and he noted the necessity of ritual greetings and condolences to secure the Iroquois' goodwill. In his introduction, Bougainville regretted the "degenerate manners" of early European settlers who "brought destruction" upon native North Americans susceptible of "progressive civilization."[33] Of course, the civilizing mission justified further imperial adventure.

The most likely explanations for Bougainville's change of tone are the Revolutionary sensitivity to the rights of man, particularly evident amid the antislavery commitment of Grégoire and his colleagues in the Class. Bougainville may also have recognized that the four-stages ideology applied to all but the most ignoble of "savages." Thus the Iroquois could benefit from easier subsistence and a more settled society.

A comparable Revolutionary sensitivity affected even the conservative cartographer Buache in his single reference to human beings in his memoir of 1798. Buache reminded the Class that no explorer should "violate the rights of man," and he asserted, a bit recklessly at this late date, that the inhabitants of areas being explored by Europeans resisted them only when offended and insulted.[34]

Certainly, the historical four-stages view permeated the work of the most subtle ethnographic analyst of the geography section, the former Navy minister and an expert cartographer, Claret de Fleurieu. From 1796 to 1799 he read to the Class excerpts of a massive four-volume account of the fur-trading voyage begun six years earlier by Captain Étienne Marchand for a Marseille firm. Fleurieu collated the journals of Marchand's crew with reports of the most noted Spanish and British explorers.[35]

Rejecting Bougainville's early climatic determinism, Fleurieu, like Montesquieu, Volney, and the hygienists, asserted the critical but limited influence of the physical environment. He resolutely assumed a progressive hierarchy of cultures, with a civilizing European mission at the top. He laboured to transcend noble–ignoble savage stereotypes to attain some empathy for other cultures.

Fleurieu thought a cultural chain of being was necessary to understand the human mind. The Fuegians remained the miserable primitives, instructive for their meagre capacities. One could then ascend a graduated scale of intelligence, from "the stupid Péscherai, who knows only how to shiver in the Tierra del Fuego, or the wild Hottentot, who differs little from the wild man of the woods; to the genius who created the Iliad, or him who anatomized light, and submitted to calculation the law of gravity."[36]

At another primitive extreme were the Marquesas islanders, who had displaced the Tahitians from the role of noble savage. They were "the most humane, most peaceable, and most generous" of any Pacific islanders. Decrying the alleged Spanish image of the "Indian" as an "animal of a species inferior to man," Fleurieu expressed horror at Spanish accounts of the dispersal of these gentle people by gunfire.[37] Here was one case where European colonial control was unnecessary. He was willing to leave the Marquesans to their indolent lifestyle, which was encouraged by their moderately fertile terrain. Yet, unlike Bougainville, Fleurieu could not abide the reports of "unbridled libertinism" and "disgusting facility" with which the Marquesan women yielded to strangers. Even more distressing were suspicions of community of property and of women, which would "debase to the level of the brute, a people who in other respects have such human form."[38] So, though the Marquesans were undeniably human, their apparent lack of fixed families and property relegated them to lower cultural status.

In an instructive comparison, Fleurieu now seized upon the very evidence of "corruption" to Rousseauist writers – luxury and social inequality – to praise how far Tahitians were from the state of nature. The more abundant crops and greater fertility in Tahiti compared to

the Marquesas had in fact fostered productivity and social development, not merely indolence.[39] Tahiti had advanced along the historical
progression.

There were no welcoming sirens at Marchand's next landfall near
modern Sitka in the Alaskan panhandle, where the sea otter trade
would begin in earnest. Here, a cold, rainy climate permitted, according to Fleurieu, only a difficult subsistence, with a small population
living by hunting, fishing, and whaling. The sailors observed in the
people a "hideous aspect, an air of ferocity." The women, with their
large labret lip ornament, seemed of a different species from the
Polynesians.[40]

But Fleurieu would still warn against simple climatic determinism.
The tropical Marquesans were apathetic about their wives' flirtations,
so unlike the "unbridled jealousy" of southern Europeans, but Alaskan
husbands displayed veritably Mediterranean emotion. Therefore, "if
climate has an influence on the character and manners of nations, this
influence is not uniform; other causes, no doubt, destroy or modify its
effects."[41] In this way Fleurieu maintained the theoretical framework
of Montesquieu and Volney, allowing for greater cultural malleability.
Indeed, Fleurieu remarked that the Tlingit, despite their forbidding
appearance, showed remarkable skill as carvers, profound respect for
the dead, and shrewd commercial ability. Hence, "the Tchinkataneans
[Tlingit] cannot be considered a savage people; the judgment and
cunning they display in their commercial concerns prove that they are
susceptible of making a very rapid progress in civilization."[42]

The same testimony to superior intelligence appeared in the architecture, sculpture, and painting of the Haida Indians of the Queen
Charlotte Islands. Yet the preconceptions of the four-stage theory of
social development could not allow a hunting people to be credited
with refined art. Hunters allegedly only had time for the pursuit of
game. These hunting tribes also had trading acumen, crafts, some
rudimentary sense of property, and some abstract ideas in their language. Fleurieu therefore proposed that the Northwest Pacific Coast
native people were descendants of ancient, more civilized tribes.
Despite linguistic differences from the peoples further south, they might
even be refugees from Cortès's conquest of Mexico who had adapted
to a harsher climate.[43]

Fleurieu displayed far more openness to Pacific Coast culture than
had Volney with the Miamis and related Appalachian tribes.[44] Defending the Haida from Dixon's unsubstantiated charges of cannibalism,
he admitted: "I am not an apologist for savage peoples; never have I
fallen into ecstasy before the man of Nature." But, he continued, "let
us not judge so precipitately, and without knowing them, the people

of that unhappy America which has so much reason to complain of us." He added that an Indian historian would rightfully describe Europeans as the destroyers of the powerful Inca and Aztec empires, as the scourges of the human species.[45]

While striving to discard the noble–ignoble polarization, Fleurieu offered an early statement of the white man's burden. Europeans could pay their debts to American natives (and reap commercial rewards) by bringing to these peaceable Northwest peoples the benefits of agriculture, the more advanced arts, and the "true principles of social order, a rational system of morality and religion."[46]

The most explicit and well-known efforts of the Institute to increase geographical knowledge came through its consultative reports for the government-funded Nicolas Baudin expedition to Australia which lasted from October 1800 to March 1804.[47] The abundant scholarly attention given to the Baudin expedition stems primarily from its link with the independent Société des Observateurs de l'Homme, in existence from 1799 to 1804, which was animated by teacher, journalist, and would-be ethnographer Louis-François Jauffret.[48] He attracted as members the Idéologue leaders Destutt de Tracy, Cabanis, and Volney, although there is no evidence of their activity in the society. Nevertheless, Jauffret's own project for an ethnographic museum and the society's publication of the instructions to Baudin by Cuvier and Degérando have become landmarks in the early history of French anthropology. Cuvier for his part discussed the importance of measuring crania of both living people and cadavers.[49]

Degérando, in his rightfully celebrated *Considérations sur les diverses méthodes à suivre dans l'observation des peuples sauvages*, shared Fleurieu's belief in a hierarchy of cultures and in a French civilizing mission. He added to existing models the concept that every people observed would represent a different stage of historical development.[50] The document was both a pointed critique of unreflective, hastily reported travel literature and a detailed blueprint for questioning, people being observed. As prominent an anthropologist as E.-E. Evans-Pritchard claimed that the "paper reads as though it might have been written yesterday." Degérando hoped to obtain knowledge on the "origin and generation of ideas, and on the formation and development of language." As befitting the author of four volumes on the influence of signs, he knew the handicap of translation from the original language into that of the observer and the importance of "describing things without judging them." Perhaps Degérando's most important legacy was his insistence on proper linguistic preparation. Travellers might try to communicate by Sicard's gestural language for deaf mutes. "The first means to the proper knowledge of the Savages, is to become after a fashion like one of them; and it is by learning their language that we shall become their fellow citizens."[51]

His questionnaire was in many ways a sequel to Volney's document. On the individual state of the "savage," "observers" should explore the influence of climate, air, food and drink, sleep, and measure physical strength. They might wish to determine how individuals educated their physical and mental faculties. One could enquire on how they judge and on how they acquire ideas of the soul, God, the good, and the beautiful. Next would come questions on domestic social phenomena – conditions in the family, importance of kinship, status of women, institutions of marriage, sexual customs, and child care. From the family one would search out phenomena of social rank, government and warfare, ideas of property and justice, use of natural resources, and subsistence by hunting, fishing, farming, or commerce. Finally, one would try to ascertain moral values and observe religious hierarchy and rituals. Degérando's philanthropic pose was actually as paternalistic as Fleurieu's, since he insisted that trade is necessary to civilize barbarous peoples.[52]

There were serious handicaps to realizing Degérando's admirable research program on Baudin's voyage. Extended anthropological observation was incompatible with its geographic objectives. Fleurieu's instructions warned Baudin that he was on "no account to lose sight of the fact that the monsoons are in control, and that a few too many days spent on one call may condemn him to six months of inactivity."[53] François Péron, the young aspiring anthropologist on the expedition, recognized that mastering a language would require a "multiplicity of associations" and a "continuity of communication" for "coherent and interesting results." Hence his efforts to compile a native vocabulary on Maria Island off Tasmania were abortive.[54]

A historian of exploration, Jean-Paul Faivre, has also called attention to the expedition's hidden strategic agenda of intelligence-gathering about a possible English settlement on Tasmania. Péron sent a long memoir in 1803 to Decaen, the bellicose governor of Mauritius, about the strategic importance, as well as the actual weaknesses, of the British colony at Port Jackson. While Péron was certainly more than just a spy, political and naval objectives made charting the coasts a higher priority than the study of the inhabitants.[55]

The unfortunate death of Baudin during the expedition had the result that it left unrevealed the ostensibly anticolonialist sentiments he expressed in his journal. To Australian Governor Philip Gidley King, Baudin wrote that humane attitudes prevented celebrating the seizure by Europeans of the territories of these "children of nature just as little civilized as your Scotch Highlanders or our Breton peasants, etc. who

if they do not eat their fellow men, are nevertheless just as objectionable." Therefore, Britain and France would each do well to "mould
for society the inhabitants of its own country" rather than "seizing the
soil" of "those very far removed from it."[56] If Baudin acted as a potentially colonialist instrument and did not surrender for a moment his
prejudices for a social hierarchy or a realistic portrait of native hostility,
he at least reflected momentarily on the injustice of colonialism.

Péron, the surviving naturalist of the expedition, had won his post
by eagerness, proclaimed in *Observations sur l'anthropologie* (1800),
a pamphlet addressed to the École de Médecine and forwarded to the
Institute, to study the effect of climate, regimen, exercise, and occupation on organic constitution, intellectual, and moral faculties. In addition to the program of the hygienists Cabanis and Hallé, Rousseauist
idealism suffused Péron's work. Postulating a great physical strength
and a moral insensitivity in "savages," he proposed to determine
whether their simpler passions and unchallenged freedom spared them
the heart and stomach afflictions of civilized, degenerate people.[57]

A few scholars have not realized that he vacillated in the same
narrative between the stereotypes of the noble and ignoble savage that
had been at least partly abandoned by the armchair ethnographers
Fleurieu and Degérando. Compared to Fleurieu's subtle comments, his
first observation of western Australian aborigines was a report of a
sullen, hostile people in an arid land. The inhabitants were miserable
and ferocious, disposed to brandish spears and clubs, and incapable
of appreciating European gifts and tools.[58] Later, in Tasmania, he could
become lyrical about the patriarchal family life which, he observed,
seemed to realize the "happiness and simplicity of the state of nature
of which I had so many times in reading felt the seductive charm." In
1984 an anthropologist consequently reasoned that, for Péron, the
"noble savage ... is alive and well in this last of the eighteenth-century
anthropological excursions."[59]

This highly selective reading disregards Péron's remarks that the
people of southern Tasmania and the coastal Maria Island were too
"ferocious and gross" to understand a kiss of greeting. The women
on Bruni Island danced with "indecent movements" that excluded the
"delicacy of sentiments and actions" of social beings.[60] By contrast,
the stolid males of Maria Island appeared so indifferent to sexual
stimulation that Péron wondered whether their desires were periodic,
like those of animals.[61] Whatever friendly communication there was
with Europeans, he nonetheless felt compelled to conclude that it was
"impossible to overcome the people's natural ferocity of character and
prejudices against us." Intimidation was the necessary European
strategy.[62]

In one respect, Péron attempted to substantiate the hygienists' theory of the indelible imprints of age and sex. The coquettish women and playful children he met during the voyage suggested to him that the "character of women and children is much more independent, compared to man, of the influence of climate, the perfection of the social order, and the imperative of physical needs."[63] Previous studies have revealed how he gave up the noble savage myth, with its assumptions of superior savage muscular strength. Testing a small sample of Malays, Timorese, Tasmanians, and Australians, along with a European control group, on a dynamometer, or "pressure machine" scale, Péron observed that the degree of strength seemed to vary proportionally with the degree of civilization. While attempting to carry out Degérando's instructions on measuring the physical strength of natives, he tended in his explanation of the results to slide back to the ignoble savage portraits of Scottish historian William Robertson and of Volney – hunting peoples must be weaker because of their fatigue and poor nutrition. The relative weakness of the Malays could be explained away by the fertility of Timor which bred indolence.[64] Modern anthropologists, however, have been sceptical that the "savages" ever understood the purpose of the machine or the test.[65] Along with Péron's endorsement of the "ignoble savage" view, appeared that of a gradation of cultures and a relative pessimism about the possible improvement of the least civilized. Péron thought the Australians were a race distinct from the more primitive and weaker Tasmanians.

Péron also concluded that the "savage" is "arbitrarily controlled by physical needs and must modify his habits to the physical nature of the soil." By contrast, he thought the British colony at Port Jackson showed how "climate and the seasons have a less general, less exclusive influence over social man," since they are "incessantly modified by laws, government, education, political and religious prejudices."[66] Péron thus reincarnated the theories of Montesquieu and Volney, while he chose to emphasize that malleability of civilized human beings which was most valued in the Revolutionary era. Unfortunately, government indifference to publishing the complete records of the expedition meant that only researchers of later generations were aware of many of Péron's unpublished notes and of the superb sketches of artists Charles-Alexandre Lesueur and Nicolas-Martin Petit.[67]

Interestingly, Cuvier's report in 1806 to the Class of Mathematical and Physical Sciences praised Péron most for his description of the transformation of incorrigible British convicts into solid Australian citizens. Severe discipline, prompt punishment, and the incentive of eventual property ownership achieved their objectives. Though rather naïvely, Péron had also claimed, to Cuvier's satisfaction, that allegedly infertile prostitutes became highly responsible mothers in this new milieu.[68] Cuvier, of course, was pleased that practices applying to convicts in Australia might promote social harmony in France.

The few geographers in the Class of Moral and Political Sciences who responded to the theoretical challenge of the hygienists, of Montesquieu, and of Volney made concerted efforts to relate people and physical environment. Coquebert de Montbret and Mentelle offered tantalizing glimpses of the new "statistical geography," but they left it either undeveloped or as compilations without theory. Volney himself insisted on debunking the noble savage myth of Rousseau and its resurrected form in Chateaubriand. He continued to stress the ferocity and repulsiveness of "savages" while claiming to interview a native spokesman for a settled, agricultural, propertied society. Nevertheless, the native Americans were not an inferior or degenerate race, as de Pauw had labelled them, but merely suffered from the disabilities of a hunting society. Bougainville and Fleurieu partly overcame the noble and ignoble savage stereotypes, while Péron tended to adopt first one, then the other; for all three, in the Revolutionary era of curiosity about culturally induced change, the four-stages model of progress related to mode of subsistence emerged triumphant over Rousseauism or cultural relativism. Bougainville's first encounter with the Iroquois was no more edifying for him than a similar encounter had been for Volney. Having been seasoned by his experiences in the South Pacific, Bougainville, amid the sensitivities of the Revolution, gave up a racial theory or simplistic climatic determinism for a nuanced view of South Pacific islanders and the Iroquois. Cuvier's instructions to the Baudin expedition of course show the continued viability of a theory of fixed races. Fleurieu was perhaps the most disposed to identify with the viewpoint of the "other," though he, too, advocated a cultural hierarchy, and used the four-stages model to promote a European civilizing mission. In his opinion, an influx of traders, missionaries, and settlers would sweep away obsolete modes of subsistence for the benefit of the inhabitants. The model could thus justify continued French commercial and colonial adventures, while it continued to be used to praise societies based on property and social inequality. Degérando produced the most anthropologically sophisticated program, but the imperatives of explorers and the tribulations of the Baudin expedition militated against its easy fulfilment.

The exemplary research of the Prussian savant and temporary French resident, Alexander von Humboldt, showed that human geography could proceed without direct institutional support from the Class of Moral and Political Sciences. Having barely missed the Baudin voyage, Humboldt financed his own five-year odyssey, lasting from

1799 to 1804, to South America, Cuba, and Mexico. His lavish thirty-volume publication (1805–36), aside from its innovative discussions of physical geography and pre-Columbian archaeology, provides an excellent statistical geography and political essay on Mexico, including comments on the Mexican census, racial composition, social rank, economic activity, and government revenue.

Elected a foreign associate of the Class of Mathematical and Physical Sciences before his return to France in 1804, Humboldt presented at least two memoirs on human geography in 1811 and 1812 to the Class of History and Ancient Literature, including a general survey of the "progress toward civilization" of the native people of the Americas.[69] Assimilating Volney's assumptions and influenced by the humanitarianism of Georg Forster, Humboldt demonstrated a surprising degree of empathy with his subjects. On the one hand, he retained the concept of a cultural hierarchy – the sixteenth-century Aztecs occupied the "very lowest degree of civilization"[70] – yet on the other he allowed each people a "particular route to civilization," in this case omitting a pastoral stage. He rejected Fleurieu's hypothesis about the Mexican origins of the Northwest Pacific Coast hunting peoples, and thought there might be uneven development in artistic creativity and moral principles. In any case, he saw in American art a "degree of civilization superior to that acknowledged by de Pauw, Raynal, and Robertson." He could not admit "those decisive distinctions between barbarous and civilized nations" since external circumstances make "infinite variations in the nuances of culture which distinguish tribes of different races."[71]

Despite Humboldt's striking success as a human geographer, the dissolution of the Class of Moral and Political Sciences in 1803 removed a potential forum for reporting the concerns of human geographers. The government would not even save the failing private Société des Observateurs de l'Homme. A decree of the Consuls in 1803 reshuffled Bougainville and Fleurieu to the Class of Mathematical and Physical Sciences, where they did no further geographic research, while Mentelle and Gossellin continued their customary communications in the Class of History and Ancient Literature. Péron and Humboldt thus faced either an audience of natural scientists or a forum for classical and historical papers. Nevertheless, the Académie des Sciences would prepare ethnological questions for the research of future French explorers, including those who accompanied the Duperrey expedition of 1824 and Dumont d'Urville's two voyages of 1826–29 and 1837–40, when longer sojourns enabled some observers to become more sensitive to the nuances of the aboriginal cultures of Australians and Pacific islanders.[72]

The demise of the Class of Moral and Political Sciences foreshadowed later difficulties in establishing societies of cultural anthropology.

The most promising research in the human sciences received considerable publicity in the bulletins of the new Paris Société de Géographie, founded in 1821 by a collection of Oriental linguists, veterans of the Egypt expedition, cartographers, and classical scholars. Of over 200 founders, fifteen were from the Académie des Sciences, and ten from the Académie des Inscriptions. Early membership lists include the names of Cuvier, Degérando, Humboldt, Coquebert de Montbret, and Louis de Freycinet, a former companion of Baudin.[73]

Other accounts demonstrate the difficulty of establishing a flourishing independent society of ethnology or ethnography. Anthropologists have compared the conspicuous strength of Paul Broca's Société d'Anthropologie, founded in Paris in 1859, which emphasized craniometry and racial classification, to the lack of theoretical coherence and institutional weakness of societies of ethnology and ethnography.[74]

In the Académie des Sciences, mathematicians and navigators most often occupied the geography chairs, while geography did not return to the Academy of Moral and Political Sciences in 1832. The Sorbonne had a separate geography chair-holder after 1812, but the rare professors of geography in the French university system were most commonly scholarly cartographers. Only in an era of soul-searching and imperial excitement after the Franco-Prussian War in 1872–74 were more geography chairs endowed. By 1890 the disciples of Paul Vidal de la Blache, professor of geography at Nancy and then at Paris, could anticipate the holistic view of social science of the modern *Annales* school, with its correlation of physical and economic features of a given region. In this "possibilist" approach, men are not prisoners of their surroundings, since they can react and adjust to them.[75] In the mid-nineteenth century, however, the lead in geographical studies had undeniably passed to the German-speaking world.

In Volney's original plan, studying the influence of the physical environment would help construct the all-important human sciences of legislation and political economy. The purpose of observing peoples in various regions of the earth, after all, was to find out how governments could best cope with or counteract the physical environment. Volney concluded, though, that government and property legislation rather than climate seemed far more important in infusing habits of personal freedom and rationality. Now, in any climate, in the agricultural or commercial stage of historical development, the problem was finding government institutions that would not only preserve social order but also guarantee individual rights. Having inherited concepts of both rights and utility, Revolutionary theorists had to balance individual fulfilment, the public good, and the need to end political turmoil.

10 Rights, Utility, and Political Institutions

The majority of members of the Class of Moral and Political Sciences wished to construct a political science that would preserve freedom without further social disorder.[1] At the very first public session in April 1796 both Henri Grégoire and Cabanis reiterated Daunou's theme of the association of freedom and knowledge. Grégoire said that a "representative government" believing in "innate rights to liberty and happiness" would encourage the "science of government," which in turn "would protect freedom" by probing the foundation of authority. An improved political science, with principles of representative government and separation of powers, would help create a government that would never despotically suppress the study of basic political principles.[2] Within the Class, aside from the wistful comments historians usually kept private, there were no formally expressed theories of royalism or desire for a return to religious authority in the style of Louis de Bonald.[3] The Idéologues were the prime developers of a political science in the Class – Destutt de Tracy, Cabanis, and Volney in the analysis of sensations and ideas section, Sieyès and Roederer in the political economy section, and Daunou in the social science and legislation section. Their innumerable constitutional schemes used representative government and, especially after 1795, separation of powers, to tame the dangerous passions aroused by a philosophy of rights. Their belief in stages of political as well as social development led to their identification of turbulent direct democracy with a bygone era of small city-states or even "savages." The heritage of Montesquieu, who had once been critical of a possibly degenerate monarchy, now inspired confidence that well-adapted republican institutions would prevent either executive or legislative tyranny. Finally, Institute authors extracted all the potential for subversion from their defence of rights by carefully restricting political rights to propertied or competent men.

Basing a political science on universal principles, deductively derived from human nature or from irrefutable historical observation, would-be experts might insist on a single correct answer for a problem. Repressing dissent in a crisis would thus invalidate Grégoire's vision of a science always protecting freedom. Intellectuals close to power during the Directory might succumb to the temptation to be élitist experts. As political actors in the Revolution, Institute authors repeatedly found that circumstances changed the balance of freedoms and the mechanisms of social control. The legacy of the Idéologues was ultimately support for a liberal individualist society, rather than a view of a positivist organic society or a technocratic totalitarianism, chiefly because they returned during the Consulate and Empire to a philosophy of individual rights for safeguarding dissent.[4]

Throughout the Revolutionary era and into the Restoration, the moderate Revolutionaries freely combined the supposedly incompatible concepts of individual rights with the principles of utility and happiness. Restricting political rights enabled a philosophy of rights to re-emerge after the Terror in a form resembling the one found in the speeches of Sieyès in 1789–90. Despite recent French Revolutionary historiography, which reads the Terror back into ideas of sovereignty and general will in 1789, Sieyès's early Revolutionary views did not logically lead to a Rousseauist or Jacobin unrepresentable general will or to the unlimited popular sovereignty of the Terror.[5]

Two of the most systematic interpretations of Idéologue political science need revision. The first interpretation correctly discerns the objective of social stability but overstresses the anticipation of organic social harmony in Saint-Simon and Comte. The second view correctly compares Idéologue thought with Benthamite utilitarianism but underestimates the return to concepts of rights after the Terror.[6] In addition, a brief consideration of the identification of the political science of the Class with "bourgeois ideology" will clarify the applicability of this concept.[7] Finally, a discussion of mathematically based political science reveals the scepticism of the Idéologues towards the great ambition of Condorcet.

INDIVIDUAL RIGHTS AND THE HISTORICAL JUSTIFICATION OF REPRESENTATION

Most of the authors in the Class of Moral and Political Sciences cited Locke, Rousseau, or the Physiocrats rather than American sources for their belief in individual rights. The most frequent justification of rights was based on an apparently empirical observation (actually more like a deduction from the definition) of the needs, pleasures, and pains of sensitive human beings. Rights were axiomatic in Condorcet, and were derived immediately from universal "needs" and "capacities" according to Sieyès in 1789 and Volney in 1793.[8] From the alleged fact of the desire for happiness and for developing "physical and mental faculties," Sieyès jumped the Humean hurdle to articulate a right to a "social guarantee of liberty, property, and security." Rights rested on the Lockean definition of personal independence – each was "proprietor of his own person." Sieyès used both natural rights terminology ("a free contract" of society) and the utilitarian goal (the "greatest happiness of all").[9] The belief in a rational social science, what Keith Baker has termed the discourse of "reason," joined the discourse of "will," based on a social contract and individual rights.[10]

In 1793 Volney similarly deduced rights from the "physical attributes that are inherent in human organization," though not from a social contract. Common human faculties and needs gave an "equal right" to life and to self-preservation. Liberty derived from the independence of each person's senses. This autonomy meant that no individual need submit to another. Each human being was also the proprietor of the immediate product (or its equivalent) of his labour.[11]

In modern political philosophy the utilitarian goal of the greatest happiness of the greatest number may be seen to threaten the freedom of the individual personality because aggregating individual fulfilments may sacrifice the individual to some community standard.[12] The utilitarian Bentham, in manuscripts unpublished until 1816, feared that proclaiming a declaration of rights would be "sowing the seeds of anarchy broadcast" and "nonsense on stilts."[13] Yet the political science of Sieyès and Volney had little anarchic potential because of their overriding concern for social order.

In 1789, long before the Terror frightened moderates and the sansculottes demand for "equal satisfactions," Sieyès called only for equality of civil rights, while he subjected political rights to a utilitarian standard. His well-known attack on noble privilege in January 1789 made it clear that advocating equal rights did not bring into question "inequality of means" and of property. As his friend Grouvelle, a social science and legislation section associate, had argued in an essay on Montesquieu, "inequality was necessary."[14] In fact inequality based on the necessity of the division of labour produced a complementary structure of classes, each playing its appropriate social role.[15] While Sieyès may have wanted a unified nation to eliminate privilege, only those worthy of exercising the function of voting would have political rights.

Later, in 1789, Sieyès spelled out the distinction between "passive citizens," whom the laws protect, and those "who take an active part in the formation of public power." The active citizens were the tax-paying "true shareholders of the social enterprise." Only those who at least voluntarily contributed to the expenses of government need be represented, and only the truly free (and therefore, excluding servants) with some degree of wealth could be electors or eligible for office.[16] Sieyès's reluctance to adopt a pure property standard seems to have derived from his reservations about giving predominance to ex-nobles or to idle absentee proprietors. Moreover, after the tax qualification was set, Sieyès contended that he had only wished to exclude the "lowliest" from active citizenship. Regardless of the details of electoral law, a more conservative Institute associate such as Ramond, who was later a covert royalist, in 1791 agreed that all citizens deserved equal protection of the laws but that political participation should be confined to "chosen citizens in whom society can personally place confidence."[17]

A historical justification of representation was an important complement to the utilitarian concept of political rights. The four-stages theory of economists, geographers, and historians explained that modern social development rested on the "division of labour, which was [both] effect and cause of the growth of wealth and the improvement of industry." In a modern commercial society, most citizens lacked "education or leisure to want to make laws directly." Therefore, pure democracy was obsolete and only a "representative government" was feasible. Contrary to Rousseau's condemnation of representation, only representation could now guarantee liberty. Moreover, the division of labour underlying political economy could now form an integrated whole with social contract theory.[18]

ROEDERER AND CAMBACÉRÈS ON SOCIAL SCIENCE

As sans-culottes demands increased after the overthrow of the monarchy, moderates such as Daunou reiterated the limitation of the Declaration of Rights to equal opportunities to acquire property, not to equal ownership.[19] Roederer, in his Lycée lectures delivered in 1793 before the Terror, insisted that universal natural rights of liberty, property, and civil equality did not suggest a dangerous "levelling." He claimed that property rights come before social convention, "civil law and popular prejudices," and should not be limited, while Robespierre called for a maximum for prices in the name of general welfare.[20] For Roederer, natural rights were not subversive but instead served social order. Like Sieyès he carefully distinguished between a "representative republic" and direct democracy.[21] Education and a social art based on political, moral, and economic sciences would tame antisocial passions.[22]

Sieyès in 1793 had proposed a single science of the "knowledge of the rights, duties, and interests of man," including natural law and morality, political law and social art, and public economy and the art of administration. This division precisely anticipated Cambacérès's 1798 discourse to the Institute which recommended a single social science with three branches – political economy based on interests, legislation based on authority, and ethics based on sentiments.[23] Cambacérès agreed with Roederer on the need to regulate the malleable moral passions. However, Cambacérès, ever the opportunistic lawyer, feared that geometric or purely rational calculation would encourage unbridled egotism. The self-interested "absurd man of the materialists" might not be a robot but paradoxically too free.[24] Historical experience and appropriate legislation should therefore temper the excesses of reason. Roederer and Sieyès were more willing to use the power of habit, as previously discussed, to channel passions in order to serve the nation.[25]

Roederer certainly planned to enlist a social science to take the emotional charge from conflicts of interest. In 1797 he proposed the neutralization of oratory in legislative chambers unprepared for debating measures by sending laws to four successive committees. Each committee in turn would discern affected interests, estimate the intensity of effects, decide on a plan, and draft the final decree. An even more technocratic provision would have reduced the number of laws passed (each would have had to be ratified in a referendum), so that the administration would have the widest possible latitude in decrees of enforcement. We see already here a remote hint of the plebiscitary tactics of Bonaparte.[26]

THE DEBATE ON RIGHTS IN 1795

While the traumatic social fears unleashed by the Terror made a social science seem more urgent, the constitutional debates of 1795 in the Convention revealed the tenacity of the concepts of a declaration of rights.[27] Almost all the interpreters of the 1795 constitution justifiably stress the changes made in the language of rights. The new Declaration of Rights introducing the constitution excluded articles such as "men are born and remain free and equal in rights," while the Convention added a Declaration of Duties to safeguard the "maintenance of property" and it again restricted political sovereignty to tax-paying citizens.[28] Yet the same Daunou who had criticized the Declaration of Rights in 1793 now insisted that some kind of Declaration of Rights should be retained as a "rallying point for republicans" against "enemies of the revolution." Unlike Roederer in 1793, Daunou thought that the natural rights argument for property might lead to undesirable claims to an equal share of property, based on pre-social conditions. Therefore, the current pragmatic defence of property that was consistent with individual rights should now enumerate "rights of man in society." But civil liberty and equality before the law were still constitutionally guaranteed rights, not merely revocable, socially utilitarian expedients.[29]

Redefining political rights was the most contentious issue in the debates of 1795. Boissy d'Anglas's notorious discourse on the virtues of government by the propertied applied not to electors but to propertied legislative representatives.[30] Daunou, supported by Baudin des Ardennes and Garran-Coulon, was the first to propose direct elections by all men, excluding only domestic servants, without a college of propertied electors.[31] However, the Convention majority, which included future Institute members Creuzé-Latouche, Merlin, and La Revellière-Lépeaux, chose a more conservative position – that of restricting primary voting rights to taxpayers and of establishing higher income qualifications (as had been done in 1791) for a much smaller number of intermediate electors. Daunou ultimately agreed that society could define political rights.[32] The common philosophy of Sieyès in 1789 and Daunou in 1795 after the Terror is apparent here – property and equal civil rights preceded any utilitarian determination of the social good. Political rights were, however, a function of fitness for citizenship, subject to an economically functional division of labour.

DIRECTORY POLITICAL SCIENCE: FROM RIGHTS TO TECHNOCRATIC ÉLITISM

Outside the constitutional debates, Institute members continued to use the language of individual rights. In an investigation of the Santo Domingo troubles he published in 1797–99, the legal scholar Garran-Coulon clearly supported the "rights of citizens anterior to society" as a "natural, social, and positive law." He praised the black leader Toussaint for "justifying the principles of the Declaration of Rights and of our constitution on the general liberty and equality of men."[33]

Baudin des Ardennes, a lawyer and deputy, was the most active author of memoirs in the legislation section of the Class of Moral and Political Sciences. He illustrated both the effort to construct a political science and the desire to preserve individual rights. Baudin firmly based political science on "principles of justice," not on "experience and observation." Once again, the "interests and needs of man as a sociable being" were the foundation of natural rights.[34] Rights were not a threat, since "ignorant and credulous crowds" would have no political sovereignty. In a representative government, leadership would have an "enlightened, wise will." The principles of social science and government required the "necessity of relations of superiority and subordination among members of political bodies." The treatises of Aristotle and Montesquieu spoke to reason, not passion, and they "did not write for the *faubourgs*," the sections of Paris where the rebellious sansculottes were dominant.[35] Hence, limits on political sovereignty were consistent with a fundamental scientific principle.

But history and experience reinforced scientific theory. By Montesquieu's allegedly scientific principle of the relativity of institutions to the spirit of laws, Baudin reasoned that factions were most incompatible with republican virtue, since they stand for "private interests, or esprit de corps." They attack not merely the élite, but the "interest of all citizens." History showed the harmful effects of the faction of the Roman Gracchi and "even their imitators are proof against them" (a pointed, highly applauded barb against "Gracchus" Babeuf, the ill-fated egalitarian conspirator of 1796).[36] Baudin's memoir on clubs also invoked the theory of representative government, which vested sovereignty only in the elected body, not in a tribune of the people or extraparliamentary pressure groups. Experience showed that the superfluous or dangerous Parisian clubs were only the "fruit of indigence and vice in part of the population of cities."[37]

Baudin here unwittingly raised the dilemma of how the supposedly unassailable principles of political science could be reconciled with civil liberties. For, if expressing dissent in clubs was to be labelled "factious," what would happen to freedom of speech or the press? Moreover, if clubs were to be closed, what would happen to freedom of assembly? Granted, the Directory was beset with opponents on both political extremes and did not have a loyal opposition. However, the name of science could be conveniently invoked to restrict what was supposed to be axiomatic and universal civil liberty.

Other Institute members crafted policies that carried out Baudin's academic principles. In the name of crushing dangerous factions, directors Merlin and La Revellière-Lépeaux, supported by Cabanis and Sieyès, carried out the antiroyalist coup of Fructidor (September 1797) and the anti-Jacobin coup of Floréal (May 1798). These Institute members did not reject the use of force or tampering with elections to save their vision of the moderate Revolution, while the Fructidor coup exiled the royalist Pastoret and chagrined the historians Delisle de Sales and Toulongeon. Government by *coup d'état* was the unintended legacy of the first coup of Fructidor.

Furthermore, the political crises of the Directory had impelled some Idéologues to approve the repression of certain newspapers and clubs. As early as in 1796 Daunou had argued that the superficial analysis of issues in newspapers could not create unified public opinion and did not enjoy full protection under constitutional guarantees of press freedom. In addition to the repression of the royalist press after the Fructidor coup, in 1799 the Directors banned the neo-Jacobin *Ami des Lois* and the *Journal des hommes libres*.[38] In the atmosphere of military collapse, financial crisis, and neo-Jacobin resurgence of 1799, Cabanis favoured closing the Manège club and other seditious clubs and limiting their membership if they encouraged conspiratorial minorities and endangered public credit. After the press attacked Sieyès, the recently installed Director, Cabanis also advocated a new calumny law preventing slander of the executive.[39] Such restrictions in the polarized atmosphere of Revolutionary politics threatened to make a mockery of the more characteristic Idéologue defence of civil liberties.

In a deeper sense, the question arises whether a belief in a science of politics, with conclusions by experts, is at all compatible with a belief in individual rights. The Idéologue moderates reached their apogee of political influence in the period from 1798 to 1801 when they also sought to construct a technocratic, élitist social science. In 1799 they supported Bonaparte's constitution even though it lacked a declaration of rights. The previous year, Destutt de Tracy's essay on public morality had reserved "knowledge of this systematic ethic in all its details" to "hardly anyone but the legislator ... [A]ll other citizens need to know some of the most important conclusions, [in the same way that] artisans, to practise their craft, are content with some proven rules and do well without studying their basis in learned theories."[40] The Idéologues undoubtedly conceived their mission as pedagogic. Destutt de Tracy's proto-positivist inclination to social control appears most notably in his 1801 pamphlet on schools which would have authorized advanced education for the "learned class," but only terminal primary schooling for the "working class destined for laborious toil."[41] Such a division resembled the one described in the journalist Petitain's public morality memoir (1798), which elicited such vigorous criticism from Roederer and Ginguené.

In their search for stability, the Idéologues helped support and rationalize Bonaparte's successful coup of November 1799. Sieyès, as a Director, at last played a decisive role in constitution-making, while his Institute colleagues Talleyrand and Roederer engineered the *rapprochement* with Bonaparte that was so vital to he successful conspiracy leading to the *coup d'état*. Both Daunou and Cabanis were active members of the rump Commission of the Council of Five Hundred, which wrote the constitution of 1799.[42]

Sieyès's constitutional ideas reveal a consistent fascination with a scientifically contrived mechanism, that of separation of powers, to manage government. Each governmental power would have a distinct function. This faith in institutions was already evident in his manuscripts of 1789. Even then he had recommended a tribunate to represent the popular will, a royal council for legislative initiative, and a legislature exercising final judgment. He had already contemplated the selection of legislators from a carefully sifted, propertied list of "eligibles" by the tax-paying, active citizens.[43]

In 1795 Sieyès proposed a constitutional jury as a "tribunal of the rights of man" to protect the constitution. When he played a significant political role in 1799, his concern to stabilize government triumphed over the guarantee of the "rights of man" that had formerly been at the apex of all the innumerable triangular constitutional schemas in his papers.[44] According to his colleague Boulay, Sieyès suggested the constitutional provisions for choosing the legislature from above, whereby a largely appointed "conservative Senate" (a modified constitutional jury) would select members from a national list of eligibles that had been sifted in stages by fellow citizens.[45]

These plans best illustrate the confidence of the Idéologue in 1799 in the supposedly scientific mechanisms of checks and balances. Cabanis's justification of the 1799 constitution still spoke of "individual rights" that derived from the "faculties and needs of men," despite his disagreement with the historical social contract idea. However, in his pamphlet he hoped the separation of powers would guarantee a strong executive, filtered lists of eligible office holders would promote a service ideal which was the best feature of aristocracy, and popular sovereignty, guided from above, would provide a "good and sound democracy."[46] He mistakenly thought that the Tribunate would guarantee strong opposition, even though it lacked the power to propose laws.[47] By 1802 Idéologue leaders had ample reason to regret their lapse in their defence of individual rights.

THE RESURGENCE OF THE LANGUAGE OF RIGHTS

During the Consulate and Empire nearly half the members and associates of the Second Class of the Institute accepted careers at the highest level of government, such as in the Senate, the Tribunate, the

Legislative Body, or the Council of State. However, Bonaparte's wrath against the "metaphysicians," which was well-known by 1801, led to the disillusionment of the Idéologue circle.[48] Only Roederer broke with his Institute colleagues to support the purge of Idéologue opponents from the Tribunate and the proclamation of the Life Consulate, and so he assumed further administrative positions in Naples and Berg during the Empire. Other Institute members, however, were equally opportunistic. Cambacérès, the advisory second Consul, became an imperial courtier as Arch-Chancellor, while Bigot de Préameneu advanced from the Council of State to the Religious Affairs ministry.

The most provocative recent interpretation of the Idéologues has concluded that their élitism after 1795 shows how their approval of utilitarianism virtually supplanted their concern for rights.[49] The issue is certainly not the compatibility of utilitarianism with Idéologue philosophy, since the language of rights and utility were both used, even in 1789. While this view has considerable merit for the Directory, it neglects the effect of the Idéologue confrontation with arbitrary power. During the Empire and Restoration, Idéologues found more safeguards in individual rights than in a standard of the common good that could more easily be twisted for reasons of state. Rights deduced from needs were still acceptable. The second major interpretation considers the Idéologues as the forerunners of positivism, yet an analysis of their political and economic thought shows they believed in liberal principles fostering individual mobility, rather than in an organic society or a consistent adherence to Destutt de Tracy's rigid demarcation of roles.

The two most famous Idéologue political treatises of the Empire and Restoration periods were Destutt de Tracy's *Commentaire sur l'esprit des lois de Montesquieu* (written in 1806–7 and published first by Thomas Jefferson in English in 1811 and then in French in 1817) and Daunou's *Essai sur les garanties individuelles* (which appeared in the *Censeur européen* periodical in 1818 and in a separate edition in 1819). Both works restated a primary concern with social stability, but both also perpetuated Sieyès's political values of 1789 – individual civil rights and "usefully" limited participation in elections.

Destutt de Tracy replaced Montesquieu's ideal types of monarchy, republic, and despotism with two models – the first, one of "special governments" based on divine right, conquest, or the rule of rank or caste, and the other, of "national governments" obedient to the general will. The latter regimes, "tempered monarchies," which he opportunistically praised in 1819, as well as representative democracies, guaranteed that "all rights and powers belong to the entire body of the nation."[50]

Destutt de Tracy now reintroduced Sieyès's historical justification of modern forms of government. Pure democracy was a "government of savages," fit only for primitive times or an early degree of civilization. Absolute hereditary monarchy, which easily degenerated into tyranny or incompetence, was a "government of barbarous peoples." With the development of printing, navigation, and free trade a new degree of civilization required monarchy to become constitutional, that is, to "declare and consecrate the principal rights of man in society."[51] In a republic, an advanced stage of civilization demanded representative institutions in which "all citizens choose their delegates," or a "democracy of enlightened reason."[52]

Though Destutt de Tracy now found formal declarations of rights superfluous, he demanded as a preamble to an ideal constitution the basic individual rights of the 1789 declaration. Just as it had equated national sovereignty with the general will, Tracy now would rest a "national" government on the "will of the majority of the governed." Secondly, equality before the law to Tracy still meant an absence of privileged social groups. Thirdly, he did not wish a governing power so fixed that "violence is needed to change it." (In 1789 the declaration had stated that "no individual may exercise authority not emanating from the nation.") Fourthly, the "careful preservation of the separation of powers" reiterated Article 16 of the 1789 declaration. Finally, Tracy's fundamental principles paralleled all the 1789 articles concerning freedom of expression and religion: "security of citizens, the right to express their sentiments on all kinds of subjects, or even the right to hold opinions on religious matters."[53]

Like Sieyès in 1789, but unlike Bentham, Destutt de Tracy saw no conflict between this language and the utilitarian goal of realizing individual desires. In his *Traité de la volonté* (1815) Tracy, too, derived rights and duties from the basic "needs and capacities" of human nature. The fulfilment of needs that bring happiness would also realize rights. Individual rights were not casual rhetoric, but founded Tracy's notion of good government. Nor was he unaware of the social problems that came from linking the happiness of some individuals to others.[54]

While wary of executive threats to legislative supremacy, Destutt de Tracy maintained the faith of Montesquieu and Sieyès in the notion of the separation of powers. He envisaged a "conservative body" that was stronger than Napoleon's submissive Senate and was elected by all citizens for choosing directly or recommending the choice of a plural executive.[55] Cut off from political power, Tracy moved away from the élitism of 1801 to defend wider individual freedoms.[56] Despite his own previous activities, he now vigorously defended all juries and doubted the usefulness of government catechisms in schools or of state-prescribed textbooks.[57]

According to Destutt de Tracy, popular sovereignty would now be sufficiently tamed by representation itself. Like Cabanis in 1799 he hoped for a "good aristocracy" of talent, and like Sieyès he warned against direct democracy, since people should "accept only suitable functions." But, having seen sham popular sovereignty under Bonaparte and the limited Restoration electorate, he now discarded a property qualification for all electors and demanded only an intermediate electoral assembly. Property had enough social advantages, and indirect election in itself would sufficiently stabilize politics.[58]

Certainly, Destutt de Tracy resembled the positivists in valuing expertise, and he believed, like the Physiocrats, that most people needed enlightenment to understand economic principles. But both freedom of expression and the diversity of opinions that were so threatened by Baudin's idea of a political science could now be defences against expert prescriptions. Nowhere in Tracy's *Commentaire* is there a sense of the sober surveillance found in Bentham's *Panopticon*. Tracy also stressed the importance of diminishing inequality, albeit by such "means not violent" as equal opportunities, luxury taxes, and equitable inheritance laws.[59] In fact, as Cheryl Welch has shown, the *Commentaire* was a rallying point for liberals, not for positivists. Despite his personal ties to harsher *laissez-faire* liberals like Charles Comte and Charles Dunoyer, Tracy did not completely share their vision of a self-regulating society.[60] In Tracy's mature social science, freedom tempered social control, and government intervention was only a minimal restriction on absolute economic freedom.

Similarly, Daunou's *Essai* of 1818 maintained a concept of individual rights despite his hope for stabilizing moral and political sciences. His ideal legislative assembly would "repulse any law against individual rights" or "limiting sovereignty." He eliminated the language of the social contract and of natural rights in the *Essai*, though not in his Collège de France lectures of 1819 and 1822.[61] But the important point is less whether he used the explicit language of *rights*, than whether his "individual guarantees" conveyed the same concepts as the 1789 declaration.[62]

Daunou defended guarantees of personal security, freedom from arbitrary state action, protection of property, freedom to exercise industry, and freedom to express opinions because of specific Restoration issues. If he advocated jury trials and a free press, the denial of juries for offences by the press in 1818 was a primary reason. The guarantee of freedom of expression targeted government censorship and the excessive security deposits required from newspaper editors.[63] His defence of the inviolability of property reflected a concern with the demands of émigrés for compensation at the expense of the

Revolutionary property settlement.[64] Moreover, he wished to extend to *all* proprietors (not just large landowners) the right to vote. Freedom of religion was a defence against Ultra demands for an intolerant state church.[65]

Daunou's guarantees were the equivalent of civil rights. In the political sphere, however, he would extend guarantees only to proprietors inclined to support social stability. Daunou supported the idea of electoral colleges of the propertied, though enlarged so that the "true shareholders of society ... all degrees of fortune would have citizenship rights."[66]

Daunou in his commitment to economic liberalism endorsed even more strongly than did Destutt de Tracy the "necessary, inevitable, and desirable" economic inequality due to the division of labour.[67] His notions of economic enterprise resembled Benjamin Constant's parallel account of "modern" liberty in a commercial society as contrasted to "ancient" Greek or Roman liberty which required ceaseless public vigilance and intervention.[68] For Daunou, meddlesome public inspectors should not encroach on the liberty of the industrial entrepreneur.[69]

Daunou's individual guarantees, like Destutt de Tracy's fundamental principles of government, enshrined individual civil rights; at the same time they avoided natural rights or social contract theory since these could be labelled fictional. Most basic freedoms were not made relative by a shifting standard of the common good. The single exception was paternal power, where social utility determined the rights of fathers and sons and limited the freedom to favour one son with excessive property. Even this exception conformed with the broader social ideals of individual mobility and the work ethic. Primarily, both Tracy and Daunou advocated civil rights as safeguards against tyranny and more serious threats to property by misguided egalitarians.

From 1789 to the Restoration, political sovereignty was a functional concept that was diluted either by indirect elections or by a property qualification. The Institute moderates thus combined concepts of individual rights with utility. From the outset, they often deduced individual rights from human attributes to make them nearly synonymous with the utilitarian pursuit of happiness. The language of rights did not have to give way entirely to that of utility since it still functioned to preclude popular democracy. Only civil rights could be envisaged as universal, at least outside of Revolutionary crises, and these did not imply social or economic equality. Thus, the moderates could use rights to assure a settled social order.

If to Institute moderates individual rights were virtually presuppositions of a political science, the same thinkers derived from Montesquieu the need to adapt institutions to a republic. Checks and balances were the hallmarks of the republican constitutions of 1795 and 1799. Rejecting the descriptive mode of Montesquieu, the Institute moderates argued that both natural law and history required representative government and the separation of powers.

The four-stages theory suggested to both Sieyès and Destutt de Tracy that a direct democracy was obsolete in a modern commercial society. Representative government was therefore the only viable option. Political liberty in representative government remained more utilitarian than did civil liberty. Writers like Baudin denied the legitimacy of extraparliamentary pressure groups or factions as contrary to the theory of representation. During the Revolution Baudin also showed the potential for portraying ideas of particular clubs and factions as contrary to the theory of the social science. At this point the distinction insulating civil liberty from repression began to break down, and the danger of a science with one correct answer was most apparent.

Thus, there remained the dilemma between scientific control and freedom of expression. The legacy of Condorcet, Montesquieu, and the Physiocrats had convinced Roederer, Daunou, Cabanis, and Destutt de Tracy that a social science was possible and necessary. The confidence in expertise and the potential for control seemed greatest during the Directory and early Consulate. At that time the Idéologues operated the most like functionaries, or "conservatives" in the parlance of the Lipset model of intellectuals. But Bonaparte appropriated the services of the more reliable functionaries like Roederer, while the non-Idéologues Cambacérès and Bigot emerged among his most prized legal experts. By the Restoration the surviving Idéologues were themselves in danger of being labelled factional. They thus found liberal guarantees a necessary defence against the policies of unfriendly governments. They had once again become outsiders, or intellectuals as moralists.

THE QUESTION OF BOURGEOIS IDEOLOGY

Historians have long debated whether moderate Revolutionary political thought represented a bourgeois ideology reflecting the demise of feudalism and the triumph of commercial and industrial capitalism. The Marxist interpretive model foundered on its failure to sustain the tight links between the terms bourgeois and capitalist. Historians have found among the leaders of the Revolution of 1789 many undynamic, non-capitalist members of the bourgeoisie who shared non-capitalist "proprietary" wealth with nobles. They have also found significant numbers of antifeudal and even capitalist nobles who participated in the Revolutionary movement.[70] Hence, recent interpretations have invalidated Sieyès's Revolutionary discourse asserting a struggle between privileged nobles and unprivileged members of the Third Estate in 1789. Bourgeois capitalism does not describe well either the largely non-entrepreneurial society of the Ancien Régime or the society of landed notables that dominated France from 1799 to 1830.

The evidence remains that the discourse of moderate revolutionaries, exemplified by six members of the Class of Moral and Political Sciences, continually celebrated a vaguely defined middle class (Sewell has not hesitated to call Sieyès's discourse the "rhetoric of the bourgeoisie"). A school principal, J.-F. Champagne, stressed in his translation of the *Politics* Aristotle's image of the "most stable of all polities ... based on the middle classes."[71] Grouvelle in 1789 called the "*classe mitoyenne* ... created by commerce and industry," the home of "sacred morals, public reason, love of the laws."[72] Roederer in 1793 spoke of the "fount of desirable virtues in the middle ranks." In the 1795 constitutional debates La Revellière-Lépeaux insisted that "those with mediocre fortune have virtue united to enlightenment."[73] Cabanis in 1799 heralded the "triumph of enlightenment and property, redistributed more justly by commerce and industry," which created the "force of the middle class where alone one finds the greatest talents and the most solid virtues."[74] In his critique of Montesquieu, Destutt de Tracy found the middle class "naturally imbued with the spirit of order, work, justice, and reason, since by its position and direct interest it is equally distant from all excesses." Tracy's attack on "idlers," of course, included capitalistic financiers and speculators, though it was largely intended for absentee landowners.[75]

Praise of a middle class does not necessarily mean "bourgeois capitalist ideology," since neither purely bourgeois capitalism nor capitalism alone was at issue. Nevertheless, there were good sociopolitical motives for this chorus: the Institute moderates opposed both aristocratic privilege and popular democracy. They vigorously defended property as the basis of any advanced society, believed in a hierarchical society, albeit one with individual social mobility, hoped to limit popular or at least uninformed participation in politics, and heralded commercial and industrial entrepreneurship. They advocated middle-class values of sobriety and work and were scandalized by aristocratic licence and popular brutality. Hence, they judged the solid, enlightened middle classes the basis of social order and appealed for productive capitalist activity, whatever the ancestry of the entrepreneurs. They were not yet reflecting a society undergoing industrialization, but they favoured adaptation to a changing economic order under the typical liberal illusion that abundance would result for all. These views may not be classic Marxist bourgeois ideology, but they favoured most forms of capitalism and idealized the industrious proprietor. The next chapter will focus on the disagreements between those who preferred the old foundation of landed wealth and those who were prophets of commercial and industrial capitalism.

If political science and liberalism seemed natural allies, what of the positivist polity of Saint-Simon and Comte? Certainly, the Idéologues and moderate Institute thinkers retained the belief that the ordinary people needed enlightenment. Yet, aside from physicians and hygienists, with their potential power in the clinic, hospital, and asylum, few other "moral and political" scientists formed an institutionalized, professional community that could exert equivalent power or control knowledge, terminology, and labels.[76] Positivist portraits of the future explicitly attacked liberal guarantees of rights and implied that disagreement with experts required not further debate but therapy. The strengthening of the belief of such thinkers as Destutt de Tracy and Daunou in individual rights, especially freedom of expression, after Napoleon's break with the Idéologues, reconstituted a shield, if not against economic exploitation, then against all would-be monopolists of knowledge and power.

SOCIAL MATHEMATICS

Another road towards a political science based on a firm knowledge of probabilities rather than on certainty was Condorcet's "social mathematics." Its purpose was to apply probability calculus to increase the degree of certainty of correct (that is, enlightened from the viewpoint of the élite) decisions in situations of highly uncertain democratic political outcomes. In the Class of Moral and Political Sciences Daunou discussed elections theory, which to him was an aspect of social mathematics. From 1785 onwards Condorcet had confused the search for an accurate expression of the voters' will with the probability of producing "true decisions." His conclusion that one needed enlightened voters for enlightened decisions raised questions about how to assure preferred outcomes in typical juries or legislatures. For example, those assemblies or juries with members who were less enlightened might require votes with larger majorities or panels to review their decisions.[77] In 1800 Daunou's memoir to the Institute aptly criticized Condorcet for confusing verification of majority will with "correctness of decisions," which "introduced an absurdity into his work."[78]

In 1795 the Institute adopted for its elections the Académie des Sciences system of summing rank-order preferences developed first by Jean-Charles Borda in 1784. But First Consul Bonaparte, as temporary president of the Institute in March 1800, suggested a review of the balloting system.[79] The following July Daunou's memoir preferred Condorcet's theory of two-by-two comparisons of leading candidates to Borda's summing of preferences. Daunou proposed to retain the rank-order preferential voting in the initial Class ballot. In the absence of an absolute majority, instead of immediately presenting the top three candidates to the Institute General Assembly, the Class would remove the lowest candidate from each successive ballot until one received an absolute majority. That candidate would be placed on the presentation list, and the same procedure would be followed for two other candidates. The Institute General Assembly would then compare each of the three candidates presented with the other two, with victory to be accorded to the candidate with the greatest relative plurality in a consistent rank order. For example, if the plurality of candidate B over candidate A was ten, of C over A was fourteen, and of C over B was twenty-two, then C, B, and A was the effective rank order and C would be the winner.[80] If the rank order was inconsistent, the election would be postponed. All such complex schemes failed, however, in the 1803 reorganization of the Institute. At that time, each Class controlled its own elections. The Class of History and Ancient Literature adopted an automatic third-ballot run-off between the top two candidates who both lacked an absolute majority, a system already rejected by Daunou. The Class of Mathematical and Physical Sciences, after hearing a ranking from the relevant section and considering the addition of more names, reduced the candidates to two on the second ballot.[81] Hence, the purity of elections theory gave way to pragmatic ease of application.

Daunou remained sceptical about the "application of calculation to moral ideas." For, without a careful analysis of each element, there could be "some inconsistencies in the observation of facts, some gap in the data, and some ambiguities in the terms; calculation established on such bases will only develop a series of perfectly linked errors, and the mathematical apparatus will have served to inspire a great respect for illusions."[82] Similarly, Destutt de Tracy's diatribe against "great calculators" who in presenting "the most defective forms of balloting" were heedless of the "nature of men and of things," did not spare Condorcet's proposals. Tracy found these expedients "absolutely impracticable, or they would have inconveniences more serious than [even those] he wished to avoid."[83]

In the prize contest on juries, Moulins central school teacher Nicolas-François Canard used the insights of Condorcet and the mathematician Laplace to assess decisions by juries. While Laplace assumed that jurors were probably correct 50 per cent or more of the time in their decisions, Canard thought that they acquitted the guilty in about three-quarters of cases. Canard fully agreed with Condorcet's precepts that enlightened decisions can come only from enlightened men, and he supported the selection of jurors from communal "lists of notables." He advocated a complex permanent jury panel review system based on the assumption that grounds for acquittal were never as sound as grounds for conviction because acquittal demanded only reasonable doubt. Like Laplace, he generally favoured raising to two-thirds the minimum majority required in juries, from the simple majority permitted in the Directory.[84] The various mathematical formulae inspired the prize commission to award him a shared first prize for a work that was "good for admiring the social science." However, another Institute colleague, Joachim Le Breton, reviewed Canard's work for the friendly *Décade philosophique* with severe scepticism about efforts to apply mathematical methods. Canard made the basic error of "treating the moral and political sciences with algebraic formulae, the very special language of quantities which is not theirs."[85] Combined with the critique of statistics in political economy, discussed in the next chapter, this judgment testifies to the limited success of Condorcet's "social mathematics" among the Idéologues and the Auteuil circle.

CONCLUSION

The Idéologues and Institute moderates anticipated aspects of positivism in believing that an authoritative political science could forever end social conflicts and assure political stability. The cautious descriptive approach of Montesquieu gave way to a confidence that rights could be deduced from human nature and that history justified representative institutions. Yet, if alleged scientific theory and empirical study limited the rights of freedom of the press and of assembly for factions, as Baudin suggested, then political science could be a pretext for discipline and control. The record of the Idéologues as would-be political actors was, of course, erratic. During the Directory they thought that maintaining moderate control of the Revolution justified *coups d'état* and press censorship. An architect of control without true civil or political liberty, such as Bonaparte, did not of course need social science theory.

The Idéologues were thus ultimately driven to defend dissent or to oppose covertly a regime in which they held office. Their liberal presuppositions meant that freedoms tempered control and scientific predictability. As Grégoire had argued, the political sciences, always seeking firmer conclusions, could also be critical and subversive of authority.

The ideas of the Idéologues had some of the defects of both positivism – the tendency to élitist manipulation – and liberalism – the alleged powerlessness before "necessary" economic inequalities. Yet the balance achieved by the Idéologues helped preserve on the one hand the positivist idea that rational, scientific arguments could determine a public interest, and on the other the liberal ideal that a discussion of contrary ideas ought not to be stilled.

In the era of the Institute, a would-be political science remained closely tied to political philosophy. Statesmen of the next generation who were convinced that human studies were becoming scientific, such as François Guizot, recreated an Academy of Moral and Political Sciences in 1832. The science of political behaviour, detached from doctrines of rights or public law, emerged under the impetus of studies of elections, colonial questions, and socialist ideas only in the last twenty years of the nineteenth century.[86]

If the defence of civil liberties and of property and praise for middle-class virtues were cornerstones of political science, the most vital issues of political economy were an intra-liberal debate about the most fruitful economic activities in the current historical stage. If the inviolability of property was taken for granted, there were still important questions to be decided concerning the role of landed wealth, the equitableness of taxing various sources of income, and the autonomy of economics from politics. While the old mercantilist view of the all-important trade balance was now discredited, Enlightenment theories of the Physiocrats and Adam Smith vied for supremacy. Academic questions of the sources of wealth reflected deeper divisions about whether commercial and industrial activities were the surest path to economic productivity.

11 Towards the Political Economy of Commercial Society

Seventeenth and eighteenth-century mercantilist economic theory sought, in an inevitable European power struggle, to enrich the royal Treasury by tariffs, bounties, and privileged trading companies and to assure a favourable foreign trade balance and the free internal circulation of goods.[1] By the late eighteenth century the production of agricultural and industrial goods assumed greater importance than did foreign trade surplus in economic theory. The doctrine of the Physiocrats that was established by François Quesnay and the Marquis de Mirabeau in 1758 sought to increase agricultural productivity by demonstrating the crucial importance of the "net product" of the landed proprietor as the source of wealth for the entire economy and the only surplus available for taxation. Predominant from 1760 to 1776, the Physiocrats believed that an agricultural society was the final term in a multi-stages theory of social development. In the 1770s the works of Condillac, Turgot, and Adam Smith envisaged a self-adjusting market model that insisted on the vital role of commercial and industrial capital. For some thinkers in the Revolutionary era, the fourth stage of commercial society had already arrived, especially with the demise of aristocratic privilege and the expected decline of great landed fortunes. While these thinkers apparently hoped to accelerate economic change, their goal paradoxically was to prevent further Revolutionary upheaval by assuring economic abundance. Only in the late 1820s did the political domination of landed *notables* seem oppressive to disfranchised merchants and professionals.

Before the Revolution, the Physiocratic ambition both to allow maximum freedom in the grain trade and to tax all proprietors, including nobles, would have upset established policies on tolls and tax privileges. Smith's similar concern to free the market and eliminate monopolies would have meant the abolition of internal customs and a controversial deregulation of colonial trade. The Revolution assured the long-term triumph of a competitive free-trade policy, at least in the domestic market, and abolished the most notorious tax exemptions and corporate privileges. In the post-Revolutionary era, the economic theories of both the Physiocrats and Smith defended the inviolability of property and the security of the earnings of agricultural and industrial entrepreneurs. In that sense, they both sought to make society safe from the demands of the sans-culottes for "equality of satisfactions" and from frightening Babouvist egalitarian schemes to hold property in common. Both theories also condemned wasteful luxury and public debt as detrimental to the economy and destabilizing to society. In 1803 J.-B. Say, a former *Décade philosophique* editor and a friend of the Idéologues, founded a new French liberal school that derived from the insights of Adam Smith. The continuing trend in the development of economic theory becomes marked only against the framework of the writings of Say and the 1815 treatise of his follower Destutt de Tracy.

As with the theory of elections and political science, probability theory and the mathematical treatment of historical evidence were suspect to economic theorists who reasoned deductively in search of universal answers with predictive power. A few economists, however, tried to use mortality tables to solve problems suggested by hygienists and geographers. The triumph of free-trade ideas brought the breakdown of the agreement between supporters of Physiocrats and Smith over sources of wealth. The logical consequence of this disagreement was a gradual shift in taxation theory from support for the Physiocratic single tax on land to a tax on all sources of wealth. Finally, the attacks on corruption and idleness associated with luxury and public debt also revealed the new disdain for the aristocratic lifestyle and for the financial practices of the Court, the symptoms of the fatal ills of the Ancien Régime. Thus, concepts of public virtue remained indelibly linked to economic theory despite efforts to construct a value-neutral science based on private interest.

THE SURVIVING PHYSIOCRAT

One pole of economic interpretation was the unrepentant Physiocracy of Du Pont, who reread memoirs in 1796 that had been first published in 1771 and 1774.[2] Although both Quesnay and Du Pont collected information about agriculture and commerce, they presented their circulation model after postulating the definition of land rent – the proprietor's net product – as the only source of wealth.[3] They assumed, beyond any empirical evidence, that industrial sales merely replaced the capital advanced and the subsistence costs of workers and managers. Du Pont was optimistic that political economy could achieve "incontestable deductions" from universally valid principles. Priding himself on his immersion in "interior and solitary meditation," he stated in his autobiography that "I found out by this method, and on my own, that land and water are the sole sources of wealth."[4]

Du Pont's main constitutional principle was the defence of property. His review of the constitution of 1795 suggested limiting political rights to landed proprietors and leaseholders. Proprietors, he wrote, were the "citizens *par excellence* ... sovereigns by decree of God, nature, their labour, and investments."[5] This implication of the Physiocratic program would be most distasteful to defenders of merchants as integral pillars of society rather than as parasites, but the divisiveness of the controversy became evident only in the Restoration.

Physiocratic taxation theory, based on the sources of wealth, coincided with the aims of some politicians in 1789. Du Pont believed that a single direct tax on the only truly surplus wealth, the net product, would be more economically sound than a combination of both direct and indirect taxes. Taxes on necessary commodities would raise their prices and therefore the labour costs of the productive cultivators. For less necessary products, consumer resistance to increased prices would mean losses for primary producers. Any decline in investments of cultivators would critically affect the net product of proprietors and, hence, all subsequent circulation of wealth. Le Mercier de la Rivière had estimated that proprietors would lose, after an indirect tax, four times the value of a comparable direct tax, while high collection costs and lost net product would deprive the Treasury of two-thirds of expected tax yields.[6]

Early in the Revolution the Constituent Assembly shifted most of the tax burden to direct land and personal taxes because of the perceived injustice of such commodity taxes as the hated salt levy. But Du Pont sadly admitted in 1790 that "despite the inseparable evils of indirect taxes . . . the nation was not mature enough for deliberations on natural law."[7] No "landed interest" would emerge as a pro-Physiocratic faction because proprietors were far from recognizing the proclaimed benefits of paying all the taxes. In practice, commodity taxes were expedient because the net product and available revenues in France together were not high enough to absorb all the burden through direct taxation.[8]

The graphic portrayal of the effect of the incidence of an excise tax on primary producers and consumers, "On Political Curves," that Du Pont reread in 1796 to the Institute had appeared first in 1774 in letters sent to the son of the Marggraf of Baden and to the mathematician Daniel Bernouilli (see Fig. 1). The curves show how the removal of an excise tax at various stages of production would increase the net price producers receive. Any such tax would generally be least burdensome at the wholesale level. A retail tax meant that all intermediate producers and distributors would seek compensation for their losses from the primary producer.[9]

Du Pont, like the theorists of rights, characteristically treated natural law as normative and not just descriptive.[10] The advances made by the proprietor justified a right to dispose of the surplus. Promoting the "proper price" for grain producers in a free market to increase the net product was the cardinal principle of the Physiocrats' program. Now that the Revolution had made "legal despotism" by an absolute monarch superfluous, freeing the market from price controls and trade regulations could be accomplished by an enlightened government.

A belief in natural laws also led to moral condemnations of luxury and slavery in addition to economic arguments. The Physiocrats detested the extravagant lifestyle of idle aristocrats and urban élites. While encouraging spending on food products, Quesnay found the "luxury of decoration" in the sterile artisan or manufacturing sectors unproductive for agriculture and total wealth. There is a trace here of the British country party ideology that held urban luxury to be dangerous to honest proprietors, and conspicuous consumption ruinous to agriculture.[11]

The Physiocrats also found public loans a fearsome spectre. While governments spent borrowed funds irresponsibly, idle *rentiers* would seek returns on government annuities rather than in agricultural enterprise.[12] Du Pont particularly attacked the life annuity, a high-interest loan in which the Treasury absorbed the capital at the creditor's death. There, "fathers preferred personal enjoyment to providing for the subsistence of their children."[13]

Aside from animosity to public and private extravagance, the Physiocrats found the slave economy archaic and wasteful. In 1771 Du Pont had introduced an ingenious economic argument against the profitability of slavery – an institution which already ran counter to the Physiocratic assumption that there is a right to the fruits of personal labour. Using prices for slaves, interest on the sums advanced, average life expectancy of slaves, and costs of overseers, Du Pont attempted to demonstrate that slaves were more expensive than free labourers in France.[14] Neither Turgot in 1774 nor Bonaparte in 1802 listened seriously to Du Pont's plan to substitute free African labourers on new sugar plantations in west Africa for the West Indies slave economy.[15]

Despite their common opposition to luxury, public debt, and slavery, critics of the Physiocrats constantly attacked their allegedly dogmatic assumptions on the sources of wealth. Economists, such as J.-B. Say and Destutt de Tracy, would idealize the empiricism of Adam Smith. Yet Say devoted his work to the exposition of definitions of value, wealth, industry, and capital.[16] Tracy worked out the implications of human desires, the will to pursue happiness, and the ownership of the personal faculties of sensitivity. Tracy could, from the theory of the will, derive a complete account of the processes of exchange and the circulation of wealth.[17] The shift to a nominally inductive credo must be explained by the epistemological heritage of Condillac. The Condillacian paradox was that once an author accepted an initial empiricist premise, he could legitimize any ingenious deduction from it.[18] On the whole, then, Say and Tracy were more remarkable for their appeals to empiricism than for their markedly innovative methods.

STATISTICS, MORTALITY, AND THE GRAIN TRADE

The one great possibility for empirical, and possibly less dogmatic, contributions to economics stemmed from the long tradition of official government inquiries (at least from the time of the memoirs of 1697–98 for the Duke of Burgundy).[19] The data from such inquiries could enable probability theory to be harnessed for the goals of concrete social policy. By predicting future outcomes with the greatest possible degree of certainty, governments and private companies could better estimate their expenditures. Condorcet's aspiration from the mid-1780s to 1793 to establish a social mathematics included acquiring data on life expectancy to assist in making calculations of private life insurance rates, public pensions, and life annuity plans. Fiscal and monetary policy would thus become more rational.[20] Condorcet's ultimate hope was nothing less ambitious than the determination of the effects of physical environment, culture, and government on life expectancy, birth and marriage rates, health, strength, intelligence, and character.[21]

A physician and amateur economist, Antoine Diannyère, consciously followed Condorcet in applying "political arithmetic" to economic doctrines. He brought together the imperatives of hygienists, human geographers, and statistical economists in relating mortality and life expectancy tables to the need for a medical topography of each department of France. Attaching himself to the Hippocratic tradition and the

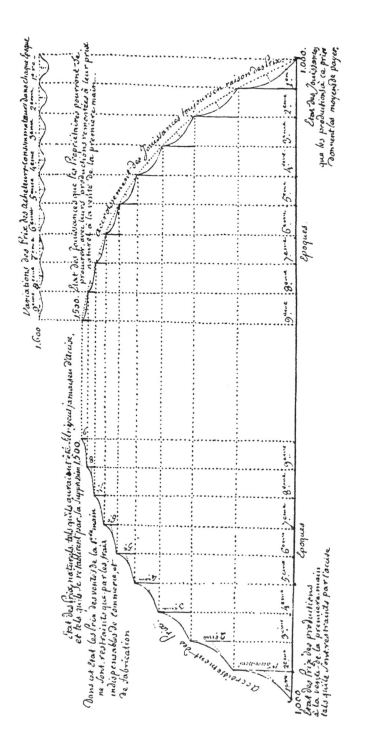

Variations des Prix des Acheteurs-Consommateurs dans chaque époque

1.600

État des Prix naturels, tels qu'ils seraient ... et tels qu'il b se rétablirent par la supposition 1.500.

Dans cet état les prix des ventes de la 1.ere main ne sont restreints que par les frais indispensables de Commerce, et de fabrication

1.000
État des Prix des productions à la vente de la première main tels qu'ils sont restraints par l'accise

1.500. État des ... d'accise que les Propriétaires pourront se procurer avec leurs productions remontées à leur prix naturel à la vente de la première main.

Accroissement des Jouissances toujours en raison des Prix

1.000.
État des Jouissances que les productions ce prix donnent les moyens de payer.

Époques

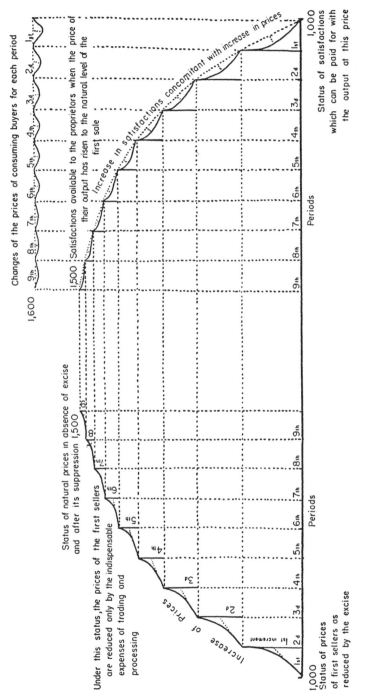

Figure 1

"On Political Curves": The Effect of the Incidence of an Excise Tax on Primary Producers and Consumers

Source: Du Pont de Nemours, *On Economic Curves*, ed. Henry W. Spiegel, 1955. Reprinted by permission of Johns Hopkins University Press.

investigations on epidemics by the Société royale de Médecine, Diannyère believed he could correlate mortality and the "situation, expo-
sure of soil, cultivation, fertility, and distance from swamps and large
cities." Indeed, the "more or less harmful miasma exhaled" in manufacturing cities could raise mortality. Having determined the "physical
causes of distinctions" in mortality, one could seek to eliminate them.[22]
Statistical demography was thus one of the most important tools in
the improvement of public health and in economic productivity.

Two other Institute members endorsed the collection of information
as a prerequisite to informed decision-making. As a member of the
finance committee of the Constituent Assembly which had to fix the
new land tax, Roederer encouraged the statistical work of Lavoisier
in his *De la richesse territoriale de la France* (1791). In Roederer's
introduction to a reprint, he argued that "the science of political, or
rather public economy, rests entirely on political arithmetic." By reasoning from the "facts of production and distribution of wealth" one
could deduce economic principles.[23] Forbonnais also believed that on
fiscal policy, "practice is better than too much speculation." He
thought the new inquiries on the state of the population by Bonaparte's
prefects could only benefit the government.[24]

The most mathematically sophisticated attempt to realize Condorcet's goals came from the search for a general law of mortality by
Duvillard, a former employee of Turgot, at the national Treasury office
in 1791 and later at Bonaparte's Bureau de Statistique. After an
elaborate interest rate analysis offered to the Académie des sciences in
1786, ten years later he constructed for the Institute a pension and life
insurance plan to "encourage industry, work, and savings" for old age
or widowhood. A secondary objective was to lower interest rates and
amortize the public debt.[25]

Alone among all Institute authors, Duvillard endorsed an egalitarian
view that was characteristic of the final democratic convictions of
Condorcet. He hoped that "as much as possible in the Republic there
should be equality of wealth, equality in means of acquiring it, and
equality of education." Thus, one could eliminate from the nation a
"poor, unfortunate, abject class." While merit inevitably brought distinctions, the inequality resulting from poverty deprives citizens of
"morals, energy, and development of talents, and diminishes the product of society, national wealth, population, and strength." Public workshops and savings banks would thus palliate the evils of inequality.
From the point of view of both national strength and humanitarianism,
Duvillard pleaded for a meaningful savings program. He even suggested that the rich might be prohibited from having such investments
to avoid further augmenting inequalities. Duvillard was thus far more

sympathetic to the poor and far less willing to justify social inequality than were his colleagues.[26]

Because of inadequate census data, Duvillard had to be content with information on average life expectancy per age decade, regardless of such other factors as gender, climate, customs, occupations, or regimen. Nevertheless, French insurance companies used his tables of mortality until 1880.[27] Duvillard's later analysis of prefects' reports for the period from 1802 to 1805 for a general law of mortality could not take into account movements of population, but it was a pioneering demographic effort in treating a stationary population.[28] In 1806 he pleaded with the government to use his laws of mortality and of proportionality of births and marriages to other variables in order to verify the information obtained from prefects. Yet Duvillard never converted Bonaparte's Bureau de Statistique, under the direction of Coquebert, to a chiefly algebraic rather than qualitative enterprise. In his aspirations, at least, he anticipated the social research of such hygienists as L.-R. Villermé in the 1820s.[29]

Diannyère represents an excellent example of someone who made conscientious use of statistical data and located their subordinate position in economic theory. The Physiocrats and Adam Smith had both advocated the removal of regulations on the grain trade. In the Revolutionary era, support of free trade meant a definitive break with the old mercantilist principle of regulating the price and supply of grain in order to protect the poor, and a complete endorsement of the idea that free trade provided a market-place solution to grain shortages. Diannyère supported free trade with evidence from historical series on grain prices and hospital mortality rates. He expected that "by facts political economy can approach a degree of certainty equal to physico-mathematical sciences."[30] Despite ingenious use of evidence, Diannyère, like Du Pont, arrived at his policy conclusions independently of the information presented.

Diannyère followed Smith's argument that the regulation of the grain trade promoted hoarding and turned dearth into famine. According to Diannyère, Necker's grain export ban in September 1788 had raised prices by 30 per cent. The correlation of grain prices with admissions to hospitals and mortality seemed to show that in London, where the grain trade was least regulated, bad harvests had the least dire consequences. In Lyon and Paris, illness and death rates seemed directly related to government regulations in crises. Diannyère assumed that government intervention in supply inevitably raised prices because of hoarding, and that the incidence of illness would have been less serious without such meddling. The excess probable mortality could be predicted according to the probable deficit in per capita bread consumption (previously estimated by mathematician Lagrange and chemist Lavoisier). He cheerfully concluded that governments should "assure liberty of commerce to agriculture."[31] He ignored all the intermediate assumptions necessary to solidify his argument. There was no discussion of the efficiency of grain supply, of whether hospital patients were representative of the general population, or of the hypothesis that free-market prices might have been even higher in a grain shortage.[32]

Despite the correspondence of statistical investigation with the nominally inductive methods of Say and Destutt de Tracy, these two were only lukewarm to the notion of any mathematical treatment of economic facts. Both were reluctant to give up the idea that economic science would present correct answers based on near certainties. Statistics for Say would only be a "recital of facts, more or less uncertain and necessarily incomplete," indifferent to the explanations required in political economy. The unreliability of data thus far collected particularly and justifiably disturbed Say. From 1827 to 1829, near the end of his life, he mellowed to the point of admitting that statistics could orient economists in their search for causes, but he never conceded that statistics or political arithmetic would prove basic economic principles.[33] Destutt de Tracy recognized the benefits of interest-rate calculations, but only attributed a minor role to probability theory. No mathematician could determine the "energy and power of passions" or even the "degrees of utility of certain inventions."[34]

Similar criticism greeted the more strictly algebraic efforts of the Institute taxation contest prizewinner, teacher Nicolas-François Canard. When he published in 1801 his elaborate mathematical theory of prices and tax incidence, Institute member and *Décade* reviewer Joachim Le Breton lamented that "really unnecessary algebraic formulas" decreased the potential audience of the book.[35] Both the uncertainty of statistical facts and the scepticism about mathematics based on doubtful assumptions ensured that verbal reasoning about fundamental principles was still the basic technique in political economy.

Diannyère's arguments for the free grain trade, however, were a leitmotif among all Institute economists. He saw his role as a latter-day Galileo, arguing against the supposed common sense of price controls in grain shortages like those who had argued against the common sense of a stationary earth. In 1792–93 Creuzé-Latouche had cited Smith in the Convention to argue that middlemen were needed to distribute grain at competitive prices. Only a monopoly, not a plethora of speculators, would result in hoarding. Hence, the laws of nature would always overturn a price maximum of the kind demanded by the sans-culottes and put into effect by the Jacobin Convention.[36]

In 1795 Creuzé-Latouche successfully obtained the creation of a political economy chair at the short-lived École normale to teach the vanity of fragmentation of property and the efficiency of free trade.[37] Similarly, Lacuée in 1797 argued that the good harvests during the period of the Terror when price maxima were in effect only proved that farmers evaded rent and tax obligations, not that price controls were desirable.[38] Free trade principles were the best defence of existing property and the best security against pandering to the popular desire for a "just" price.

THE SOURCES OF WEALTH

While free trade was the common doctrine of both the Physiocrats and the supporters of Smith, they diverged markedly on the sources of wealth. An old-guard neo-mercantilist bureaucrat like Véron de Forbonnais attacked the Physiocrats as early as 1767 for "disdaining the observation of facts when the peremptory mind dominates." He defended the productivity of commerce and manufacturers. In 1775 the Church canon Sieyès, who had read Condillac, found the Physiocrats' maxims to be based on "false, contradictory ... reasoning more ingenious than just."[39] Against the exclusive productivity of land, he offered a labour theory of value, probably derived from Locke or Cantillon, and asserted that the "production of industry was not just equal to the part of reproduction consumed by the *industrieux*."[40] All work that produced something useful produced wealth. In a tripartite class division, Sieyès allotted the same economic value to intermediary merchants as he did to proprietors, and he also recognized even beyond Adam Smith the productivity of services, including the work of the "political class" of government employees. Sieyès would also accept "public works as productive."[41]

The only real mediator between the Physiocrats and the disciples of Smith was the eclectic author Germain Garnier. In his 1796 manual he had already stressed the division of labour, capital accumulation, and entrepreneurial profit. Yet he insisted that "proprietors are responsible for the sole distribution of wealth" and that "in the last analysis, all revenue comes from land, even in mercantile cities." In his notes to his widely used translation (1802) of Smith's *The Wealth of Nations*, he defended the Physiocrats' notion of the net product but conceded that the epithet sterile humiliated merchants and manufacturers. In fact, all labour was productive of convenience or utility, but not necessarily of new value. Unlike Roederer, he thought that proprietors could do without others, but non-landed producers still depended on proprietors.[42] Destutt de Tracy in 1815 labelled him among those who believe that "culture alone is productive."[43] Yet Garnier stated that even though the Physiocrats might be theoretically correct, the works of Smith were more useful, since non-agricultural labour was necessary.[44] By 1822, in the posthumous second edition of the Smith translation, Garnier had evolved even closer to the views of Smith. He admitted that the weak point of the Physiocrats was their refusal "to appreciate all the influence of labour of arts and manufacturing on the increase of wealth." He had virtually subscribed to a labour theory of value.[45]

Still, the political and social perspectives of Garnier aligned him firmly with a nostalgic view of landowners' dominance. He believed in a political monopoly for a landowning "geocracy," defined as a necessary aristocracy of proprietors with revenues equal to a worker's annual subsistence. Garnier was more rigid than Roederer or Cabanis on the question of social mobility. He believed that wealthier societies inevitably accentuated the division between "mechanical and intellectual labour" and he worried about overeducation of the people, who merely needed moral instruction and minimal safeguards against ignorance and superstition.[46] In the Restoration Garnier adamantly supported more substantial landed property as the only qualification for active citizenship. Hence, despite his concessions to the labour theory of value, he remained in spirit a Physiocratic advocate of the landowning élite.[47]

At the opposite pole from the Physiocrats, the most systematic critic of the theory of land as sole source of wealth was Roederer, a lawyer and the owner of a glass-making enterprise. Attracted to Adam Smith's ideas by at least about 1780, he asserted in a 1788 pamphlet the rights of industrial proprietors to representation in the Estates-General. Fearing political domination by great landowners, he reasoned that the "institution of landed property is not the essence of society ... Mobile property, the fruits of the earth, is alone essential for society." As in Smith's historical account, the cultivation of land expanded in response to the demands of new urban manufacturers. Roederer also thought that "capitals" were formed by savings and included the mobile property of farmers and lenders as well as land. By 1793 he saw all profit after expenses as a form of *rente*, including the profits of manufacturers and merchants.[48]

Previous study of Roederer's Lycée lectures of 1800–1 has shown how he extracted the social implications of this view. Even wage-earners were *propriétaires d'industrie*, who needed social harmony, but only *capitalistes d'industrie*, that is, substantial proprietors, deserved political participation. Among capitalists, landowners had no primacy. Citing both Turgot's *Réflexions sur la formation et la distribution des richesses* and Smith, Roederer argued that the *fermier* is an entrepreneur earning a true *rente*, while the profits of manufacturers included compensation for risk, a rate of return on capital, and a salary for subsistence.[49]

Roederer thus bridged the era of Turgot and Smith with that of Say and Destutt de Tracy.[50] Tracy completely displaced land from any privileged place. For him the "undertaker of industry" was the "heart of the body politic, and their capital its blood." He bitterly attacked the idle *rentier* who created no new capital.[51] Industrial, entrepreneurial activity, wherever conducted, was now the essential source of wealth. These views carried a pointed political message during the Restoration. The social eminence of the landed proprietor should not allow him to monopolize political power at the expense of other entrepreneurs.

TAXATION THEORY

Physiocratic taxation theory provoked a major fiscal policy controversy as a consequence of the theory of the sources of wealth. If only land was productive, the Physiocrats claimed, then only land should be taxable. Indirect taxes damaged the source of wealth by rippling back through all the intermediaries from retail sale to primary producer, resulting in a surcharge on the proprietor. As the primacy of landed wealth was discarded, there was a slow and fitful movement, propelled by fiscal necessity, towards accepting the legitimacy of indirect taxes. Hence taxation theory became another index of the acceptance of the new commercial and industrial society.

The pre-Revolutionary critique of Physiocracy by Forbonnais and Sieyès extended to the single tax. Forbonnais believed Quesnay's "incredible suppositions" vastly exaggerated both the amount of the net product available for taxation and the collection costs for indirect taxes. In 1800 he admitted that it might be "theoretically true" that all taxes burden the landed proprietor, but he rejected the contention that there was an effective surcharge. Indirect taxes in fact could free capital for agricultural investment.[52]

After the Constituent Assembly in 1790–91 had in fact shifted more than half the tax burden to direct land and personal taxes, Garnier defended the Physiocratic view as a theoretical proposition. Commodity taxes, he claimed, would raise wages and therefore the labour costs of proprietors, who could never be compensated by additional charges to the consumer. Indirect taxes "fall on the proprietor with a surcharge." By a strange line of reasoning Garnier asserted, however, that indirect taxes would stimulate the worker to raise his own wage in order to be able to afford more tea, sugar, coffee, tobacco, wine, and beer. Also, taxpayers might prefer to pay small indirect taxes than large land taxes. Nonetheless, his nuanced conclusion was that moderate direct taxes and borrowing would on the whole be more constructive fiscal policies than heavy commodity taxes.[53]

Roederer had read the taxation theories of "Schmitt" (i.e. Adam Smith) even by 1781.[54] Yet, as late as 1796 he supported the Physiocratic surcharge theory of indirect taxes at a time when he had abandoned the theory of land as the unique source of wealth.[55] The final shift in Roederer's views seems directly associated with the taxation prize contest of 1799–1800. As the prize commission reporter he helped recommend the winning entry of Canard. In the long run, Canard argued, a tax assessed at any point in the circulation of goods from producer to consumer would have the same effects. As in a hydraulic system, a temporary change in fluid levels would end in a new equilibrium level. The Physiocrats were incorrect to claim that proprietors bore the entire tax burden, since taxes affected all economic actors.[56]

By 1800–1 Roederer's new Lycée lectures reiterated Canard's arguments without acknowledgment, and he even proclaimed that taxation theory had a success "not often obtained in the moral and political sciences." While Canard had used the concept of *rente* rather than capital, Roederer proclaimed that a tax on any capital return, whether from land, loans, commerce, or industry, would be equally burdensome.[57] Any sector burdened by a tax might suffer a flight of capital investment, but competition in the capital market among land, bonds, and commercial or industrial investments would eventually bring all rates of return to an equivalent level. Canard's work is an obvious source for the altered theory, despite Roederer's faint praise for it in the prize report.[58]

Destutt de Tracy also rejected the Physiocratic tax theory in a long essay that tended to downplay the frictional effects of new taxes feared by Canard. While all taxes were inherently evil, at least luxury taxes would not inhibit essential production. More than Roederer, Tracy remained cautious enough to conclude that in taxation policy "practice was more reasonable than theory."[59]

Since many proprietors had never seen the benefits of a single tax on the net product, they supported government efforts to shift the burden to indirect taxes. Already in 1797 the Directory had approved new retail commodity taxes. By 1813, in fact, Napoleon collected 71 per cent of his tax revenue from indirect taxes, and there would be no non-landed income taxes in France until the era of the First World War.[60]

LUXURY

Both the Physiocrats and Adam Smith had envisaged political economy in a framework of moral principles. Their concern with productivity and the free market retained the old humanist goal of the virtuous citizen. While the "invisible hand" seemed to suggest that pursuing private gain automatically produced public virtue, in fact shared attitudes towards luxury and the public debt did not justify tolerance for any "private vice."

Attitudes in the Institute towards luxury reflected the delicate balance of this humanist moralism, with the reluctance to interfere in private consumption habits. Several authors defended the economic benefits of luxury. In the old neo-mercantilist framework of Forbonnais in 1767, luxury goods had helped maintain the favourable trade balance and had suited a monarchy. Large consumer expenditures also created jobs and wealth. Thus, Quesnay's critique of the "luxury of decoration" was unfounded.[61] Garnier also thought that the "sensuality and vanity of the rich" stimulated the economy, and that agriculture benefited from the "extension of artificial wants" encouraged by new trade routes and industries. But the Revolutionary context lent itself to a continued moralistic opposition to aristocratic idleness and extravagance. Garnier therefore shared the Physiocrats' condemnation of the vain luxury of refinements.[62]

The tolerance of others for luxury stemmed partly from antipathy to the sans-culottes' doctrine of "equality of satisfactions." Creuzé-Latouche found the illusory Spartan ideal of 1793 only fit to "proscribe what helps industry and the arts."[63] Roederer in his 1793 lectures feared that any maximum placed on fortunes would discourage large, efficient farmers and stifle large industrial enterprises. Diannyère in 1800 warned that flourishing agriculture and industry always required the incentive of additional earnings for exercising talent and providing enlightened supervision.[64]

Yet the economics of J.-B. Say and Destutt de Tracy found luxury wasteful and public debt an invitation to unproductive government spending. Therefore, economic maxims would be consistent with moral behaviour.[65] Say and Tracy integrated public virtue with their vision of a commercial society. Certainly, in the Revolutionary era there was a distinct rhetorical bias in favour of republican simplicity. Prudent consumption happened to be congruent with the economic necessity of saving for capital formation. In his utopian essay, *Olbie*, Say had especially stressed that "great wealth is also disastrous to good morality" and "luxury should be restrained." His advocacy of a public censorship system, moralized theatre, and tax rebates for virtue were not explicable merely on free-market principles.[66]

Destutt de Tracy went further than Say by bringing the indictment of wasteful consumption into a treatise of economics itself. For Tracy, Garnier's defence of luxury was unacceptable. The sterile habits of those "living nobly" diverted capital that was needed elsewhere. Luxury to Tracy was "always harmful ... a great evil ... immoral."[67] The full emergence of the thrifty entrepreneur as model remained tied to an attack on extravagance. The idle rentier was both morally reprehensible and economically inefficient. The message was intended for Restoration courtiers as well as for the edification of a liberal reading audience. Luxury would create the perception of undue extremes of wealth which had to be controlled for social stability.

PUBLIC DEBT

Even more than the debate on private extravagance, the opinion of Institute authors on public loans demonstrated the attack on wastefulness. The proponents of both Physiocratic political economy and Smith were akin to the British country party campaign against Court corruption. French and British authors in the eighteenth century had provided an assortment of arguments on the evils of public debt. Government plans would divert capital from agriculture and create a sterile monied interest. Loans might cause wage and price inflation, higher interest rates, and a high tax burden to pay off the debt.[68] In the Revolutionary context, spiralling public debt and, later, unsupported paper money were leading causes of economic and social turmoil. Yet, with the Treasury unable to tax sufficiently to meet expenses, there had to be a more subtle view of loans.

The most sympathetic author to the older financiers' viewpoint was Garnier, who found borrowing "less than an absolute evil." Building canals or other public works would later raise revenues and thus justify government debt. The total debt would be dangerous only if it rose disproportionately to government revenue and overly increased the tax burden.[69] Similarly, Forbonnais in 1800 thought moderate borrowing in wartime or to increase monetary circulation was preferable to a precipitous tax increase. He still feared high interest rates, which would distort the flow of capital.[70] Roederer, in his review of the public loans contest and in his own reflections on the subject in 1797, justified some loans for public works or for small savings bonds to reduce the tax burden of poor relief. Thus, while he did not share the perceived overconfidence the English placed in paper credit, Roederer would not promote excessive fears of bankruptcy.[71]

Sieyès in his manuscripts called attention to the loanable-funds theory of modern economics. He expressed fears that capital-poor private investors would be outbid by government in borrowing and hampered by high interest rates.[72] Roederer refuted this view by reasoning that only an additional 1 per cent of available capital would be attracted by a new government loan. Thus, there would be no crowding out of loanable funds. Furthermore, even if capital were temporarily scarce, a rise in interest rates could always be reversed by an influx of foreign capital. Developing Turgot's arguments on capital returns, Roederer claimed that all capital returns on land, loans, and commercial and industrial profit tended towards an equal equilibrium rate. Therefore, a decrease in interest rates would drive funds to agricultural or other business sectors until their declining profit rates equalled the new interest rate.[73]

However, the Class of Moral and Political Sciences as a whole remained reluctant to praise a benevolent view of public credit.[74] The trend of French economic theory was not towards Roederer's pragmatism but rather towards the implacable hostility to debt of Say and Destutt de Tracy. Their economic assumption was that government spending was inherently unproductive and created no new wealth, and their moral assumption was that spending in excess of revenue was incompatible with virtue. Tracy saw no rationale whatever for regarding public credit as a sign of strength. For one thing, a bloated government budget enriched government ministries, so that they arbitrarily carried out "sterile and destructive" projects without consulting the people. Secondly, loans unjustly burdened future generations with the equivalent of a perpetual tax at onerous rates to repay interest and principal. Thirdly, the idle *rentier* was a drain on entrepreneurial lifeblood, since he produced nothing himself and his purchase of government bonds threatened capital investment in more fruitful enterprises. Lending produced "a crowd of licentious gamblers in the funds." He fervently hoped that legislators would refuse to guarantee government loans so that funds would dry up.[75] Public debt was therefore profoundly corrosive of the entire society.

CONCLUSION

The most important commitment of Institute political economists was to the defence of a society founded on private property. While equal treatment of all proprietors may have been a revolutionary principle in 1760, to defend property after the Revolution was to defend the existing social order against threats from the unpropertied. The general attack by everyone except Duvillard on "levellers" and the reluctance of some even to criticize luxury consumption were based on a view of the necessity of unhindered private possession and consumption in the face of sans-culottes threats to limit great fortunes. The second general consensus, given the eclipse of the neo-mercantilists, was that there should be no obstacles to a freely operating market-place. Heirs of both the Physiocrats and Adam Smith believed in the maximum possible free trade, especially in grain. Producers' incentives would assure a guaranteed supply in the future. Despite the advocacy of modest public works and public education by a few thinkers, the emerging liberals opposed price controls and neo-mercantilist tariffs. They cleared the way for the harsher *laissez-faire* individualism of the leading French economists of the July Monarchy, Charles Dunoyer and Frédéric Bastiat, and for the steadfast opposition to tariffs by disciples of J.-B. Say.[76]

The sources of wealth issue, however, divided partisans of agriculture as the culmination of social development from those who expected a commercial and industrial society. Du Pont himself remained firmly committed to the exclusive productivity of land, while a brief reference by Cambacérès, Garnier's moderate views, and a note by the otherwise egalitarian Duvillard registered agreement. However, the significant trend, represented by Roederer, Destutt de Tracy, and J.-B. Say, the most important economist outside the Institute, resolved the issue against the Physiocrats. Neo-mercantilists had already envisaged a commercial society, but Institute economists, except Forbonnais, firmly rejected a balance of trade theory. Roederer's concept of the equivalence of capitals, based on Turgot and Smith, helped end the stereotype of the parasitic merchant. In economic theory, growth through agricultural capitalism yielded to entrepreneurial growth of all kinds. This theory anticipated the era of industrialization in France, though it gained credence from the contemporary transformation of the British economy. Bonaparte's electors were still largely defined by land tax payments, and the political dominance of landed proprietors remained a live issue that helped provoke the revolution of 1830.[77]

There was no simplistic correlation between economic and political views. However, Du Pont and Garnier, the two who were most sympathetic to Physiocracy, were both more favourable to royalism. The adversary of the Physiocrats, Sieyès, certainly supported the antiroyalist Fructidor coup in September, 1797, though Roederer, the partisan of industry, had been highly critical before the Fructidor coup of the Directors' fears of a royalist plot.[78] Du Pont was endangered enough by the Fructidor coup to embark eventually for the United States. However, there was no alignment during the Revolutionary decade of a landed, pro-Physiocratic party against a progressive interest favouring Adam Smith. In the Restoration, however, Garnier sided with the great landed proprietors against Destutt de Tracy and Daunou, both of whom wished to expand the electorate to include merchants and industrial entrepreneurs who might own modest parcels of land.

The controversy on sources of wealth entailed divergences on theory of taxation. Motivated by the need for government revenue, Roederer gradually adjusted to the legitimacy of indirect taxes. The Institute prize contest of 1799–1800 in effect intensified support for the increased indirect taxes initiated in 1797. While Du Pont was an unrepentant advocate of the single land tax, by 1800 Roederer had accepted Canard's contention that indirect taxes would not overburden landowners. The prize memoirs had helped furnish arguments for a revision in fiscal policy to proceed apace in the Directory and Consulate. In this context, Institute intellectuals undertook no great initiatives that opposed the governments, although in the future liberal economists would often contradict powerful manufacturing and mining interests which demanded heavy tariffs.

A few authors were able to engage in Mandevillian detachment separating the economic benefits of luxury and public debt from moral concerns. There was considerable support for luxury consumption, if only to challenge socially radical levellers. But the works of Say and of Destutt de Tracy reveal that the emerging liberal view, which provided economic rationales for savings and capital accumulation, retained the concern of the Physiocrats to create virtuous citizens. Both agricultural and industrial entrepreneurs were productive, while extravagance by the aristocratic and urban élite threatened the reconciliation of social groups. Such luxury appeared to postpone the more equitable distribution of goods that was expected from higher productivity. Roederer, Say, and Tracy all believed that enlightened capital formation needed moral guidance. Therefore, they were strongly biased against both private and public waste.

Given the deplorable state of the government Treasury, some Institute members advocated pragmatic public borrowing as necessary. The major liberal theorists – the Physiocrats, Smith, Say, and Destutt de Tracy – were ferociously hostile to public debt. Their view happened to coincide with Bonaparte's inclination to avoid open borrowing and to requisition wealth from satellite territories.

With political overtones to such basic issues as the primacy of landed wealth, there could hardly be the value-free, autonomous, technical science envisaged by J.-B. Say. The Physiocrats and their critics both reasoned deductively from defined premises that were allegedly based on observation. Despite the nominal allegiance of Say and Destutt de

Tracy to an inductive model, the effort to ground inductive reasoning on "political arithmetic" and to pursue Condorcet's ideals did not, on the whole, find a warm Institute reception. Duvillard's ambitions at generalizing a law of mortality were relatively unappreciated by his scientific colleagues, while Diannyère could not convince critics that his mortality and price tables were really essential to the defence of free trade. Nevertheless, they all took up the call of Condorcet to attempt to correlate social variables with age, life expectancy, and health. Social statisticians of the 1830s would continue to search for the average human condition along with laws of mortality.

The Institute intellectuals seemed on the whole to have sanctioned prevailing government economic policies. The abolition of the Class of Moral and Political Sciences in 1803 troubled writers like Du Pont, who lamented his reassignment to the Class of History and Ancient Literature.[79] Outside the Institute, Say found free trade doctrine sometimes unwelcome to a government committed to administrative intervention, though he did not himself object to Napoleon's Continental blockade as a policy of economic warfare.

Despite the opposition between the theory of free international trade and a protectionist policy, Bonaparte could well boast that he had consolidated the property interests of the Revolution. The didactic purpose of the Class of Moral and Political Sciences had been, after all, to dissuade misguided agitators who misunderstood the natural laws of the economic order and thereby threatened the Revolutionary property settlement. The Continental System created new industrial markets in some sectors, while fifteen years of warfare were disastrous for French merchants. From 1830 to 1848, however, few could contest the diagnosis that France was abandoning the era of an overwhelmingly agricultural economy. A more vocal school of liberal economists, the heirs of Say and Destutt de Tracy, had definitively discarded the doctrines of the Physiocrats.

12 Suppression and Resurrection of an Academy

The Revolutionaries' self-image of breaking completely with the past does not accurately represent continuities with Ancien Régime institutions. After 1789 new Revolutionary language, diffused by a burgeoning press, helped create a new political culture expressing popular sovereignty and citizenship, and symbols that pervaded even the dress and speech of everyday life.[1] Yet, for all the cascading, if ephemeral, onslaught of Revolutionary symbols, the composition of "academic" élites, the forms of academic culture, and the practice of public service persisted across the Revolutionary divide as if they were in the stratum of "long duration" as described by Fernand Braudel.[2] To heal the wounds of the Revolution after tragic personal losses and suffering, the Institute tended to select for membership many former academy members and to preserve previous academic rituals. These continuities helped reinforce the intellectual and political objectives of stability. The Class of Moral and Political Sciences also successfully enshrined the self-consciously constructed Enlightenment models of the human sciences, though Revolutionary imperatives had altered their meaning.

Previous studies of the Idéologues and of the Second Class have not directly focused on how the new institutional practices of academies affected the Enlightenment Encylopedist ideal. By its very existence the Institute replaced separate corporate academies and fulfilled Enlightenment goals of extending the scientific method to human problems.

At the first public session on 4 April 1796 poet Collin d'Harleville offered an ode to the "Great United Family" with the "touching mission of making human beings happier and better, spreading talents, moral conduct, and honouring genius everywhere."[3]

Yet, even the apparently minor matter of common quarterly public sessions ultimately threatened Encyclopedism. For, whatever genuine private interactions there were among members of the three classes, the Institute offered on public display a polyglot series of readings with many rigorous or esoteric papers that tested the patience of an audience eager for light verse and oratorical eloquence. Even the correspondents of the *Décade philosophique*, so friendly in principle to the human sciences, lamented the restrictions on literary genius, while the conservative press waxed nostalgic for the Académie française as an arbiter of language and literature. Celebrations of literary eloquence sometimes became a code word for hostility to Revolutionary language. Former Enlightenment philosophes, such as Morellet, now found scientific culture detrimental to the intellectual sovereignty of literature. Amid press complaints about common public sessions, historians and scientists hoped for their own autonomy. The result was a waning of the Encyclopedist ideal which guaranteed a special niche for moral and political sciences. The government could re-establish in 1803 three separate classes with separate public sessions, more like the old academies, though under the administrative and financial umbrella of the Institute. Even the re-establishment by the Restoration government in 1816 of a single annual public showcase session for the four academies did not resurrect the Encyclopedist spirit. Nor did the abolition of the Second Class in 1803 elicit widespread protests about a gap in the Encyclopedic table of knowledge.

In other respects, the Institute contrasted less with the former academies than its founders envisaged. Before the Revolution the internal structures of the Paris Académie des Sciences and Académie des Inscriptions had mimicked the surrounding society with honorific member-patrons and senior "pensioners." The republican academic élite of 1795 nominally discarded all internal hierarchy and honorific members. Yet there was a quasi-honorific inactive contingent of retired military or naval officers and diplomats, especially in the Class of Moral and Political Sciences geography section. The Second Class even managed to evade the provisions of 1795 for equal state stipends for all members. A de facto hierarchy of seniority ensured that newly elected members of the Class subsidized the founding members through a differential scale of stipends from at least 1798 to 1803.

Even the social composition of the Class at first effectively minimized and concealed the Directory's punitive measures against counter-

Revolutionary aristocrats. The long-term trend towards a reduced clerical membership in the academies continued, but a surprising number of former nobles remained members and associates even through the crisis of the antiroyalist Fructidor coup. In a group that otherwise celebrated the triumph of the middle classes, the disproportionate persistence of aristocratic membership displayed in academic microcosm the much-remarked post-Revolutionary social fusion of former Second and Third Estate élites.[4] In addition, more than one-third of the members and associates were Ancien Régime celebrities who had achieved their greatest renown before election to the Institute and, in most cases, before 1789.

The political convictions of Class members were also not so solidly republican as might be expected. To the extent that legal prohibitions prevented overt royalism and that the election system most likely assured the exclusion of neo-Jacobins, the members and associates were a moderate republican élite. But there was still in the history and geography sections a surprising number of covert royalists, such as the noisy and troublesome Delisle de Sales. The sensitive issue of the reintegration of émigrés showed the limits of tolerance in 1800 for royalist aims. However, the reorganization of 1803 restored the remaining royalist exiles and soothed the consciences of people who held out, like the former refractory priest, J.-J. Garnier.

Academic culture included two equally strong, but opposed ideals – public utility to justify state sponsorship and the necessary independence of the man of letters. The ideal of an intellectual who advised and served government was not strictly compatible with the image of the independent heir to the philosophe. From its foundation the Class willingly adopted the familiar ideal of public service, that consultative mode already characteristic of Ancien Régime academies. The Institute was even more a creature of the state than the earlier bodies of savants which received royal charters.[5] The Directory asked the Institute to provide a questionnaire for the Egyptian expedition, and even Bonaparte's Navy ministry allowed the Institute to set the scientific agenda for Baudin's voyage to Australia. Interior Minister Lucien Bonaparte also promoted interest in public health and secular funeral ceremonies with an Institute prize contest in 1800, though the government would refuse to accept the contestants' prescriptions for civic morality. The Directory Legislative Councils encouraged cooperation with the Institute on issues of public education and public assistance, though financial difficulties sidetracked the more ambitious proposals. The Directory Interior ministry employed six members of the Auteuil circle to coordinate in the ten-seat Council of Public Instruction in 1799–1800 the curriculum and books of central (secondary) school teachers.[6] The Idéologues successfully aroused interest in Condillac and in the human sciences among teachers, but the demise of the central schools soon neutralized the Council's aims. In the atmosphere of the Concordat of 1801–2 the goal of secularizing the human sciences became anathema. The Church was a more efficient institution for reconciling believers to the existing social order.

The Consulate government generally used the talents of pliable individuals rather than the Class as a collective repository of expertise in the moral and political sciences. Second Consul Cambacérès, Bigot, and Merlin helped draft the Civil Code, Third Consul Lebrun was a financial adviser, Roederer and Degérando served the Interior ministry, Coquebert and Duvillard were statisticians, Talleyrand and Reinhard were diplomats, Lacuée was a military administrator, and Fleurieu worked in the Navy ministry. The assistance of such Idéologues as Sieyès and Cabanis in Bonaparte's coup of 1799 procured them high salaries as appointed senators but gave them neither effective political power nor fulfilment of their intellectual agenda. When a sensitive issue such as the re-establishment of slavery emerged in 1802, the antislavery opinion expressed by Grégoire and others in the Second Class carried little weight. The goals of secularization and civil liberty, despite conspicuous violations in coups and press restrictions, that were so prominent in the Directory, could not be the objectives of trusted advisers to Bonaparte.

Neither during the Ancien Régime nor after the Revolution could academies fully represent Jürgen Habermas's concept of a public sphere of equal, freely communicating citizens, which could, however, be applied to salons, the press, clubs, and the Masonic lodges. Because they were funded by the Crown or government Treasury, the academicians were not an independent élite. Yet they certainly interacted with the public space of the Republic of Letters. Except for a covert royalist minority, they promoted politically moderate republican views during the Directory, while struggling against the suffusion of public space with government propaganda during the Consulate.[7]

At the founding of the Institute, the image it projected, as expressed at a public session by Daunou and Grégoire, was that science and freedom were mutually reinforcing. Men of letters were independent, not subordinate to anyone. Science and learning could not flourish without freedom, while the self-correcting nature and spirit of scientific inquiry allegedly helped promote freedom and establish free political institutions. This ideal supposedly replaced the tainted royal supervision of Ancien Régime academies, which had always been at the mercy of a rarely practised royal veto on elections. However, the Directory's rapid purge of the Institute after the 1797 Fructidor coup and

Bonaparte's reorganization of 1803 mocked the idea of self-determining men of letters insulated from political winds of change. The reintegration of the Fructidor exiles was possible only when the First Consul no longer feared royalism. In 1805 the Emperor even humiliated astronomer Jérôme Lalande at a special session of the Institute, which enjoined him to cease publishing atheistic principles "destructive of all morality, if not in individuals, at least in nations."[8] The Emperor's heavy-handed attempt to censor Chateaubriand's reception speech in 1811 illustrated the potential for meddling, even when the majority of the Literature Class agreed on Chateaubriand's lack of tact.

Just as patronage had intruded upon the image of the autonomous Enlightenment philosophe, during the Revolution government imperatives disturbed a critical intellectual pose.[9] The Idéologues may have wished to be moralists in Lipset's sense, whereby they weighed all government policies in the balance of principles of moral and political sciences. In practice they wished to preserve the Directory against royalist and neo-Jacobin threats, and hence they became implicated in the compromises and excesses of the regime. Having cast their lot with Bonaparte in 1799 to further the search for political and social stability, they suffered alienation when he ignored the need they perceived for expertise in the social sciences. When they did not brood silently, they could revert to a moralistic intellectual stance in their writings, which they sometimes kept in the cabinet until after Bonaparte's fall. Their ambivalent desire for public service, however, often kept them in honorific or politically innocuous positions on the government payroll. In this relationship they found the role of secular priest or expert no longer available, and they could no longer legitimize an authority they contested. Yet the regime's censors and ministers who controlled government positions and pensions could silence any would-be prophet. The deist royalists, such as Delisle de Sales, or more politically conservative Institute members had to make similar compromises with Bonaparte as the best of evils, though an irrepressible spirit such as de Sales, with little but his Institute stipend to lose, tested the limits of tolerance for unconventional political opinion. The saga of intellectuals in this era, as in many other times, shows that they vacillated between the subservient consultant and the isolated, often intimidated critical voice.

While no one would contest the novelty of the very existence of the Class of Moral and Political Sciences, its composition, its academic culture, its notions of public utility, and its effective subordination to governments demonstrated significant similarities to pre-Revolutionary practice. The Class also conspicuously endorsed Enlightenment models for the social sciences but these could not survive the Revolution intact. In going beyond previous studies of the Idéologues as being in the era of the "sunset of Enlightenment" or as representative of the "Revolutionary consciousness," we have demonstrated the alteration of Enlightenment thought-patterns by specific Revolutionary events. Doctrines that once challenged Ancien Régime abuses and social privilege now articulated the urgent post-Revolutionary message of social stability. The Idéologues in the Class of Moral and Political Sciences had new motives for proclaiming the intervention of scientific reason in a society torn asunder by passions. Other former Enlightenment philosophes, such as Mercier, de Sales, and Bernardin de Saint-Pierre, sought a return to traditional moral virtues after the Jacobins had employed the very word virtue as a mask for the Terror. Their counter-Revolutionary colleagues in the history section sought the tranquillity of conventional religion as the firmest guarantee of social order.

Certain issues re-emerged in the post-Revolutionary period deceptively similar to those in late Enlightenment debates. Three out of the sixteen prize questions – on paternal authority, on the incidence of taxation on proprietors, and on founding public morality – repeated pre-Revolutionary academy prize subjects. The liberalization of Revolutionary family law had shifted attention from containing the abuses of the patriarchy of Roman law to reaffirming paternal control over wayward youth and women. Both secular and religious techniques for moralizing the people seemed more imperative after crowds in the streets had contested élite guidance. When budget deficits rose uncontrollably despite the shifting of the tax burden to land, economists reconsidered Physiocratic disdain for the burdensome retail commodity taxes of the Ancien Régime. The Class choice of prize contest questions also directly elicited solutions which could be studied by the Directory Councils or Bonaparte's Council of State. The paternal power contest coincided with the work of Civil Code framers, while the taxation contest followed debates during the Directory on re-establishing indirect taxes. Jury reform seemed urgent in 1800 at a time of apparent leniency to brigands. The prizewinner's view of propertied jurors actually resembled the final Council of State decision of 1808.

In theories of the mind, of morality, and of history the Institute Second Class reflected competing strategies for stabilizing the Revolution – the Idéologue route of secular moral and political sciences, the deist route of civic rituals promoting social solidarity, and the counter-Enlightenment return to the Catholic faith. Vocal opponents of secularization within the Class formed a discordant chorus in this supposed "fief of the Idéologues." Despite the eminent intellectual role the Idéologues played and their importance as Class secretaries and prize contest commissioners, they did not thoroughly control the agenda or elections. Non-Idéologue geography and history memoirs occupied much reading time in both private and public sessions, while the less politically active critics of the Idéologues, the theists Delisle de Sales, Bernardin de Saint-Pierre, and Mercier had more time to attend Class meetings.

The self-image of Idéologue hygienists was that they would be technicians of temperament – promoting social harmony by modifying the innate, possibly fractious inclinations of each individual temperament. Yet critics saw the enterprise of manipulating temperament without acknowledging an independent soul or will as irredeemably materialistic. Moreover, the metaphysical monism of Cabanis and Destutt de Tracy did not sway their younger colleagues Degérando and Laromiguière, who both recommended modifying Condillac's questionable transformed sensations model. For Maine de Biran only the personal experience of will could establish the self, the foundation of introspective psychology. Hence, internal disarray among the Idéologue circle over post-Revolutionary "materialism" complicated the Enlightenment project of a science of mind.

The replacement of priests by medical experts which Cabanis desired in the post-Revolutionary period raises Foucault's issues of the hierarchical gaze at patients and of normalizing judgments in clinic and asylum. There was always a potential for the manipulative abuse of power in the nineteenth-century asylum. Since the therapeutic capability of nineteenth-century physicians was severely limited, medical authority no doubt sometimes exceeded its legitimacy. Yet the moral treatment of the hygienists, which employed diet, regimen, exercise, and work, was less potentially harmful than heroic drug therapy.[10] The theory of temperament itself also did not require "normalizing" to a single correct model, and individual treatment always had to adjust to eccentricity.[11] However, the particularly rigid view of an indelible feminine temperament that hygienists held culturally construed the sensitivity of women so as to confine them to conventional gender roles in a private sphere. This was social stabilization with a vengeance. The promotion of sensitive, sympathetic temperaments for social harmony valued some feminine qualities, but did not advance the rights of women.

By the 1820s new statistical hygienists like Louis-René Villermé continued the correlation of physical environment and health.[12] The attacks by physiological determinist François-Joseph-Victor Broussais against introspective psychology maintained the importance of medical jurisdiction over mind, though by the time he endorsed the innate dispositions enumerated by phrenology in 1831 his vision of society was more hierarchical and organic than akin to Idéologue liberalism.[13]

Destutt de Tracy, Degérando, and some prize contestants metamorphosed Condillac's potentially democratic method of analysis of sensations into a dangerous tool against the primitive and uneducated. "Savages" with less refined sensations might need European tutelage, while the uneducated Frenchmen were unsuited for political rights or even for serving on juries. Hence, whatever Idéologue intentions, Volney's deduction of rights from needs of a sensitive being could justify withholding political rights from beings with as yet unrefined sensitivity.

The Revolution also helped cast doubt on Condillac's well-made language, despite the rush to construct synoptic tables and etymological dictionaries. Suppressing disagreements and misunderstandings by a perfect language seemed unrealistic after Revolutionary battles over meanings. Degérando pointedly urged philosophers to live virtuous lives rather than to try to invent perfect signs. In his view definitions in the moral and political sciences were too often either vacuous or tools of the powerful.

The most vocal critics of the Idéologues found the very idea of a secular moral science unacceptable. To Cabanis and Destutt de Tracy, a rationally indefensible religion only handicapped morality. Volney thought happiness under natural law almost infallibly assured benevolence towards others. For Mercier and Bernardin de Saint-Pierre, enlightenment of self-interest and cultivation of sympathy by education or legislation too easily became an immoral endorsement of greed or sensuality. Without celestial inspiration, self-sacrifice and heroic virtue would disappear. For converted Kantians like Mercier after 1800, virtue had to be a struggle of duty against inclination. Hence, after the Revolution there were still serious differences among adherents of various Enlightenment discourses on how much morality could become secular and scientific.

Deists such as La Revellière-Lépeaux rejected full secularization because of the perceived need of civic festivals for social solidarity. The Catholic Church had lost its privileged ethical jurisdiction. Yet, in the Consulate the competing, ultimately successful, government strategy for moral order was for a reconciliation with the Church tempered by religious toleration. Moralizing the people remained both a political and academic goal throughout the nineteenth century.[14]

While authors like Destutt de Tracy would have constructed moral science through natural law rather than history, almost all Institute historians agreed that history was a series of moral experiments, furnishing *exempla* for imitation or avoidance. The philosophical program of Condorcet and Volney sought historical guidance for linking culture and prosperity while preserving the principles of 1789. Acute political and religious divisions, however, crystallized in the debate on the Revolution itself as the fountainhead of vice. Counter-Revolutionary historians, awash in plot theories, wished to return to monarchy and Catholic doctrine. Anticlericals pointed to the allegedly pernicious influence of the clergy.

Like the geographers, economists, and political scientists, historians accepted the model of stages of civilization that linked mode of subsistence to complexity of society and refinement of culture. They were conscious of the unique features of each era, but showed no empathy with the unenlightened past. Lévesque's survey of three stages from savagery to civilization associated progress with social inequality and attempted to prove, as had Sieyès, the obsolescence of democracy. Hence, historical analysis would help stifle incipient popular revolutionism. While Burke and de Maistre would use historical tradition against natural law arguments, nineteenth-century liberal historians, such as François Guizot, François Mignet, and Augustin Thierry, turned history into a new anti-aristocratic instrument. For them, the historical emergence of the bourgeoisie represented a higher stage of civilization.[15] History could thus justify a government representing a new commercial and professional élite, rather than perpetuating aristocratic and corporate institutions.

Despite the opposition of many Class members to slavery, the prevailing four-stages model had the connotation of justifying the European mission of cultural diffusion, even if it did not condone crass commercial domination. Audiences at public sessions cheered the French civilizing mission around the globe. For Institute geographers, settled agricultural, propertied societies with social inequality were further advanced on the path to civilization than were hunting societies which could not display cultural refinement. This view consigned to myth both the golden age and the new Romantic idealization of the "savage."

The activities of Institute geographers continued the theoretical tradition of Montesquieu, Volney, and the physician-hygienists who correlated climate and topography with culture and politics. The Revolutionary imperative of human rights fostered an environmentalist theory of susceptibility of peoples to civilization rather than a more facile racism. For Volney, the disadvantages of a hunting society or of tyrannical government were even more critical than race or an unfavourable climate. Charting the interaction of climate and culture initiated the development of a qualitative statistical science and prefigured the human geography of Alexander von Humboldt and the late nineteenth-century regional topography of Vidal de la Blache.

The social and political implications of the stages-of-progress scheme justified a social hierarchy without aristocratic privilege or idleness.

Social inequality was part of the fabric of modern civilization, and the innovative, diligent middle classes, possessors of property and enlightenment, deserved to have political leadership in a modern commercial society. Whereas conservatives, including Germain Garnier and Delisle de Sales, repeated eighteenth-century fears of overeducation or blatantly proclaimed unequal rights to happiness, their more moderate colleagues Roederer and Cabanis envisaged historical progress through individual social mobility.

Montesquieu's descriptive, implicitly conservative approach to politics in various physical and cultural environments seemed excessively to justify the status quo in contrast to the social regeneration sought by Revolutionaries. But another aspect of Enlightenment political ideas, the apparently liberating doctrine of natural rights, could now be converted to a more conservative credo. Even in 1789 Sieyès's notion of the general will did not imply unlimited popular sovereignty. Functional limits on political rights, as compared to civil liberty for all citizens, prefigured the restricted electorate of 1795. Equal rights never implied social or economic equality. The institutional mechanisms of representative government and separation of powers, justified both by natural law and history, were the antidotes to obsolete, turbulent popular democracy. The vocabulary of utility was already used almost interchangeably with rights, but rights posed no threat of anarchy or disorder. The principles of 1789, for Idéologue thinkers like Sieyès, did not logically lead to the Terror, but rather to a balanced government run by propertied citizens.

A deductive science of politics searching for universally valid laws posed definite threats to individual rights. Especially from 1798 to 1801 Idéologues like Destutt de Tracy condoned a passive acceptance of political science formulated by experts, while Cabanis justified Bonaparte's 1799 constitution without a bill of rights. During the Directory, Baudin also unfurled the banner of natural law and representative government to attack allegedly illegitimate factions. In crises the Idéologues approved violations of the civil liberties of the press and of clubs. And Roederer's casual combination of Condillac's power of language and symbols with the calculations of Machiavelli could signal the dangerous use of moral and political sciences for state propaganda.

Idéologue scientism, however, did not ultimately negate the ideal of freedom.[16] In the late Empire and Restoration, Destutt de Tracy and Daunou gave new value to political dissent and civil liberties as necessary safeguards against despotic government. Tracy's mature concept of "democracy of enlightened reason" was not equivalent to technocracy. The language of "fundamental principles" and "individual guarantees" in practice validated the ideals of the Declaration of 1789. Hence, the Idéologues vacillated between a Saint-Simonian and pre-positivist deference to experts and a liberal defence of individual rights. The Idéologues' liberal and individualist social imagery rejected a frozen social hierarchy, at least for men. As Cheryl Welch has argued, it was not the Saint-Simonians but the liberals of the 1820s and 1830s, Auguste and Victorin Fabre, Armand Carrel, and the young Joseph Rey, who respected the political theory of Daunou and Tracy.[17]

For the Idéologues property was the basis of economic life as much as the indispensable prerequisite for political sovereignty. While the Physiocrats and Adam Smith both opposed Ancien Régime privilege and monopoly, the defence of property after 1795 discouraged a revival of the claims of the sans-culottes to an "equality of satisfactions." The principle of freeing the market-place, previously upsetting to mercantilists and defenders of just prices for the poor, now made incentives to all producers the basis of prosperity.

The general interest in the stages of social development by 1795 divided disciples of the Physiocrats, who viewed agricultural society as the culmination of civilization, from partisans of a fully commercial society. For the Physiocrats, only the net product of land produced wealth and was fit for taxation. Their opponents, like Roederer, idealized mobile property and admitted that taxation should be imposed on all capital returns. Destutt de Tracy, following J.-B. Say, made entrepreneurial skill the lifeblood of the economy. By the Restoration, there were definite political overtones to such views, which pitted aristocrats against non-landed financiers, merchants, or professionals. In seeking to accelerate the social acceptability of merchants and industrialists and in heralding the entrepreneurial age, Institute economists were not wishing for social upheaval, only for recognition of the wealth produced by all forms of capital.

The science of political economy preserved the Physiocratic ideal of a complete science of government. J.-B. Say's aspiration for a value-free technical science ran afoul of residual ethical commitments. For disciples of both the Physiocrats and Smith, virtuous saving and prudence, the foundations of political economy, extended to moral condemnations of wasteful luxury and extravagant public debt.[18] The market-place itself would work against existing inequality, while liberalized inheritance laws would discourage the consolidation of great fortunes. Entrepreneurial risk might yield productive results, while government debt promoted the indolence of creditors. Proponents of nineteenth-century *laissez-faire* liberalism still castigated unproductive public debt and government spending, but there were generally fewer moral qualms about the costs of economic growth, with the exception

of child labour. By the mid-nineteenth century, even non-socialist philosophers and historians expressed reservations about an economics
that was uncontrolled by ethics.

In political science and economics, Institute authors sought to reconcile social order and progress. As a component of Enlightenment
political theory and economics, the program of individual rights and
free trade would have been a reformist challenge to the Ancien Régime.
In the Revolutionary context after 1795, the defence of property and
social hierarchy was a message of stability to safeguard against another
round of social revolution. The head of Minerva radiated this conso-
lation of social harmony, not further strife.

THE SUPPRESSION OF THE CLASS

Most accounts of the Class of Moral and Political Sciences have
accepted Jules Simon's traditional explanation of its abolition on
23 January 1803: "Bonaparte kicked it because it troubled him. That
is the judgment of contemporaries and it will be that of history."[19]
Certainly, the suppression of the Class would have been unimaginable
without Idéologue opposition to Bonaparte on civil liberties and the
Concordat. Their opposition in the Senate to the unjustified deportation of neo-Jacobins and their protests in the Tribunate against special
tribunals for brigands and political criminals resulted in police surveillance of Idéologue coteries.

Bonaparte then could castigate the Idéologues, a word that had been
coined by the royalist press early in 1800. Disdain for the Auteuil circle
was evident in an article inspired by Bonaparte in the *Journal de Paris*,
which complained about the "twelve or fifteen obscure metaphysicians" who "believed themselves a party" and dared challenge the First
Consul – "making long speeches they think perfidious, but which are
only ridiculous."[20] More concretely, the Interior ministry dissolved the
Council of Public Instruction in 1800, the Senate failed to re-elect
Ginguené, Chénier, Daunou, and Laromiguière to the Tribunate in
March 1802, and the Legislative Body ratified the Concordat in April
1802 and abolished the central schools in May 1802. Bonaparte's
correspondence with conservative newspaper editor Joseph Fiévée suggests that the Institute needed to be "gagged, but not too rudely," since
the Idéologues sought to overturn traditional values.[21]

Bonaparte's vendetta against the Idéologues was, however, only one
motive for reorganizing the Institute. Historians had long felt that the
old Académie des Inscriptions had been torn asunder. Its former permanent secretary, Dacier, helped reform the Institute, and Delisle de
Sales anticipated some features of Chaptal's plan.[22] Men of letters

hoped to revive academic literary culture. In fact, despite Bonaparte's rejection of a new Académie française, some survivors were receiving government pensions.[23] In November 1800 Chaptal planned a new eloquence section in the Institute and lamented the "excessive neglect of ancient languages." He thought that the eulogies of a permanent secretary would also revive an honoured literary form.

A strange article appeared in Roederer's *Mémoires d'économie publique* in 1800 under the heading: "Sceptical considerations on our moral sciences." Even after thirty years of study, claimed the author, he found no agreement by moralists on how to reach happiness. A happy person was more likely to be a "robust, merry peasant, who is sooner cured of sorrows than the melancholy philosopher." Like Degérando, he saw only misunderstanding from "all our abuses of language." Hence, moral science was like a "labyrinth, where a thousand blind men, each having in their hands a thread they believe unbreakable, wander, for a long time, jostling each other, but end up at their point of departure."[24]

As Speaker of the Council of State to the Legislative Body in May 1802, Roederer denied the need to teach legislation in the schools, for the "state should not teach sciences [that are] not mature, well-defined, or recognized, and whose methods are still diverse and uncertain." Moreover, the danger of critical thinking was apparent to this servant of Bonaparte: it was "not good for the state to have a large number of men who believe they have a right to pretend to [know] all."[25]

Yet the suppression of human sciences from the school curriculum was not a foregone conclusion. In August 1802 Roederer, as Director-General of Public Instruction, submitted an elaborate *lycée* curriculum plan for the teaching of the *sciences métaphysiques* (in one draft they were even named *sciences idéologiques*) of morality, law, political economy, statistical geography, and history. Even more remarkably, the final two years in the plan featured Destutt de Tracy's favourite subjects, analysis of the faculties of the understanding, theory of the art of speaking and writing, and logic. Perhaps Roederer was privately more sympathetic to the human sciences in this last gasp of the Encyclopedist ideal. In any case, the commission on Latin literature for *lycées* in 1803 included only old-style grammar and logic, although the University Council in 1809 reintroduced a philosophy chair under its general parameters of compatibility with religion.[26] Legislation totally vanished from the secondary school curriculum, and even elements of natural law and French public law did not appear in the École de Droit curriculum of 1804.[27] History fared better in the schools because Bonaparte valued military and legal history, as well as the potential glorification of his dynasty.[28]

Clearly the greatest scepticism and opposition to the human sciences came from conservative thinkers. The pro-Catholic *Journal des Débats* separated happiness from scientific progress and attacked Degérando's moral philosophy as too secular.[29] In reviewing Cabanis's *Rapports du physique et du moral de l'homme*, the *Mercure* lamented the "absence of morality if all our reactions are produced by internal or external impressions." The author wondered if sugar promoted social affections, and coffee, benevolence and philanthropy.[30]

Further attacking materialism, the *Gazette de France* argued that it necessarily leads to the amorality of a Marquis de Sade.[31] This interpretation is a stronger version of the modern critique of the Enlightenment by Lester Crocker – the view that materialism created the conditions for the emergence of a philosophy like that of Sade. In the spring of 1800 the *Gazette* editors were scandalized to see that in pushing the "consequences of Helvétius's views on virtue to their end results, an author has produced in the name of Justine, or the Misfortunes of Virtue, the most execrable conception that has ever dishonoured the world of letters."[32]

The critique of materialism accompanied the arguments for a reaffirmation of eloquence. In October 1801 the *Journal des Débats* thought that the absence of great poets in the Institute was correlated to the "dangerous ascendancy of metaphysics and the exact sciences in scholarly companies."[33] We have previously quoted Roederer's argument in his public instruction report of 1802 for a Class of the Institute "constituted for the decent, systematic praise of the government."[34] These conservative and administrative goals reinforced the aims of former Enlightenment philosophes Delisle de Sales and Morellet to promote history and eloquence. In short, the demise of the Class was assisted by lukewarm philosophes who had been frightened, even in 1789, by the Revolution as well as by conservative enemies of the Enlightenment.

There were few controversial utterances in Class publications to provoke the First Consul. The 1802 prize contest on the Reformation did not contradict Portalis, the minister of cults who had introduced the Concordat with praise for religious tolerance. Moreover, the government exerted no effort to prevent the successor of the Class of Moral and Political Sciences, the Class of History and Ancient Literature, from judging in 1804 the contest on the Reformation.

Chaptal's report of January 1803 never even mentioned the Class of Moral and Political Sciences.[35] He first advocated separate public sessions and permanent secretaries. Accepting Morellet's charges, Chaptal also indicted the "mediocre men" holding the "sceptre of literature." He warned that the absence of eloquence had been a "dangerous influence on the fate of letters, corrupting the lessons of great writers, drying up the sources of true erudition, displacing the arbiters and destroying the authorities of good taste."[36] Chaptal intended, by recalling the survivors of the old Académie française and reintegrating the Fructidor exiles, to create a "durable peace in the Republic of Letters" and to enforce respect of the older generation.[37]

However, all was not harmonious in the supposedly reconciled company. Marie-Joseph Chénier's progress report, *Tableau du progrès de la littérature française* (1808), celebrated the achievements of the Idéologues so much that it was not published until the Restoration.[38] In 1810 the new Class of French Language and Literature had to satisfy both advocates and critics of eighteenth-century ideas by giving a joint award after five long rounds of a prize contest on the "Literary portrait of eighteenth-century France." In 1811 the Class as as whole, after a split on its public session commission, prohibited Chateaubriand from reading his reception speech after his election. In a blatant violation of academic custom, he had proposed indecorously to criticize his predecessor, Chénier, for regicide opinions and had also implied that he was responsible for the guillotining of his brother, poet André Chénier. The Emperor personally ordered alterations to the speech, but Chateaubriand refused to edit it or to read it in closed session. Later that year the Emperor hoped the Institute would mollify Chateaubriand with a decennial prize in literature for his *Le Génie du Christianisme*. However, the Class of French Language and Literature refused the Interior minister's suggestion to nominate Chateaubriand for a literature prize, on the ostensible grounds that there was no category for a combined work of literature and philosophy. Chateaubriand never attended the Institute sessions during the Empire.[39]

In the Third Class of History and Ancient Literature most of the old apolitical Académie des Inscriptions group could cheerfully carry on their work with little concern for the outward organization. Bouchaud's series of memoirs on Roman law had begun in the Académie des Inscriptions in 1777, and Pastoret re-read in 1804 an ancient history memoir of 1792.[40] Gosselin, a specialist in ancient navigation near Asia and Africa, linked the old and new Inscriptions academies with a series of memoirs beginning in 1791 and ending in 1826 through four different academic regimes.[41]

The rules of the new Class of History and Ancient Literature illustrated the triumph of the Académie des Inscriptions ethos of 1786, when regulations provided that "no term of scorn or bitterness will be used [by members] against each other in speeches or writings." In 1803 the internal regulations of the Class stated that "those members occupied with research relative to these [sciences] will avoid in their memoirs any historical, religious, or political discussions, which, by their object or proximity in time, can disturb the harmony which must prevail among the members of the Class."[42] There could be no greater sign that academic culture was intact.

THE RESURRECTION OF THE MORAL AND POLITICAL SCIENCES

The decline of Idéologue élan did not mean that early nineteenth-century thinkers abandoned the desire to apply scientific method to human beings and society. In addition, while devoutly Catholic thinkers always questioned the idea of secular ethics, the threat of revolution as a viable option in France accentuated the desire to moralize systematically the people. So, although outsiders like Saint-Simon and Auguste Comte carried on the project of a social science, a diverse group of liberals at the University wished after 1830 to restore a moral and political sciences academy.

The paradox of early nineteenth-century liberals was that their desire for social stability did not outweigh their concern to preserve the Revolutionary settlement of constitutional government, unprivileged inheritance, and religious toleration. Consequently, partisans of the social sciences became stalwarts of political opposition after 1815. Restoration liberals used slogans of individual freedom against religious and political despotism, though they would have repressed social disorder as much as the aristocratic and clerical oligarchy.

The human sciences now reappeared in the private forum of the Athénée royal (formerly the Lycée), in the Conservatoire des Arts et Métiers, and in the Collège de France.[43] On at least four occasions a group of Restoration liberals, linked through salons or newspaper editorial offices, discussed the re-establishment of a new society of moral and political sciences, with prominent participation of former members of the Auteuil circle and with divisions resembling the old Class of Moral and Political Sciences. Benjamin Constant, deputy and political analyst, hosted the fourth and longest-lived project for a society from the spring of 1826 to late in 1828 or early 1829. This group overlapped in membership with the electoral lobby for liberal candidates, Paris history lecturer François Guizot's Aide-toi, le Ciel t'aidera society, which also had as members deputy Victor de Broglie, historian of the Revolution and moderate liberal François Mignet, philosopher Victor Cousin, liberal economists Charles Comte and Charles Dunoyer, and lawyer Odilon-Barrot.[44]

By 1829 Guizot had certainly arrived at the conviction that the moral and political sciences had laws just like the physical sciences.[45]

His Sorbonne history lectures, resumed in 1828 after six years of interruption by the government, updated the four-stages theory to include the class struggle of the triumphant bourgeoisie with the aristocracy.[46] Meanwhile, Charles Comte, who was J.-B. Say's son-in-law, and Charles Dunoyer developed in the pages of the *Censeur européen* in 1817–18 a philosophy of "industrialism," which advocated the rule by manufacturers, merchants, and financiers. In the mid-1820s these were all decidedly anti-aristocratic doctrines that were directed against the political élite, though without sympathy for industrial workers. The attack on the idle ruling class resembled Saint-Simon's condemnation of the idle and support of all productive agents whom he termed *industriels*.[47]

Despite his opposition to the heritage of the Idéologues, Cousin discussed with Degérando in 1830 the possibility of restoring an academy of moral and political sciences. Continuing social unrest in Paris and Lyon made social stabilization again an urgent necessity. In January 1832 Roederer suggested to King Louis-Philippe that the new regime could benefit from a restored academy of moral and political sciences. "This institution should place in a respected body the authority of political science, which is so popular among schoolboys [but] which lacks a rallying point for healthy doctrines in France or a centre for discussing and examining new ideas." Similarly, the deputy Charles Comte argued one month later that such an academy could correct errors in the press, and conduct research into "healthy systems of ethics."[48]

Guizot's program as minister of public education in the new cabinet of October 1832 included primary education, historical publications, and the foundation of a new academy to help direct intellectual and cultural life. He conceived the academy not as a direct agent of government; rather, as he wrote in his memoirs, "learned societies give a healthy direction to elevated and enlightened intelligence, a salutary influence for the benefit of a sound intellectual position and can lend to a power wise enough to maintain intelligent relations with them, an indirect or useful support."[49]

In the preface to the founding decree of 26 October 1832, Guizot reiterated his confidence in the moral and political sciences, which were now "supported on certain data, rigorous, and positive." No government need fear these sciences because the "stability of our Charter can withstand speculative errors." Furthermore, one would not foresee continued conflict between religion and philosophy: "reason is honoured to consolidate the foundation of the most noble beliefs of humanity, and the moral and political sciences will henceforth serve (one can hope) to make firmer what they once shook."[50] When founded, the new Academy of Moral and Political Sciences reintegrated all the survivors of the old Second Class.[51]

While the Academy investigated troubling social problems of labour and poverty, population and statistical demography, education, and commerce, its members were notably reluctant to criticize the government administration.[52] A topos of the speeches by Academy presidents was the reminder that it was not a governing body.[53] When in 1848 the chief executive, Eugène Cavaignac, asked the Academy to write "little treatises" on the sanctity of property and the family, both socialists and conservatives criticized it for surrendering its pose of neutrality.

The new Academy, like the Second Class before it, played on the themes of freedom and control. Dedicated to economic freedom and civil liberty, its nineteenth-century members most definitely spoke for the triumph of the middle classes and therefore the discipline of artisans and industrial workers. Economic freedom could be seen as a force for social stability in that it allowed the strongest economic actors to maintain their domination. There were few occasions of dissent from the reigning economic orthodoxy, though a notable exception was the "Christian political economy" of Alban de Villeneuve-Bargemont.[54] At no time before 1848 were academicians receptive to universal male suffrage, much less female suffrage.

The compatibility of free-market economics with ethics remained a sensitive issue. As Charles Dunoyer and Adolphe Franck consolidated the *laissez-faire* position through the *Journal des économistes*, established in 1841, scepticism grew among their academic colleagues, such as Mignet and Cousin. Mignet wondered whether more schools and the regulation of child labour were necessary to avoid industrial materialism. Cousin feared that the economists' materialism would itself provoke socialism, and he cautiously advocated state participation in poor relief and state leadership in both instruction and moral education. He wondered aloud if self-interest was the key to durable moral foundations of society. To his colleague Joseph Droz, he commented, late in 1847, "Let's raise political economy to ethics, but let's not drag down ethics to political economy."[55] Hence, the relative role of pure political economy in relation to ethics remained a vital question in the mid-nineteenth century.

Minerva's message of social stability remained crucial. The durability of the academic ethos is obvious still in 1983 in the statement of the Academy's permanent secretary, Bernard Chenot. He celebrated the academic "calm, where, dominated by the spirit of reason dear to the Encyclopedists, the Academy approached subjects ... in serenity, thanks to a style of work in which perfect courtesy is the supreme elegance, thanks to a reserve which, in safeguarding the zone of action of governments, obligates them to respect our independence." While no longer in the avant-garde of research, the Academy investigates problems of the highest social importance and urgency, though it has "never taken itself for a Council of State or for a political or judicial Parliament." And so, under the majestic cupola of the Palais des Quatre Nations across from the Louvre on the Left Bank of the Seine, the Academy still discusses educational reform, problems of housing and urbanization, bioethics, public assistance, rights of prisoners, violence and group aggression, labour conditions, capital punishment, international law, foreign aid, international monetary relations, economic growth, and the problems of the Paris region.[56]

Any analysis of the emergence of the social sciences in the Enlightenment and Revolutionary eras cannot avoid the notorious contention of Michel Foucault that the ostensibly liberating knowledge of human beings and society arose only amid expert practices of disciplinary control, hierarchical relationships, normalizing judgments, and a penchant for surveillance. Our entire argument has certainly reinforced the links between the construction of knowledge and the preservation of social and political power. The hope of some Institute academicians for a universal morality could lead to tendentious, manipulative claims about both health and ethics. Similarly, the search for the one correct answer in the deductive sciences of politics and economics could stifle dissent through the power to define universal human nature. The dangers in the human sciences ever since their emergence have been their use as rationales for the infallibility of government, private employers, and the experts themselves in manipulating and dominating the weak. Too frequently, politically and socially dominant groups used nineteenth-century social sciences to belittle or exploit the human potential of women, ethnic or racial minorities, and inmates of prisons and asylums.

The idea of the existence of general laws of the social sciences may be moribund. Apart from some economists and philosophers of science, few enthusiasts in the social sciences or in the historical profession believe in a single objective truth or in universal laws independent of particular culture and perspective.[57] The demise of positivist empiricism in the natural sciences has meant increasingly the belief that facts are theory-laden and explanations value-laden.

The expected logical conclusion is that the emergence of the social sciences fostered a misplaced faith in emulating the knowledge and approaches of the natural sciences, flawed as they themselves were. But such an estimate of the state of the natural sciences is, to say the least, premature. The elements of social construction in all scientific theories do not reduce them all to mere ideology or invalidate them for their limited puzzle-solving purposes. Moreover, verification of the historical misuse of power that is implicated in the formation of "social scientific" knowledge does not imply the supremacy of some other "hermeneutic" or "conversational" approach. Must "social sciences" inevitably be used for an exploitative will to power without the production of any true "knowledge"? There is no need to idealize the Enlightenment project to cast doubt on the expected answer.

Foucault's critique of the emergence of social sciences by no means solves the problems of social cohesion and discipline in modern societies, even if only non-universalizable solutions are now deemed possible. An empathetic or hermeneutic approach may arouse necessary compassion, but provides insufficient rationale for policymaking. Given pluralistic societies that tolerate divergent moral codes, governments would abdicate all aspirations to inspiring public purpose unless they can provide some "examinations and investigations" with testable information on the human condition. One might turn Foucault's perspective around to ask whether there is any hope for those who are marginal, illiterate, or handicapped without some kind of psychological study that tailors programs to their individual needs. In a purely competitive power struggle among interest groups, the marginal could easily be foreordained to lose to the dominant; for example, current backlashes against employment equity and affirmative action testify to dangers. Sifting through the conflicting advice of experts who are sensitized to human diversity and suffering might just be a preferable choice.

Faced with the need for assisting individual learning and motivation and for explaining the boundaries between the physiological and the cultural, a human science of psychology is likely to survive. In the swamps of public policymaking, governments still feel the need for the informed advice of expert economists (can one imagine designing a health care policy or a budget without them?) and political scientists. Whether or not government is considered an art or a science, if it genuinely aspires to solve social problems it will require more solid evidence from a professional élite than empty slogans designed to maintain a ruling party in power. Philosophical conversations of the kind advocated by such neo-pragmatist philosophers as Richard Rorty speak vainly across ever widening chasms, rather than arbitrate among interest groups. The moral and political sciences which emerged so triumphantly in the eighteenth century are therefore likely to endure in a less pretentious form, despite the attack of post-modernists and hermeneutic theorists.

APPENDIX I
Joseph Lakanal's List of Nominees for the Class of Moral and Political Sciences for Consideration by the National Convention, October 1795 (cancelled by the Directory)

SECTION 1
ANALYSIS OF SENSATIONS AND IDEAS

D.-J. Garat, P.-C.-F. Daunou

SECTION 2
ETHICS

J.-H. Bernardin de Saint-Pierre, L.-S. Mercier

SECTION 3
SOCIAL SCIENCE AND LEGISLATION

E.-J. Sieyès, J.-A.-C. Gallois

SECTION 4
POLITICAL ECONOMY

P.-S. Dupont, Anne-François-Joachim Fréville

SECTION 5
HISTORY

J.-J. Garnier, L.-P. Anquetil

SECTION 6
GEOGRAPHY

Alexandre-Gui Pingré, J.-N. Buache

Members and Associates of the Class of Moral and Political Sciences, Established in 1795

Listed in the order of their nomination by the Directory on 20 November 1795 or by the date of their election

SECTION 1, ANALYSIS OF SENSATIONS AND IDEAS
Members: Constantin-François Chassebeuf de Volney,[1,2,10] Dominique-Joseph Garat,[1,2,10] Joachim-Jean Lebreton,[2a] Alexandre Deleyre, Pierre-Louis Ginguené,[2] Pierre-Jean-Georges Cabanis,[2] François-Emmanuel Toulongeon[4]
Associates: Antoine-Louis-Claude Destutt de Tracy,[2,4] Paul-Victor de Sèze,[2a] Pierre Laromiguière,[2] Louis-Marie-Joseph-Maximilien Caffarelli du Falga,[4] —— Sicard, Frédéric-François-Venceslas Jacquemont,[2a] Joseph-Marie Degérando,[2] Pierre Prévost

SECTION 2, ETHICS
Members: Jacques-Henri Bernardin de Saint-Pierre,[1,10] Louis-Sébastien Mercier,[1] Henri Grégoire,[9] Louis-Marie La Revellière-Lépeaux,[9] Jacques-André Naigeon, Joseph Lakanal[9]
Associates: Pierre Roussel,[2] Michel-Guillaume-Jean, dit Saint-John de Crèvecœur, Jean-Gervais Labène, Dominique Ricard, Alexandre-Louis Villeterque,[4] François Ferlus, Jacques-Maurice Gaudin

SECTION 3, SOCIAL SCIENCE AND LEGISLATION
Members: Pierre-Claude-François Daunou,[1,2] Jean-Jacques Régis de Cambacérès,[1,9] Philippe-Antoine Merlin de Douai,[9] Claude-Emmanuel-Joseph-Pierre de Pastoret,[3,9] Jean-Philippe Garran-Coulon,[9] Pierre-Charles-

Louis Baudin des Ardennes,[9] Jean-François Champagne, Félix-Julien-Jean Bigot de Préameneu[9]
Associates: Louis-Auguste Legrand-Laleu, David Houard,[3] Julien Raimond, Louis-François-Élisabeth Ramond de Carbonnières, Philippe-Antoine Grouvelle,[2a] Félix-Julien-Jean Bigot de Préameneu,[7] Ruffin-Castus Massa[9]

SECTION 4, POLITICAL ECONOMY
Members: Emmanuel-Joseph Sieyès,[1,2] Jacques-Antoine Creuzé-Latouche,[1,9] Charles-Maurice de Talleyrand,[5,9] Pierre-Louis Roederer,[2] Jean-Gérard Lacuée,[4,9] Pierre-Samuel Du Pont de Nemours,[9] Charles-François Lebrun[9]
Associates: François Véron de Forbonnais, Jean-Antoine-Cauvin Gallois,[2a] Germain Garnier,[9] Emmanuel-Étienne Duvillard de Durand, Antoine Diannyère, Philippe-Rose Roume de Saint-Laurent

SECTION 5, HISTORY
Members: Jean-Baptiste-Claude-Izouard Delisle de Sales,[1] Pierre-Charles Lévesque,[1,3] Louis-Pierre Anquetil,[3a] Guillaume-Thomas Raynal, Bon-Joseph Dacier,[3] Gabriel-Henri Gaillard,[3,8] Mathieu-Antoine Bouchaud,[3] Pierre-Jean-Baptiste Legrand d'Aussy, Germain Poirier[3]
Associates: Pierre-Louis Gaillard, Christophe-Guillaume de Koch, Edme Gautier de Sibert,[3] Jean Senebier, Jean-Jacques Garnier,[3] Jean-Pierre Papon, Paul-Philippe Gudin de la Brenellerie

SECTION 6, GEOGRAPHY
Members: Jean-Nicolas Buache de la Neuville,[1,6,10] Edme Mentelle,[1,10] Carl-Friedrich Reinhard,[5] Charles-Pierre d'Eveux Claret de Fleurieu,[4] Paschal-François-Joseph Gosselin,[3] Louis-Antoine de Bougainville[4]
Associates: Pierre-Joseph de Beauchamp, Jean-François de Bourgoing,[5] Jean-René-Antoine Verdun de la Crenne,[4] Jean-Claude Éléonor Le Michaud d'Arçon,[4] Guillaume-Jacques-Constant de Liberge de Granchain de Semerville,[4] François de Barthélemy,[5] Daniel Lescallier,[5] Nicolas-Charles Romme,[6] Charles-Étienne Coquebert de Montbret[5]

Legend
1 Nominated by the Directory
2 Idéologues, defined as authors of a major work in medical or philosophical Ideology or in elements of ethics, politics, economics, and having at least two of the following attributes: (1) attendance at the salons of Mme Helvétius, Destutt de Tracy, or Mme de Condorcet in the period 1794–1809; (2) on the staff of or a contributor to *La Décade philosophique*; (3) and moderate republican after 1794 and in opposition to Bonaparte after 1801

2a Member of the Auteuil circle
3 Former member of the Académie royale des Inscriptions et Belles-Lettres
3a Correspondent of the Académie royale des Inscriptions et Belles-Lettres
4 Active or retired military officer
5 Diplomatic service or colonial administration
6 Navy connections
7 Associate and later elected member
8 Declined position as full member but became associate
9 Member of a non-Idéologue politically active group
10 École normale lecturer in 1795

DIRECTORY NOMINATIONS
Volney, Garat, Bernardin de Saint-Pierre, Mercier, Daunou, Cambacérès, Sieyès, Creuzé-Latouche, Delisle de Sales, Lévesque, Buache de la Neuville, Mentelle

IDÉOLOGUES
Volney, Garat, Ginguené, Cabanis, Destutt de Tracy, Laromiguière, Degérando, Roussel, Daunou, Sieyès, Roederer

AUTEUIL CIRCLE
Volney, Garat, Lebreton, Ginguené, Cabanis, Destutt de Tracy, de Sèze, Laromiguière, Degérando, Jacquemont, Roussel, Daunou, Sieyès, Roederer, Grouvelle, Gallois

PATRONAGE APPOINTMENTS BY MEMBERS OF THE AUTEUIL
CIRCLE (sponsor's name followed by names of appointees)
Sieyès: Roederer, Grouvelle, Laromiguière, Reinhard, Lakanal
Garat: Cabanis, Grouvelle, Laromiguière
Cabanis: de Sèze, Roussel
Ginguené: Le Breton, Grouvelle, Jacquemont
Roederer: Villeterque

FORMER MEMBERS AND CORRESPONDENTS OF THE ACADÉMIE
ROYALE DES INSCRIPTIONS ET BELLES-LETTRES
Pastoret, Houard, Lévesque, Anquetil, Dacier, Gaillard, Bouchaud, Poirier, Gautier de Sibert, J.-J. Garnier, Gossellin

MILITARY AND DIPLOMATIC SERVICE ÉLITE
Toulongeon, Caffarelli du Falga, Villeterque, Lacuée, Buache de la Neuville, Reinhard, Fleurieu, Bougainville, Coquebert de Montbret, Bourgoing,

Verdun de la Crenne, Le Michaud d'Arçon, de Liberge de Granchain, Barthélemy, Lescallier

PATRONAGE APPOINTMENTS BY MEMBERS OF THE MILITARY AND DIPLOMATIC SERVICE ÉLITE (sponsor's name followed by names of appointees)
Carnot and Lacepède: Lacuée
Lacuée: Toulongeon
Buache de la Neuville: Fleurieu
Borda, Pingré, and Fleurieu: Verdun de la Crenne, Liberge de Granchain
Talleyrand: Reinhard, Le Michaud d'Arçon
Monge: Caffarelli du Falga
Fourcroy, Monge, Berthollet, and Guyton: Coquebert
Lalande: Romme

MEMBERS OF A NON-IDÉOLOGUE POLITICALLY ACTIVE GROUP
Cambacérès, Creuzé-Latouche, Grégoire, La Revellière-Lépeaux, Lakanal, Merlin, Garran-Coulon, Baudin, Bigot, Massa, Talleyrand, Du Pont, Lebrun, G. Garnier

MEMBERS AND ASSOCIATES IN MORE THAN ONE CATEGORY (political-Idéologue, political-military, or Military–Idéologue)
Garat, Cabanis, Siéyes, Daunou, Roederer, Lacuée

OTHER MEMBERS APPOINTED THROUGH PATRONAGE (sponsor's name followed by names of appointees)
La Revellière-Lépeaux (as Director): Bernardin de Saint-Pierre
Bernardin de Saint-Pierre and Sieyès: Lakanal
Lakanal: Ferlus
Sicard: Ricard
Grégoire and Garran-Coulon: Raimond
Creuzé-Latouche and Lacuée: Diannyère
Du Pont: Gudin
Creuzé-Latouche and Garran-Coulon: Roume de Saint-Laurent

APPENDIX 3
The National Institute after
the Reorganization of 1803

CLASS OF FRENCH LANGUAGE AND LITERATURE
Members carried forward from the Class of Moral and Political Sciences
Idéologues: Volney, Garat, Cabanis, Sieyès
Bonapartist Opportunists: Roederer, Cambacérès, Bigot, Merlin, Lacuée
Others: Bernardin de Saint-Pierre, Naigeon

Members carried forward from the Class of Literature and Fine Arts
Idéologues: François-Guillaume-Jean-Stanislas Andrieux, Marie-Joseph Chénier
Grammarians: François-Urbain Domergue, Roch-Ambroise Sicard
Others: Gabriel Villar, Nicolas François de Neufchâteau, Jean-François Cailhava, Ponce-Denis Lebrun-Écouchard, Jean-François Ducis, Jean-François Collin-Harleville, Gabriel-Marie-Jean-Baptiste Le Gouvé, Antoine-Vincent Arnault

Reintegrated Fructidor exile
Louis Fontanes

Returned émigrés
Jean-François de la Harpe, Jacques Delille

Survivors of the Académie française of 1793
Jean-François Saint-Lambert, Jean-Baptiste-Antoine Suard, André Morellet, Guy-Jean-Baptiste Target, Stanislas-Jean Boufflers, Claude de Thyard, Comte de Bissy, Jean-Armand de Bessuejoules, Comte de Roquelaure, Jean de Dieu-

Raymond de Boisgelin de Cuce, Henri Cardin Jean-Baptiste de Fresnes, Comte d'Aguesseau

Government officials
Lucien Bonaparte, Jean Devaines, Louis-Philippe Ségur, Jean-Étienne-Marie Portalis, Michel-Louis-Étienne Regnaud de Saint-Jean-d'Angély

CLASS OF HISTORY AND ANCIENT LITERATURE
(as listed in the government decree of 28 January 1803)
Carried Forward from the Class of Moral and Political Sciences

Bon-Joseph Dacier
Charles-François Lebrun
Germain Poirier
Louis-Pierre Anquetil
Mathieu-Antoine Bouchaud
Pierre-Charles Lévesque
Pierre-Samuel Du Pont
Pierre-Charles-François Daunou
Edme Mentelle
Charles Reinhard
Charles-Maurice Talleyrand
Pascal-François-Joseph Gossellin

Pierre-Louis Ginguené
Jean Delisle de Sales
Jean-Philippe Garran de Coulon
Jean-François Champagne
Joseph Lakanal
François-Emmanuel Toulongeon
Joachim Lebreton
Henri Grégoire
Louis-Marie La Revellière-Lépeaux
Louis-Sébastien Mercier
Jean-Jacques Garnier

Carried Forward from the Class of Literature and Fine Arts

Paul-Jérémie Bitaubé
François-Jean-Gabriel Laporte du Theil
Marie-Charles-Joseph Pougens
Antoine Mongez
Gaspard-Michel Le Blond
Armand-Gaston Camus

Louis-Mathieu Langlès
Pierre-Henri Larcher
Jean-Baptiste-Gaspard Villoison
Charles-François Dupuis
Hubert-Pascal Ameilhon

Survivors from the Académie royale des Inscriptions et Belles-Lettres
Abraham-Hyacinthe Anquetil-Duperron, Antoine-Isaac Silvestre de Sacy, Guillaume-Emmanuel-Joseph-Guilhem Sainte-Croix, Marie-Gabriel-Auguste-Florent, Comte de Choiseul-Gouffier, Gabriel-Henri Gaillard (also an associate of the Class of Moral and Political Sciences)

APPENDIX 4
Members of the Class of Moral and Political Sciences Carried Over into the Revived Academy of Moral and Political Sciences in 1832

	Section Membership in the Class of Moral and Political Sciences	Section Membership in the Academy of Moral and Political Sciences, 1832
Garat	Analysis of sensations and ideas	Ethics
Tracy	Analysis of sensations and ideas	Philosophy
Laromiguière	Analysis of sensations and ideas	Philosophy
Prévost	Analysis of sensations and ideas	Philosophy
Degérando	Analysis of sensations and ideas (Associate)	Philosophy
Lakanal	Ethics	Ethics
Daunou	Social Science and legislation	Legislation, public law, and jurisprudence
Merlin	Social Science and legislation	Legislation, public law, and jurisprudence
Pastoret	Social Science and legislation	History (declined seat)
Sieyès	Political economy	Political economy and statistics
Talleyrand	Political economy	Political economy and statistics

	Section Membership in the Class of Moral and Political Sciences	*Section Membership in the Academy of Moral and Political Sciences, 1832*
Roederer	Political economy	Ethics
Dacier	History	Ethics
Reinhard	Geography	History
Lacuée	Political economy	Ethics

APPENDIX 5
Number of Memoirs Read before the Class of Moral and Political Sciences and Published in Its Collection

SECTION I, ANALYSIS OF SENSATIONS AND IDEAS

	Memoirs Read	Memoirs Printed
Members		
Constantin-François Chassebeuf de Volney (1757–1820)	1	0
Dominique-Joseph Garat (1749–1833)	0	0
Pierre-Louis Ginguené (1748–1816)	0	0
Alexandre Deleyre (1726–1797)	0	0
Joachim-Jean Le Breton (1760–1819)	0	0
Pierre-Jean-Georges Cabanis (1757–1808)	8	6
François-Emmanuel Toulongeon (1748–1812)	13	2
Associates		
Antoine-Louis-Claude Destutt de Tracy (1754–1836)	9	7
Paul-Victor de Sèze (1754–1830)	0	0
Pierre Laromiguière (1756–1837)	3	2
Louis-Marie-Joseph-Maximilien Caffarelli du Falga (1756–1799)	0	0
Sicard of Marseille (?–1800)	0	0
Frédéric-François-Venceslas Jacquemont (1757–1836)	0	0
Joseph-Marie Degérando (1772–1842)	4	0
Pierre Prévost (1751–1839)	0	0

SECTION 2, ETHICS

	Memoirs Read	Memoirs Printed
Members		
Jacques-Henri Bernardin de Saint-Pierre (1737–1814)	5	0
Louis-Sébastien Mercier (1740–1814)	13	0
Henri Grégoire (1750–1831)	7	2
Louis-Marie La Revellière-Lépeaux (1753–1824)	3	0
Jacques-André-Naigeon (1738–1810)	1	0
Joseph Lakanal (1762–1845)		0
Associates		
Michel-Guillaume-Jean Crèvecœur (1735–1813)	0	0
Jean-Gervais Labène (1764–1844)	0	0
Dominique Ricard (1741–1803)	0	0
Alexandre-Louis Villeterque (1759–1811)	5	0
François Ferlus (1748–1812)	0	0
Jacques-Maurice Gaudin (1735–1810)	2	1

SECTION 3, SOCIAL SCIENCE AND LEGISLATION

	Memoirs Read	Memoirs Printed
Members		
Pierre-Claude-François Daunou (1761–1840)	4	2
Jean-Jacques Régis de Cambacérès (1753–1824)	3	1
Philippe-Antoine Merlin de Douai (1754–1838)	2	0
Claude-Emmanuel-Joseph-Pierre de Pastoret (1756–1840)	1	0
Jean-Philippe Garran-Coulon (1748–1816)	0	0
Pierre-Charles-Louis Baudin des Ardennes (1748–1799)	6	4
Jean-François Champagne (1751–1813)	3	1
Félix-Julien-Jean Bigot de Préameneu (1747–1825)	1	0
Associates		
Louis-Auguste Legrand-Laleu (1755–1819)	2	0
David Houard (1725–1802)	0	0
Julien Raimond (1740?–1802)	0	0
Louis-François-Élisabeth Ramond (1755–1827)	0	0
Philippe-Antoine Grouvelle (1757–1806)	0	0
Ruffin-Castus Massa (1742–1829)	1	0

SECTION 4, POLITICAL ECONOMY

Members	Memoirs Read	Memoirs Published Separately	Memoirs Published by Institute
Emmanuel-Joseph Sieyès (1748–1836)	0		0
Jacques-Antoine Creuzé-Latouche (1749–1800)	1		0
Charles-Maurice Talleyrand (1754–1838)	2		2
Pierre-Louis Roederer (1754–1835)	17	12	0
Pierre-Samuel Du Pont (1739–1817)	31	17	1
Jean-Gérard Lacuée (1752–1841)	1	0	
Charles-François Lebrun (1739–1824)	0	0	
Associates			
François Véron de Forbonnais (1722–1800)	2	1	1
Jean-Antoine-Cauvin Gallois (1755–1828)	0		0
Germain Garnier (1754–1821)	0		0
Emmanuel-Étienne Duvillard de Durand (1755–1832)	2		0
Antoine Diannyère (1762–1802)	8	5	1
Philippe-Rose Roume de Saint-Laurent (1743–1804)	0		0

SECTION 5, HISTORY

Members	Memoirs Read	Memoirs Printed
Jean-Baptiste-Claude Izouard Delisle de Sales (1741–1816)	30	9 excerpted
Pierre-Charles Lévesque (1736–1812)	21	13, 2 excerpted
Louis-Pierre Anquetil (1723–1806)	39	3
Bon-Joseph Dacier (1742–1833)	1 (report)	
Mathieu-Antoine Bouchaud (1719–1804)	21	12
Pierre-Jean-Baptiste Legrand d'Aussy (1737–1800)	10	4
Germain Poirier (1724–1803)	1	0
Gabriel-Henri Gaillard (1726–1806) (became an associate when declined to live in Paris)	0	0

	Memoirs Read	Memoirs Printed
Associates		
Christophe-Guillaume de Koch (1737–1813)	3	2
Edme Gautier de Sibert (1725–1797)	0	0
Jean Senebier (1742–1809)	0	0
Jean-Jacques Garnier (1729–1805)	0	0
Jean-Pierre Papon (1734–1803)	7	0
Paul-Philippe Gudin de la Brenellerie (1738–1812)	0	0
SECTION 6, GEOGRAPHY		
Members		
Jean-Nicolas Buache de Neuville (1741–1825)	16	7
Edme Mentelle (1730–1815)	13	1
Carl-Friedrich Reinhard (1761–1837)	0	0
Charles-Pierre d'Eveux, Claret de Fleurieu (1738–1810)	8	0
Paschal-François Gosselin (1751–1830)	9, 1 report	0
Louis-Antoine Bougainville (1729–1811)	2, 1 report	2
Associates		
Pierre-Joseph de Beauchamp (1752–1801)	1	0
Charles-Étienne Coquebert de Montbret (1755–1831)	0	0
Jean-François de Bourgoing (1748–1811)	1	0
Jean-René-Antoine Verdun de la Crenne (1741–1805)	0	0
Jean-Claude-Éléonor Le Michaud d'Arçon (1733–1800)	0	0
Guillaume-Jacques-Constant de Liberge de Granchain (1744–1805)	0	0
François de Barthélemy	0	0
Nicolas-Charles Romme	2	0
Daniel Lescallier	2	2

Sources: Archives de l'Académie des Sciences morales et politiques, A9, 10; "Liste chronologique des Mémoires qui ont été lus par personne et par section," ans IV-V, through to an XI; A1, 2, 3; Procès-verbaux de la Classe des sciences morales et politiques, an IV–an XI.

APPENDIX 6
Prize Contests of the Class of Moral and Political Sciences

LEGEND

1 Text of questions for prize contests
2 Number of contests for each question; opening and closing dates of the contests
3 Number of memoirs received in each contest
4 Names of the prizewinners and of those receiving honourable mentions and their subsequent links to the Institute

SECTION 1, ANALYSIS OF SENSATIONS AND
IDEAS

First Subject
1 Determine the influence of signs on the formation of ideas. (1) Is it true that sensations cannot transform ideas except by signs? Do the very first ideas need signs? (2) Would the *art de penser* be perfect if an *art de signes* were perfect? (3) In sciences where no dispute arises, is this condition owing to perfection of the signs? (4) Where there are eternal matters for dispute, is the divergence in opinions a necessary effect of the inexactitude of signs? (5) Is there a way to correct poorly formulated signs to make all sciences susceptible of demonstration?
2 2 contests
   contest 1: 15 Messidor 4 to 15 Messidor 5
   contest 2: 15 Messidor 5 to 15 Germinal 7
3 contest 1: 13 memoirs; contest 2: 10 memoirs

4 contest 1: honourable mentions to Degérando (subsequently associate of the Class of Moral and Political Sciences in March 1800 and member of the Class of History and Ancient Literature, April 1805) and Lancelin contest 2: prize to Degérando; 1st honourable mention to Prévost (Class of Moral and Political Sciences associate January, 1801), 2nd honourable mention to P.-R.-F. Butet
Source: Archives de l'Institut, Académie des Sciences morales et politiques (AI-SMP), B1, B2

Second Subject
1 The influence of habit on the faculty of thought; show the effect of frequent repetitions of the same operations on each of our intellectual faculties.
2 2 contests
contest 1: 15 Nivôse 8 to 15 Nivôse 9
contest 2: 15 Germinal 9 to 15 Germinal 10
3 contest 1: 4 memoirs; contest 2: 7 memoirs
4 2nd contest: prize to Maine de Biran, honourable mention to Canard
Source: AI-SMP, B6

Third Subject
1 Determine how one should decompose the faculty of thought, and what elementary faculties should be recognized.
2 2 contests
contest 1: 20 Vendémiaire 11 to 15 Nivôse 12
contest 2: 15 Nivôse 12 to 1 Nivôse 13
3 contest 1: 15 memoirs, contest 2: 18 memoirs
4 contest 1: honourable mention, anonymous
contest 2: prize to Maine de Biran (correspondent of the Class of History of Ancient Literature, November 1805); honourable mention to Nicolas Canard
Source: AI-SMP B10, Archives de l'Institut, Académie des Inscriptions et Belles-Lettres (AI-IBL), 1H9

SECTION 2, ETHICS

First Subject
1 After political revolutions, what means are most appropriate to restore a people to the principles of ethics? Revised to: What are the most appropriate means to establish the morality of a people? Revised 15 Vendémiaire 6 to: What are the most appropriate institutions to establish the morality of a people? Revised 15 Vendémiaire 7 to specify: What are the most suitable institutions to give man in society habits capable of making him happy? Discuss the nature of habit.

2 2 contests
  contest 1: 15 Messidor 5 to 15 Germinal 6
  contest 2: 15 Vendémiaire 7 to 15 Vendémiaire 8
3 contest 1: 16 memoirs, contest 2: 8 memoirs
4 contest 1: honourable mentions to Villaume, Silvestre, Petitain
  contest 2: honourable mentions to Petitain, J.-B. Say, Canolle
Source: AI-SMP, B4

Second Subject
1 Is emulation a useful means of education? Changed to: Is emulation a good means of education?
2 1 contest: 15 Nivôse 8 to 15 Germinal 9
3 16 memoirs
4 prize to Feuillet (member at large, Academy of Moral and Political Sciences in 1833); honourable mentions to Petitain, Raymond, Brun
Source: AI-SMP, B7

Third Subject
1 What is the true character of goodness in a public man?
2 1 contest, 15 Nivôse 9 to 15 Nivôse 10
3 11 memoirs
4 honourable mentions to Ponce and two anonymous
Source: AI-SMP, B8

Fourth Subject
1 To what point do barbarous treatments of animals interest public morality? Is it a question for legislation?
2 1 contest, 17 Messidor 10 to 15 Messidor 11
3 26 memoirs
4 honourable mentions to Grandchamp, Salaville, and "L.H.R.," an author from Amiens
Source: AI-IBL, 1H8

SECTION 3, SOCIAL SCIENCE AND LEGISLATION

First Subject
1 What should be, in a well-constituted republic, the extent and limits of the power of the father? Revised 15 Nivôse 8 to specify rights and duties of the father, the influence of paternal power on social order, public and private morality, and political constitutions.
2 3 contests
  contest 1: 15 Messidor 6 to 15 Messidor 7
  contest 2: 15 Vendémiaire 8 to 15 Vendémiaire 9

contest 3: 15 Nivôse 9 to 15 Nivôse 10
3 contest 1: 3 memoirs; contest 2: 7 memoirs; contest 3: 6 memoirs
4 contest 1: honourable mention to Petitain denied by Class
  contest 2: honourable mentions to Nougarède, Delacour, (Deproge?)
  contest 3: honourable mentions to Dulçat, Bodmann, Besgueil du Puy
Source: AI-SMP, B5

Second Subject
1 What are the means of improving the institution of the jury in France?
2 1 contest, 15 Nivôse 9 to 15 Nivôse 10
3 8 memoirs
4 prize doubled and shared by Bourguignon and Canard; honourable mention to Louvet
Source: AI-SMP, B9

SECTION 4, POLITICAL ECONOMY

First Subject
1 For what objects and under what conditions is it suitable for a republic to open public loans? to give credit to citizens in savings banks? to give public assistance? Consider the question in all respects – political, economic, and ethical.
2 4 contests
  contest 1: 15 Messidor 4 to 15 Germinal 5
  contest 2: 15 Messidor 5 to 15 Germinal 6
  contest 3: 15 Messidor 6 to 15 Vendémiaire 8
  contest 4: 15 Nivôse 8 to 15 Nivôse 9
3 contest 1: 4 memoirs; contest 2: 2 memoirs; contest 3: 3 memoirs; contest 4: 6 memoirs
4 contest 1: honourable mention, anonymous
  contest 2: none
  contest 3: honourable mention to Girard de Villesaison
  contest 4: 1st honourable mention to Girard de Villesaison; 2nd honourable mention to Giraud; 3rd honourable mention to Charpentier de Beaumont overruled by Class
Source: AI-SMP, B3

Second Subject
1 Is it true that in an agricultural country any kind of tax falls in the last analysis on proprietors of land, and, if so, do indirect taxes fall on these same proprietors with a surcharge?
2 1 contest, 15 Vendémiaire 8 to 15 Vendémiaire 9
3 4 memoirs

4 prize to Canard
Source: AI-SMP, B8

Third Subject
1 How has the progressive abolition of servitude in Europe influenced the development of enlightenment and the wealth of nations?
2 2 contests
contest 1: 17 Messidor 10 to 15 Vendémiaire 12
contest 2: 1 Nivôse 12 to 15 Nivôse 13
3 contest 1: 1(?) memoir; contest 2: 6 memoirs
4 contest 2: honourable mention to Leuliette
Source: AI-SMP, B11

SECTION 5, HISTORY

First Subject
1 Research and give observations on public spirit in France from François Ier to the convocation of the Estates-General in 1789. Revised 15 Germinal 7 to: By what causes has the spirit of liberty developed in France from François Ier to 1789?
2 2 contests
contest 1: 15 Messidor 5 to 15 Nivôse 7
contest 2: 15 Germinal 7 to 15 Messidor 8
3 contest 1: 0 memoirs; contest 2: 3 memoirs
4 prize to Nicolas Ponce (correspondent of the Académie royale des Beaux-Arts, July 1827)
Source: AI-SMP, B8

Second Subject
1 What influence did the Reformation of Luther have on the political situation in the different states of Europe and on the progress of enlightenment?
2 1 contest, 15 Germinal 10 to 15 Germinal 11
3 7 memoirs
4 prize to Charles Villers (correspondent of the Class of History and Ancient Literature, September 1804); honourable mentions to Leuliette, Maleville, fils
Source: AI-IBL, 2H2

SECTION 6, GEOGRAPHY

First Subject
1 Determine what great changes occurred on the globe, that are either indicated or proved by history.

2 2 contests
   contest 1: 15 Messidor 6 to 15 Vendémiaire 8
   contest 2: 15 Nivôse 8 to 15 Germinal 9
3 contest 1: 0 memoirs; contest 2: 2 memoirs
4 none
Source: AI-SMP, B8

Second Subject
1 Compare the geographic knowledge of Ptolemy on the interior of Africa
   with that transmitted by later geographers and historians, excepting the
   areas of Egypt and the Barbary Coast from Tunis to Morocco.
2 2 contests
   contest 1: 15 Messidor 9 to 15 Vendémiaire 11
   contest 2: 20 Vendémiaire 11 to 15 Messidor 12 (withdrawn by the
   Class of History and Ancient Literature, 30 Germinal 11)
3 0 memoirs in both contests
Source: AI-SMP, B10

SUMMARY

CSMP *Section*	*Number of Prize Memoirs*	*Number of Contests*	*Average Number of Memoirs per Contest*
Analysis of sensations and ideas	67	6	11.2
Ethics	76	5	15.2
Social science and legislation	24	4	6.0
Political economy	25	7	3.6
History	10	3	3.3
Geography	2	3	0.7

Notes

CHAPTER ONE

1 Guillaume, *Procès-verbaux* 6:796–8, 869–73; Aucoc, *L'Institut*, 3–47; Simon, *Une Académie*, 60–80; Moravia, *Il tramonto*, 410–26; Hahn, *The Anatomy of a Scientific Institution*, 286–312, to which I am heavily indebted.

2 *Institut de France: Catalogue*, 7; for the use of Minerva in eighteenth-century Montpellier see Roche, *Le Siècle*, 1:150.

3 Cabanis, *Œuvres philosophiques* (hereafter OP), 1:162.

4 Arrêté du Directoire exécutif, 29 brumaire IV (20 November 1795), in Aucoc, *L'Institut*, 13.

5 Among recent interpretations of the Idéologues, the most significant are Moravia, *Il tramonto* and *Il pensiero*; Kaiser, "The Idéologues"; Kennedy, *A Philosophe*; Gusdorf, *La Conscience révolutionnaire*; Welch, *Liberty and Utility*; Margerison, *P.-L. Roederer*; Head, *Ideology*; Matucci, ed., *Gli "idéologues"*; Azouvi, ed., *L'Institution de la raison*; Picavet, *Les Idéologues,* remains the classic, though now outdated, work.

6 Gusdorf, *La Conscience révolutionnaire*, 295.

7 Ibid., 96.

8 Baker, *Inventing the French Revolution*, 8–11.

9 Baker, "On the Problem of the Ideological Origins of the French Revolution," in LaCapra and Kaplan, eds. *Modern European*, 198–9.

10 Furet, *Interpreting the French Revolution*; Chartier, *The Cultural Origins*, 19.

11 Gay, *The Enlightenment*, 1:23, and d'Alembert, *Essai sur les élémens de philosophie*, cited in Lively, ed., *The Enlightenment*, 4–5.

12 Vovelle, *La Mentalité révolutionnaire*, 184.

13 Chartier, *The Cultural Origins*, 5, 83–91, 92–110, 187–98.

14 See the forum on Furet's interpretation in *French Historical Studies*, 16 (1990): 766–802; Baker, *Inventing*, 305; my interpretation in early drafts of this work has since been confirmed by William Sewell in *A Rhetoric of Bourgeois Revolution*, 192–3.

15 Masseau, *L'Invention*, 6n; Coser, *Men of Ideas*, 215–25.

16 Masseau, *L'Invention*, 45–63; Goodman, *The Republic of Letters*, 2, 12–23, on the republic of letters and the related concept of Jürgen Habermas's public sphere of critical discussion.

17 Bourdieu, *Les Règles*, 461–72, esp. 468–72; Said, *Representations*, xvi–xvii, 7, 11, 121; see also Richard Hofstadter's contrast of critical, creative "intellectuals" against merely manipulative and practical users of "intelligence" in Lipset and Basu, "Des types," 62.

18 Ibid.

19 Ibid., 68–79; a weakness of this model is its failure to differentiate "operationally" between gatekeeper and moralist.

20 Ibid., 79–88.

21 Masseau, *L'Invention*, 52–5.

22 Darnton, "The High Enlightenment," 83–5, 115; on Morellet, see Darnton, "Une carrière littéraire exemplaire," in *Gens de lettres*, 47–67; Kors, *D'Holbach's Coterie*, 246.

23 Coser, *Men of Ideas*, 189–97, on Idéologues; page 140, for the citation taken from Robert Merton, "Role of the Intellectual in Public Bureaucracy," in *Social Theory and Social Structure*, New York: The Free Press, 1957, 222.

24 For Goodman on academies as "compromised," see *The Republic of Letters*, 21.

25 Burke, *The Fabrication of Louis XIV*, 50–4; Hahn, 8–15. The dates of foundation of major Paris academies are as follows: the Académie française, 1635; the Académie royale de Peinture et de Sculpture, 1648; the Académie royale des Inscriptions et Belles-Lettres, 1663; the Académie royale des Sciences, 1666; the Académie royale d'Architecture, 1671.

26 Amiable, *Une Loge maçonnique d'avant 1789: Les Neuf Sœurs*, ed. Porset, commentary, 95–123; Porset, "Maçonnerie et idéologie: Le précédent de la Loge des Neuf Sœurs," in *Les Idéologues*, 9–15; Pilâtre de Rozier's Lycée carried on similar lectures in 1785.

27 For example, a *prix d'utilité* was awarded for Gudin de la Brenellerie's history of the Estates-General in 1789; *Biographie Universelle* (Michaud), 18:30.

28 Roche, *Le Siècle des lumières en province*, 1:345–55, 2:139.

29 See ibid., 1:351–5, 363, 102 on social conformism.

30 Roche, *Le Siècle*, 1:136–81, and Hahn, *The Anatomy*, 150–8, 183–93; Fayet, *La Révolution française*, 50–67, 129–30; Françoise Waquet, "La Bastille académique," in Bonnet, ed., *La Carmagnole des muses*, 19–36.
31 Fayet, *La Révolution française*, 198–9; Hahn, *The Anatomy*, 212–6.
32 Franqueville, *Le Premier siècle de l'Institut*, 1:22; "Mélanges," *Magasin encyclopédique*, 16 (1797): 83–8.
33 Archives de l'Institut (hereafter AI), 3A1, Répertoire des procès-verbaux des séances générales de l'Institut, 1:69; Rousseau, *The First and Second Discourses*, 36.
34 Taillandier, *Documents biographiques sur P.-C.-F. Daunou*, 103.
35 Cabanis, *OP*, 1:161.
36 Nelson, "The Economics Profession," 80.
37 MacIntyre, *After Virtue*, 84, 101.
38 Ross, *The Origins of American Social Science*, 472.
39 Horkheimer and Adorno, *Dialectic of Enlightenment*, xii, 4, 6, 23, 36; on Sade, see Ibid., 81–119.
40 Winch, *The Idea of a Social Science*, 40–94; Gardiner, *Theories of History*, 35, 213–25.
41 Hanson, *Patterns of Discovery*, 4–30; Kuhn, *The Structure of Scientific Revolutions*; Feyerabend, *Against Method*, 295–309. For the "strong program" in sociology of knowledge, see Barnes, *Interests and the Growth of Knowledge*; for a critique of relativism in the social sciences without concessions to positivism, see Trigg, *Understanding Social Science*, chapters 2, 4, 6, 10.
42 Foucault, *Discipline and Punish*, 23, 25–8, 102–3, 138, 143–4, 176–7, 200, 220–7; for a convenient anthology, see Rabinow, ed., *A Foucault Reader*; for critiques of Foucault's simplistic representation of the Panopticon, see Semple, *Bentham's Prison*.

CHAPTER TWO

1 Gay, *The Enlightenment*, 2:174–87; for an excellent study of the intellectual background to eighteenth-century social science, see Olson, *The Emergence of the Social Sciences*, who differentiates between psychological, economic, and philosophical history models.
2 Montesquieu, *De l'esprit des lois* (1748), in *Œuvres complètes*, ed. D. Oster, book 1, i and iii, 529–32.
3 For a discussion stressing anti-Cartesian elements, see Shackleton, *Montesquieu*, 259–61; *De l'esprit des lois*, I, i, 529–31; II, III, 532–39.
4 Shackleton, 245–51, sees Montesquieu's natural laws as descriptive, while Waddicor, *Montesquieu and the Philosophy of Natural Law*, 31–8, sees them as prescriptive; Klosko, "Montesquieu's Science of Politics," 153–77; *De l'esprit des lois*, I, ii, 530–1.

5 Ibid., III, x, 539–40, and XI, vi, 586–90; "Réflexions extraites d'un
   ouvrage du citoyen Grégoire sur les moyens de perfectionner les sciences
   politiques" (1796), *Mémoires de l'Institut national des sciences et arts.
   Sciences morales et politiques* (hereafter MSMP), 1:555.
6 [Grouvelle], *De l'autorité de Montesquieu*, 12–13, 46–7, 53–4, 93, 137–9.
7 Olson, *The Emergence*, 146–55.
8 "Observations de Condorcet sur le vingt-neuvième livre de l'Esprit des
   lois," in A.-L.-C. Destutt de Tracy, *Commentaire sur l'Esprit des lois* 404,
   420–1.
9 Condorcet, "On the Influence of the American Revolution," in Baker, ed.,
   Condorcet, 72–3.
10 Imbert, *Destutt de Tracy critique de Montesquieu*, 38, 46.
11 Montesquieu, *Esprit des lois*, XIX, iv, 641.
12 See Shackleton, *Montesquieu*, 313; Cabanis, "Rapports du physique et du
   moral de l'homme," in *Œuvres philosophiques*, 1:460–512; Volney,
   Voyage en Égypte et en Syrie, 371–98.
13 Shackleton, *Montesquieu*, 306.
14 Staum, *Cabanis*, 159, 232–5, 354–5, 381–2; on the environmental imperative in eighteenth-century social science, see Moravia, "The Enlightenment and the Sciences of Man," 254–7; L.J. Jordanova, "Earth Science
   and Environmental Medicine: The Synthesis of the Late Enlightenment,"
   in Jordanova and Porter, eds., *Images of the Earth*, 119–46.
15 Hampson, *Will and Circumstance*, 25; *De l'esprit des lois*, III, iii–iv, 536–
   8; VIII, ii–iv, 570–2; VIII, xvi, 575.
16 Archives nationales (hereafter AN), F^{17}1339, F^{17}1344$^{6-7}$; see Staum,
   "Human, not Secular Sciences," 60.
17 Baker, *Condorcet: From Natural Philosophy*, 391–5; Head, "Origins of
   'La Science Sociale,'" 115–32.
18 Roederer, "Cours sur l'organisation sociale," *Œuvres*, vol.8; Cambacérès,
   "Discours sur la science sociale," in MSMP, 3:1–14.
19 Olson, *The Emergence*, 57–70, 118–37.
20 On Quesnay and circulation, see Foley, *The Social Physics of Adam
   Smith*, 120–31; for background on Physiocracy, see Fox-Genovese, *The
   Origins of Physiocracy*; Meek, *The Economics of Physiocracy*; Larrère,
   L'Invention de l'économie au XVIIIe siècle, 173–213; Perrot, *Une Histoire
   intellectuelle de l'économie politique (XVIIe–XVIIIe siècle)*, 217–36.
21 Perrot, "The Golden Age of Regional Statistics (Year IV-1804)," in Perrot
   and Woolf, *State and Statistics in France*, 1789–1815, 8.
22 *Quesnay's Tableau économique*; see Meek, *The Economics*, 265–96;
   Ibid., 70, for the citation of Mirabeau; for an insistence on profit as an
   integral Physiocratic notion, see Vaggi, "The Role of Profit," 367–84.
23 Fox-Genovese, *The Origins*, 14; Daire, ed., *Physiocrates*, 445.

24 Du Pont, "Discours de l'éditeur," *Physiocratie*, xiv, xv, xxvi, reprinted in *Œuvres politiques et économiques*, 1:434–5, 443; on Montesquieu, see *Éphémérides du citoyen*, 1769, 6:144n; and Larrère, *L'Invention*, 195.

25 Saricks, *Pierre-Samuel Du Pont de Nemours*, 46.

26 *Éphémérides du citoyen*, 1769, 6:63n–65n.

27 Ibid., 6:43–4; Le Mercier de la Rivière, *L'Ordre naturel et essentiel des sociétés politiques*, in Daire, 482–7, 495–7, 504–7, 514–18; Archives de l'Institut-Sciences morales et politiques (hereafter AI–SMP), B3, Premier concours sur les emprunts publics, manuscript report of Du Pont, 5–6.

28 Quesnay, "Natural Right," in Meek, *The Economics*, 43–5.

29 Turgot, *Réflexions sur la formation et la distribution des richesses* (1770), in *Œuvres de Turgot*, 2:533–604, esp.570, 589–91; see Groenewegen, "Turgot's Place in the History of Economic Thought," 585–616.

30 Condillac, *Le Commerce et le gouvernement* (Paris, 1776), 45, 374; Klein, "Deductive Economic Methodology in the French Enlightenment," 51–71.

31 On Roederer's background, see Margerison, "P.-L. Roederer," 473–88.

32 For Smith as a sound empirical Newtonian scientist, see Campbell, *Adam Smith's Science of Morals*, 21, 28, 39, 54; for more balanced views, see Thomson, "Adam Smith's Philosophy of Science," 212–33; Campbell and Skinner, introduction to Adam Smith, *Wealth of Nations*, 19–31; Skinner, "Science and Role of Imagination," in *A System of Social Science*, 14–41; for Say on Smith and the Physiocrats, see *A Treatise on Political Economy*, xxxiii–iv, xxxix.

33 Smith, *Wealth of Nations*, book IV, 1:428; see also Chapter 11 below.

34 For the Physiocratic scheme, see Quesnay and Mirabeau, *Philosophie rurale* (1763), in Meek, *The Economics*, 60–4; for Smith, *Wealth of Nations*, book III, 1:376–427; for a discussion of Smith's use of history, introduction to *Wealth of Nations*, 1:50–60; for a general analysis of the four-stage schema, see Meek, *Social Science and the Ignoble Savage*, 68–176.

35 See Chapter 9 below on human geography.

36 AN, $F^{17}1339$; $F^{17}1344^{2-3}$; see Staum, "Human, not Secular," 56. For background on Condillac, see Le Roy, *La Psychologie de Condillac*; Knight, *The Geometric Spirit*; Sgard, ed., *Condillac et les problèmes du langage*; Rousseau, *Connaissance et langage chez Condillac*. For Revolutionary interest in Condillac, see Auroux, "La vague condillacienne," 107–10.

37 Condillac, *Essai sur les origines des connaissances humaines* (1746), in *Œuvres philosophiques*, 1:105–6; *Traité des systèmes* (1749), 1:213; *Grammaire* (1775), 1:435; "Art de penser" (1775), 1:773; *Logique* (1780), 2:374–6, 379, 382, 405; cf. Descartes, *Regulae ad directionem*

ingenii, in *Œuvres philosophiques*, 1:100–2, 154. For the use of analysis by Cabanis and its impact on clinical medicine, see Staum, *Cabanis*, 156–9, and Moravia, "Philosophie et médecine," 1124, 1139, 1146–51.

38 Condillac, *Essai sur les origines*, in *Œuvres philosophiques*, 1:47; *Traité des sensations*, in *Œuvres philosophiques*, 1:239–55A.

39 On the Revolutionary impact of Condillac, see Albury, "The Order of Ideas," 203–25.

40 See the discussion of Helvétius's *De l'esprit* (1758) and *De l'homme* (1771) in Staum, *Cabanis*, 44–8; Cabanis, *Œuvres philosophiques*, 1:142.

41 Condillac, *Essai* (1746), in *Œuvres philosophiques*, 1:20–5; *Traité des animaux* (1755), 1:365–66, 370; *Cours d'études* (1775), 1:416–18; see Chapter 6 below. For Condillac's sparse physiological remarks, see Paganini, "Psychologie et physiologie," 165–78.

42 Condillac, *Traité des systèmes*, in *Œuvres philosophiques*, 1:216; *Logique*, 2:394.

43 Rousseau, *Connaissance et langage chez Condillac*, 38–9, 63–4, 73, 291–2.

44 Auroux, in *Langue des calculs*, ed. Auroux and Chouillet, i–xxx; on the mixed reception of this work, see Auroux, "Idéologie et Langue des calculs," 53–7; Auroux, "Empirisme et théorie linguistique chez Condillac," in Sgard, ed., *Condillac*, 177–219.

45 Lavoisier, Guyton de Morveau, Berthollet, and Fourcroy, *Méthode de nomenclature chimique* (Paris, 1787).

46 See the references to a universal symbolic language in AI-SMP, A4, Procès-verbaux de la Classe des Sciences morales et politiques (hereafter PV-CSMP), 17 brumaire–12 floréal VIII, and 2 ventôse, 12 germinal IX; for etymological dictionaries, see the prize submission of Butet in AI-SMP, B2.

47 "Discours prononcé dans l'Académie française 21 février 1782," in *Œuvres de Condorcet*, 1:392; Baker, ed., *Condorcet*, 6,19.

48 Condorcet, *Essai sur l'application de l'analyse à la probabilité des décisions rendues à la pluralité des voix*, in Baker, ed., *Condorcet*, 33; Gillispie, *Science and Polity* (Princeton, 1980), 4; Crépel, "À quoi Condorcet a-t-il appliqué le calcul des probabilités?" in Crépel and Gilain, eds., *Condorcet mathématicien*, 76–86; Daston, *Classical Probability in the Enlightenment*, 216–17, 342–51.

49 Baker, *Condorcet*, 235–4; see passages in Baker, ed., *Condorcet* 45–9, 61–2; for Laplace, see Gillispie, "Probability and Politics," 3, 8–11, 15.

50 Olsen, "A Failure of Enlightened Politics," 303–34; Baker, "Politics and Social Science," 108–30.

51 Condorcet, "Tableau général de la science qui a pour objet l'application du calcul aux sciences politiques et morales," in *Œuvres*, 1:539–73.

52 For a discussion of Emmanuel Duvillard de Durand and Antoine Diannyère, see Chapters 10 and 11 below; David G. Troyansky, "Condorcet et

l'idée d'assurance vieillesse: risque, dette sociale et générations," in Crépel and Gilain, *Condorcet mathématicien*, 174–80.

53 Condorcet, *Œuvres*, 1:544, 552; "Fragment sur l'Atlantide," 6:612–19; Condorcet, *Sketch*, 174–5, 185–6, 199–201.

54 Perrot, "The Golden Age," 4–5, 38, 51–2.

55 Condorcet, *Œuvres*, 1:543, 6:628; Baker, ed., *Condorcet*, 185–6.

CHAPTER THREE

1 Waquet, "La Bastille," 27; Mirabeau, *Travail sur l'éducation publique*, 15, 20, 43–5; Simon, *Une Académie sous le Directoire*, 57–8.

2 Simon, *Une Académie*, 59–61; Hahn, *The Anatomy*, 203–6.

3 Azouvi, "L'Institut national: une 'encyclopédie vivante'?" in Azouvi, ed., *L'Institution de la raison*, 55.

4 Talleyrand-Périgord, *Rapport sur l'instruction publique*, 17, 57–60, 65, 69, 101, 109, tables I and III.

5 Azouvi, "L'Institut," 57–8.

6 Condorcet, *Rapport* in *Œuvres*, ed. Arago, 7:449–573, esp.544–7, 550, 557; see the discussion in Baker, *Condorcet*, 388–90; Hahn, *The Anatomy*, 207–13; see also Coutel and Kintzler, eds., *Écrits sur l'instruction publique*; J.-J. Garnier's *De l'éducation civile* (1765) anticipated Condorcet's interest in teaching morality, public law, natural law, and the law of nations in the collèges; see Thuillier, "Aux origines," 434–40. On 28 September 1795 the Public Instruction Committee of the National Convention proposed schools of "political sciences" with five chairs in legislation, public law and law of nations, political economy, analysis of human understanding, and ethics and philosophical history of peoples; see Thuillier, "Les projets," 125.

7 Condorcet, *Œuvres*, 7:519.

8 Fayet, *La Révolution*, 20–49; Hahn, *The Anatomy*, 150, 183–93, 211–25, 237–41; see Ibid., 296–304 on foundation of the Institute.

9 On Ginguené's cultural patronage policy, see Hesse, *Publishing and Cultural Politics*, 158–9; Guillaume, *Procès-verbaux*, 6:324–5.

10 Ibid., 339–42.

11 Ibid., 576, 580–2, 644–5.

12 Ibid., 789, 791.

13 AI, 3A, I, 15 germinal IV, reprinted in Taillandier, *Documents biographiques*, 103, 105. Cf. Azouvi, "L'Institut," 52–3.

14 Lakanal, *Exposé sommaire*, 21–35, reprinted in Aucoc, *L'Institut de France*, 16–19.

15 Aucoc, *L'Institut*, 54; three others purged from the First and Third Classes were L. Carnot, R.-A. Sicard, and L. Fontanes.

16 Gusdorf, *La Conscience révolutionnaire*, 308–9.

17 Lakanal, *Exposé*, 16–19; see also AN, F[17]1094, letter of Interior Minister Bénézech to the Directory, 3 frimaire IV, urging acceptance of Lakanal's list, and Ginguené's apparently delayed letter to Lakanal, 29 brumaire, requesting the list.

18 Guillaume, 6:839; see Malandain, *Delisle de Sales*.

19 Biographical information in this chapter comes from Franqueville, *Le Premier siècle*, and from the relevant articles of the *Biographie universelle*, with verification against published *éloges* or dossiers at the Archives de l'Institut where possible and a systematic inspection of photocopies of baptismal certificates from the French departmental archives.

20 Gramsci, *Selections from the Prison Notebooks*, 3.

21 Another source on social relationships among the Idéologues is Guillois, *Le Salon de Mme. Helvétius*.

22 On the *Décade*, see Kitchin, *Un Journal "philosophique,"* and Régaldo, *Un Milieu intellectuel*; for Garat-Cabanis links, see Guillois, *Le Salon*, 109.

23 Amiable, *Une Loge maçonnique*, 17–18, 28, 31–2, 66, 357, 389–93.

24 AI-SMP, B2.

25 See, for example, Edme Mentelle, "Essai statistique sur les villes principales de la Russie," *Séances des écoles normales*, 5:109–20, and for Mentelle's plan to employ diplomats as geographical correspondents, see AI-SMP, A5, extrait, "Aperçu des travaux à exécuter par la section de géographie" (1796).

26 Doneaud du Plan, *Histoire de l'Académie de Marine*, 1:5.

27 AI, 3A[I], Registre des procès-verbaux des séances générales de l'Institut, 15 frimaire IV.

28 Chassériau, *Notice*, 23–4.

29 Guillois, *Le Salon*, 123, 138.

30 AI-SMP, A1, PV-CSMP, 27 floréal V, and AI, 3A[I], Séances générales de l'Institut, 5 thermidor V.

31 Information on titles and reading of memoirs is available in the PV-CSMP and also in the manuscript, "Liste chronologique des mémoires lus par personne et par section," in AI-SMP, A9 and A10.

32 AI, Séances générales, 3A[I], 19 thermidor IV; Aucoc, *L'Institut*, 45–6; AN, F[17] 1094 and F[17] 1218 for budgets and signatures for stipends received for the years VI to VIII; cf. Crosland, *Science under Control*, 66n.

33 On the Ancien Régime academy, see Maury, *Les Académies d'autrefois*; on the Third Class of the Institute (Littérature et Beaux-Arts), see Dussaud, *La Nouvelle Académie*.

34 For other patronage relationships, see Appendix 2.

35 Roche, "Milieux académiques provinciaux et société des lumières," in Bollème et al., eds., *Livre et société*, 1:114, 118–19, 129, 132, 148; "Sciences et pouvoirs," 747, n.26–29; Roche, *Le Siècle*, 1:286–7; 2:381–4, 387, 437.

36 Ibid., 2: 398–403, 437, 457; see McClellan, "The Académie Royale des Sciences," 541–67, esp.558, which gives the figure as 15 per cent. Cf. the decline of clergy from 32 per cent (1757) to 20 per cent (1784) in all of the identifiable authors of *La France littéraire* in Darnton, "The Literary Revolution of 1789," 8.

37 Barksdale, "Liberal Politics," 19–20.

38 McClellan, 556; Darnton's figures for nobles in *La France littéraire* increase from 9 per cent in 1757 to 14 per cent in 1784; see Darnton, "The Literary Revolution," 8.

39 Bouclon, *Étude historique*, 497, 530; dossier of Liberge in the Archives de l'Académie des Sciences.

40 Roche, *Le Siècle*, 2:375.

41 Roche, "Milieux," 176. Cf. Giesselmann, *Die brumairianische Elite*, 81; for a fuller set of tables, see Staum, "The Class," 378–9.

42 For a verification of legislative terms, see Robert et al., *Dictionnaire des parlementaires français*; see Darnton's chart for *La France littéraire* authors in "The Literary Revolution," 10.

43 Barksdale, "Liberal Politics," 39, indicates that in the new Academy of Moral and Political Sciences in 1832–52, 22 per cent still had Ancien Régime titles of nobility, and another 18 per cent acquired nobility in the Napoleonic or Restoration eras.

44 Popkin, *Revolutionary News*, 44–5, 50, indicates a relative stability in the occupational origins of journalists from the mid-eighteenth century through to the Revolution as well as higher pay for successful Revolutionary journalists.

45 Outram, "The Ordeal of Vocation," 251–73.

46 For voting in the Convention, see Patrick, *The Men of the First French Republic*, 317–39. For each of the nine situations, I awarded positive or negative points. The resulting quantities (plus 5 for a radical revolutionary tendency or minus 5 for a conservative one, for example) have no real significance, but are general indicators of which individuals and sections were most fervently committed to the Revolution.

47 The average age at election of seventy-one members and associates in 1795–96 was 49.6; for thirteen new members elected by 1803, 55.7; and for all eighty-four members, 50.6. The comparable figures for the 120 in the First Class of Mathematical and Physical Sciences, given by Hahn, *Anatomy*, 301, are 53.7 for those elected in 1795–96, 51.3 for fourteen new members, and 53.5 for all members; the average age for the eleven Idéologues was 41.1, for the geographers 52.1, and for the historians 64.9.

48 Maury, *Académie des Inscriptions*; besides the biography in *Biographie universelle* (Michaud), see eulogies by Dacier of Germain Poirier, Garnier, Gaillard, and Anquetil in *Histoire et mémoires de l'Institut royal de*

France, Classe d'Histoire et Littérature ancienne (hereafter CHLA), 1:285–99, 335–51, and 3:3–20, 21–40; on Dacier, see Georges Perrot, 69–105. Personal dossiers of Ancien Régime members are in the Archives de l'Académie des Inscriptions; for Delisle de Sales, see Malandain, *Delisle de Sales.*

49 For the designation of officers, see PV-CSMP every six months at vendémiaire and germinal. See also Ginguené, *Rapports*; Daunou wrote the 1814 report.

50 Prize commission membership is most accessible in AI-SMP in the B1–11 series, and in AI-Inscriptions et Belles Lettres, 1H8, 1H9, and 2H2, for post-1803 contest decisions. See also PV-CSMP.

51 For the necessary comparisons, one may check the manuscript chronological lists of memoirs in AI-SMP with the published MSMP. Printing commission decisions are also in AI-SMP, A8.

52 *MSMP*, 1:247–82 and 2:231–9.

53 Ibid., 3:80–91.

54 *Notice des travaux de la Classe des Sciences morales et politiques* [report by Daunou], 1er trimestre, an XI, 3.

55 La Revellière-Lépeaux, *Réflexions sur le culte*, 19–22, 45; see also Chapter 7.

56 *MSMP*, 3:13.

57 PV-CSMP, 12, 27 prairial VI; AI-3, A2, Registre des procès-verbaux des séances générales, 15 messidor VI; *De la nature de la morale*, Paris, an VI; see also Aimé-Martin, ed., *Œuvres complètes*, 7:401–41. In fact, sixteen of twenty-three prize memoirs expressed reverence for God; see AI-SMP, B4.

58 Souriau, *Bernardin de Saint-Pierre*, 331–2.

59 See Hahn, *The Anatomy*, 183–5, for Saint-Pierre's attacks on academies.

60 On Mercier, see *Biographie universelle* (Michaud), 28:12–16; see Chapter 6 for Mercier on Kant; on Delisle de Sales, see Chapter 7.

CHAPTER FOUR

1 Crosland, *Science under Control*, 65.

2 Aucoc, *Institut de France*, 33n.

3 For the relatively unsuccessful agricultural inspection program, see Aucoc, 9–10; for the budget cuts, see AN, $F^{17}1094$; see AN, $F^{17}1095$, doss.6, for Institute budgets for ans VI, VIII; see AN, $F^{17}1218$, for *an* X budget; for Du Pont as a member of the Institute travelling to the United States, see the physical geography and natural history memoirs in Du Pont, *Quelques mémoires*; on the metric system, see Bibliothèque de l'Institut (hereafter BI), Usuels AA 33, vol.18, no.23. Metric measures had first been approved by the Convention on 7 April 1795; see Kula, *Measures and Men*, 120, 237–8, 241–3.

4 For the engagement of scientists in serving the Napoleonic state, see Dhombres, *Naissance d'un pouvoir,* 709–63.

5 AI, 3A¹, Registre des procès-verbaux des séances générales de l'Institut, 5 thermidor IV; see also AI-SMP, PV-CSMP, 17 prairial IV, for a committee of Baudin, Roederer, and Lacuée on the "gaps in national instruction" to strengthen primary schools.

6 Daunou, *Rapport,* 25 floréal V, 6–8, 14–20, 26–7; reprinted in Duruy, *L'Instruction publique,* 419–71; Roger-Martin, *Rapport général fait ... sur l'organisation de l'instruction publique,* 19 brumaire VII, 31–5; Palmer, *The Improvement of Humanity,* 242–68.

7 Destutt de Tracy, *Observations,* 48–9, 51; see speech by Fourcroy to the Tribune, 30 germinal X, in A. de Beauchamp, *Recueil des lois,* 1:68.

8 Staum, "Human, not Secular Sciences," 58, 67, 74; Beauchamp, *Recueil des lois,* 1:249–50, 305–6.

9 AN, F¹⁷*1011, Rapport du Conseil de l'instruction publique; see Staum, "Human," 52–3; Palmer, *Improvement,* 268–78. For the reprinted report and Destutt de Tracy's circulars, see "Pièces relatives à l'instruction publique," *Éléments d'idéologie,* 4, and recent editions of documents in *Corpus,* n° 26/27, 209–30.

10 Forrest, *The French Revolution and the Poor*; Staum, *Cabanis,* 136–46; PV-CSMP, A1, PV, 2 thermidor IV, 12; 27 fructidor IV; 12 vendémiaire V.

11 *Décade philosophique,* 11:87–91, 20 vendémiaire V; Imbert, *Le Droit hospitalier,* 122; Forrest, *The French Revolution and the Poor,* 116–33.

12 Ibid., 2–3; Imbert, *Le Droit hospitalier,* 105–10.

13 MSMP, 2:288–95, 299–301.

14 MSMP, 2:301; *Décade philosophique,* 14:104, 20 messidor V; *Clef du cabinet des souverains,* 20 messidor V; *Journal de Paris,* 17 messidor V, 1170–1; *Nouvelles politiques,* 23 messidor V.

15 MSMP, 2:298; see Silvera, "The Origins," 26.

16 Gillispie, "Historical Introduction," in Gillispie and Dewachter, eds., *Monuments of Egypt,* 1:3; see Dhombres, *Naissance d'un pouvoir,* 107, on Tallien's article in Cairo on toleration of Islam.

17 Dhombres, 93–149, sees this expedition as the "laboratory" for Napoleon's construction of a viable scientific community and as a springboard for careers; see Ibid., 824–6, for the Commission on Modern Egypt divisions.

18 BI, Usuels AA 33, vol.18, no.31, *Procès-verbaux des séances de l'Institut des Sciences et des Arts d'Égypte*; Charles-Roux, *Bonaparte: Governor of Egypt,* 120–74, 313–34; Thiry, *Bonaparte en Égypte,* 203–14; Goby, "Les séances," 59–67.

19 [Volney], *Questions de statistique.*

20 MSMP, *Histoire,* 3:5–21, esp.13–17.

21 Gillispie, *Monuments,* 1:11, 15, 20; Boussif Ouasti, "La *Description de l'Égypte*," 73–82, esp.77.

22 Gillispie, "Scientific Aspects," 447–74, especially 471–3; see also Godlewska, "Traditions, Crisis, and New Paradigms," 192–213; Gillispie and Dewachter have edited a magnificent reproduction of the antiquities plates. See also Gillispie, "Historical Introduction," 1–29, and bibliography, 40–6.

23 Godlewska, "Napoleon's Geographers (1797–1815): Imperialists and Soldiers of Modernity," in Godlewska and Smith, *Geography and Empire*, 45–9, 53. This article argues for an imperialism inherent in the very concept of modernity.

24 Hubert-Pascal Ameilhon of the Third Class analysed in 1801 and 1803 the Greek inscription of the Rosetta Stone discovered in 1799, and outside the Institute Silvestre de Sacy speculated about the meaning of the hieroglyphs, which were finally deciphered by his pupil Jean-François Champollion in 1821–22; see also Dhombres, "L'image du monde arabe," 151–64.

25 Faivre, *L'Expansion française*, 104–6, 110–11, 121–2.

26 Horner, *The French Reconnaissance*, 40, 336–7; Péron and Freycinet, *Voyage de découvertes*, 1:ix.

27 For Buache on the French Guiana boundary, see AI-SMP, A1, PV, 17 floréal IV; MSMP, 3:15–39; *Notice des travaux de la Classe ... 1er trimestre, an IX*, 3; for Anquetil on judicial institutions in the Holy Roman Empire to plan for peace with Austria, see AN, AD XVIIIe 474, *Compte rendu et notice des travaux ... an VI*, 101–10 .

28 Caput, *L'Académie française*, 15; Roche, *Le Siècle*, 1:322–85, esp.326–7, 336, 344–56; 2:146–9.

29 J.-P. Brissot, *Théorie des loix criminelles*; Marat, *Plan de législation criminelle*; Hampson, *The Life and Opinions*, 11–18; Darnton, "The High Enlightenment."

30 Fox in Fox and Weisz, eds., *The Organization of Science*, 246–50, and in Baker and Harrigan, eds., *The Making of Frenchmen*, 544–7, 559–64.

31 Pastoret, Lévesque, J.-J. Garnier, Gossellin, and Legrand-Laleu were prizewinners and members of the Académie des Inscriptions; Volney (an Inscriptions prizewinner), Gaillard, and Garat were either in the Académie française or the Class of French Language and Literature.

32 Biographical information from *Biographie universelle* (Michaud) and Franqueville, *Le Premier siècle*. See Appendix 6 for prizewinners who became academicians.

33 Prize dossiers in AI-SMP, B1–11; AI-Inscriptions et Belles-Lettres (hereafter AI-IBL), 1H8–9, 2H2.

34 AI-SMP, A5, Pièces annexes aux registres des procès-verbaux, ans IV–V.

35 AI-SMP, A6, Pièces annexes, ans VI–VII, Cambacérès note to Baudin, 27 prairial VI; Review of Daunou in *Dissertations sur l'autorité paternelle ...*

Berlin 1788, in *Journal encyclopédique ou universel*, 1 May 1789, 3:379–403 (I wish to acknowledge Ruth Graham for this reference).

36 *Œuvres de Turgot*, G. Schelle, ed., 2:431–3, 504, 515, 630–55, 665–72; Roederer's notes are in AN, 29 AP 86, 110.

37 Roche, *Le Siècle*, 2:148.

38 A manuscript note claims the 1798–1800 geography subject on the historical proof of changes in the globe was proposed by Turgot for a contest in 1774–76; AI-SMP, A7, Pièces annexes, ans VIII–IX.

39 For poetry contests, see AI-Académie française, 1D1, Registre des Prix. See Appendix 6 for a precise contest-by-contest breakdown of the numbers of memoirs submitted and of the prolongations in each contest.

40 Roederer, *Des Institutions funéraires*, 4–5, 8.

41 *MSMP*, 2 (1799):681–94, esp.683 (5 frimaire VII).

42 Hintermeyer, *Politiques de la mort*, 16, 27, 72–7, 82–100, 162, 167.

43 Hallé's report in BI, Usuels AA 33, vol.18, no.34; Hintermeyer, *Politiques*, 21, 105–6, 137–41.

44 For a detailed discussion of the five contests in ethics, legislation, and political economy, see Staum, "The Enlightenment Transformed"; PV, 7 messidor V; BI, Usuels AA 33, vol.17, no.57, and Roederer, *Journal d'économie publique*, 30 vendémiaire VI, 309–15; Destutt de Tracy, "Quels sont les moyens de fonder la morale d'un peuple?" (1798), in *Commentaire*, 437–77.

45 "Rapport à l'Institut sur le catéchisme universel de Saint-Lambert ..." (20 brumaire VII), and "De la composition d'un catéchisme moral," in Roederer, *Œuvres*, 5:107–17, 122–29.

46 *Journal d'économie publique*, 30 vendémiaire VI (11 October 1797), 314.

47 Bernardin de Saint-Pierre, *De la nature de la morale*; Bernardin de Saint-Pierre, *Œuvres*, 7:424–6; PV-CSMP, 17, 22 germinal VI; AN, 29 AP III, Roederer's report, 261–3, and abstracts of memoirs, 265–369.

48 BI, Usuels AA 33, vol.17, no.57, Développements, 15 vendémiaire VII, 3–4.

49 AI-SMP, B4, Rapport de Ginguené, 15 nivôse VIII, 3, 6–7, 12.

50 Printed excerpts of Louis-Germain Petitain, no.5, 1st contest, public morality, in *Mémoires d'economie publique*, 1, 5 (1800):298–308; 2, no.1 (1802): 63–65; for the attack on perfectibility, see *Mémoires*, 1, no.5:279, 285, 288–97 and 2, no.1:65–85, 90.

51 AI-SMP, B4, 2nd contest, Rapport de Ginguené (15 nivôse an VIII), 9.

52 AN, 29 AP III, rapport, 261–3; cf. Kenneth Margerison, *P.-L. Roederer*, 94–113.

53 Staum, "Images of Paternal Power," 425–45; AI-SMP, B5, Rapport de Champagne, 15 vendémiaire VIII, 19–24; Ibid., Rapport de Daunou, 15 nivôse IX, 3–4, 9–10.

54 Ibid., Compte rendu de Dissertations sur l'autorité paternelle.

55 Staum, "Images," 421–3; for a provocative interpretation of revolt against father images and "rehabilitation of the family," see Hunt, *The Family Romance*, 153–65. More than other scholars, Hunt explores the theme of paternal status in novels and iconography.

56 AI-SMP, A6, Note to Baudin, 27 prairial VI.

57 Cambacérès, *Projet de Code Civil, messidor an IV*, 11–12, 29–30.

58 AI-SMP, B5, twelve contestants in three competitions (1798–99, 1799–1801, and 1801–2)

59 AI-SMP, B5, 1st contest, no.1, 9, and 2nd contest, no.6; printed excerpts in Roederer's *Mémoires d'économie publique*, 2, no.3 (1801):210–12, 214–19, 221, 224; see Montesquieu, *De l'esprit des lois*, book V, ch.7.

60 AI-SMP, B5, 2e concours, no.3, 1, 37, 145–51; a revised version is in A.-J.-S. Nougarède, *Essai sur l'histoire*, 91, 96–7, 204.

61 AI-SMP, B5, 1st contest, Rapport de Champagne, 15 vendémiaire VIII, 19–23.

62 AI-SMP, B5, 2nd contest, Rapport de Daunou, 15 nivôse IX, 9–10.

63 Sagnac, *La législation civile*, 350, 363.

64 J.-G. Locré, éd., *Procès-verbaux du Conseil d'État*, 2:368, 775.

65 Staum, "Images," 441–4.

66 AI-SMP, A6, Cambacérès to Baudin, 27 prairial VI, manuscript note suggesting the contest; Esmein, *A History*, 453–7, 461.

67 AI-SMP, B9 (January 1801–April 1802).

68 For the actual acquittal rates and practices of juries, see Woloch, "'Le Palladium de la Liberté'? Vicissitudes du juré criminel," in Vovelle, ed., *Images de la Révolution française*, 2:983–9.

69 Taillandier, *Documents biographiques*, 185–6; Godechot, *Les Institutions de la France*, 627.

70 Locré, ed., *La Législation civile*, 24:48, 443, 591.

71 AI-SMP, B9, no.4 Louvet opposed special courts.

72 Bourguignon, *Deuxième mémoire*, 55.

73 Bourguignon, *Mémoire*, 27; Bourguignon, *Deuxième mémoire*, 83; Bourguinon, *Troisième mémoire*, 41; Godechot, *Les Institutions*, 633.

74 Esmein, *A History*, 484; Bigot in Locré, ed., *La Législation civile*, 24:26, 28, 439, 447, 584, 591; AI-SMP, B9, Rapport de Garran-Coulon, 15 germinal X.

75 Staum, "The Enlightenment," 171–2.

76 *Mémoires d'économie publique*, 1, no.3 (30 nivôse VIII):179–83.

77 For Roederer's economic theory, see James, "Pierre-Louis Roederer," and Kaiser, "Politics and Political Economy"; see also Margerison, *P.-L. Roederer*, 94–108; Roederer, "Mémoires sur quelques points d'économie publique," *Œuvres*, 8:41–97.

78 *Mémoires d'économie publique*, 1, no.3 (30 nivôse VIII):179–81.

79 Staum, "The Enlightenment," 172–3; de Villesaison, *Mémoire sur cette question*, 6–7, 13–18, 22–4, 28, 42, 44n.

80 PV-CSMP, A5, 7 germinal IX.

81 Bergeron, *L'Épisode napoléonien*, 51–2; AI-SMP, B8; Canard, *Principes d'économie politique*, 3–6, 153–74; Roederer, *Œuvres*, 8:68–72.

82 Cf. the contrary view in Régaldo, *Un Milieu intellectuel*, 1:531; Moravia, *Il tramonto*, 576–81.

83 Portalis, *Discours*, 7, 24, 46, 48–9; Villers, *Essai sur l'esprit et l'influence*, 202–3n.

84 Ponce, *Essai historique*, 98–9; Leuliette, *Discours*, 59; Villers, *Essai sur l'esprit et l'influence*, 3, 17–18, 32, 40, 55–6, 95, 228, 260, 345.

85 *Mercure de France*, 14 fructidor XII–1 September 1804, 11:486, 494.

CHAPTER FIVE

1 Brunel, *Les Philosophes*, 199–201, 232.

2 See Popkin, *The Right-Wing Press*, 79–80, 177–8, 196, for police reports and P.-L. Roederer's estimates; Cabanis, *La Presse sous le Consulat*, 320–1. The above estimates include *L'Ami des lois* (5,000); the pro-Directory moderate *Clef du cabinet des souverains* (1,100); the scholarly, pro-Idéologue *La Décade philosophique* (1,000); Joseph Fiévée's royalist *Gazette française*, later the *Gazette de France* (1,700–3,750); two dailies, the *Journal de Paris* (2,600–3,600) and, in the Consulate, the very conservative *Journal des débats* (6,000–10,000); the scholarly, pro-Institute *Magasin encyclopédique*, edited by Aubin-Louis Millin (500), Louis Fontanes's right-wing *Mercure de France* (1,500); the daily semi-official *Moniteur* (6,000); and the royalist J.-B.-A. Suard's *Nouvelles politiques*, later *Le Publiciste* (4,000–5,000). See Popkin, *Revolutionary News*, 84–5.

3 *Clef du cabinet des souverains* (hereafter CCS), 19 vendémiaire VI.

4 "Description de la salle des séances publiques de l'Institut national," *Décade philosophique* (hereafter DP), 15:152–6, 30 vendémiaire VI; CCS, 5:3259, 23 nivôse VI, and 14:9809–10, 21 germinal VIII; *Journal de Paris* (hereafter JP), 17 germinal VIII.

5 For efforts to reform public sessions, see AI, Registre des assemblées générales de l'Institut, 3A1, 5 floréal IV; 3A 2, 5 fructidor VI; and 3A3, 5 germinal IX; Crosland, *Science under Control*, 356. For press complaints, see DP, 9:125, 20 germinal IV, 17:110, 20 germinal VI, and 19:107, 20 vendémiaire VII. See also JP, 17 messidor IV, 1150–1; CCS, 14:9809–10, 21 germinal VIII; *Journal des Débats* (hereafter JD), 17 nivôse IX.

6 DP, 29:119, 20 germinal IX.

7 Aucoc, *Institut de France*, 30–31; for restrictions on auditors to an élite, scientifically sophisticated group in the Class of Mathematical and Physical

Sciences, and for later prohibitions on debate with the public, see Crosland, *Science under Control,* 26–7.

8 DP, 9:125, 20 germinal IV; CCS, 19 nivôse and 22 germinal V; see *Magasin encyclopédique* (hereafter ME), 14:252, on the 15 messidor V session, and the citation on erudition is from Roederer in *JP,* 17 messidor IX.

9 Du Pont, *Quelques mémoires,* 263–4, 274, 316; see favourable reaction in CCS, 19 nivôse and 19 germinal V, and a more critical tone in DP, 13:110, 20 germinal V.

10 JP, 17 germinal IV, 787–8; 17 nivôse X, 639; CCS, 19 nivôse V; 17 nivôse X, 7–8; DP, 32:113, 20 nivôse X.

11 Taillandier, *Documents biographiques,* 103, 107–8.

12 See the discussion in Chapter 10 on political science.

13 MSMP, 5 (1804):317–30, esp.330; *Le Publiciste,* 17 germinal VII.

14 Toulongeon, *De l'esprit public;* DP, 31:116, 20 vendémiaire X.

15 For Talleyrand on trade see MSMP, 2 (1799):86–106; see also reactions in CCS, 18 germinal V, 788; ME, 12:526.

16 Fleurieu, *Voyage autour du monde,* 1:373–402, esp.376, 380, 398–400; see also Chapter 9.

17 Lettre de Talleyrand à Papon, 8 vendémiaire VII, AI-SMP (unclassified); MSMP, *Histoire* 3:22–26; MSMP *Histoire,* 4:68–9; *Mémoires de l'Institut royal de France, Classe d'Histoire et Littérature ancienne, Histoire,* 3:85–9.

18 MSMP, 3:40–60, esp.59; CCS, 20 vendémiaire VII, 5441; JP, 17 vendémiaire VII, 768–9; Martin-Allanic, *Bougainville navigateur,* 2:1329.

19 Buache's memoir in MSMP, 3:264–321; DP, 27:141–5, 30 vendémiaire IX. Faivre, *L'expansion française,* 109–10, 158, 164; for Bernardin de Saint-Pierre, see DP, 27:141–5, 30 vendémiaire IX.

20 MSMP, 4:27–44; Bibliothèque nationale, MSS NAF 9373, cited by F.C.T. Moore in Degérando, *The Observation of Savage Peoples,* 13, 110.

21 JP, 17 germinal IV, 788.

22 Doyle, *The Oxford History,* 331–7, 370–1.

23 Bellanger et al., *Histoire générale de la presse française,* 1:525, 536, 543–7.

24 Aucoc, *L'Institut,* 55; AN, AD XVIII[C] 439, Daunou, *Compte rendu et présenté au Corps législatif par l'Institut national ... an V,* 169.

25 Malandain, *Delisle de Sales,* 1:368, 375–8; 2:709–10.

26 Delisle de Sales, *À l'Institut National de France,* 1–21, esp.16–17, 21; *Mémoires pour les Académies,* 139–48.

27 Delisle de Sales, *À l'Institut,* 55, 76, 115; JP, 19 germinal VIII, 871–2, 3 floréal VIII; *Gazette de France* (hereafter GF), 5 floréal VIII; on Joseph Fiévée, see Popkin, "Conservatism under Napoleon."

28 Cf. analogous speeches in the Academy of the Moral and Political Sciences in the 1840s; see also Chapter 12.

29 JP, 10 floréal VIII, reprinted in Roederer, *Œuvres,* 5:363–5. François Guizot, interior minister in 1830, used this precedent to refuse the

administrative reintegration in the Académie française and the Académie des Inscriptions of those purged in 1816; see Barksdale, "Liberal Politics," 193–4.

30 *JP*, 6 floréal VIII, 947, 8 floréal VIII, 972, and 29 floréal VIII; see also *GF*, 6 floréal VIII, *JD*, 7 floréal VIII, and *Le Publiciste*, 7 floréal VIII.

31 *Ami des lois*, 15 floréal VIII, and 7 prairial VIII; see also *Le Publiciste*, 7 prairial VIII; *JD*, 8 prairial VIII; *GF*, 9 prairial VIII; *DP*, 25:441–3, 10 prairial VIII.

32 See Cabanis, *La Presse*, 20–1, for the suppression and Napoleon's letter.

33 For elections of Bonaparte and Sicard, see AI-3A2, 5 nivôse VI, and AI-3A3, 5 messidor IX.

34 *JD*, 7 floréal VII; *DP*, 22:493, 20 fructidor VII.

35 See Désirat and Hordé, "Les écoles normales," 37–9, 46–7, for the École normale debate of 1795 between Laharpe defending eloquence and Garat condemning it as serving tyranny and superstition. Even Voltaire in 1775 had questioned the utility of eulogies as eloquence prize subjects; see Brunel, *Les Philosophes*, 303.

36 [Chaptal], *Analyse des procès-verbaux*, 539–57.

37 *GF*, 12, 19, 24 messidor VIII; *Le Publiciste*, 14 messidor VIII; Louis Fontanes in *Mercure de France*, 16 messidor VIII, 106.

38 *DP*, 10:111–12, 20 messidor IV; see also 18:114–17, 20 messidor VI, and 23:111, 20 vendémiaire VIII.

39 *DP*, 27:116, 20 vendémiaire IX; see also *DP*, 17:109, 20 germinal VI; *CCS*, 18 messidor VI; *ME*, 14:252; and *JD*, 3 ventôse VIII, 2 messidor VIII, and 17 nivôse IX.

40 Beale, "Academies to Institut," 122–7.

41 Lucien Bonaparte was also a patron of Louis Fontanes; see Iung, *Lucien Bonaparte et ses mémoires*, 1:390; *Mémoires (inédits) de l'Abbé Morellet*, 2:81–106, esp.81–9; *JD*, 2 messidor VIII.

42 Morellet, *Mémoires*, 2:88–9; *GF*, 12 messidor VIII.

43 Napoleon's letter to Lucien Bonaparte is cited by Gaffarel, "L'opposition littéraire sous le consulat," 312.

44 *DP*, 30:34, 10 messidor IX.

45 Morellet, *Mémoires*, 2:90; *ME*, 32:261–2.

46 Delisle de Sales, *Académies*, 182–6, 192–7; Burton, *Napoleon and Clio*, 54–5; the *Décade* mischievously suggested that de Sales would soon write memoirs in favour of the Parlements, clergy, and the Merovingian dynasty: *DP*, 27:438, 10 frimaire IX.

47 *Mercure*, 16 thermidor VIII; *JP*, 19 thermidor VIII.

48 Chaptal, *Rapport et projet de loi sur l'instruction publique*, 59–60, 82; Morellet, *Mémoires*, 2:103–6.

49 *DP*, 29:333–4, 30 floréal IX.

50 A1-3A3, 5 floréal IX (other members of the Dictionary commission were
J.-B.-J. Delambre, Lacepède, Laplace, L.-B. Guyton de Morveau, J.-A.
Naigeon, Dacier, Daunou, Gabriel Villar, and M.-C.-J. Pougens); see
Andrieux's first report at the public session of 15 messidor IX in *DP*,
30:85, 20 messidor IX; Morellet, *Du projet annoncé par l'Institut national*, 13, 15–6, 18. Morellet's defence of "politesse" seems a typical
instance of Darnton's Voltairean Enlightenment, which was so much
shaken by the Rousseauist and Revolutionary disdain for social refinement; Darnton, "The Literary Revolution of 1789," 20–6.

51 See Chapter 3. The Institute did include less socially prestigious engineers
in the mechanical arts section and actors in the music and declamation
section. For Morellet's defence of the Philosophes and his attack on the
Revolution, see Christian Albertan, "Lumières et Révolution, le point de
vue de Morellet," in *L'Écrivain devant la Révolution*, ed. Sgard, 121–30,
esp.122–5; Mortier, "André Morellet devant la Révolution," in Matucci,
9–18. On Morellet's dictionary project, see Jean-Claude Perrot, "Les dic-
tionnaires de commerce au XVIIIᵉ siècle," in *Une Histoire intellectuelle*,
97–125.

52 Roederer, *JP*, 17 messidor VII, 1258–9; *CCS*, 18 messidor VII, 7583–8.

53 Morellet, *Du projet*, 24–7; for Morellet's scorn of Sieyès, see Darnton,
"Un philosophe face à la Terreur," in *Gens de lettres*, 145.

54 AN, AF^{IV} 1050, dossier 9, 7–8.

55 Morellet, *Mémoires*, 2:112; the Chaptal report in Aucoc, 67–72, esp.68.

56 Villenave, "Garat," in *Biographie universelle*, 15:541.

57 Morellet, *Mémoires*, 2:119–20; for the careers of Morellet, Suard, Saint-
Lambert, see Kors, *D'Holbach's Coterie*; Goodman, *The Republic of Letters*, 309–10; Darnton, *Gens de lettres*, 47–67, 139–50.

58 See Malandain on Delisle de Sales, and the Weiss article in *Biographie
universelle*, 24:598–602.

59 Dhombres and Dhombres, *Naissance d'un pouvoir*, 271; Hahn, *The
Anatomy*, 155–7; Souriau, *Bernardin de Saint-Pierre*, xl–xli, 320.

60 Hermann Hofer, "Mercier devant la Révolution," in *L'Écrivain*, ed.
Sgard; Dhombres and Dhombres, *Naissance*, 443–4; Jacques Solé,
"L'image de la Révolution française dans *Le Nouveau Paris* de Louis-
Sébastien Mercier," in Vovelle, ed., *L'Image de la Révolution française*,
3:1899–1904. See Chapter 6 for a discussion of Mercier on Kant.

61 Dhombres and Dhombres, *Naissance*, 276–8, 314–6.

62 Morellet, *Mémoires*, 2:119–20; *GF*, 16 vendémiaire IX, 1028.

63 *GF*, 23 nivôse XI, 189; *JD*, 16 nivôse XI.

CHAPTER SIX

1 Destutt de Tracy, "Mémoire sur la faculté de penser," *MSMP*, 1:344–5.

2 *OP*, 1:126; 2:209–10; on "physical and mental," see 1:142; on denial of materialism, see de Luppé, *Les Idées littéraires de Madame de Staël*, 70–1.

3 Condillac, "Traité des sensations," 1:230, and "Traité des animaux (1755)," in Condillac, *Œuvres philosophiques*, 1:374–7. On the legacy of Condillac, see Albury, "The Order of Ideas," in Schuster and Yeo, *The Politics*, 218–19.

4 See Dowd, *Pageant-Master of the Republic*, 45–77, on festivals as a propaganda technique, and 125–42 on social control of public opinion; on the broader attempt to create a utilitarian, patriotic republican art, see Leith, *The Idea of Art as Propaganda*, 104–56 esp.109–10, 132–3; Leith, *Media and Revolution*, 6–7; Hunt, *Politics, Culture, and Class*, 91–2; Ozouf, *Festivals in the French Revolution*; see Leith, *Space and Revolution*, for architecture.

5 Staum, *Cabanis*. Cabanis read six memoirs to the Institute in 1796–97, a seventh in 1800, and added five more in *Rapports du physique et du moral de l'homme* (1802).

6 Teysseire, "Lien social et ordre politique chez Cabanis," 353–400.

7 Cabanis, "Du degré de certitude de la médecine" (1798), *OP*, 1:99–101n.

8 Foucault, *Discipline and Punish*, 25–8, 102–3; and, on the Idéologues, 138, 143–4, 176–7, 220–8; for the abuses of labelling, see Goldstein, *Console and Classify*.

9 Staum, *Cabanis*, 220–32.

10 Cabanis, *OP*, 1:356–8.

11 Laqueur, *Making Sex*, viii, 11, 149–51, 153, 195–9, 281. A confirmation of this view appears in Fraisse, *Reason's Muse*, 73–96, esp.78, who more controversially ascribes women's exclusion to premises of democratic thought about citizenship.

12 Imbert, *Décade philosophique*, 30 pluviôse and 10 ventôse XI, 321–8, esp.325; 385–94, and Laya, *Décade philosophique*, 10 prairial and 10 messidor XIII, 403–12 and 11–26.

13 Hoffmann, *La Femme dans la pensée des lumières*, 153–6; Teysseire, "Fonctionnalisme sexuel et privatisation de la femme chez Cabanis et quelques autres," *Les Femmes et la Révolution française*, 1:343–50.

14 Roussel, *Système physique et moral de la femme*, 16, 62, 91.

15 Ibid., 30–4, 100–4, 288.

16 Cabanis, *OP*, 1:273, 278–9, 284, 291–3, 297–9.

17 For the exclusion of women from the public space of Revolutionary Stoic heroism, see Outram, *The Body and the French Revolution*, 33, 84, 124–52; see Landes, *Women and the Public Sphere*, 66–89, on Rousseau, and 169–89 on Comte; Hunt, *The Family Romance*, 156–9.

18 Destutt de Tracy, *De l'amour*, 28, 45–6, 49–50; reprinted in 1994 with *Traité de la volonté*, ed. Deneys and Deneys.

19 Garat, *Séances des écoles normales*, 1:145–8; 2:4–5; 36–7, 39; a new French edition of selected École normale lectures is available. For Garat on signs, see Joël Ganault, "Idéologie et organisation du savoir à l'Institut national," in Azouvi, ed., *L'Institution de la raison*, 70–2; Cabanis, *OP*, 1:157; Marcelo Dascal, "Signs and Cognitive Processes: Notes for a Chapter in the History of Semiotics," in Eschbach and Trabant, eds., *History of Semiotics*, 169–90, and Knowlson, *Universal Language Schemes*, 150–60 on pasigraphy, 161–82 on signs and thought, and 183–209 on the perfect language.

20 Alfaric, *Laromiguière et son école*, 31, 34.

21 Chouillet and Auroux, eds., *Condillac: Langue des calculs*, xxxii–iii, and, in the same work, "Note des éditeurs," by Laromiguière, 478–80.

22 Laromiguière, *Paradoxes de Condillac*, 55–7, 80–4, 114, 145–6, 156.

23 Ibid., 105, 188, 235–6; Auroux, *Langue des Calculs*, xviii; Laromiguière, *Leçons de philosophie*, 1:32, 62; 2:130, 305.

24 Degérando, *Des signes*, 4:468–86, 543–56.

25 Lavoisier, *Traité élémentaire de chimie*, i–xxxii; Albury, "The Order of Ideas," 207–10, on Lavoisier; Rousseau, *Connaissance et Langage chez Condillac*, 291–2.

26 AI-SMP, A2, PV-CSMP, 17 prairial and 2 messidor an IV; the memoirs are in AI-SMP, B1 and B2; Ganault, "Idéologie et organisation du savoir," 63–81.

27 See Butet, *Abrégé d'un cours complet de lexicologie*; Brigitte Schlieben-Lange, "Les idéologues et l'écriture," in Busse and Trabant, *Les Idéologues*, 185–6; Dougnac,"La néologie," 67–72.

28 Lancelin, *Introduction à l'analyse des sciences*, 1:34–5n, 63, 75, 336, 353–4, 375–7, 410, 436n; 2:90–6, 136, 203, 283.

29 Knowlson, *Universal Language Schemes*, 150–60.

30 Degérando, *Des signes*, 4:436–41.

31 PV-CSMP, PV, 7 prairial VI, 17 prairial VII, 7 ventôse VIII, 27 floréal VIII, 27 germinal IX.

32 Destutt de Tracy, "Réflexions sur les projets de pasigraphie," *MSMP*, 3:535–51.

33 Degérando, *Des signes*, 3:550–1, 572; 4:80, 109, 355, 363, 390–407, 436–41.

34 *MSMP*, 1:414–16.

35 Destutt de Tracy, *Éléments d'idéologie: Grammaire*, 369–80; *Éléments d'idéologie, Idéologie proprement dite* (1970 ed.), 1:345–6, 2:279–80.

36 Destutt de Tracy, *Éléments d'idéologie: Idéologie proprement dite*, 1:340–9; Auroux, "Idéologie et Langue des calculs," 53–7.

37 Auroux, *Langue des calculs*, xii–xiii.

38 Destutt de Tracy, *Grammaire*, 384–9.

39 Degérando, *Des signes*, 1:194, 294; 2:162–3; 3:37, 74–5, 151; Bowman, "Degérando et la théorie des signes," in Matucci, ed., *Gli "Idéologues" e*

la Rivoluzione, 209–19; comparable views were expressed by runner-up Pierre Prévost, *Des signes*, 20.

40 Degérando, *Des signes*, 4:576.

41 Ibid., 3:241; 4:324–5, 328–9; cf. Prévost, 26–7, and AI-SMP, B2, no.7, 84–5; AI-SMP, B6, 2nd contest, no.6 (Isnard), 40, 43.

42 Degérando, *Des signes*, 3:260–1, 266.

43 Ibid., 1:127, 151; 2:345; 3:156; Degérando, *De la génération des connaissances humaines*, 125, 171, 218; AI-SMP, B1, no.7, 6 (Ricard); B2, no.4, 14, 39 (Escher).

44 Lakanal, "Rapport sur l'organisation des écoles normales, 2 brumaire an III," in Hippeau, *L'Instruction publique en France pendant la Révolution* (Paris, 1883), 2:416–17, cited in Moravia, *Il tramonto*, 384n.

45 Condillac, "Cours d'études: grammaire," in *Œuvres*, 1:434; "Logique," 2:398.

46 Garat, *Séances*, 1:150.

47 Roederer, "Cours d'organisation sociale," in *Œuvres*, 8:182, 224–5.

48 Ibid., 207; for Roederer's political and scientific thought, see Margerison, *P.-L. Roederer*.

49 Kennedy, *A Philosophe*; Head, *Ideology and Social Science*; Goetz, *Destutt de Tracy*.

50 "Mémoire sur la faculté de penser," in MSMP, 1:288, 320, 323–4, for ideology (this memoir now available in a 1992 Fayard edition by A. and H. Deneys); for "branch of zoology," see *Éléments d'idéologie*, 1:xiii.

51 MSMP, 1:392; "De la métaphysique de Kant," MSMP, 4:549 (also available now in the 1992 re-edition by the Deneys); Kennedy, "Destutt de Tracy and the Unity of the Sciences," 223–39.

52 Laromiguière, "Sur la détermination des mots, analyse des sensations," MSMP, 1:452, 454–6, 466; "Extrait d'un mémoire sur la détermination du mot Idée, "1:471; the lost memoir of November 1796 on the "Système des opérations de l'entendement," critical of Condillac, is reported in AN, AD XVIIIᶜ 439, *Compte-rendu et notice des travaux de la Classe des Sciences morales et politiques*, an v, 4; Ricken, "Les Idéologues et la sensation transformée," in Busse and Trabant, 19–43.

53 AI-SMP, B1; Joseph-Marie Degérando, *Des signes*, 4:101n.

54 *Journal des Débats*, 12 frimaire x (4 December 1801); Degérando, *Des signes*, 1:11; *De la génération*, 109, 154, 232–6; on Degérando, see also Moravia, *Il pensiero*, 417–56.

55 Degérando, *Histoire comparée des systèmes de philosophie*, 1:33, 50, 345–6; 2:466; 3:316, 324, 374–5, 378n.

56 Degérando, "Philosophie," 278–355, esp.340, 347, in Dacier, ed., *Rapport historique*.

57 Degérando, *Histoire comparée* (1804), 1:xv, cited in Donald R. Kelley, "What is Happening to the History of Ideas?" 8.

58 Laromiguière, *Leçons de philosophie* (1815), 1:6, 63, 91, 149, 213; *Leçons de philosophie* (1820–23), 1:12–13, 74n120, 151, 169, 188, 245; 2:58, 67–9, 272, 428; Victor Cousin, *Fragments philosophiques*, 5:341–78.

59 For a similar separation of Condillac's empiricism from materialism, see Daunou, Bibliothèque nationale, Manuscrits NAF 21910, fol.56, "Note historique sur une opinion de Condillac."

60 AN, 284 AP 2, dossier 2, 1773–76, "Les deux statues de Condillac et de Bonnet," 8, 12, 14, 51.

61 Passage previously published in Forsyth, *Reason and Revolution*, 42, 47.

62 AN, 284 AP 17 (1796), dossier 4, letters of Reinhard to Sieyès, 18, 30 nivôse and 2 pluviôse IV; see Azouvi and Bourel, eds., *De Königsberg à Paris*, 77–83.

63 AN, 284 AP 5, dossier 1/1.

64 AN, 284 AP 5, dossier 3/1, fol.b.

65 Ibid., dossier 3/1 "Du cerveau et l'instinct," fols.4, 6, 7, 10; see also dossier 3/2, "Travail sur la vie," fols.2, 43.

66 The first contest memoirs are in AI-SMP, B 10, and the second set is in AI-Archives de l'Académie des Inscriptions et Belles-Lettres (hereafter IBL), 1H9.

67 See AI-SMP, B 10, no.13 (Blank), 1–2, 6–7, for the strongest support of Cabanis, and AI-IBL, 1H9, no.17, 1–3; on the antireligious or monist side, see AI-IBL, 1H9, no.15, 2–3, 6–7, for the deist side, see Ibid., no.10 (Louilliet), 15, 89–90, 113, 121; AI-SMP, B10, no.8 (anon); Ibid., no.3 (J.-B. Garnier), 3–4; on the dualist side, see Ibid., no.10 (Maugras), 5, 7, 9, 12, 19, 21, 26, 42, 45, 61; Serre, *Nouvelle théorie des facultés de l'âme*, vi, 6, 23–4, 28–9, 98–100n; AI-IBL, 1H9, no.9 (Fontaine), also AI-SMP, B 10, no.2, 6, 8, 12–13, 45, 47; AI-IBL, 1H9, no.8 (Bonot-Vuillier), 3, 8–9.

68 J. Garebeuf, *Réflexions sur l'ouvrage de M. Cabanis*, iv, 5–8, 13, 24; AI-IBL, 1H9, no.12, 5, 9, 14, 20, 29, 60, 67, 69–70, 114–15, 130–1; [Caze], *Essai sur la décomposition de la pensée*, 38, 42, 58, 83–4, 86, 97; AI-IBL, 1H9, no.14 (Sédillot), 10, 14, 52–4.

69 On Maine de Biran, see Dimitri Voutsinas, *La Psychologie de Maine de Biran*; F.C.T. Moore, *The Psychology of Maine de Biran*; Moravia, *Il pensiero*, 484–5, 508; G. Romeyer-Dherbey, *Maine de Biran*; Letter of Biran to Degérando, 26 vendémiaire XI, in Maine de Biran, *Œuvres complètes*, ed. Tisserand, 6:148–9; cf. Henri Gouhier, *Les Conversions de Maine de Biran*, 163; Maine de Biran, "Note sur les signes," in *Œuvres*, ed. Tisserand, 1:245; appearing too late for consultation was the important new doctoral thesis on Maine de Biran by Azouvi.

70 Maine de Biran, *Œuvres, tome 3: Mémoire sur la décomposition de la pensée*, ed. Azouvi, 24–5, 308, 385; the prizewinning memoir text is at 18:298, while the revised version for the incomplete and unpublished printing on 301–439 contains innumerable editorial corrections to the Tisserand edition.

71 Ibid., 318, 321–3, 331, 362n; Madinier, *Conscience et mouvement.*

72 Maine de Biran, *Mémoire sur la décomposition*, 337–8, 344–6, 396–7.

73 Summary tables appended to the text in *Œuvres, tome* 3, ed. Azouvi.

74 Roederer, "Cours," in *Œuvres*, 8:185–6, 227–8; see also "Deux éléments de la sociabilité humaine, l'imitation et l'habitude," *Journal d'économie publique* (hereafter *JEP*, 10, 20, 30 pluviôse V), 2:311–30, 349–57, 399–410, reprinted in *Œuvres* 5:258–72.

75 Roederer, "Cours," 8:215, 221–2; on Revolutionary architecture plans as integrating antiroyalist or antifeudal propaganda, see Leith, *Space and Revolution.*

76 *JEP*, 313, 402–5, 409–10.

77 Destutt de Tracy, "Quels sont les moyens de fonder la morale chez un peuple?" in *Commentaire*, 451, 461–2; Cabanis, *Œuvres complètes*, ed. Thurot, 2:444–50; Cabanis, *OP*, 2:428, 440.

78 Destutt de Tracy, *MSMP*, 1:429, 437, 439–42.

79 Destutt de Tracy, *Idéologie proprement dite*, 255–8.

80 Ibid., 294–6.

81 Destutt de Tracy, *Logique*, 312; *Supplément aux Éléments d'idéologie* (1826 ed.), 4:45–6.

82 AI-SMP, PV 12, vendémiaire VIII.

83 Rapport de Tracy, AI-SMP, B6, 17 messidor X (reprinted in Maine de Biran, *Œuvres: Influence de l'habitude sur la faculté de penser*, ed. Romeyer-Dherbey, 2:338–9). AI-IBL, 1H9, no.5 (Canard).

84 AI-SMP, B6, Mullot, no.4, 33, 64, 69, 88, 103, 125–6, 136; cf. Caze's similar view in AI-IBL, 1H9, no.4, 22, 26, 45–6.

85 See Bibliothèque de l'Institut, MS 2128, 39–40, for a copy of the draft memoir of 1799 endorsing Cabanis on organic sensations; cf. the contest submission of 1801 contesting transformed sensations.

86 Maine de Biran, *Œuvres*, ed. Romeyer-Dherbey, 2:17, 22, 31–2, 65, 69, 74, 76, 132–61, 362.

87 Staum, *Cabanis*, 259–64 for the discussion with Destutt de Tracy; see letter to Tracy on Biran's disappointment at the changed emphasis on motility, *Œuvres*, ed. Tisserand, 6:231–3; Moravia, *Il pensiero*, 399–400, 405–6.

88 Maine de Biran, *Œuvres*, ed. Romeyer-Dherbey, 138–40, 147–8; Staum, 262.

89 Ibid., 212, 323; see critique by Tracy, Rapport, 17 messidor X, in Maine de Biran, *Œuvres*, ed. Romeyer-Dherbey, 346–7; by Degérando in *Décade*, 20 nivôse XI, in Ibid., 358.

90 Ibid., first memoir, 100, second memoir, 204–14, esp.205.

91 Ibid., 229–31, 259, 267.

92 Romeyer-Dherbey, "Maine de Biran et les signes," 514–41; Maine de Biran, *Œuvres*, ed. Romeyer-Dherbey, 243n, 277n, 278, 287–8, 290.

93 Voutsinas, *La Psychologie de Maine de Biran*, 69, 73, 115.

94 On the general subject of the introduction of Kant's thought in France, see Azouvi and Bourel, eds., *De Königsberg à Paris*, 86–183; Mercier, Bibliothèque de l'Arsenal, Manuscrits, 15087(c), "Vues sur la morale" (1799), fols.82v, 83r, 101, 103; see also "Vues politico-morales" (1799), fols.78–9.

95 Mercier, "Mémoire sur Kant" (1801), fols.106–8, 112–13, 121–2, 124–5; for a summary of memoir on innate ideas, see *Décade philosophique*, 20 floréal VIII, 306–9.

96 *Notice des travaux de la Classe ... Ier trimestre de l'an X*, 6–7.

97 *Journal des Débats*, 1 germinal VIII, 3; letters of Mercier, 14, 20, and 30 nivôse X, 2–3; *Décade*, 30 floréal VIII, 375–6.

98 AI-SMP, B2, no.9, part 2, chapter 8, pages not numbered.

99 Azouvi and Bourel, eds., *De Königsberg à Paris*, 238–59; Kant, *Critique de la raison pratique*, Introduction by François Picavet, vi and xxi–xxiv on Mercier; J.-M. Degérando, *Histoire comparée* (1804), 1:33; 2:179, 183–5, 193, 199–200.

100 Ibid., 3: 520, 525, 544–52.

101 See Destutt de Tracy's letter in *Décade philosophique*, 10 vendémiaire IX, 54–7 (attribution by Marc Régaldo).

102 "De la métaphysique de Kant," MSMP, 4:548, 552–3, 558–60, 570, 604 (a new reprint is available in the Deneys edition of 1992). Paradoxically, Morellet, the great critic of Institute literary efforts before 1803, commented adversely on Villers's Kantianism in favour of the empiricism of Locke and Condillac; see his manuscripts cited in Simone Meyssonier, "Deux économistes sous la Révolution: Véron de Forbonnais et l'Abbé Morellet," in *Colloque: La pensée économique pendant la Révolution française* (Vizille, 1989), 2, 6th paper, 15–7.

103 On Maine de Biran's use of the term eclectic, see Gouhier, *Les Conversions*, 248.

104 See Maine de Biran, *Journal*, ed. Gouhier (Paris, 1954), 1:8, and 22 September 1814, 17 March 1817, as cited in Barksdale, "Liberal Politics," 126, 203, 205.

105 For an informative survey of medical disciples of Cabanis and spiritualist physicians in the Restoration, see Jacyna, "Medical Science and Moral Science," 111–46; for other reflections on ideology and phrenology, see Staum, "Physiognomy and Phrenology."

106 Barksdale, "Liberal Politics," 350–1 on the 1837–38 memoirs of the new Academy of Moral and Political Sciences.

CHAPTER SEVEN

1 See Chartier, *The Cultural Origins*, 103–6, for popular cultural disengagement from the Church, stemming as much from the excessive rigour of Jansenist priests as the hypocritical laxity of Jesuits and non-Jansenist

priests and the urban decline of a coherent parish. Despite Vovelle's conclusions about long-term changes in birth control practices and attitudes toward death, the Catholic revival of the nineteenth century raises doubts about how long this alienation lasted. Cf. Kennedy, *A Cultural History*, 384–92.

2 Helvétius, "De l'esprit," *Œuvres complètes*, 1:314; "De l'homme" [1772], 3:431–2n.

3 Ibid., 1:375; 3:430, 436.

4 Ibid., 3:51, 54n, 74, 78; 4:86–7.

5 D'Holbach, *Système de la nature*, 1:142, 145, 151, 345.

6 Mercier, *L'An* 2440, 69, 79, 87n.

7 Ibid., 109, 122, 137, 158–9, 168.

8 [Delisle de Sales], *De la philosophie de la nature*, 1:271–5, 281, 286, 295, 311, 328; 2:7, 108, 162, 241, 262; 5:200, 219; *Biographie universelle* (Michaud), 24:598–600; and Malandain, *Delisle de Sales*, 1:354. For the post-Revolutionary definition of happiness, see Delisle de Sales, *De la philosophie du bonheur*, 2:24, 70, 99, 117; cf. Mauzi, *L'Idée du bonheur*, 408–9. For other Institute efforts to reconcile happiness and virtue, see Du Pont, *Philosophie de l'univers*, and *Sur la liberté morale*; Villeterque, *Les Veillées philosophiques*.

9 McManners, *The French Revolution and the Church*, 61–131; Vovelle, *La Révolution contre l'Église*; Lyons, *France under the Directory*, 100–15.

10 For Roederer on Volney, see *Mémoires d'économie publique*, vol.1, no.8 (1800), 361–81; Cabanis, *OP*, 1:119.

11 Volney, *La Loi naturelle*, 39.

12 Destutt de Tracy, "Quels sont les moyens," in *Commentaire*, 45.

13 Volney, *La Loi naturelle*, 9–10; Gaulmier, *L'Idéologue Volney*, 270–8; see Deneys and Deneys on the *Moniteur* announcement of the catechism in *Corpus*, n° 11/12 (1989): 106–7.

14 Volney, *La Loi naturelle*, 12, 17.

15 Olson, *The Emergence of the Social Sciences*, 53–4.

16 Volney, *La Loi naturelle*, 45–8.

17 Ibid., 51–3, 58–9.

18 Ibid., 47, 49, 66.

19 Ibid., 60–1.

20 For the shared assumptions of regeneration and more austerely Rousseauist and patriotic Jacobin morality, see Serge Leroux, "L'idée de morale: un outil idéologique au service de la Révolution," in Vovelle, ed., *L'Image de la Révolution française*, 1:458–67.

21 Volney, *La Loi naturelle*, 42, 53, 56.

22 Cabanis, *OP*, 1:156, 199; 2:209–10.

23 Tracy, "Quels sont les moyens," 458.

24 On Naigeon, Kors, *D'Holbach's Coterie*, 276–7; Naigeon, *Philosophie ancienne et moderne*, 1:xvii, xxiii–iv, 3, 29–30, 35; *Adresse à l'Assemblée nationale* (1790), 53–5 cited in Lough, *The Philosophes*, 199.

25 Grégoire, *Mémoires*, 2:9–10.

26 Souriau, *Bernardin de Saint-Pierre*, 326; Grégoire, *Histoire des sectes religieuses*, 1:liii, lvi.

27 Necheles, *The Abbé Grégoire*, 9–39, 60–125; Grégoire, *De la littérature des nègres*, v–vi; the antislavery phalanx in the Second Class included Bernardin de Saint-Pierre, Mercier, Volney, Garat, Roederer, Sieyès, and associates Destutt de Tracy, Crèvecœur, Diannyère, Raimond, and Lescallier.

28 Grégoire, *De la littérature*, 19–33, 44, 81, 87, 89, 174–5, 185, 279.

29 *MSMP*, 4:45–75; esp.46–9, 62, 64, 70; for modern evaluations, see Wagner, *The Life and Writings of Bartolomé de las Casas*, 22–3, 40–1, 245–7; Friede and Keen, eds., *Bartolomé de Las Casas in History*, 505–6. For a curious lament on the dishonesty of servants that shows Grégoire's concept of limited social mobility, see Grégoire, *De la domesticité*, read partly as an Institute memoir in 1803.

30 La Revellière-Lépeaux, *Réflexions sur le culte*, 4, 7, 10–11; members included Du Pont on the directing committee and Creuzé-Latouche; see Grégoire, *Histoire des sectes*, 2:90, 101–2, 113–5; Mathiez, *La Théophilanthropie*, 106n, 107, 136, 207.

31 Ozouf, *La Fête révolutionnaire*, 145–6, 326–7; La Revellière-Lépeaux, *Réflexions*, 10, 33–4.

32 Malandain, *Delisle de Sales*, 1:436–49, details the furore over Delisle de Sales's *Mémoire en faveur de Dieu* (1802); see his *Mémoire*, 4–7, 151, 219, 230, 243.

33 De Sèze, *Recherches phisiologiques et philosophiques*, 31, 73, 275.

34 Staum, *Cabanis*, 189–91; Cabanis, *OP*, 1:578; 2:26.

35 Staum, *Cabanis*, 207–43; Cabanis, *OP*, 2:28, 211.

36 Head, *Ideology and Social Science*, 79–83, 86–7; Destutt de Tracy, *Traité de la volonté*, 491, 502–3, 507–8, 512–16.

37 Destutt de Tracy, "Quels sont les moyens," 438–9, 453, 461–5, 469.

38 Ibid., 451, 460–2; Cabanis, *op*, 2:449, 449–50n.

39 Bernardin de Saint-Pierre, "Études de la nature, XII" (1783), *Œuvres complètes*, 5:1–135; Racault, "Paul et Virginie et l'utopie," 419–71, esp.456–8.

40 Bernardin de Saint-Pierre, *De la nature de la morale*, 31, 34; *Œuvres complètes*, 7:424–8.

41 Bernardin de Saint-Pierre, *De la nature*, 5–6, 9.

42 Bibliothèque de l'Arsénal, Manuscrits de Mercier, MS 15087(c), 82v, 107, 115, 119, 130v.

43 Jacques Solé, "L'image de la Révolution française dans le 'Nouveau Paris' de Louis-Sébastien Mercier," in Vovelle, ed., *L'Image*, 3 (1989): 1899–03.

44 Roederer, *Œuvres*, 5:153–6, and *Journal d'économie publique*, 30 vendé-miaire an VI (11 October 1797), 314; see also Chapter 4 on the funeral ceremonies and public morality contests.

45 Ozouf, *La Fête*, 140, 236, 244, 269–77, 331; see Dowd, *Pageant-Master of the Republic*, for precedents furnished by David; Staum, "The Enlightenment Transformed, 157; Say, *Olbie*, 64, 69, 129; AI-SMP, B4, see second contest, no.6, 59–60.

46 AI-SMP, B4, first contest, no.1, 3–4, 6, 14; Dowd, *Pageant-Master*, 125–7.

47 Say, *Olbie*, 59, 63; AI-SMP, B4, first contest, no.1, 4, 8, 9, 10, 13; Ibid., second contest, no.2, 6, 8.

48 Memoirs in AI-IBL, 1H8 were studied by Pelosse in "Imaginaire social et protection de l'animal," 5–33 and 33–51; Agulhon, "Le sang des bêtes," 81–109.

49 Robert Darnton, *The Great Cat Massacre*, 75–106.

50 Pelosse, "Imaginaire social," 25, 27, 43–4; Grandchamp, *Essai philosophique*, 72, 99.

51 Say, *Olbie*, 25; see also 3–4, 6, 10–11, 33–4, 112.

52 Cabanis, *op*, 1:30; 2:247.

53 Roederer, "Cours," *Œuvres*, 8:265–6.

54 See Malandain, *Delisle de Sales*, 1:209, 279–81; Delisle de Sales, *De la philosophie du bonheur*, 2:24, 70, 99, 113, 117; MSMP, 1:573–8.

55 Delisle de Sales, *Philosophie du bonheur*, 2: 130–1; MSMP, 1:591.

56 Toulongeon, *Histoire de France*, 1:21.

57 See Chapter 4.

58 AI-SMP, B7 (January 1800–July 1801).

59 *Encyclopédie, ou Dictionnaire raisonné ...*, 12:303–4.

60 Bernardin de Saint-Pierre, *Œuvres complètes*, 3:413–4.

61 AI-SMP, B7, Rapport de Daunou, 15 messidor IX, 1–3.

62 Zeldin, *France, 1848–1945: III, Intellect and Pride*, 267–8.

63 AI-SMP, B7, no.8, 14; see also Petitain, *Question proposée*, 31, 44.

64 AI-SMP, B7, no.2, 10–11, 24–5, 32.

65 Brun, *Mémoire sur cette question*, 59, 97, 105, 112–3.

66 Feuillet, *Mémoire couronné*, 10.

67 Ibid., 102–7; for similar analogies, see AI-SMP, B7, no.1, 3; no.4, 6, 13, 15; no.12, 36; no.13, 12.

68 Feuillet, *Mémoire couronné*, 57, 66–7, 108–9 (citation); see also Raymond, *Essai sur l'émulation*, 172–3; AI-SMP, B7, no.3, 2, 42; no.5, 13–14; no.12, 8.

69 On Cousin's derivation and differences from Kant, see Stock-Morton, *Moral Education for a Secular Society*, 33–5.

70 Hume, *A Treatise of Human Nature* (1739–40), 468–9.

71 Stock-Morton, *Moral Education*, 35; Comte, *A General View of Positivism*, 366–7.

72 Durkheim, *Moral Education*, ed. Everett K. Wilson, 5; Stock-Morton, *Moral Education*, 101–7, 125–37; Isambert, "Durkheim: Une science de la morale," 129–46.

73 For modern British ethical naturalism, see Warnock, *The Object of Morality*, and John Searle, "How to Derive 'Ought' from 'Is,'" in Foot, ed., *Theories of Ethics*, 101–14.

74 Volney, *Leçons d'histoire*, 106, 113–14.

CHAPTER EIGHT

1 Volney, *Leçons d'histoire*, 94–106.

2 Ibid., 83–4, 139–42; Destutt de Tracy, "Pièces relatives à l'instruction publique," *Éléments d'idéologie*, 4:282–3; for the sixteenth-century origins of ideals of historical scholarship, see Kelley, *The Foundations of Modern Historical Scholarship*, esp.133–5; Huppert, *The Idea of Perfect History*, 9–10, 104, 116, 141; for eighteenth-century historical craftsmanship, see *L'Histoire au XVIIIe siècle*.

3 See the *Esquisse* translated in Baker, ed., *Condorcet*, 256–7; the education report is in *Œuvres de Condorcet*, 7:348–52, 417–9; Baker, ed., *Condorcet*, 343–82, 389, or Coutel, ed., *Écrits sur l'instruction publique*, vol. 2; Gusdorf, *La Conscience révolutionnaire*, 504–17.

4 Destutt de Tracy, "Pièces," in *Éléments d'idéologie*, 4:283–9, 346; for a discussion and a bibliography, see Staum, "Human, Not Secular Sciences," 50, 67–74.

5 Volney, *Leçons*, 90–7, 123, 130, 132; Gaulmier, "Volney et ses *Leçons d'histoire*," 52–65; Henri Deneys, "Le récit de l'histoire selon Volney," *Corpus*, n° 11/12 (1989): 43–72.

6 Volney, *Leçons*, 106, 113–14, 130.

7 Destutt de Tracy, "Pièces," in *Éléments*, 4:283, 287; Baker, *Condorcet: From Natural Philosophy to Social Mathematics*, 352–5.

8 Volney, *Leçons*, 143; Destutt de Tracy, "Pièces," in *Éléments*, 4:346.

9 Delisle de Sales, *Histoire des hommes*, 1:v; 17:17, 44; 18:101–7; 40:267–8; MSMP, 1:593–616.

10 Delisle de Sales, *Histoire des hommes*, 1:cxlviii; 39:148, 254; 40:188–91.

11 Toulongeon, *Histoire de France*, 1:i–iii.

12 Anquetil, *L'Esprit de la Ligue*, 1:viii; Garnier, *Histoire de France*, 29:6–7; Toulongeon, 1:i–ii.

13 Meek, *Social Science and the Ignoble Savage*, 68–176.

14 Lévesque, MSMP, 1:209–46, esp.230–1, 241–6; cf. Lévesque, *L'Homme moral*, 393–490; MSMP, 3:238–9; for similar comments on agriculture and social order, see the views of a legal historian, Pastoret, in *Histoire de la législation des peuples*, 1:19–22.

15 *Notice des travaux de la Classe des Sciences morales et politiques* (hereafter NTSMP), 4e trim. an X, 1–3.

16 Lévesque, *MSMP*, 2:21, 56–60, 67; 5:233; *CHLA*, 2:393.

17 Delisle de Sales, *Histoire des hommes*, 17:43.

18 Legrand d'Aussy, *MSMP*, 2:417; 3:407–8, 432; Legrand d'Aussy, *Fabliaux ou contes du XIIe et du XIIIe siècles*, 1:lxv; 4:xxxv.

19 Papon, *Histoire générale de Provence*, 1:572–3; 2:195–7; Lévesque, *La France sous les cinq premiers Valois*, 1:161, 165; Anquetil, *Histoire de France*, 2:25–6.

20 AI-SMP, A1, A3; PV-CSMP, 7 messidor an V, 7 ventôse an X; AI-SMP, B8, for manuscripts of the three contestants.

21 Ponce, *Discours qui a remporté le prix d'Histoire*, 32, 52.

22 Toulongeon, *Histoire de France*, 1:1; 3:ii, v (read as Institute memoir on 8 fructidor X); 2:194, 287.

23 Gaillard, *Histoire de François Ier*, 1:xxxv–xxxvi; Delisle de Sales, *Histoire des hommes*, 1:cxli; 18:101–7; Lévesque, *La France*, 1:viii–ix; Toulongeon, *Histoire de France*, 3:xiii.

24 Legrand d'Aussy, *MSMP*, 2:320–1; Pastoret, *Législation des peuples*, 1:74–5, 102, 168; the 1797 memoir is in PV-CSMP, 27 pluviôse, 2 ventôse V; Bouchaud, *MSMP*, 3:114–221; 4:76–112.

25 Lévesque, *MSMP*, 3:222–31; NTSMP, 1er trim. an X, 12–13; *CHLA*, 2:307–93, esp.318–24, 330, 393; *MSMP*, 4:279–90.

26 Delisle de Sales, *Histoire des hommes*, 1:x, cxxix–cxxx; see also Malandain, *Delisle de Sales*, 1:312, 319.

27 Delisle de Sales, *Histoire des hommes*, 2:16, 234, 275; Malandain, 1:309, 315, 322–36; see Bailly's speculations that Spitzbergen was Atlantis in Ramage, "Perspectives Ancient and Modern," in Ramage, ed., *Atlantis: Fact or Fiction?* 30–1.

28 Garnier, *Histoire de France*, 29:2; Papon, *Histoire générale de Provence*, 1:x, xxviii.

29 Ibid., 1:1–477; 2:219; 4:191–5, 634–711.

30 De Sales, *MSMP*, 1:617–642; for Anquetil, see NTSMP, 2e trim. an IX, 5–6 and 4e trim. an IX, 1; PV-CSMP, 22 frimaire, 12 pluviôse, 12 fructidor an VIII; for Legrand d'Aussy, see *Biographie universelle* (Michaud), 23:641; for Lévesque, see *Biographie universelle* (Michaud), 24:299–401.

31 On Lacurne de Sainte-Palaye, see Gossman, *Medievalism and the Ideologies of the Enlightenment*; Legrand d'Aussy, *Fabliaux*, 1:iiin, xiii, lxv, lxxii, xcvi; 4:v, xxxviii.

32 Legrand d'Aussy, *Histoire de la vie privée des Français*, 1:vii, liv.

33 Ibid., 1:267; 2:39, 360; 3:88, 93, 114, 264–5.

34 Legrand d'Aussy, *MSMP*, 2:411–12, 663–81; see Hintermeyer, *Politiques de la mort*.

35 Legrand d'Aussy, *MSMP*, 2:675–8; Christopher M. Greene, "Alexandre Lenoir and the Musée des monuments français," 211, 215–19.

36 On the burial of riches, see Legrand d'Aussy, *MSMP*, 2:417–42, 449; for the periodization, see Ibid., 2:461–80; on menhirs and dolmens, see Ibid., 2:543, 564; and on statues, Ibid., 2:607, 620.

37 Ariès, *The Hour of Our Death*, 205 on coffins, 233–4 on epitaph tombs, 240–50 on statues, 260 on sculpture.

38 Koch, *MSMP*, 4:234–366, esp.344–8, 364.

39 Gautier de Sibert, *Variations de la monarchie française*, 3:382–5.

40 Legrand d'Aussy, *MSMP*, 3:424; 2:677; 4:426, 467–8; Legrand d'Aussy, *Contes dévots*, 4: xxvii, xxxiii, 153.

41 Gautier de Sibert, *Variations*, 3:131–5; Lévesque, *La France*, 4:80–159, esp.86, 91.

42 Anquetil, *Histoire de France*, 4:275–308; *Précis d'histoire universelle*, 1:3, 5–8, 12, 135.

43 Delisle de Sales, *Histoire des hommes*, 2:14; Malandain, *Delisle de Sales*, 1:316.

44 Papon, *Histoire générale de Provence*, 2:195–6.

45 Ibid., 2:351–2; Anquetil, *L'Esprit*, 1:xxiv, 3:375–6; cf. Anquetil, *Histoire de France*, 7:173, 12:302.

46 Anquetil, *L'Esprit*, 1:xiv, 2; *MSMP*, 1:19; Anquetil, *Histoire de France*, 13:203; Papon, *Histoire de la révolution de France*, 1:xlviii, lii; Papon, *Histoire générale de Provence*, 2:352.

47 Gautier de Sibert, *Variations*, 3:1–2, 10; for pre-Revolutionary use of historical arguments to support Third Estate demands, see Margerison, "History, Representative Institutions, and Political Rights," 77, 86, 94, on Gautier de Sibert and Gudin.

48 Dale van Kley contends that there was a turning away from historical arguments late in 1788 as the "ministerial" and "magisterial" factions could reach no consensus on the meaning of history and as the election of the Estates produced an unprecedented situation; see "New Wine in Old Wineskins," 461–2; Lévesque, *La France*, 1:xv, 12–13; *MSMP*, 4:222–3, 247, 294–310; [Gudin], *Essai sur l'histoire des comices de Rome*, 1:177; 2:179; 3:322–3. For the contrary view that the nation was represented under Charlemagne, see Legrand d'Aussy in *MSMP*, 3:463–6.

49 Lévesque, *MSMP*, 3:349–50, 358, 374–5; on the appeal to antiquity, see Parker, *The Cult of Antiquity*, 89–118, 178–9.

50 Lévesque, *MSMP*, 4:119, 160–1, 264.

51 Lévesque, *NTSMP*, 1er trim. an x, 13–16; *MSMP*, 4:316. Cf. Anquetil, *Esprit*, 1:xxv, for a similar warning against any civil war.

52 Lévesque, *L'Homme moral*, 46, 58, 62, 90, 95.

53 Lévesque, *MSMP*, 3:231, 235, 238; for the secretarial position, see PV-CSMP, A1–A3, vendémiaire an V–germinal an VI; germinal an VIII–germinal an X; *NTSMP*, 1er trim. an X, 1–2.

54 This moderately royalist work has not yet received adequate interpretation, but see Smith, "François-Emmanuel Toulongeon: Contemporaneous Historian of the French Revolution," in Slavin and Smith, eds., *Bourgeois, Sans-Culottes, and other Frenchmen*, 97–111.

55 Toulongeon, *Histoire de France*, 1:2–6, 18–19.

56 Ibid., 1:41–3, 71, 91, 186.

57 Ibid., 1:81, 2:72–3, 177, 273; 3:136, 229

58 Ibid., 6:190, 106–7, 217.

59 Ibid., 1:107.

60 Millot, *Éléments de l'histoire de France*, 9th ed., 4:10, 40, 198 (continuation by Delisle de Sales); see Malandain, 2:596–8 for a description of the 1800 pamphlet, *De la paix de l'Europe et de ses bases*.

61 *Correspondance de Napoléon 1er*, 8:374, (24 June 1803), cited in Burton, *Napoleon and Clio*, 54–5; cf. Malandain, *Delisle de Sales*, 1:461–2.

62 Anquetil, *Histoire de France*, 12:404; 13:292.

63 Anquetil, *L'Esprit*, 3:2.

64 Anquetil, *Précis*, 9:201–2; *Histoire de France*, 13:280, 288, 301, 308.

65 Pastoret, *Législation des peuples*, 2:484.

66 Delisle de Sales, *De la fin de la Révolution française*, 45–6.

67 Papon, *Histoire de la Révolution*, 1:lxxi, cix–cxii, 135; Anquetil, *Histoire de France*, 12:288.

68 Papon, *Histoire de la Révolution*, 1:228; 3:56.

69 Ibid., 1:xv, xx; 2:339; 3:467; 4:206–7, 309.

70 Ibid., 1:i.

71 Dussaud, *La Nouvelle Académie des Inscriptions et Belles-Lettres*, 1:12; *CHLA, Histoire*, 1:14–15.

72 Papon, *Histoire de la Révolution*, 5:346–7; for Papon's two failures to be elected a full member, see PV-CSMP, 7 germinal an VI, 22 nivôse an IX; Registre des assemblées générales de l'Institut, 3A2, 5 prairial an VI.

73 *CHLA*, 2:44–110.

74 Georges Perrot, "Notice," 81–2; Archives de l'Académie des Inscriptions, dossier of Dacier in C26; Silvestre de Sacy, *Notice sur B.-J. Dacier* (Paris, 1834), 9.

75 Delisle De Sales, *Mémoire pour les académies*, 176–8, 187–92; Millot, *Éléments*, 4:412–3; Aucoc, *L'Institut*, 68.

76 Ibid., 74; see the index of memoirs submitted in Procès-verbaux de la Classe d'Histoire et Littérature ancienne, Archives de l'Académie des Inscriptions.

77 Daunou, *Cours d'études historiques*, 1:xv–xix; Anquetil, *Histoire de France*, 1:x.

78 Daunou, *Cours*, 20:29–30.

79 Cf. Kelley, *Historians and the Law in Postrevolutionary France*, 14.

80 Olson, *The Emergence of the Social Sciences*, 138–61, particularly accentuates the philosophical history of Montesquieu and Adam Ferguson as preparing Burke's conservatism.

81 Mellon, *The Political Uses of History*, 5–30, esp.10–12 for Thierry on the communes and the middle class, and 12–13 on Guizot. See Crossley, *French Historians and Romanticism*, 45–70 on Thierry, and 71–104 on Guizot; see also the introductory chapter on post-revolutionary ideas of history, 1–44.

CHAPTER NINE

1 Moravia, "Philosophie et géographie," 937–1011; *Il pensiero*, 533–671; Gusdorf, *La Conscience révolutionnaire*, 477–503.

2 See "Mémoire du Roi," written by Claret de Fleurieu, in La Pérouse, *Voyage de La Pérouse autour du monde*, 1:48.

3 On the status of geography in the eighteenth century, see Broc, *La géographie des philosophes*, and, more recently, Livingstone, *The Geographic Tradition*; on the Institute members, see Archives de l'Institut, Procès-verbaux des séances générales de l'Institut, 3A3 for elections; 40 of 52 memoirs were barely related to human geography.

4 Godlewska, "Napoleon's Geographers," in *Geography and Empire*, 31–54, develops the theoretical association among geography, the state, modernity, and imperialism. While she argues with some justice that surveying and statistics-gathering in themselves were activities tied to state control or to economic imperialism, on the other hand she finds Idéologues such as Volney more understanding of other cultures than the technocratic military engineers. This opposition of the latter seems overdrawn, given Volney's estimate of native Americans. See also the same author's "Geography under Napoleon."

5 Charlton, *New Images of the Natural in France*, 105–34.

6 Meek, *Social Science and the Ignoble Savage*, 68–176.

7 Blanckaert, "Les vicissitudes de l'angle facial," 434–5.

8 Helvétius, "De l'homme," *Œuvres complètes*, 3:170n, 176.

9 Condorcet, *Journal d'instruction sociale*, no.4 (9 June 1793): 121; see also Baker, *Condorcet*, 336–7, 472.

10 "Airs, Waters, Places," paragraphs 13, 19–24, in Hippocrates, *The Works*, 1:109–11, 121–37; Jean-Noël Hallé, "Précis d'un cours d'hygiène," *La Médecine éclairée par les sciences physiques*, 4 (1792): 225–35; see Jordanova, "Earth Science and Environmental Medicine," in

Jordanova and Porter, eds., *Images of the Earth*, 124–8, 131; Cabanis, *OP*, 1:407, 443, 455–7, 482–95; Staum, *Cabanis*, 222–7.

11 On modern regional geography, see James and Martin, *All Possible Worlds*, 190; Buttimer, *Society and Milieu*, 43–58.

12 Robert Shackleton, "The Evolution of Montesquieu's Theory of Climate," 317–29; *De l'esprit des lois* (1748), books XIV–XIX, on the four gradations of legal complexity, book XVIII, viii; see above, Chapter 2.

13 Volney, *Voyage en Égypte et en Syrie* (1787), 33–40, 198–214, 361–75, 401–5; on Volney, see Gaulmier, *L'Idéologue Volney*, 87–121, 459–82; Moravia, "Philosophie et géographie," 997–1007, and *Il pensiero*, 645–71; cf. Désirat and Hordé, "Volney, l'étude des langues dans l'observation de l'homme," in Rupp-Eisenreich, *Histoires de l'anthropologie*, 133–41.

14 Volney, *Questions de statistique à l'usage des voyageurs* (1795), 6; *Leçons d'histoire*, 130–2.

15 Volney, *A View of the Soil and Climate of the United States of America* (1804), xviii–xx, 331–427; "Tableau du climat et du sol des États-Unis," in *Œuvres complètes*, 7:iii–iv, xii–xiii, 358–82, esp.363, 374, 382.

16 Ibid., 7:383–481, esp.423–4, 469n, against Chateaubriand; Moravia, *Il pensiero*, 645–50; Anne Deneys, "Géographie, histoire et langue dans le *Tableau du climat et du sol des États-Unis*," *Corpus*, n°11/12 (1989): 73–90, esp.85; Denise Brahimi, "Volney chez les sauvages: un idéologue contre l'idéologie," in Roussel, ed., *Volney et les idéologues*, 73–81.

17 Statistics first appeared in works of the 1740s and 1750s by German authors Gottfried Achenwall and Anton-Friedrich Büsching as a synonym for political science; see Rupp-Eisenreich, "Aux 'origines' de la *Völkerkunde* allemande," in Rupp-Eisenreich, ed., *Histoires*, 95; Bowen, *Empiricism and Geographical Thought*, 154–7.

18 J.C. Perrot, "L'âge d'or," 217; Bourguet, "Des préfets aux champs," in Rupp-Eisenreich, ed., *Histoires*, 259–72.

19 Bibliothèque historique de la ville de Paris, MS 815, Lycée républicain, an VI, fols.80–1.

20 See Coquebert, *Journal des Mines*, 4 (1796): 39–50; 5, no. 25 (1796): 49–73, for the departments of the Ain and Aisne; J. C. Perrot, "L'âge d'or," 254, 257, 262, 267; Doë de Maindreville, *Généalogie de la Maison Coquebert*, 44–6; Biraben, "La statistique de population," 361; de Silvestre, *Notice biographique sur Coquebert de Montbret*, 15, 20.

21 AI-SMP, A5, Mentelle, Extrait, "Aperçu des travaux à exécuter par la section de géographie."

22 MSMP, *Histoire*, 4:43; AN, AD XVIII^c 474, 106, *Compte-rendu et notices des travaux de l'Institut an VI*; Mentelle, *Cours d'histoire*, 2e année, 386–7.

23 Mentelle in *Séances des écoles normales, Leçons*, 4:421–51, 5:109–20, 279–308; PV-CSMP, 22 floréal, 2, 7 prairial an IV.

24 Mentelle in *Séances*, 4:440–2; 5:114, 304.
25 Moravia, "The Enlightenment and the Sciences of Man," 254, 257–60. For other efforts at making a correlation between physical and political, see the diplomat Bourgoing's *Tableau de l'Espagne moderne*, 3:308, 315, 321; see the mostly folkloric *Promenades dans les Vosges* by Grégoire, 35–45; and the essay, now lost, on the Vendée in 1802–3 by La Revellière-Lépeaux, PV-CSMP, 22, 29 vendémiaire, 6, 13, 20 brumaire XI.
26 Survey in Jaenen, *The French Relationship with the Native Peoples*, 61–3; Bougainville, *Adventure in the Wilderness*, 41, 123–4, 127, 133.
27 Bougainville, *Voyage autour du monde*, 1:289–302; B. Smith, *European Vision and the South Pacific*, 64. Such visions persisted as late as 1927; see Gamble, "Archaeology, History, and the Uttermost Ends of the Earth," 712–20.
28 Bougainville, *Voyage*, 2:142, 186–8, 225; the Institute botany associate Palissot de Beauvois also read to the Class of Moral and Political Sciences at a public session a highly unflattering description of the "frenzied fanaticism," human sacrifices, theft, and superstition of the despotically governed people of Benin in west Africa; he even thought the European slave trade resulted in fewer deaths than did native murders; see *Décade philosophique*, 28 (30 nivôse IX): 141–51.
29 Bougainville, *Voyage*, 2:30–32, 45, 87, and Bougainville, *Voyage*, ed. Hérubel, 209–13; see also Martin-Allanic, *Bougainville navigateur*, 1:660–87.
30 Charlton, *New Images of the Natural*, 113; Duchet, *Anthropologie et histoire*, 407–75; Diderot, *Supplément au voyage de Bougainville* in Hérubel, 435–500. For the kinship of Diderot to Herder's sceptical views on the relative superiority of European civilization, see Pagden, *European Encounters*, 141–72.
31 Bougainville, *Voyage*, ed. Hérubel, 213–14, 225–31.
32 Porter, *The Enlightenment*, 62–3, and Charlton, *New Images*, on Tahiti. For the view that Cook's behaviour in Tahiti, the New Hebrides, and Hawaii foreshadowed cultural relativism, see Frost, "The perception of culture's relativity," 137–9.
33 Bougainville, MSMP, 3:322–46, esp.322, 327–8. Bougainville borrowed his remarks on wampum belts, but without acknowledgment, from Lafitau, *Customs of the American Indians*, 1:310; a similar evaluation of brutal Carolina Creeks and Cherokees as susceptible to civilization is in Palissot de Beauvois, *Décade philosophique*, 30 (30 messidor IX): 94.
34 Buache, MSMP, 3:306.
35 Namely Mendaña, Quiròs, Cook, the Forsters, George Dixon, John Meares, and Vancouver; Chassériau, *Notice sur M. le Comte de Fleurieu*, 12–16; PV-CSMP, 17, 22 messidor an V; 12, 17 thermidor an V; 17

ventôse an VI; *Voyage autour du monde … par Étienne Marchand*; Dunmore, *French Explorers in the Pacific*, 1: 342–53.

36 Fleurieu, *Voyage*, 1:287, translated as *Voyage Round the World*. English references, except where noted, are in parentheses.

37 Fleurieu, *Voyage* 1:63–4 67–8, 141, 126.

38 Ibid., 1:121–2n (1:108–10).

39 Ibid., 1:130, 156–8 (1:117, 133, 141–2).

40 Ibid., 1:241–3, 251 (1:217–21, 226–7); on the landfall, see Dunmore, *French Explorers in the Pacific*, 1:350; on the natives, see Drucker, *Indians of the Northwest Coast*, 10.

41 Fleurieu, *Voyage*, 1:278–9 (1:250–1).

42 Ibid., 1:213, 266, 272–3, 278 (1:192, 232, 239, 245, 249).

43 Ibid., 1:301, 312, 376–81 (1:271–2, 279, 338–42); cf. J. R. Forster's degeneration theory for the Fuegians.

44 Volney, *A View*, 354–5.

45 Fleurieu, *A Voyage Round the World*, 1:322–3; Archer, "Cannibalism in the Early History of the Northwest Coast," 476–7.

46 Fleurieu, *Voyage*, 1:398–400 (1:358–60); cf. the similar civilizing mission for Madagascar advocated by geography associate Daniel Lescallier in *MSMP*, 4:25–6.

47 Faivre, *L'Expansion française dans le Pacifique*, 102–3, 106, 121; for a translation of Fleurieu's memoir, see Cornell, ed., *The Journal of Post Captain Nicolas Baudin*, 1–6.

48 Faivre, *L'Expansion*, 100–83; Bouvier and Maynial, *Une aventure dans les mers australes*; Dunmore, *French Explorers in the Pacific*, 2:9–40; the most thorough recent work is Frank Horner, *The French Reconnaissance*; the juxtaposition with little critical comment of the four-stages theory with Péron's views also occurs in Rhys Jones, "Philosophical Time Travellers," 744–57. See also F.C.T. Moore in his introduction to Degérando, *The Observation of Savage Peoples*, 1–58; Moravia, *La scienza dell' uomo*, 212–47, and *Il pensiero*, 574–84. Some of the essays attributed to Jauffret by Moravia and other scholars are actually translations, not necessarily by Jauffret, of works published from 1787 to 1789 in Göttingen by university lecturer Christoph Meiners; see Rupp-Eisenreich, "The 'Société des Observateurs de l'Homme' and German Ethno-Anthropology," 5–11, and "Des choses occultes," 134–5.

49 On the society, besides the above works, see Stocking, "French Anthropology in 1800," reprinted and revised in *Race, Culture, and Evolution*, 13–41; Faivre, "Les idéologues de l'an VIII," 3–15; Copans et Jamin, *Aux origines de l'anthropologie française*. The Jauffret memoir is discussed by Faivre and translated in the Cornell edition of Baudin, 594–6; the Cuvier memoir is reprinted in Copans and Jamin, 173–6.

50 Degérando, *Considérations*, as reprinted in Copans and Jamin, *Aux origines de l'anthropologie française*, 127–69, and Degérando, *Observations*, 59–104; see also Stocking, "French Anthropology," 21–8.

51 Degérando, *The Observation*, p. ix-x (preface by E.E. Evans-Pritchard), 65, 70, 72.

52 Ibid., 80–1, 84–6, 91–101.

53 Cornell, *The Journal*, 5.

54 Jones, "Images of Natural Man," in Bonnemains, Forsyth, and Smith, eds., *Baudin in Australian Waters*, 40.

55 Faivre, *L'Expansion*, 109–10, 158, 164; for Moore on Péron as a spy, see Degérando, *The Observation*, 43.

56 Letter, Baudin to the King, 23 December 1802, cited in Horner, *The French Reconnaissance*, 271–2.

57 Péron, *Observations sur l'anthropologie*, in Copans and Jamin, *Aux origines*, 179–85; on Péron, see Laissus in Bonnemains, Forsyth, and Smith, eds., *Baudin*, 31; Baudin, *The Journal*, 510; Bouvier and Maynial, *Une Aventure*, 158–60, 164; Stocking, "French Anthropology," 31–4.

58 On Péron's manuscripts, see Faivre, *L'Expansion*, 176; Moravia, *Il pensiero*, 583, and Bonnemains, Forsyth, and Smith, eds., *Baudin*; Péron et Freycinet, *Voyage de découvertes*, 1:79–82, 89–90.

59 Péron, *Voyage*, 1:231–8; see Bonwick, *The Last of the Tasmanians*, 18–27; Fagan, *Clash of Cultures*, 114, 120.

60 Péron, *Voyage*, 1:221, 238–9, 253, 282; Bouvier and Maynial, *Une Aventure*, 60.

61 Manuscript cited in Copans and Jamin, *Aux origines*, 32–5. See similar suggestions by the Royal Society of Medicine in 1785 to La Pérouse mentioned in *Voyage de La Pérouse*, 1:184–5, and Fleurieu's recommendation to Péron of these instructions in Baudin, *Journal*, 6.

62 Péron, *Voyage*, 1:285, 287. His vacillation has been acknowledged in Horner, *French Reconnaissance*, 197; Jones, "Images," 45, and Miranda Hughes, "Tall Tales or True Stories?" in Macleod and Rehbock, *Nature in Its Greatest Extent*, 73.

63 Péron, *Voyage*, 1:228.

64 "Expériences sur la force physique des peuples sauvages de la Terre de Diemen, de la Nouvelle-Hollande, et des habitans de Timor," in Péron, *Voyage*, 1:446–84, esp.458, 465–6, 472; see Stocking, "French Anthropology," 32–3, and, more recently, Hughes, "The Dynamometer," in Le Grand, ed., *Experimental Inquiries*, 81–98.

65 Copans and Jamin, *Aux origines*, 37.

66 Péron, *Voyage*, 1:375; 2:214–5.

67 See Bonnemains, Forsyth, and Smith, eds., ed., *Baudin*, 65–8, on the rediscovery of these materials, after 1874, in the Musée d'Histoire naturelle in Le Havre.

68 Péron, *Voyage*, 1:375–7; 2:400–3, 409–10; Cuvier, Rapport, 9 juin 1806, in Ibid., xiii–xiv.

69 Ginguené, *Rapport sur les travaux de la Classe d'histoire et de littérature ancienne*, 3 juillet 1812, 45; 2 juillet 1813, 60–4.

70 Humboldt, *Political Essay on the Kingdom of New Spain*, 1:139.

71 Humboldt, *Vues des cordillères*, ix, xii–xiii, xv, 58–9, 86; on the calendar, Ibid., 125–95, and on barbarism, see 194; for Humboldt on Fleurieu, see *Essay*, 1:134–43; on racial features, 1:152–3.

72 Laguérenne and Kernéis, "French Interest in the Australian Aborigines," in Hardy and Frost, eds., *European Voyaging*, 147–8. See also recent translated excerpts from Dumont d'Urville in Dumont d'Urville, *Two Voyages*, ed. Rosenman.

73 Lejeune, "La 'Société de Géographie' de Paris"; Lejeune, *Les sociétés de géographie en France*; Fierro, *La Société de Géographie*, 8–28. See Godlewska, "Traditions, Crisis, and New Paradigms," 209, on the shift from cartography to interest in commercial or racial questions from the era of the *Description de l'Égypte* to the *Exploration scientifique* of Algeria in 1840–42.

74 On the Société ethnologique de Paris, founded in 1839 by the physiologist and racial theorist William Edwards, and the culturally oriented Société d'Ethnographie américaine et orientale, founded by the linguist Léon Rosny in 1859, see Stocking, "Qu'est-ce qui est en jeu dans un nom?: La 'Société d'ethnographie' et l'historiographie de l'anthropologie en France," in Rupp-Eisenreich, ed., *Histoires*, 421–31; Williams, "The Science of Man," PH.D. thesis; see also her more recent *The Physical and the Moral*; Blanckaert, "On the Origins of French Ethnology: William Edwards and the Doctrine of Race," in Stocking, ed, *Bones, Bodies, and Behavior*, 19–55.

75 See *Journal des Débats*, 10 pluviôse XI, for the composition of new Institute classes; Broc, "L'établissement de la géographie," 558–62; Buttimer, *Society and Milieu*, 52–7.

CHAPTER TEN

1 On the politics of the Idéologue circle, see Moravia, *Il tramonto dell' illuminismo*; Moravia, *Il pensiero degli Idéologues,* 675–804; and Gusdorf, *La Conscience révolutionnaire*, 173–284, 392–427.

2 Cabanis, OP, 1:161–2n; Grégoire,"Réflexions sur les moyens de perfectionner les sciences politiques," MSMP, 1:552, 554–5, 558–60.

3 For a juxtaposition of Bonald and the Idéologues, see Gérard Gengembre, "Bonald: la contre-révolution à l'école," in Azouvi, *L'Institution de la raison*, 209–17, and Jennings, "The *Déclaration des Droits de l'Homme et du Citoyen* and its Critics," 839–59; see also Klinck, "Aristocracy,

Counter-Revolution, and the Search for an Organic Community in France."

4 Hayek, *The Counter-Revolution of Science*, 103–88.

5 See the forum on François Furet's *Interpreting the French Revolution* in *French Historical Studies*, 16 (1990): 766–802; Baker, *Inventing the French Revolution*, 305; for a convincing parallel to this reading of Sieyès, see Sewell, *A Rhetoric of Bourgeois Revolution*, 49.

6 Kaiser, "The Idéologues: From Enlightenment to Positivism," 310–23, 518–22, 634; Welch, *Liberty and Utility*, 6–42, 97–134. Despite these criticisms, Kaiser and Welch have contributed immeasurably to our understanding of the Idéologues.

7 For summaries of the historical controversy, see Doyle, *Origins of the French Revolution*; Blanning, *The French Revolution*; Sewell, *A Rhetoric*, 39, argues for a concept of "rhetoric from a bourgeois [well-to-do, urban, educated non-noble] perspective," independent of all Marxist definitions.

8 On rights in Condorcet, see Baker, *Condorcet*, 198, 225–44, 352; for Destutt de Tracy's attitude toward facts, see Head, *Ideology and Social Science*, 35–7. Sieyès, however, in 1789 exalted "principles" over "facts" as the basis of the "science of the state of society"; see Forsyth, *Reason and Revolution*, 23–4. Jean Ehrard, "Volney et les droits de l'homme," in Matucci, ed., *Gli "Idéologues,"* 133–50 corrects the traditional views that Volney and Garat opposed the Declaration of Rights of Man.

9 Sieyès, *Préliminaire de la constitution*, 20, 23, 26; reprinted in Zapperi, ed., *Écrits politiques*, 191–206; see also Forsyth, 113, for the utilitarian and moralistic arguments conjoined.

10 As applied to Sieyès, see Baker, "Sieyès and the Creation," in Valtz, ed., *The Languages*, 199–201.

11 Volney, *La Loi naturelle*, 60–1, 75.

12 Hart, "Between Utility and Rights," in Ryan, ed., *The Idea of Freedom*, 78–98.

13 See "A Critical Examination of the Declaration of Rights," in *Bentham's Political Thought*, 259, 269.

14 [Grouvelle], *De l'autorité de Montesquieu*, 16, 35, 67–8, 137.

15 Sewell, *A Rhetoric*, 98.

16 Sieyès, *Qu'est-ce que le tiers état?* 57–9, 208; *Préliminaire*, 25, 36–7, 46; ostensibly he regretted the customary exclusion of women. Bastid, *Sieyès et sa pensée*, 89, stresses the voluntary aspect of the contribution, but see the combination of voluntary and compulsory criteria in AN, 284 AP 3, dossier 2/1, 10; 284 AP 18, dossier 2; and in 1799, 284 AP 5, dossier 2/4, fol.44; see the discussion in Sewell, *A Rhetoric*, 161–80, citation on 179.

17 Ramond, *Opinion énoncée à la Société de 1789*, 20.

18 Sewell, *A Rhetoric*, 66–72; Sieyès, *Observations sur le rapport du comité de constitution, concernant la nouvelle organisation de France*, 2 octobre 1789, in Zapperi, *Écrits*, 257–62; *Dire de l'Abbé Sieyès sur la question du veto royal* ... *7 septembre 1789* (Versailles, 1789), in Zapperi, *Écrits*, 236; see Baczko, "The Social Contract of the French," S98–S125, esp.S120; Larrère, *L'Invention de l'économie*, 269–307, esp.298–9; Pasquino, "Emmanuel Sieyès, Benjamin Constant et le 'gouvernement des modernes,'" 219–21.

19 Daunou, *Essai sur la Constitution*, 3, 5–6; Moravia, *Tramonto*, 195–6; Welch, *Liberty and Utility*, 26–7; Jennings, "The *Declaration*," 855.

20 Roederer, "Cours d'organisation sociale," *Œuvres*, 8:146, 229–30, 232, 234, 245–6; see Robespierre's draft Declaration of Rights, 5 May 1793, in Stewart, *A Documentary History*, 431; see also Margerison, *P.-L. Roederer*, 94–113.

21 Roederer, "Cours," in *Œuvres*, 8: 141–3, 148, 265–6; *Journal d'économie publique*, 30 messidor v, in *Œuvres*, 5:155–6.

22 Roederer, "Cours," in *Œuvres*, 8:131, 181–2, 187–90, 199–201.

23 Sieyès, Prospectus of *Journal d'instruction sociale*, cited in Forsyth, *Sieyès*, 28–9; Cambacérès, MSMP, 3:10–11, 13.

24 Ibid., 4, 10, 13–14.

25 Roederer, "Cours," in *Œuvres*, 8:194, 206, 209–15, 221, 228.

26 Roederer, "De l'organisation des assemblées," in *Œuvres*, 7:71–84; Margerison, *P.-L. Roederer*, 109–10.

27 Godechot, *Les Institutions de France*, 396–7; Church, "Du nouveau sur les origines," 607, 609, 619; *Mémoires de La Revellière-Lépeaux* 1:227–45.

28 Lefebvre, *The French Revolution*, 160–2.

29 *Moniteur universel. Réimpression*, 25: 150, 214, 219; on the change to social definitions of property, see also Martin, "Aux sources thermidoriennes du Code Civil, 107–16, and Dorigny, "Les Girondins et la propriété," 15–31.

30 *Moniteur universel*, 25:92–3, 108–9.

31 Ibid., 252, 260.

32 Ibid., 171, 195, 215–6, 219.

33 Garran-Coulon, *Rapport sur les troubles de Saint-Domingue*, 2:89; 3:121–2; 4:23, 647. Garran and Grégoire may have engineered the election to the Institute of social science and legislation associate Julien Raimond, a mulatto proprietor; see Kates, *The Cercle Social, the Girondins, and the French Revolution*, 217–8; Necheles, *The Abbé Grégoire*, 84, 120, 126; Garran-Coulon, *Rapport sur Julien Raimond*, 24 floréal III, 22, 33.

34 Baudin des Ardennes, "De l'origine de la loi," MSMP, 2:376–7, 387–8, 390.

35 Ibid., 2:387–8; AI-SMP, A6, "De la seconde classe de l'Institut," 9.

36 Baudin des Ardennes, "De l'esprit de faction," MSMP, 1:497–503; *Magasin encyclopédique*, 8:231–5, messidor IV.

37 Baudin des Ardennes, "Sur les clubs et leurs rapports avec l'organisation sociale," MSMP, 1:509–11, 529, 538.

38 Popkin, *Revolutionary News*, 176–7.

39 Cabanis, *Opinion ... sur les réunions s'occupant d'objets politiques,* [6 thermidor VII]; *Discours ... sur le message du Conseil des Anciens ...* 1 fructidor VII.

40 Cabanis, "Quelques considérations sur l'organisation sociale," in OP, 2: 460–90; Destutt de Tracy, "Quels sont les moyens de fonder la morale d'un peuple," in *Commentaire*, 438, 461, 467.

41 See Staum, "Human, not Secular Sciences," 49–76; Head, 195–200; Kennedy, *A Philosophe in the Age of Revolution*, 91; Sewell's *A Rhetoric*, 154–61, uncovers similar dichotomies in Sieyès's papers.

42 Bastid, *Sieyès et sa pensée*, 249–58.

43 AN, 284 AP 3, dossier 2/1; on the separation of powers, see Forsyth, *Sieyès*, 183.

44 *Opinion de Sieyès sur plusieurs articles des titres IV et V du projet de constitution, 2 thermidor an III; Sur les attributs et l'organisation du jury constitutionnaire, 18 thermidor III*, 17; AN, 284 AP 5, dossier 1/11.

45 Boulay de la Meurthe, *Théorie constitutionnelle de Sieyès*, 15; cf. AN, 284 AP 5, dossier 2/4, where, contrary to Boulay's proposal, property qualifications for citizenship are combined with a voluntary tribute; see also Mignet, *Histoire de la Révolution française*, 2:227–81, and diagram.

46 Cabanis, OP, 2:462, 471–5 (citation, page 474).

47 Ibid., 482–3, 486–7.

48 Kennedy, *A Philosophe*, 89–90.

49 Welch, *Liberty and Utility*, 114–34.

50 Destutt de Tracy, *Commentaire*, 12, 21, 26–7.

51 Ibid., 66, 135, 211n, 358; 38–44, and discussion of these points in J.-Paul Frick, "Destutt de Tracy et la démocratie de la raison éclairée," in Matucci, *Gli "Idéologues"*, 151–62, esp.158–9.

52 Destutt de Tracy, *Commentaire*, 21–2, 42–3, 57.

53 Ibid., 231–2; for a translation of the 1789 text, see Stewart, *A Documentary Survey*, 113–5.

54 Destutt de Tracy, *Traité de la volonté et de ses effets*, 51–52; cf. Jennings, "The *Declaration*," 858, who finds Tracy's concept of individual happiness detached from any social bond.

55 Destutt de Tracy, *Commentaire*, 203–8; Kennedy, *A Philosophe*, 176.

56 Ibid., 175–8; Head, *Ideology*, 181–2, 200–1; cf. Welch, *Liberty and Utility*, 146.

57 Destutt de Tracy, *Commentaire*, 45, 57, 60, 72; cf. "Quels sont les moyens," 441–2; see Kennedy, *A Philosophe*, 174–5; Head, *Ideology*, 180–1.

58 Destutt de Tracy, *Commentaire*, 57, 172, 178–80; cf. Head, *Ideology*, 165.

59 Destutt de Tracy, *Commentaire*, 306.

60 Welch, *Liberty and Utility*, 157–71.

61 Daunou, *Essai sur les garanties individuelles*, 6, 228; cf. *Cours d'études historiques*, 2:136, 270.

62 For a contrary interpretation which supports Welch, see Jennings, "The Declaration," 857–9.

63 Daunou, *Garanties*, 5, 10–32, esp.27–9.

64 Ibid., 33–47.

65 Ibid., 94–9, 115, 123; on religion, see also Daunou, *Cours d'études*, 2:74, 132.

66 Daunou, *Garanties*, 104, 189, 200.

67 Ibid., 58–9, 211.

68 Holmes, *Benjamin Constant*, 31.

69 Daunou, *Garanties*, 41, 45, 48–65.

70 For the revised image of the nobility, see Chaussinand-Nogaret, *The French Nobility*.

71 For Champagne's "republican" translation of Aristotle, which may have earned him election to the Institute, see Palmer, *The School of the French Revolution*, 172–5; *The Politics of Aristotle*, 179, chapters 4, 11; Head, *Ideology*, 184, on Destutt de Tracy's praise of middle classes as an Aristotelian convention.

72 Grouvelle, *Montesquieu*, 83.

73 Roederer, "Cours," in *Œuvres*, 8:48; *Moniteur universel*, 25:308.

74 Cabanis, *OP*, 2:481.

75 Destutt de Tracy, *Commentaire*, 44–5, cited in Head, 181.

76 The charge is of course made against late Enlightenment thought and Bentham in particular by Foucault, *Discipline and Punish*; on positivism, see Frank E. Manuel, *The New World of Henri Saint-Simon* (Cambridge, Mass.: Harvard University Press 1956), and *The Prophets of Paris* (Cambridge, Mass.: Harvard University Press 1962), 103–93, 249–96.

77 Baker, *Condorcet*, 235–42; for background, see Borda's memoir in de Grazia, "Mathematical Derivation of an Election System," 42–7; Black, *The Theory of Committees and Elections*, 156–84; Gillispie, "Probability and Politics," 14. For a more recent discussion, see Crépel and Gilain, eds., *Condorcet*, 65–100.

78 Daunou, *Mémoire sur les élections au scrutin*, read in July 1800, 60.

79 De Grazia, "Election System," 51; see also the complex system of presentation lists and supplementary choices in a second column advocated by

Daunou in the constitution debates of 1795 in Daunou, *Rapport et projet de loi sur les élections*, 23 fructidor III.

80 Daunou, *Mémoire*, 74–7.

81 Aucoc, *Institut de France*, 186; Crosland, *Science under Control*, 211.

82 Daunou, *Mémoire*, 79–80.

83 Destutt de Tracy, *Traité de la volonté*, 31–3; see also Daston, *Classical Probability in the Enlightenment*, 354–5.

84 Laplace, *A Philosophical Essay on Probabilities* (1814), 136; AI-SMP, B9, Mémoire de Canard, no.7, fols.3v, 6–7, 25v, 31v, 35r, 38v, 47v–54, 71r.

85 AI-SMP, B9, Rapport de Garran-Coulon, 15 germinal X, 11–12; Le Breton, "Extrait de Canard," *La Décade philosophique*, 20 frimaire XI, 35:285.

86 On Guizot, see Rosanvallon, *Le Moment Guizot*; though a liberal, Guizot was against the social contract theory, popular sovereignty, and a utopianism of the free market, 45–50; Favre, "La constitution d'une science du politique," 181–219, 365–402.

CHAPTER ELEVEN

1 On the views of neo-mercantilist Véron de Forbonnais, see Larrère, *L'Invention de l'économie*, 99, 113, 140.

2 Saricks, *Pierre-Samuel Du Pont de Nemours*, 26–62; McLain, ed., *The Economic Writings of Du Pont de Nemours*, 52–122, 162–209.

3 On the Physiocrats, see Weulersse, *La Physiocratie à l'aube de la Révolution*; Fox-Genovese, *The Origins of Physiocracy*; Meek, *The Economics of Physiocracy*; on Quesnay's collection of data, see J.-C. Perrot, *Une Histoire intellectuelle de l'économie politique*, 221–2.

4 Du Pont, *L'Enfance et la jeunesse de Du Pont de Nemours* (1906), cited in McLain, 68; on Quesnay's refusal to allow empirical information to refute his basic assumptions, see Larrère, 193.

5 Du Pont, *Observations sur la constitution*, 6–7, 9.

6 Du Pont, *Éphémérides* (1769, no.6), 43–4; see AI-SMP, B8, for Du Pont's similar taxation views in reviewing the public loans prize memoirs of 1797; Le Mercier de la Rivière, *L'Ordre naturel et essentiel des sociétés politiques* (1767), in Daire, ed., *Physiocrates*, 482–7, 495–7, 504–7, 514–18; see somewhat different ratios in Quesnay, "Second Economic Problem" (1767) in Meek, *The Economics*, 186–202, 242.

7 Du Pont, *Rapport fait ... sur les impositions indirectes*, 2–3, 5, 12; Marcel Marion, *Histoire financière de la France*, 4:94, 113, 117–20, 134–5, 203.

8 On Du Pont's practical modification of theoretical principles, see Pierre-Henri Goutte, "Dupont de Nemours et la transition vers l'ordre naturel," in Servet, ed., *Idées économiques sous la Révolution*, 145–233.

9 AI-SMP, A3, PV-CSMP, 12 floréal IV; Du Pont, *On Economic Curves*, 3, 16, diagrams between 12–13; McLain, *The Economic Writings*, 132–5.

10 Du Pont, *De l'origine et progrès d'une science nouvelle*, 10, 17–18.

11 Quesnay, "General Maxims," in Meek, *The Economics*, 236; Pocock, *Virtue, Commerce, and History*, 48, 123.

12 Meek, *The Economics*, 237–8.

13 Du Pont, *Discours sur l'état et les ressources des finances*, 81, 98.

14 PV-CSMP, 2 ventôse IV; Du Pont, *Ephémérides* (1771, no.6), 179–246, esp.206–18.

15 AN, AD XVIII^c 383, no.6, *Compte rendu et présenté au Corps législatif des travaux des diverses classes de l'Institut, an IV*, 153.

16 Say, *A Treatise on Political Economy*, xx, xxiv–v, xxxix, 101, 234–60, 306–14. On Say, see Allix, "La méthode et la conception," 335–9; Breton, "La place de la statistique et de l'arithmétique politique," 1053. On Destutt de Tracy as an economist, see Klein, "Deductive Economic Methodology"; Kennedy, *A Philosophe*, 197–207; Welch, *Liberty and Utility*, 73–96; Head, *Ideology*, 129–62.

17 For the psychological assumptions of Destutt de Tracy's economics, see Allix, "Destutt de Tracy, économiste," 425–30; Welch, *Liberty and Utility*, 74–5.

18 For Condillac's influence on Say, see Allix, "La méthode," 321–34. An exception to the trend away from the Physiocrats was central school teacher Guillaume Grivel; see Allix, "L'œuvre économique," 321.

19 J.-C. Perrot, *Une Histoire intellectuelle*, 24.

20 Moravia, *Il pensiero*, 675–715; Baker, *Condorcet*, 198–201, 225–44, 335–8.

21 Condorcet, *Journal d'instruction sociale*, no.4 (29 juin 1793), 110–12, 121.

22 Diannyère, *Journal des arts et manufactures*, 2:431–41, esp.432, 436.

23 Cited in Breton, "La place de la statistique," 1050; see Perrot, *Une histoire intellectuelle*, 378–9, and, more generally, 377–423.

24 Forbonnais, MSMP, 3:483, 485–8; *Analyse des principes sur la circulation des denrées*, 12, 18.

25 Baker, *Condorcet*, 280, 460; Duvillard, *Recherches sur les rentes*, introduction; *Notice des travaux de M. du Villard*, part 2, 3–6, 9–10; for a comparison of Duvillard and Condorcet, see Crépel, "Les calculs économiques et financiers de Condorcet," *Colloque la pensée économique pendant la Révolution, Vizille* (hereafter *Vizille*), vol.4, fourth paper.

26 Bibliothèque nationale, NAF 20580, "Travail sur l'établissement d'une caisse nationale d'épargnes," fols.10, 22–3, 27, 32.

27 Bibliothèque nationale, NAF 20580, cited in Jonckheere, "La table de mortalité de Duvillard," 867–70; "Duvillard et la statistique en 1806," in *Histoire économique*, 425–35, esp.425.

28 Jonckheere, "La table de la mortalité de Duvillard," 873.

29 "Duvillard" in *Histoire économique*, 429, 433–4; J.-C. Perrot, *L'Âge d'or de la statistique régionale*, 217; Coleman, *Death is a Social Disease*; Lécuyer, "Démographie statistique et hygiène publique," 215–45.

30 Diannyère, *Essais d'arithmétique politique*, viiin, 18; see also Moravia, *Il pensiero*, 741–2.

31 Diannyère, *Essais*, 1–11, 18; citation on 11; see Smith, *Wealth of Nations*, 1:539.

32 Diannyère, *Essais*, 18, and, generally, 12–24.

33 Say, *A Treatise*, xx, xxvi–ii; see also Moravia, *Il pensiero*, 788–9, Perrot, *Une Histoire intellectuelle*, 86 and especially Breton, "La place de la statistique," 1044–5, 1052, 1057–8.

34 Destutt de Tracy, *A Treatise on Political Economy*, 25, and, generally, 17–31; Moravia, *Il pensiero*, 739–41.

35 Le Breton, "Extrait de N.-F. Canard, Principes d'économie politique," *La Décade philosophique*, 10 ventôse x, 385–99, 399 (citation).

36 Creuzé-Latouche, "Opinion sur le commerce des blés," *Journal des débats*, 18 décembre 1792, 316–17; *Supplément*, 12; Creuzé-Latouche, *Discours ... sur les subsistances*, 28 avril 1793, 9.

37 Diannyère, *Essais*, xv; Creuzé-Latouche, *Discours sur la nécessité*, 3, 9–10 (citation).

38 Lacuée, *Opinion sur la résolution*, 3 floréal v, 2, 6, 11–13.

39 Véron de Forbonnais, *Principes et observations économiques*, 1:iii–iv; 2:97; AN, 284 AP 2, dossier 10, Sieyès, "Lettres aux économistes sur leur système de politique et de morale" (1776), fols.3, 15; Sieyès, *Écrits politiques*, 27, 37.

40 Forbonnais, *Principes*, 1:75, 234; 2:116, 122; Sieyès, AN, 284 AP 2, dossier 10, fols.5, 14–15, 19; dossier 6, "Impôts," fol.1; cf. Sieyès, *Écrits*, 32, 35–43, 51–2.

41 Sieyès, AN, 284 AP 2, dossier 4, "Rapports et valeurs" (1772?), dossier 7, "Tableaux des différentes classes des citoyens" (1772); dossier 10, fol.10; see also the differing analysis by Dorigny, "La formation de la pensée économique," 17–34, which depicts Sieyès not as a *laissez-faire* liberal but as an advocate of a protective and active state in the tradition of Colbert and Necker and anticipating the Saint-Simonians more than did Constant, 29–33; Larrère, *L'Invention de l'économie*, 273; Sewell, *A Rhetoric*, 94–5, argues that Sieyès saw division of labour as an end in itself and never developed the concept of a free market to increase productivity.

42 Smith, *Recherches sur la nature*, trans. Germain Garnier, 5:171, 262, 280, 283, 294–5.

43 Tracy, *A Treatise*, 180–1n; Allix, "La rivalité," 336–8.

44 Cf. Moravia, *Il pensiero*, 772–4; Garnier, *Abrégé élémentaire*, 16, 155; Allix, "L'œuvre économique de G. Garnier," 317–42, esp.327; Smith, *Recherches*, trans. Garnier, 1:iv–xii.

45 Yves Breton, "Germain Garnier (1754–1821), l'économiste et l'homme politique, tradition et modernité," 12–14, in *Vizille*, vol.1, fifth paper; see also Bernard Delmas and Thierry Demals, "Dupont et les 'Éclectiques': La controverse sur la stérilité pendant la période révolutionnaire," in *Vizille*, vol.1, last paper, 20–5.

46 Smith, *Recherches*, trans. Garnier, 5:4.

47 Despite Duvillard's egalitarianism, his manuscript, "Travail sur l'établisse-ment d'une caisse nationale d'épargnes," in BN, NAF 20580, fol.34, calls "land the producer of profits of funds of all kinds of capitals, as well as all salaries." The royalist Toulongeon, by contrast, thought "human industry increases the value of goods," in *Histoire de la France*, 1:250. Hence, theories of value are not infallibly testimony to democratic or conservative political views.

48 Roederer, AN, 29 AP 86, "Extrait de Smith," July 1780, 64, 137; on Roederer's early economic ideas of 1787–88, see Weulersse, *La Physio-cratie*, 107–8, 344–7, 353–5 (citation, 344); Margerison, *P.-L. Roederer*, 22, 25–7; Roederer, "Cours," in *Œuvres*, 8:140–3.

49 For a survey of the economic thought of the Idéologues, see Kaiser, "Pol-itics and Political Economy," 141–60; on Roederer's 1800–1 lectures, see James, "Pierre-Louis Roederer," 460–1; Margerison, 94–8, 106–8; Gilbert Faccarello, "Le legs de Turgot," *Vizille*, vol.4, eighth paper, 3–6; Delmas and Demals, "Dupont et les 'Éclectiques,'" *Vizille*, 1:25–8; Roederer's discourse on taxation is in "Mémoires sur quelques points d'économie publique," *Œuvres*, 8:71–4; for related passages in Smith, see *Wealth of Nations*, 1:351, 2:847–8.

50 James, "Pierre-Louis Roederer," 466–7.

51 Destutt de Tracy, *A Treatise*, 19–20, 24–5, 168, 171; Say, *A Treatise*, 74–7, 329–32.

52 Forbonnais, *Principes*, 1:78, 86–91, 97, 208, 210; MSMP, 3:486–7. For a controversial interpretation of Forbonnais as an "egalitarian liberal," see Simone Meyssonier, "Deux économistes sous la Révolution: Véron de For-bonnais et l'Abbé Morellet," in *Vizille*, vol.2, sixth paper, 22–6; Sieyès, AN, 284 AP 2, dossier 6, "Impôts," fol.2; Bastid, *Sieyès et sa pensée*, 327.

53 Garnier, *Abrégé élémentaire*, 212–13, 219, 422–40; Allix, "L'œuvre éco-nomique," 340; Smith, *Recherches*, trans. Garnier, 5:398–9, 425, 436–8; for Lacuée's unsuccessful support for a new salt tax in 1799 see *Opinion de Lacuée sur la résolution*, 1 ventôse VII, 7, 16–18.

54 Roederer in AN, 29 AP 86, 29, 33–4, 57; on the reasons for the fame of Smith in France, see Allix, "L'œuvre économique," 318n; see also Roederer's

comment in the *Journal de Paris*, 20 thermidor V, that Smith became famous in the 1787 discussion of financial problems in the Assembly of Notables.

55 Roederer, *Journal de Paris*, 21 (30 thermidor IV, 4 fructidor IV): 1324, 1339–40; 22 (20 frimaire V, 7 nivôse V): 322, 389–90.

56 Canard, *Principes d'économie politique* (Paris, an X-1801), 161–7, 179–81; for a possible derivation from Pietro Verri of Canard's formula, see Condorcet's critique of Verri in Baker, *Condorcet*, 337–8; for Canard as an anti-Physiocratic partisan of distribution of "net product" in equilibrium form to all holders of *rentes* (industrial, commercial, and land), see Ramon Tortajada, "Produit net et latitude (Nicolas-François Canard, 1754–1833)," *Vizille*, vol.4, last paper.

57 Another recent advocate of a progressive tax on all forms of revenue was Condorcet in the *Journal d'instruction sociale* in 1793; see J.-C. Perrot, "Condorcet," 13–37, esp.24.

58 Roederer, "Mémoires," in *Œuvres*, 8:68–72; for Roederer's support of Canard as a teacher and admission that he was "capable of appreciating his [Canard's] research and observations," see AN, F¹⁷ 7886, cited in Thuillier, "Les idées monétaires," 45, 54.

59 Destutt de Tracy, *A Treatise*, 195–232, esp.195, 197, 224–5, 232.

60 Bergeron, *L'Épisode napoléonien*, 51–2.

61 Forbonnais, *Principes*, 1:237–8, 242, 246–51.

62 Garnier, *Abrégé*, 183, 223, 240; Allix, "L'œuvre économique," 327; Smith, *Recherches*, trans. Garnier, 5:191.

63 Creuzé-Latouche, *Discours sur l'école normale*, 7–8.

64 Roederer, "Cours," in *Œuvres*, 8:147–8, 150–1; Diannyère, *Essais*, 60, 65, 67.

65 Say, *A Treatise*, xv; Say, *Olbie*, 1, 16–17, 79; see also Frick, "Philosophie et économie politique," 51–66, esp.55.

66 Say, *Olbie*, 3–6, 25, 27, 29, 33–4, 59–67, 122; *A Treatise*, 124.

67 Destutt de Tracy, *A Treatise*, 176–84, 193, 253.

68 Pocock, 194–6; Staum, "The Enlightenment Transformed," 171.

69 Garnier, *Abrégé*, 234–7, 240; Smith, *Recherches*, trans. Garnier, 5:440.

70 Forbonnais, MSMP, 3:484–5; "Analyse des principes sur la circulation," 21, 34; on the monetary ideas of Nicolas Canard as a contestant in the fourth public loans contest of 1801 and as favourable at least to private credit, see Thuillier, "Les idées."

71 AI-SMP, B3; Bibliothèque de l'Institut, Usuels, AA 33, vol.17, no.53, 3n, 3–4, 6–7; Roederer, *Mémoires d'économie publique* 1, no.3 (30 frimaire VIII): 179–83.

72 Sieyès, "Emprunts du gouvernement," in AN, 284 AP 2, dossier 12.

73 Roederer, *Journal d'économie publique* 5 (30 vendémiaire VI): 368–75, esp.373; see *Œuvres de Turgot*, 2:589–92, or R.L. Meek, ed., *Turgot on Progress*, 170–2.

74 See Chapter 4 on the prize contest on public loans.

75 Destutt de Tracy, *A Treatise*, 180–1n, 236–47.

76 Welch, *Liberty and Utility*, 157–8, 175–6; Allix, "Destutt de Tracy," 431–2.

77 Bergeron and Chaussinand-Nogaret, *Les "masses de granit*,*"* 23.

78 Margerison, *P.-L. Roederer*, 141–4.

79 Saricks, *Pierre-Samuel Du Pont de Nemours*, 327–8; 423 for the citation of the letter to Hennin, 23 Pluviôse XII.

CHAPTER TWELVE

1 Jeremy Popkin, "The Press and the French Revolution," 664–83, esp.671–6, referring to Hunt, *Politics, Culture, and Class*, and Claude Labrosse and Pierre Rétat, *Naissance du journal révolutionnaire* (Lyon, 1989).

2 Emmet Kennedy, *A Cultural History*, 17, 391, on the persistence of academic practices and ideas.

3 Collin d'Harleville, "La grande famille réunie," published in the *Mémoires de l'Institut. Classe de Littérature et Beaux-Arts*, 2:18–24, cited in Hahn, "From the Académie des Sciences to the Institut National," 202–9.

4 For the persistence of aristocratic representation in academies, see Barksdale, "Liberal Politics," 19–20, 35, 38–9.

5 Hahn, "From the Académie," 202–9.

6 Staum, "Human, not Secular Sciences," 50–1.

7 Nathans, "Habermas's 'Public Sphere,'" 620–44, esp.631.

8 Dhombres and Dhombres, *Naissance d'un pouvoir*, 262.

9 For a parallel discussion on the ideal of the independent artist and the imperative to create patriotic or didactic art, see Leith, *The Idea of Art as Propaganda*, esp.129–56.

10 For a different slant on the "moral treatment," see Goldstein, *Console and Classify*, 72–119.

11 Destutt de Tracy, *De l'amour*; see the discussion in Welch, *Liberty and Utility*, 118–9, 122–3; Kennedy, *A Philosophe*, 261–7.

12 Coleman, "Health and Hygiene in the *Encyclopédie*," 399–421 and *Death Is A Social Disease*.

13 See Jacyna, "Medical Science and Moral Science," 111–46, and Braunstein, "Broussais et le matérialisme," 33–6.

14 See Barksdale, "Liberal Politics," 612–64.

15 Lévesque, MSMP, 1:209–46, esp.230–1, 241–6; see Comninel, *Rethinking the French Revolution*, 53–76, on the "liberal materialism" of Guizot, Thierry, Mignet, and their forerunners among the advocates of the four-stage theory. See below on the new historical consciousness of the nineteenth century.

16 Cf. the argument of Mitchell in "Tocqueville's Mirage or Reality?" 28–54, especially on Cabanis's support of Bonaparte's constitution as a symbol of misunderstanding of the *practice* of politics.

17 Welch, *Liberty and Utility*, 157–71.

18 Say, *A Treatise on Political Economy*, xv.

19 Simon, *Une Académie sous le Directoire*, 452–72, esp.459; Moravia, *Il tramonto*, 452–70, 564–9; on Idéologue opposition to Bonaparte, see Gobert, *L'Opposition des assemblées*, 117, 155, 175–8, 366, 373; Ville-fosse et Bouissonouse, *L'Opposition à Napoléon I*; Polowetzky, *A Bond Never Broken*.

20 *Mercure de France*, 16 pluviôse IX (16 January 1801), 320–4, reprinted from the *Journal de Paris*; see remarks made by Bonaparte in the Council of State in Kennedy, *A Philosophe*, 89.

21 *Correspondance et relations de Joseph Fiévée avec Bonaparte*, 1:118–9, cited in Polowetzky, *A Bond Never Broken*, 97.

22 Delisle de Sales, *Mémoires pour les académies*, 179–89, 197.

23 AN, 29 AP 75, fol.751, Roederer, "Hommes de lettres pensionnés par le département de l'instruction publique," which records pensions to Gaillard, Saint-Lambert, and Morellet.

24 Roederer, *Mémoires d'économie publique*, 1, no.7:329–32; reprinted with derisive comments about Idéologues in the *Gazette de France*, 14 floréal an VIII, 895–6.

25 Roederer in AN, 29 AP 75, 252–3, 255, 256, 264; *Recueil de lois et règlements concernant l'instruction publique*, 11 floréal an X, 3, 6, and 24 floréal an X (14 May 1802), 2:252–5; see AN, 29 AP 75, 652–5, for Roederer's "Plan d'un lycée de neuf professeurs" and "Projet d'arrêté – an XI, 31 août 1802"; Thuillier, "Aux origines de l'enseignement des sciences politiques," 40:434–40, notes some anticipations of Roederer's scheme in a work of 1765 by Garnier to enhance the philosophy classes of the *collèges*.

26 *Recueil de lois et règlements concernant l'instruction publique*, 2:378–401.

27 De Beauchamp, *Recueil des lois et règlements sur l'enseignement supérieur*, 1:165; *Bulletin des lois*, 3ᵉ série, 24:701–9.

28 Burton, *Napoleon and Clio*, 3–17, 34; *Recueil de lois et règlements concernant l'instruction publique*, 2:305–6, 378–401.

29 *Journal des Débats*, 13 messidor VIII, 4; 12 frimaire IX; *Gazette de France*, 16 vendémiaire IX, for Degérando's memoir on observation of savages.

30 G., *Mercure*, 16 nivôse X, 140; P.M., *Mercure*, 2 pluviôse XI, 217–24, 265–76, esp.265, 273; cf. similar sentiments by A. in *Journal des Débats*, 25 fructidor X, for a review of Cabanis; see also Ibid., 22 nivôse XI, 12 January 1803.

31 Crocker, *An Age of Crisis; Nature and Culture.*

32 *Gazette de France*, no.867, 8 floréal VIII, 871; see also the review of Destutt de Tracy, in Ibid., no.1486, 22 nivôse X, 51, and of Cabanis, in Ibid., no.1710, 6 fructidor X.

33 *Journal des Débats*, 2 brumaire X.

34 Roederer in AN, AF^{IV} 1050, dossier 9, 7–8.

35 Chaptal, *Rapport présenté aux Consuls*, 17 nivôse XI (7 January 1803), in Aucoc, *L'Institut de France*, 67–72; on the Institute budget, see Bradley, "The Financial Basis," 468–9. Budgetary motives seem to have been minimal in the reorganization of 1803; the budget, averaging 280,000 FF in the Revolutionary era, jumped to 497,000 in 1806, and stabilized at 440,000 in 1812, while the number of members increased from 144 to 171.

36 See Aucoc, *L'Institut de France*, 68–71, and Appendix A for the redistribution of members; see AN, F^{17} 3590, Organisation de l'Institut, 1803, 3, 8 pluviôse XI, for the government reorganization commission that included Dacier and Roederer from the second class.

37 Aucoc, *L'Institut de France*, 69, 71.

38 Lyon-Caen, *Notice sur l'Académie*, 71.

39 Archives de l'Institut, Académie française, 1D1, Registre des prix; Fayolle, "Le XVIIIe siècle jugé par le XIXe," in *Approches des lumières*, 181–96; Mortier, *Le "Tableau littéraire de la France au XVIIIe siècle"*; Welschinger, *Chateaubriand*; Polowetzky, *A Bond Never Broken*, 151–2.

40 Archives de l'Académie des Inscriptions, C15, dossier de Bouchaud; *Histoire de l'Académie royale des Inscriptions et Belles-Lettres*, vols.47–50; *Mémoires de l'Institut royal de France. Classe d'Histoire et de Littérature ancienne*, vols.1–3.

41 *Mémoires de l'Académie royale des Inscriptions*, 9:86–127.

42 Dussaud, *La Nouvelle Académie des Inscriptions*, 1:12; Aucoc, *L'Institut de France*, 74, 184.

43 Powell, "The History and Influence of the Athénée," 178–82; Haines, "The Athénée de Paris," *History and Technology*, 5:249–71. Benjamin Constant lectured on the English constitution in 1819; Say on political economy in the Athénée in 1818–19, and then in the Conservatoire after 1819 and in the Collège de France after 1830; Charles Dunoyer and Charles Dupin in the Athénée in 1824–25 and 1827; see Ventre-Denis, "Sciences sociales et université," 321–42.

44 Barksdale, 117–20, 128–32, 153–5. This discussion is heavily indebted to Barksdale's excellent dissertation, which deserves publication. Sophie Leterrier is revising a doctoral thesis she defended in December 1992 at the Université de Paris-I on "Les sciences morales et politiques à l'Institut de France 1795–1850." I have not had access to this text, though I have seen a short summary in January 1994 in the Bulletin de la Société française de l'Histoire des Sciences de l'Homme.

45 On Guizot's vision of psychology as a tool against political enemies, see Chase, "The Influence of Psychology on Guizot," 177–93.

46 Barksdale, "Liberal Politics," 167–8, 170–5; see Walch, *Les Maîtres de l'histoire*, 116–17, 135, 137; Mellon, *The Political Uses of History*, 5, 18; Rosanvallon, *Le Moment Guizot*, 182–98.

47 Allix, "J.-B. Say et les origines de l'industrialisme," 303–13, 341–63, esp.350–7.

48 Barksdale, "Liberal Politics," 190, 198, 200–1, 293–4.

49 Guizot, *Mémoires*, 3:149, cited in Barksdale, "Liberal Politics," 301, and 3:158–9, cited in Rosanvallon, *Le Moment Guizot*, 226; see also Rosanvallon, *Le Moment Guizot*, 93–7, 125–8, 145, 164–7, 227.

50 Aucoc, *L'Institut de France*, 124.

51 Lakanal was forgotten for a year; see Roederer, *Œuvres*, 5:371, on the importance of general culture rather than specialization. See Appendix 4 for the list of former members of the Class of Moral and Political Sciences.

52 Ibid., 5:374–7, 459, 534; see also Feller and Gœury, "Les Archives de l'Académie," 567–83; Bonnefous, "Le cent-cinquantième anniversaire de l'Académie," 15–23, esp.18.

53 Barksdale, "Liberal Politics," 413–15.

54 Ibid., 547.

55 Ibid., 505, 564, 570–73, 586.

56 *Institut de France. Catalogue de l'Exposition*, 205, 228–32.

57 See the lively discussion in Novick, *That Noble Dream*, 535–72.

Bibliography

MANUSCRIPTS

Archives de l'Académie des Sciences
Dossier de Liberge de Granchain.

Archives de l'Institut
3 A^{1-2-3} Registres des procès-verbaux des séances générales de l'Institut, an IV–an XI (contains information on all elections).

Archives de l'Institut, Académie des Inscriptions et Belles-Lettres
C15 Dossier de Bouchaud.
C26 Dossier de Dacier.
1H5, 6, 7 Concours de l'Institut sur les sépultures et les cérémonies des funérailles, 40 mémoires.
1H8 Concours sur la barbarie envers les animaux, 26 mémoires.
1H9 2e Concours sur la décomposition de la pensée, 18 mémoires.
2H2 Concours sur l'influence de la Réformation de Luther, 7 mémoires.
Indice des personnes.

Archives de l'Institut, Académie des Sciences morales et politiques
A1, 2, 3 Procès-verbaux de la Classe des sciences morales et politiques, 3 registres an IV–an XI.
A4 Feuilles de présence.
A5, 6, 7, 8 Pièces annexes aux procès-verbaux, an IV–an XI.
A8 Liste de mémoires à imprimer.

A9, 10 Liste chronologique des mémoires lus par personne et par section.

B1 Concours, l'influence des signes sur les idées, 13 mémoires.

B2 Deuxième concours–signes, 10 mémoires.

B3 Concours sur les emprunts publics, 4 concours, 4, 2, 3, 6 mémoires.

B4 Concours sur la morale d'un peuple, 2 concours, 15, 8 mémoires.

B5 Concours sur le pouvoir paternel, 3 concours, 3, 7, 6 mémoires.

B6 Concours sur l'habitude, 2 concours, 4, 7 mémoires.

B7 Concours sur l'émulation, 16 mémoires.

B8 Concours sur la bonté d'un homme public, 11 mémoires. Concours sur les impôts dans les pays agricoles, 4 mémoires. Concours sur les changements dans le globe, 2 mémoires. Concours sur l'esprit public depuis François Ier, 3 mémoires.

B9 Concours sur le perfectionnement du jury, 8 mémoires.

B10 Concours sur l'intérieur de l'Afrique, 1 mémoire non admis. Concours sur la décomposition de la pensée, 15 mémoires.

B11 Concours sur l'abolition progressive de la servitude, 6 mémoires.

Archives de l'Institut (Académie française)
1D1 Registres des prix.

Archives départementales, consulted for baptismal certificates
Aisne: Legrand de Laleu.
Allier: Ardennes-Baudin, dossier Destutt de Tracy, Diannyère.
Ariège: Lakanal.
Aude: Ferlus.
Aveyron: Laromiguière.
Bouches-du-Rhône: Barthélemy, Pastoret.
Corrèze: Cabanis.
Côte-d'Or: Champagne.
Eure: Liberge de Granchain.
Gironde: de Sèze.
Haute-Saône: Beauchamp, Toulongeon.
Hérault: Cambacérès.
Ille-et-Vilaine: Bigot, Ginguené, Le Breton.
Lot-et-Garonne: Labène, Lacuée.
Marne: Buache.
Meurthe-et-Moselle: Grégoire.
Meuse: Villeterque.
Nièvre: Bourgoing.
Pas-de-Calais: Daunou, Jacquemont.
Puy-de-Dôme: Romme.
Pyrénées-Atlantiques: Garat transcription de la Ville de Bayonne.
Sarthe: Véron de Forbonnais.

Seine: Bougainville, Mercier, Gudin (reconstitution)
Seine-Maritime: Saint-Pierre.
Somme: Legrand d'Aussy.
Var: Sieyès.
Vendée: La Revellière-Lépeaux.
Vienne: Creuzé de la Touche.
Yonne: Gautier de Sibert.

Archives municipales, consulted for baptismal certificates.
Aix-en-Provence: Gallois.
Bouxwiller-Musée: Koch.
Gorron: J.-J. Garnier.
Lyon: Delisle de Sales, Fleurieu, Lescallier.
Menton: Massa.
Metz: Roederer.
Pontarlier: Le Michauc d'Arçon.
Saint-Maixent-L'École: Garran de Coulon.
Strasbourg: Ramond.

Archives nationales
AD XVIII^c 383, no. 6 *Compte rendu et notice des travaux des diverses classes de l'Institut, an IV*. Paris, an V.
AD XVIII^c 439 *Compte rendu et notice des travaux de la Classe des sciences morales et politiques*. Paris, an V.
AD XVIII^c 474 *Compte rendu et notice des travaux de la Classe des sciences morales et politiques au Corps législatif*. Paris, an VI.
AF^{IV} 1050, dossier 9 (Institute finances).
29 AP 75, 86, 110, 111 Papiers de Roederer (includes draft reports on public morality contest, education plans).
284 AP 2 Sieyès sur Condillac et Bonnet, "Lettres aux économistes" (economic manuscripts).
284 AP 3, 5, 18 Papiers de Sieyès (includes papers on life and on the brain).
284 AP 17 Correspondance de Sieyès.
C 465 Compte rendu et notice des travaux de l'Institut national au Corps législatif, an VII.
F $^{17^*}$ 1011 Rapport du Conseil d'Instruction publique [1800].
F^{17} 1094 Fondation de l'Institut.
F^{17} 1095, dossier 6 Budgets de l'Institut.
F^{17} 1218 Budget de l'Institut, Indemnités reçues.
F^{17} 1339 Conseil d'Instruction publique, Correspondance.
F^{17} 1344$^{2-3,6-7}$ Écoles centrales, Cahiers et réponses des professeurs – grammaire générale, réponses des professeurs de législation.
F^{17} 3590 Organisation de l'Institut, 1803.

Bibliothèque de l'Arsenal
MS 15087(c) Manuscrits de Mercier, Vues sur la morale, Vues politico-morales, Mémoire sur Kant.

Bibliothèque de l'Institut
Usuels AA 33, vols.17, 18 Programmes des prix, Procès-verbaux des séances de l'Institut d'Égypte.
MS 2128 Manuscrits de Maine de Biran, Copie du brouillon pour le premier mémoire sur l'habitude.

Bibliothèque historique de la Ville de Paris
MS 815, Lycée républicain.

Bibliothèque nationale
NAF 20580 Manuscrits de Duvillard, "Travail sur l'établissement d'une caisse nationale d'épargnes."
NAF 21910 Manuscrits de Daunou.

PERIODICALS

Ami des lois. An VIII.
La Clef du cabinet des souverains. An IV–an XI.
La Décade philosophique, littéraire et politique. An II [1794]–1807.
Éphémérides du citoyen. 1769–71.
Gazette de France. An VIII–an XI.
Journal d'économie publique. Ed. P.-L. Roederer. An V–an VII.
Journal de Paris. An IV–an XI.
Journal des arts et manufactures. 1796.
Journal des débats. 1792.
Journal des débats. An VIII–an XI.
Journal des mines. 1796.
Journal d'instruction sociale. 1793.
Journal encyclopédique ou universel. Vol.3, part 3. 1789.
Magasin encyclopédique. An IV–1803.
La Médecine éclairée par les sciences physiques. Ed. Antoine-François Fourcroy. 1791–92.
Mémoires d'économie publique. Ed. P.-L. Roederer. An VIII–an IX.
Mercure de France. 1800–4.
Moniteur universel. Réimpression ... Vol.25. Paris: Plon 1847.
Notice (s) des travaux de la Classe des Sciences morales et politiques. Paris an IX–an XI (contains quarterly reports of class secretaries).
Nouvelles politiques. An V.
Le Publiciste. An VIII.

Rapport(s) lu(s) à l'assemblée générale de l'Institut sur les travaux de la Classe d'Histoire et Littérature ancienne (8 annual reports). Paris 1807–14.

BOOKS, ARTICLES, AND DOCUMENTS

Agulhon, Maurice. "Le sang des bêtes: Le problème de la protection des animaux en France au xixe siècle." *Romantisme*, 31 (1981): 81–109.

Albury, W.R. "The Order of Ideas: Condillac's Method of Analysis as a Political Instrument in the French Revolution." In John Schuster and Richard Yeo. *The Politics and Rhetoric of Scientific Method: Historical Studies.* Dordrecht: Reidel 1986. 203–25.

Alfaric, Prosper. *Laromiguière et son école.* Paris: Éditions Ophrys 1929.

Allix, Edgard. "Destutt de Tracy, économiste." *Revue d'économie politique*, 26 (1912): 425–30.

– "J.-B. Say et les origines de l'industrialisme." *Revue d'économie politique*, 24 (1910): 303–13, 341–63.

– "La méthode et la conception de l'économie politique dans l'œuvre de J.-B. Say." *Revue d'histoire des doctrines économiques et sociales*, 4 (1911): 321-60.

– "L'œuvre économique de G. Garnier, traducteur d'Adam Smith et disciple de Cantillon." *Revue d'histoire des doctrines économiques et sociales*, 5 (1912): 317–42.

– "La rivalité entre la propriété foncière et la fortune mobilière sous la Révolution." *Revue d'histoire économique et sociale*, 6 (1913): 297–348.

Amiable, Louis. *Une Loge maçonnique d'avant 1789: Les Neuf Sœurs.* Paris 1897. Ed. Charles Porset. Paris: Edimaf 1989.

Anquetil, Louis-Pierre. *L'Esprit de la Ligue, ou histoire politique des troubles de France pendant les XVIe et XVIIe siècles.* 3 vols. 3rd ed. Paris: Moutard 1783.

– *Histoire de France depuis les Gaulois jusqu'à la mort de Louis XVI.* 14 vols. Paris: Garnery an XIII-1805.

– *Précis d'histoire universelle.* 2nd ed. 12 vols. Paris: Lesguilliez an IX-1801.

Archer, Christon I. "Cannibalism in the Early History of the Northwest Coast: Enduring Myths and Neglected Realities." *Canadian Historical Review*, 61 (1980): 453–79.

Ariès, Philippe. *The Hour of Our Death.* Harmondsworth: Penguin 1982.

Aucoc, Léon. *L'Institut de France: Lois, statuts, et règlements concernant les anciennes académies et l'Institut, de 1635 à 1889.* Paris: Imprimerie nationale 1889.

Auroux, Sylvain. "Idéologie et *Langue des calculs.*" *Histoire épistémologie langage*, 4 (1982): 53–7.

– "La vague condillacienne." *Histoire épistémologie langage*, 4 (1982): 107-10.

Azouvi, François, ed. *L'Institution de la raison: La Révolution culturelle des Idéologues*. Paris: J. Vrin 1992.

– *La Science de l'homme selon Maine de Biran*. Paris: J. Vrin, 1995. I have not been able to consult this very important new work.

– and Dominique Bourel, eds. *De Königsberg à Paris, la réception de Kant en France (1788–1804)*. Paris: J. Vrin 1991.

Baczko, Bronislaw. "The Social Contract of the French: Sieyès and Rousseau." *Journal of Modern History*, 60, suppl. (1988): S98–125.

Baker, Donald, and Patrick Harrigan, eds. *The Making of Frenchmen: Current Directions in the History of Education in France, 1679–1979*. Waterloo, Ont.: Historical Reflections Press 1980.

Baker, Keith. *Condorcet: From Natural Philosophy to Social Mathematics*. Chicago: University of Chicago Press 1975.

– *Inventing the French Revolution*. Cambridge: Cambridge University Press 1990.

– "On the Problem of the Ideological Origins of the French Revolution." In Dominick LaCapra and Steven L. Kaplan, eds. *Modern European Intellectual History: Reappraisals and New Perspectives*. Ithaca: Cornell University Press 1982. 197–219.

– "Politics and Social Science in Eighteenth-Century France: The Société de 1789." In J.F. Bosher, ed. *French Government and Society (1500–1850)*. *Essays in Memory of Alfred Cobban*. London: Athlone Press 1973. 208–30.

– "Sieyès and Revolutionary Discourse." In Loretta Valtz, ed. *The Languages of Revolution*. Milan 1989. 195–205.

Barksdale, Dudley. "Liberal Politics and Nascent Social Science in France: The Academy of Moral and Political Sciences, 1803–1852." ph.d. dissertation, University of North Carolina 1986.

Barnes, Barry. *Interests and the Growth of Knowledge*. London: Routledge and Kegan Paul 1977.

Bastid, Paul. *Sieyès et sa pensée*. 2nd ed. Paris: Hachette 1970.

Baudin, Nicolas. *The Journal of Post Captain Nicolas Baudin*. ed. Christine Cornell. Adelaide: Libraries Board of South Australia 1974.

Beauchamp, Alfred de. *Recueil des lois et règlements sur l'enseignement supérieur*. 5 vols. Paris: Typographie de Delalain Frères 1880–98.

Beale, Georgia Robison. "Academies to Institut." *Consortium on Revolutionary Europe, Proceedings 1972*. Gainesville: University of Florida Press 1973. 110–27.

Bellanger, Claude, et al. *Histoire générale de la presse française*. 5 vols. Paris: Presses universitaires de France 1969.

Bentham, Jeremy. *Bentham's Political Thought*. Ed. Bhiku Parekh. London: Croom Helm 1973.

Bergeron, Louis. *L'Épisode napoléonien: Aspects intérieurs*. Paris: Le Seuil 1972.

Bergeron, Louis, and Guy Chaussinand-Nogaret. *Les "Masses de granit." Cent mille notables du Premier Empire.* Paris: Éditions de l'École des hautes Études en sciences sociales 1979.

Bernardin de Saint-Pierre, Jacques-Henri. *De la nature de la morale.* Paris: Imprimerie-Librairie du "Cercle social" an VI.

– *Œuvres complètes de Jacques-Henri-Bernardin de Saint-Pierre.* Ed. L. Aimé-Martin. 12 vols. Paris: Méquignon-Marvis 1818.

Biographie universelle (Michaud) ancienne et moderne. Ed. Joseph-François Michaud. 45 vols. Paris: Michaud; Delagrave 1854–62.

Biraben, Jean-Noël. "La statistique de population sous le Consulat et l'Empire." *Revue d'histoire moderne et contemporaine*, 17 (1970): 359–72.

Black, Duncan. *The Theory of Committees and Elections.* Cambridge: Cambridge University Press 1958.

Blanckaert, Claude. "On the Origins of French Ethnology: William Edwards and the Doctrine of Race." In George W. Stocking, Jr., ed. *Bones, Bodies, and Behavior: Essays in Biological Anthropology.* Madison: University of Wisconsin Press 1988. 19–55.

– "Les vicissitudes de l'angle facial et les débuts de la craniométrie (1765–1875)," *Revue de synthèse*, 4ᵉ série, 3–4 (1987): 417–53.

Blanning, T.C.W. *The French Revolution: Aristocrats vs. Bourgeois?* Atlantic Highlands, N.J.: Humanities Press 1987.

Bollème, G., et al., eds. *Livre et société dans la France du XVIIIᵉ siècle.* Paris and The Hague: Mouton 1965.

Bonaparte, Lucien. *Lucien Bonaparte et ses mémoires, 1775–1840.* Ed. Th. Iung. 2 vols. Paris: G. Charpentier 1882.

Bonnefous, Édouard. "Le cent-cinquantième anniversaire de l'Académie des Sciences morales et politiques." *Nouvelle Revue des deux mondes*, n.s. (juillet 1982): 15–23.

Bonnemains, Jacqueline, Elliott Forsyth, and Bernard Smith, eds. *Baudin in Australian Waters.* Melbourne: Oxford University Press 1988.

Bonnet, Jean-Claude, ed. *La Carmagnole des Muses: L'homme de lettres et l'artiste dans la révolution.* Paris: Armand Colin 1988.

Bonwick, James. *The Last of the Tasmanians.* London: S. Low, Marston, Searle, and Rivington 1884.

Bouchaud, Mathieu-Antoine. *Lettre détaillant les titres de Bouchaud...* Paris an V.

Bouclon, Adolphe de. *Étude historique sur la marine de Louis XVI: Liberge de Granchain, capitaine des vaisseaux du roi.* Paris: A. Bertrand 1866.

Bougainville, Louis-Antoine de. *Adventure in the Wilderness: The American Journals of Louis-Antoine de Bougainville, 1756–1760.* Ed. Edward Hamilton. Norman, Okla: University of Oklahoma Press 1964.

– *Voyage autour du monde par la frégate du roi "Boudeuse" et la flûte "l'Étoile."* 2nd ed. 2 vols. Paris: Saillant et Nyon 1772.

– *Voyage de Bougainville autour du monde*. Ed. Michel Hérubel. Paris: Union générale des Éditions 1966.

Boulay de la Meurthe, Antoine-Jacques-Claude-Joseph. *Théorie constitutionnelle de Sieyès*. Paris: P. Renouard 1836.

Bourdieu, Pierre. *Les Règles de l'art: Genèse et structure du champ littéraire*. Paris: Le Seuil 1992.

Bourgoing, Jean-François de. *Tableau de l'Espagne moderne*. 3 vols. Paris: chez l'auteur an v.

Bourguignon, Claude-Sébastien. *Mémoire qui a remporté le prix... "Quels sont les moyens de perfectionner en France l'institution du jury?"* Paris: Imprimerie de la République an x.

– *Deuxième mémoire sur les jurés*. Paris: C.F. Patris an xii-1804.

– *Troisième mémoire sur les jurés*. Paris: Léopold Collin 1808.

Bouvier, René, and Édouard Maynial. *Une Aventure dans les mers australes*. Paris: Mercure de France 1947.

Bowen, Margarita. *Empiricism and Geographical Thought*. Cambridge: Cambridge University Press 1981.

Bradley, Margaret. "The Financial Basis of French Scientific Education and Scientific Institutions in Paris 1790–1815." *Annals of Science* 36 (1979): 451–91.

Braunstein, Jean-François. "Broussais et le matérialisme." *Histoire des sciences médicales*, 21 (1988): 33–6.

Breton, Yves. "La place de la statistique et de l'arithmétique politique dans la méthodologie économique de Jean-Baptiste Say: Le temps des ruptures." *Revue économique*, 37 (1986): 1033–62.

Brissot, Jacques-Pierre. *Théorie des lois criminelles*. [1781]. 2 vols. Paris: J.P. Aillaud 1836.

Broc, Numa. "L'établissement de la géographie en France (1870–1890)." *Annales de géographie* 83 (1974): 545–68.

– *La Géographie des philosophes: Géographes et voyageurs français au XVIIIe siècle*. Paris: Éditions Ophrys 1975.

Bruce, James. *Voyage aux sources du Nil, en Nubie, et en Abyssinie ...* Trans. Jean Castéra. 5 vols. Paris: Hôtel de Thou 1790–92.

Brun, J.-B. *Mémoire sur cette question ... L'émulation est-elle un bon moyen d'éducation? ...* Paris: Bernard an ix.

Brunel, Lucien. *Les Philosophes et l'Académie française au dix-huitième siècle*. Paris: Hachette 1884.

Bulletin des lois. 3e série. Vol.24. Paris: Imprimerie de la République an xii-1804.

Burke, Peter. *The Fabrication of Louis XIV*. New Haven: Yale University Press 1992.

Burton, June. *Napoleon and Clio: Historical Writing, Teaching, and Thinking during the First Empire*. Durham, N.C.: Duke University Press 1979.

Busse, Winfried, and Jürgen Trabant, eds. *Les Idéologues: Sémiotique, théories et politiques linguistiques pendant la Révolution française.* Amsterdam: J. Benjamins 1986.

Butet, P.-R.-F. *Abrégé d'un cours complet de lexicologie.* Paris: Crapelet an IX-1801.

Buttimer, Anne. *Society and Milieu in the French Geographic Tradition.* Chicago: University of Chicago Press 1971.

Cabanis, André. *La Presse sous le Consulat et l'Empire (1799–1814).* Paris: Société des Études robespierristes 1975.

Cabanis, Pierre-Jean-Georges. *Discours ... sur le message du Conseil des Anciens, relatif aux journaux calomniateurs des premières autorités ... 1 fructidor VII.* Paris: Imprimerie nationale an VII.

– *Œuvres complètes.* Ed. François Thurot. 5 vols. Paris: Bossanges 1823–25.

– *Œuvres philosophiques.* Ed. Claude Lehec and Jean Cazeneuve. 2 vols. Paris: Presses universitaires de France 1956.

– *Opinion ... sur les réunions s'occupant d'objets politiques.* [6 fructidor an VII]. Paris n.d. (misdated an V in *Catalogue de l'histoire de France*).

Cambacérès, Jean-Jacques-Régis. *Projet de Code Civil, messidor an IV.* Paris: Imprimerie nationale an IV.

– *Résultat des opinions sur l'institution des jurés en matière civile, 17, 19 juin 1793.* Paris 1793.

Campbell, T.D. *Adam Smith's Science of Morals.* London: Allen and Unwin 1971.

Canard, Nicolas-François. *Principes d'économie politique.* Paris: F. Buisson an IX-1801.

Caput, Jean-Pol. *L'Académie française.* Paris: Presses universitaires de France 1986.

[Caze, Pierre]. *Essai sur la décomposition de la pensée.* Bordeaux: P. Baume 1804.

[Chaptal, Jean-Antoine]. *Analyse des procès-verbaux des Conseils généraux des Départements, session de l'an IX.* Vol.2. Paris: Imprimerie de la République an X.

– *Rapport et projet de loi sur l'instruction publique.* Paris: Deterville an IX.

Charles-Roux, François. *Bonaparte: Governor of Egypt.* London: Methuen 1937.

Charlton, D.G. *New Images of the Natural in France.* Cambridge: Cambridge University Press 1984.

Chartier, Roger. *The Cultural Origins of the French Revolution.* Durham, N.C.: Duke University Press 1991.

– "Intellectual History or Sociocultural History? The French Trajectories." In Dominique LaCapra and Steven Kaplan, eds. *Modern European Intellectual History: Reappraisals and New Perspectives.* Ithaca: Cornell University Press 1982. 13–46.

Chassériau, Frédéric. *Notice sur le M. le Comte Fleurieu*. Paris: F. Didot frères 1856.

Chaussinand-Nogaret, Guy. *The French Nobility in the Eighteenth Century.* [1976]. Cambridge: Cambridge University Press 1985.

Church, Clive. "Du nouveau sur les origines de la Constitution de 1795." *Revue historique de droit français et étranger*, 52 (1974): 594–627.

Coleman, William. *Death Is a Social Disease: Public Health and Political Economy in Early Industrial France.* Madison: University of Wisconsin Press 1982.

– "Health and Hygiene in the *Encyclopédie*: A Medical Doctrine for the Bourgeoisie." *Journal of the History of Medicine* 29 (1974): 399–421.

Colloque la pensée économique pendant la Révolution française, Vizille, 1989. 4 vols. Grenoble: Presses de l'Université de Grenoble 1989.

Comninel, George. *Rethinking the French Revolution.* London: Verso Press 1987.

Comte, Auguste. *A General View of Positivism.* New York: R. Speller 1957.

Condillac, Étienne Bonnot de. *Le Commerce et le gouvernement considérés relativement l'un à l'autre.* Paris: Jombert et Cellot 1776.

– *Langue des calculs.* [1798]. Ed. Sylvain Auroux and Anne-Marie Chouillet. Villeneuve-d'Ascq: Presses universitaires de Lille 1981.

– *Œuvres philosophiques.* Ed. Georges Le Roy. 3 vols. Paris: Presses universitaires de France 1951.

Condorcet, M.-J.-A. N. Caritat, Marquis de. *Condorcet: Selected Writings.* Ed. Keith Baker. Indianapolis: Bobbs-Merrill 1976.

– *Écrits sur l'instruction publique.* Ed. Charles Coutel and Catherine Kintzler. 2 vols. Paris: Edilig 1988–89.

– *Œuvres de Condorcet.* Ed. A. Condorcet O'Connor and François Arago. 12 vols. Paris: Firmin Didot 1847–49.

– *Sketch for a Historical Picture of the Progress of the Human Mind.* Ed. June Barraclough. London, Weidenfeld and Nicholson 1955.

Copans, Jean and Jean Jamin. *Aux Origines de l'anthropologie française.* Paris: Le Sycomore 1978.

Coser, Lewis. *Men of Ideas.* New York: The Free Press 1965.

Cousin, Victor. *Fragments philosophiques pour servir à l'histoire de l'humanité.* 5 vols. Paris: Didier 1866.

Crépel, Pierre, and Christian Gilain, eds. *Condorcet mathématicien, économiste, philosophe, homme politique.* Paris: Minerve 1989.

Creuzé-Latouche, Jacques-Antoine. *Convention nationale. Discours et projet de décret sur les subsistances, 28 avril 1793.* Paris: Imprimerie nationale 1793.

– *Convention nationale. Discours sur la nécessité d'ajouter à l'École normale un professeur d'économie politique, 12 pluviôse II.* Paris: Imprimerie nationale an II.

Crocker, Lester. *An Age of Crisis: Man and World in Eighteenth-Century Thought.* Baltimore: The Johns Hopkins University Press 1959.

– *Nature and Culture: Ethical Thought in the French Enlightenment.* Baltimore: The Johns Hopkins University Press 1963.

Crosland, Maurice. *Science under Control: The French Academy of Sciences, 1795–1914.* Cambridge: Cambridge University Press 1992.

Crossley, Ceri. *French Historians and Romanticism: Thierry, Guizot, the Saint-Simonians, Quinet, Michelet.* London: Routledge 1993.

Dacier, Bon-Joseph, ed. *Rapport historique sur les progrès de l'histoire et de la littérature ancienne depuis 1789, et sur leur état actuel.* Paris: Imprimerie impériale 1810.

Darnton, Robert. *Gens de lettres, gens du livre.* Paris: Odile Jacob 1992.

– *The Great Cat Massacre.* New York: Vintage Books 1984.

– "The High Enlightenment and the Low-life of Literature." *Past and Present,* 51 (1971): 81–115.

– "The Literary Revolution of 1789." *Studies in Eighteenth-Century Culture,* 21 (1991): 3–26.

Daston, Lorraine. *Classical Probability in the Enlightenment.* Princeton: Princeton University Press 1988.

Daunou, Pierre-Claude-François. *Cours d'études historiques.* 20 vols. Paris: F. Didot 1842–49.

– *Essai sur la Constitution.* Paris: Imprimerie nationale 1793.

– *Essai sur les garanties individuelles que réclame l'état actuel de la société.* Paris: Foulon 1819.

– *Mémoire sur les élections au scrutin, juillet 1800.* Paris: Baudouin an XI-1803.

– *Rapport et projet de loi sur les élections, 23 fructidor III.* Paris: Imprimerie de la République an III.

Degérando, Joseph-Marie. *De la génération des connaissances humaines.* Berlin: G. Decker 1802.

– *Des signes, et de l'art de penser considérés dans leurs rapports mutuels.* 4 vols. Paris: Goujon fils, Fuchs, Henrichs an VIII-1800.

– *Histoire comparée des systèmes de philosophie.* 3 vols. Paris: Henrichs, 1804. 3rd ed. 4 vols. Paris: Ladrange 1847.

– *The Observation of Savage Peoples.* [1800]. Ed. F.C.T. Moore. Berkeley: University of California Press 1969.

Dejace, André. *Les Règles de la dévolution successorale sous la Révolution, 1789–1794.* Bruxelles: E. Bruylant 1957.

Delisle de Sales, Jean-Baptiste-Claude Izouard. *À l'Institut national de France, sur la destitution des citoyens Carnot, Barthélemy, Sicard, et Fontanes.* Paris: sans nom an VIII-1800.

– *De la fin de la Révolution française.* Leipzig: A. Grieshammer 1800.

– *De la philosophie de la nature.* [1770]. 3rd ed. 6 vols. London: sans nom 1777.

– *De la philosophie du bonheur.* 2 vols. Paris: l'auteur an IV.
– *Éléments de l'histoire de France.* 9th ed. Vol.4 (continuation by Abbé Millot). Paris: Libraires associés 1814.
– *Histoire des hommes, ou histoire nouvelle de tous les peuples du monde.* 52 vols. Paris: sans nom 1779–85.
– *Mémoire en faveur de Dieu.* Paris: J.J. Fuchs an X-1802.
– *Mémoires pour les académies.* Paris: Guerebart et J.J. Fuchs an VIII-1800.
Deneys, Henry, and Anne, eds. *Corpus*, n° 11/12 (1989): *Volney.*
– and Deneys-Tunney, Anne, eds. *Corpus*, n° 26/27 (1994): *A.-L.-C. Destutt de Tracy; l'Idéologie.*
Descartes, René. *Œuvres philosophiques.* Ed. Ferdinand Alquié. 2 vols. Paris: Garnier 1963.
Désirat, Claude, and Tristan Hordé. "Les Écoles normales: une liquidation de la rhétorique." *Littérature*, 18 (1975): 31–50.
Destutt de Tracy, Antoine-Louis-Claude. *Commentaire sur l'esprit des lois de Montesquieu.* 2nd ed. Paris: Delaunay 1819.
– *De l'amour.* Ed. Gilbert Chinard. Paris: Les Belles Lettres 1926. Reprinted also in Fayard 1994 edition, ed. A. and H. Deneys.
– *Éléments d'idéologie I: Idéologie proprement dite.* [1817]. Paris: Vrin 1970.
– *Éléments d'idéologie II: Grammaire* (1817). Paris: Vrin 1970.
– *Éléments d'idéologie.* 4 vols. Paris: Veuve Courcier 1825.
– *Éléments d'idéologie.* 5 vols. Brussels: A. Wahlen 1826–27.
– *Observations sur le système actuel de l'instruction publique.* Paris: Panckoucke an IX.
– *Traité de la volonté et de ses effets.* [2nd ed. 1818]. Geneva and Paris: Slatkine 1984. Also available in 1994 Fayard edition of A. and H. Deneys.
– *A Treatise on Political Economy.* [Georgetown, 1817]. New York: Augustus M. Kelley 1970.
Dhombres, Jean. "L'image du monde arabe dans le bilan des activités scientifiques dressé par l'Institut de France sous l'Empire." *Sciences et techniques en perspective*, 20 (1991–92): 151–64.
Dhombres, Nicole et Jean. *Naissance d'un pouvoir: Sciences et savants en France (1793–1824).* Paris: Payot 1989.
Diannyère, Antoine-Louis. *Essais d'arithmétique politique.* Paris: Goujon an VIII.
Dictionnaire de biographie française. 13 vols. Paris: Letouzey et Ane 1933–86.
Dictionnaire des parlementaires français. Ed. A. Robert, et al. 5 vols. Paris: Bourloton 1889–90.
Doë de Maindreville, Henri. *Généalogie de la Maison Coquebert.* Paris 1953.
Doneaud du Plan, Alfred. *Histoire de l'Académie de Marine.* 2 vols. Paris: Berger-Levrault 1878–82.
Dorigny, Marcel. "La formation de la pensée économique de Sieyès d'après ses manuscrits (1770–1789)." *Annales historiques de la Révolution française*, 271 (1988): 17–34.

- "Les Girondins et la propriété." *Bulletin d'histoire économique et sociale de la Révolution française*, 1980–81: 15–31.

Dougnac, F. "La néologie." *Histoire épistémologie langage*, 4 (1982): 67–72.

Dowd, David L. *Pageant-Master of the Republic: Jacques-Louis David and the French Revolution*. [1948]. New York: Books for Libraries Press 1969.

Doyle, William. *Origins of the French Revolution*. Oxford: Oxford University Press 1980.

- *The Oxford History of the French Revolution*. Oxford: Oxford University Press 1989.

Drucker, Philip. *Indians of the Northwest Coast*. New York: Natural History Press 1955.

Duchet, Michèle. *Anthropologie et histoire au siècle des lumières*. Paris: François Maspero 1971.

Duguit, L., et al. Ed. G. Berlia. *Les Constitutions et les principales lois politiques de la France depuis 1789*. Paris: Librairie générale de Droit et de Jurisprudence 1952.

Dumont d'Urville, Jules-Sébastien-César. *An Account in Two Volumes of Two Voyages to the South Seas ...* Ed. Helen Rosenman. Honolulu: University of Hawaii Press 1987.

Dunmore, John. *French Explorers in the Pacific*. 2 vols. Oxford: Oxford University Press 1965.

Du Pont de Nemours, Pierre-Samuel. *Assemblée nationale. Discours sur l'état et les ressources des finances, 24 septembre 1789*. Versailles: Baudouin 1789.

- *De l'origine et progrès d'une science nouvelle*. Paris: Desaint 1768.

- *The Economic Writings of Du Pont de Nemours*. Ed. James J. McLain. Newark, Del.: University of Delaware Press 1977.

- *Observations sur la constitution proposée par la Commission des Onze, et sur la position actuelle de la France*. Paris: Du Pont an III.

- *Œuvres politiques et économiques*. 10 vols. Nendeln: KTO Press 1979.

- *On Economic Curves*. Ed. Henry W. Spiegel. Baltimore: The Johns Hopkins University Press 1955.

- *Philosophie de l'univers*. 3rd ed. Paris: Goujon fils an VII.

- *Physiocratie*. Paris: Merlin 1767.

- *Quelques mémoires sur différens sujets: La plupart d'histoire naturelle, ou de physique générale et particulière*. Paris: Delance 1807.

- *Rapport fait ... sur les impositions indirectes ... 29 octobre 1790*. Paris: Imprimerie nationale 1790.

- *Sur la liberté morale*. [Paris: sans nom an XI].

Durkheim, Émile. *Moral Education: A Study in the Theory and Application of the Sociology of Education*. Ed. Everett K. Wilson. New York: The Free Press 1973.

Duruy, Albert. *L'Instruction publique et la Révolution*. Paris: Hachette 1882.

Dussaud, René. *La Nouvelle Académie des Inscriptions et Belles-Lettres (1795–1914)*. 2 vols. Paris: P. Geuthner 1946.

Duvillard de Durand, Emmanuel-Étienne. "Duvillard et la statistique en 1806." In *Histoire économique et financière de la France. Études et documents I.* Paris: Imprimerie nationale 1989. 425–35.

– *Notice des travaux de M. du Villard.* Paris 1814.

– *Recherches sur les rentes, les emprunts, et les remboursements.* Paris: l'auteur 1787.

Encyclopédie, ou Dictionnaire raisonné... 36 vols. Geneva: Pellet 1778.

Eschbach, Achim and Jürgen Trabant, eds. *History of Semiotics.* Amsterdam: John Benjamins 1983.

Esmein, Adhémar. *A History of Continental Criminal Procedure.* Revised Ed. Boston: Little, Brown, and Co. 1913.

Fagan, Brian. *Clash of Cultures.* New York: Freeman 1984.

Faivre, Jean-Paul. *L'Expansion française dans le Pacifique de 1800 à 1842.* Paris: Nouvelles Éditions Latines 1953.

– "Les idéologues de l'an VIII et le voyage de Nicolas Baudin en Australie (1800–1804)." *Australian Journal of French Studies,* 3 (1966): 3–15.

Favre, Pierre. "La constitution d'une science du politique, le déplacement de ses objets, et l'irruption de l'histoire réelle." *Revue française de science politique,* 33 (1983): 181–219, 365–402.

Fayet, Joseph. *La Révolution française et la science.* Paris: M. Rivière 1960.

Fayolle, Roger. "Le XVIIIe siècle jugé par le XIXe: à propos d'un concours académique sous le premier Empire." In *Approches des lumières: Mélanges offerts à Jean Fabre.* Paris: Klincksieck 1974. 181–96.

Feller, Élise and Jean-Claude Gœury. "Les archives de l'Académie des Sciences morales et politiques, 1832–1848." *Annales historiques de la Révolution française,* 47 (1975): 567–83.

Feuillet, Laurent-François. *Mémoire couronné ... L'émulation est-elle un bon moyen d'éducation?* Paris: Renouard an IX-1801.

Feyerabend, Paul K. *Against Method: Outline of an Anarchistic Theory of Knowledge.* Atlantic Highlands: Humanities Press 1975.

Fierro, Alfred. *La Société de Géographie, 1821–1946.* Geneva: Droz 1983.

Fleurieu, Charles-Pierre Claret de. *Voyage autour du monde ... par Étienne Marchand.* 4 vols. Paris: Imprimerie de la République ans VI–VIII.

– *Voyage Round the World.* 4 vols. London: Longman and Rees 1801.

Foley, Vernard. *The Social Physics of Adam Smith.* West Lafayette, Ind.: Purdue University Press 1976.

Forrest, Alan. *The French Revolution and the Poor.* Oxford: Oxford University Press 1981.

Forsyth, Murray. *Reason and Revolution: The Political Thought of the Abbé Sieyès.* Leicester and New York: Leicester University Press 1987.

Foucault, Michel, *Discipline and Punish.* [1975]. New York: Random House 1978.

Fox, Robert, and George Weisz, eds. *The Organization of Science and Technology in France, 1808–1914.* Cambridge: Cambridge University Press 1980.

Fox-Genovese, Elizabeth. *The Origins of Physiocracy.* Ithaca: Cornell University Press 1976.

Fraisse, Geneviève. *Reason's Muse: Sexual Difference and the Birth of Democracy.* [1989]. Chicago: University of Chicago Press 1994.

Franqueville, A.-C.-F., Comte de. *Le Premier siècle de l'Institut de France.* 2 vols. Paris: J. Rothschild 1895.

Frick, Jean-Paul. "Philosophie et économie politique chez J.-B. Say." *Histoire, économie, et société,* 60 (1987): 51–66.

Friede, Juan, and Benjamin Keen, eds. *Bartolomé de Las Casas in History: Toward an Understanding of the Man and His Work.* De Kalb, Ill.: Northern Illinois University Press 1971.

Frost, Alan. "The Perception of Culture's Relativity in the Second Half of the Eighteenth Century." In J.P. Hardy and J.C. Eade, eds. *Studies in the Eighteenth Century, 5.* Oxford: Oxford University Press 1983. 129–41.

Furet, François. *Interpreting the French Revolution.* [1977]. Cambridge: Cambridge University Press 1981.

Gaffarel, Paul. "L'opposition littéraire sous le Consulat." *La Révolution française: Revue d'histoire contemporaine,* 9 (1889): 307–26, 397–432.

Gaillard, Gabriel-Henri. *Histoire de François Ier.* 7 vols. Paris: Saillant 1766–69.

Gamble, Clive. "Archaeology, History, and the Uttermost Ends of the Earth – Tasmania, Tierra del Fuego and the Cape." *Antiquity,* 66 (1992): 712–20.

Garat, Dominique-Joseph. *Mémoires de Garat.* 3rd ed. Paris: Poulet-Malassis 1862.

Gardiner, Patrick. *Theories of History.* Glencoe, Ill.: Free Press 1959.

Garebeuf, J. *Réflexions sur l'ouvrage de M. Cabanis ... Rapports du physique et du moral ...* Limoges: Chapoulaud an xi.

Garnier, Germain. *Abrégé élémentaire des principes économiques.* Paris: H. Agasse an iv.

Garnier, Jean-Jacques. *Histoire de France depuis l'établissement de la monarchie.* Vol.29. Paris: Saillant et Nyon, Veuve Desaint 1786.

Garran-Coulon, Jean-Philippe. *Rapport sur Julien Raimond ...* Paris: Imprimerie de la République 24 floréal an iii.

– *Rapport sur les troubles de Saint-Domingue.* 4 vols. Paris: Imprimerie nationale an v–an vii.

Gaulmier, Jean. *L'Idéologue Volney, 1757–1820.* [1951]. Geneva and Paris Slatkine, 1980.

– "Volney et ses leçons d'histoire." *History and Theory* 2 (1962): 52–65.

Gautier de Sibert, Edme. *Variations de la monarchie française dans son gouvernement politique, civil, et militaire.* 4 vols. Paris: Saillant 1765.

Gay, Peter. *The Enlightenment: An Interpretation.* Vol.1: *The Rise of Modern Paganism.* Vol.2: *The Science of Freedom.* New York: Knopf 1966–69.

Giesselmann, Werner. *Die brumairianische Elite.* Stuttgart: Klett 1977.

Gillispie, Charles C. "Probability and Politics: Laplace, Condorcet, and Turgot." *Proceedings of the American Philosophical Society,* 116 (1972): 1–20.

– *Science and Polity in France at the End of the Old Regime*. Princeton,: Princeton University Press 1980.

– "Scientific Aspects of the French Egyptian Expedition, 1798–1801." *Proceedings of the American Philosophical Society* 133 (1989): 447–74.

– and Michel Dewachter, eds. *Monuments of Egypt, The Napoleonic Edition. The Complete Archaeological Plates from La Description de l'Égypte*. 2 vols. Princeton: Princeton Architectural Press 1987.

Ginguené, Pierre-Louis. *Rapports lus à l'assemblée générale de l'Institut sur les travaux de la Classe d'Histoire et Littérature ancienne*. Paris 1807–13.

Girard de Villesaison, Laurent-René-Philippe. *Mémoire sur cette question ... Pour quels objets ... convient-il d'emprunter?* Paris: Desenne an IX-1801.

Gobert, Adrienne. *L'Opposition des assemblées pendant le Consulat*. Paris: E. Sagot 1925.

Goby, Jean-Édouard. "Les séances du premier Institut d'Égypte." *Revue de l'Institut Napoléon*. 150 (1988): 59–67.

Godechot, Jacques. *Les institutions de France sous la Révolution et l'Empire*. Paris: Presses universitaires de France 1951. 2nd ed. 1968.

Godlewska, Anne. "Geography under Napoleon and Napoleonic Geography." *The Consortium on Revolutionary Europe, Proceedings 1989*. Athens: University of Georgia Department of History 1990. 1:281–302.

– "Traditions, Crisis, and New Paradigms in the Rise of the Modern French Disciplines of Geography, 1760–1850." *Annals of the Association of American Geographers*, 79 (1989): 192–213.

– and Neil Smith, eds. *Geography and Empire*. Oxford: Basil Blackwell 1994.

Goetz, Rose. *Destutt de Tracy. Philosophie du langage et science de l'homme*. Geneva: Droz 1993.

Goldstein, Jan. *Console and Classify: The French Psychiatric Profession in the Nineteenth Century*. Cambridge: Cambridge University Press 1987.

Golinski, Jan. "The Theory of Practice and the Practice of Theory: Sociological Approaches in the History of Science." *Isis*, 81 (1990): 492–505.

Goodman, Dena. *The Republic of Letters: A Cultural History of the French Enlightenment*. Ithaca: Cornell University Press 1994.

Gossman, Lionel. *Medievalism and the Ideologies of the Enlightenment*. Baltimore: The Johns Hopkins University Press 1968.

Gouhier, Henri. *Les Conversions de Maine de Biran*. Paris: J. Vrin 1948.

Gramsci, Antonio. *Selections from the Prison Notebooks of Antonio Gramsci*. [1929–1935]. Ed. Quentin Hoare and Geoffrey Nowell Smith. New York: International Publishers 1971.

Grandchamp, J.-L. *Essai philosophique, jusqu'à quel point les traitemens barbares exercés sur les animaux intéressent la morale publique*. Paris: Fain jeune an XII-1804.

Grazia, Alfred de. "Mathematical Derivation of an Election System." *Isis*, 44 (1953): 42–7.

Greene, Christopher M. "Alexandre Lenoir and the Musée des monuments français during the French Revolution." *French Historical Studies*, 12 (1981): 200–22.

Grégoire, Henri. *De la domesticité chez les peuples anciens et modernes*. Paris: A. Egron 1814.

– *De la littérature des nègres, ou recherches sur leurs facultés intellectuelles, leurs qualités morales, et leur littérature*. Paris: Maradan 1808.

– *Histoire des sectes religieuses*. 2 vols. Paris: Potey 1810.

– *Mémoires ecclésiastiques, politiques, et littéraires*. Ed. Hippolyte Carnot. 2 vols. Paris: A. Dupont 1837.

– *Promenades dans les Vosges*. Épinal: Imprimerie vosgienne 1895.

Groenewegen, Peter. "Turgot's Place in the History of Economic Thought." *History of Political Economy*, 15 (1983): 585–616.

[Grouvelle, Philippe-Antoine]. *De l'autorité de Montesquieu dans la Révolution présente*. Paris: sans nom 1789.

[Gudin, Paul-Philippe]. *Essai sur l'histoire des comices de Rome, des États-Généraux de la France, et du Parlement d'Angleterre*. 3 vols. Paris: Maradan 1789.

– *Supplément au Contrat social*. Paris: Maradan 1791.

Guillaume, James, ed. *Procès-verbaux du Comité d'Instruction publique de la Convention nationale*. 6 vols. Paris: Imprimerie nationale 1891–1907.

Guillois, Antoine. *Le Salon de Mme. Helvétius. Cabanis et les idéologues*. Paris: Calmann Lévy 1894.

Guiral, P. *Mélanges géographiques offerts au Doyen Ernest Benevent*. Gap 1954.

Gusdorf, Georges. *La Conscience révolutionnaire, les idéologues*. Paris: Payot 1978.

Habermas, Jürgen. *The Structural Transformation of the Public Sphere: An Inquiry into a Category of Bourgeois Society*. [1962]. Cambridge Mass.: MIT Press 1989.

Hahn, Roger. *The Anatomy of a Scientific Institution: The Paris Academy of Sciences, 1666–1803*. Berkeley: University of California Press 1971.

– "From the Académie des Sciences to the Institut National." In *Annalen der Internationalen Gesellschaft für Dialektische Philosophie/Societas Hegeliana*, 6 (1989): 202–9.

Haines, Barbara. "The Athénée de Paris and the Bourbon Restoration." *History and Technology*, 5 (1988): 249–71.

Hampson, Norman. *The Life and Opinions of Maximilien Robespierre*. Oxford: Blackwell 1974.

– *Will and Circumstance: Montesquieu, Rousseau and the French Revolution*. Norman, Okla: University of Oklahoma Press 1983.

Hanson, Norwood. *Patterns of Discovery: An Inquiry into the Conceptual Foundations of Science*. Cambridge: Cambridge University Press 1961.

Hart, H.L.A. "Between Utility and Rights." In Alan Ryan, Ed. *The Idea of Freedom.* Oxford: Oxford University Press 1979. 78–98.

Hayek, Friedrich A. *The Counter-Revolution of Science.* Glencoe, Ill.: Free Press 1955.

Head, Brian W. *Ideology and Social Science: Destutt de Tracy and French Liberalism.* Dordrecht: Martinus Nijhoff 1985.

– "Origins of 'La Science Sociale' in France, 1770–1800." *Australian Journal of French Studies,* 19 (1982): 115–32.

Helvétius, Claude-Adrien. *Œuvres complètes.* 4 vols. Paris an III.

Hesse, Carla. *Publishing and Cultural Politics in Revolutionary Paris 1789–1810.* Berkeley: University of California Press 1991.

Hintermeyer, Pascal. *Politiques de la mort tirées du Concours de l'Institut, germinal an VIII–vendémiaire an IX.* Paris: Payot 1981.

Hippocrates. *The Works of Hippocrates.* Ed. W.H.S. Jones. 4 vols. London: W. Heinemann 1940–44.

Histoire de l'Académie royale des Inscriptions et Belles-Lettres avec les mémoires de littérature ... Vols.47–50. Paris: Imprimerie impériale 1808.

Histoire et mémoires de l'Institut royal de France. Classe d'Histoire et Littérature ancienne. Vols.1–3. Paris: Imprimerie royale 1815–18.

Hoffmann, Paul. *La Femme dans la pensée des lumières.* Paris: Éditions Ophrys 1977.

[Holbach, Paul Thiry, Baron d']. *Système de la nature, par Mirabaud.* 2 vols. London [Paris]: sans nom 1774.

Holmes, Stephen. *Benjamin Constant and the Making of Modern Liberalism.* New Haven: Yale University Press 1984.

Horkheimer, Max, and Theodor Adorno. *Dialectic of Enlightenment.* [1944]. New York: Herder and Herder 1972.

Horner, Frank. *The French Reconnaissance: Baudin in Australia.* Melbourne: Melbourne University Press 1987.

Hughes, Miranda. "The Dynamometer and the Diemenese." In H.E. Le Grand, Ed. *Experimental Inquiries: Historical, Philosophical, and Social Studies of Experimentation in Science.* Dordrecht: Kluwer Academic Publishers 1990. 81–98.

– "Tall Tales or True Stories? Baudin, Péron, and the Tasmanians, 1802." In Roy Macleod and Philip F. Rehbock, eds. *Nature in Its Greatest Extent: Western Science in the Pacific.* Honolulu: University of Hawaii Press 1988. 65–88.

Humboldt, Alexander von. *Political Essay on the Kingdom of New Spain.* [London 1811]. 4 vols. New York: AMS Press 1966.

– *Vues des cordillères et monuments des peuples indigènes de l'Amérique.* [Paris 1810–13]. Nanterre: Érasme 1989.

Hume, David. *A Treatise of Human Nature.* [1739–40]. Ed. L.A. Selby-Bigge and P.H. Nidditch. Oxford: Oxford University Press 1978.

Hunt, Lynn. *The Family Romance of the French Revolution*. Berkeley: University of California Press 1992.
- *Politics, Culture, and Class in the French Revolution*. Berkeley: University of California Press 1984.
Huppert, George. *The Idea of Perfect History*. Chicago: University of Chicago Press 1970.
Imbert, Jean. *Le Droit hospitalier de la Révolution et de l'Empire*. Paris: Recueil Sirey 1954.
Imbert, Pierre-Henri. *Destutt de Tracy critique de Montesquieu*. Paris: A.G. Nizet 1974.
Institut de France: Catalogue de l'exposition, Conservatoire national des Arts et Métiers, 12 avril – 29 mai 1983. Paris: Gauthier-Villars 1983.
Isambert, François-A. "Durkheim: Une science de la morale pour une morale laïque." *Archives de sciences sociales des religions*, 69 (1990): 129–46.
Jacyna, L.S. "Medical Science and Moral Science: The Cultural Relations of Physiology in Restoration France." *History of Science*, 25 (1987): 111–46.
Jaenen, Cornelius. *The French Relationship with the Native Peoples of New France and Acadia*. Ottawa: Department of Indian and Northern Affairs Canada 1984.
James, Michael. "Pierre-Louis Roederer, Jean-Baptiste Say and the Concept of 'industrie.'" *History of Political Economy*, 9 (1977): 455–75.
James, Preston E., and Geoffrey J. Martin. *All Possible Worlds: A History of Geographic Ideas*. 2nd ed. New York: Wiley 1981.
Jennings, Jeremy. "The *Déclaration des Droits de l'Homme et du Citoyen* and its Critics in France: Reaction and 'Idéologie.'" *Historical Journal*, 35 (1992): 839–59.
Jonckheere, Werner J. "La table de mortalité de Duvillard." *Population*, 20 (1965): 865–74.
Jones, Rhys. "Philosophical Time Travellers." *Antiquity*, 66 (1992): 744–57.
Jordanova, L.J. "Earth Science and Environmental Medicine: The Synthesis of the Late Enlightenment." In L.J. Jordanova and Roy S. Porter, eds. *Images of the Earth: Essays in the History of the Environmental Sciences*. Chalfont St Giles: British Society for the History of Science 1981. 119–46.
Kaiser, Thomas. "The Idéologues: From Enlightenment to Positivism." ph.d. dissertation, Harvard University 1976.
- "Politics and Political Economy in the Thought of the Idéologues." *History of Political Economy*, 12 (1980): 141–60.
Kant, Immanuel. *Critique de la raison pratique*. Ed. François Picavet. Paris: Alcan 1888.
Kates, Gary. *The Cercle Social, the Girondins, and the French Revolution*. Princeton: Princeton University Press 1985.
Kelley, Donald R. *The Foundations of Modern Historical Scholarship*. New York: Columbia University Press 1970.

- *Historians and the Law in Postrevolutionary France.* Princeton: Princeton University Press 1984.
- "What is Happening to the History of Ideas?" *Journal of the History of Ideas,* 51 (1990): 3–25.

Kennedy, Emmet. *A Cultural History of the French Revolution.* New Haven: Yale University Press 1989.
- "Destutt de Tracy and the Unity of the Sciences." *Studies on Voltaire and the Eighteenth Century,* 171 (1977): 223–39.
- *A "Philosophe" in the Age of Revolution: Destutt de Tracy and the Origins of "Ideology."* Philadelphia: American Philosophical Society 1978.

Kitchin, Joanna. *Un Journal "philosophique": La Décade (1794–1807).* Paris: M.J. Minard, 1965.

Klein, Daniel. "Deductive Economic Methodology in the French Enlightenment: Condillac and Destutt de Tracy." *History of Political Economy,* 17 (1985): 51–71.

Klinck, David. "Aristocracy, Counter-Revolution, and the Search for an Organic Community in France: An Intellectual Biography of Louis de Bonald (1754–1840)." Unpublished manuscript.

Klosko, George. "Montesquieu's Science of Politics: Absolute Values and Ethical Relativism." *Studies on Voltaire and the Eighteenth Century,* 189 (1980): 153–77.

Knight, Isabel. *The Geometric Spirit: The Abbé de Condillac and the French Enlightenment.* New Haven: Yale University Press 1968.

Knowlson, James. *Universal Language Schemes in England and France 1600–1800.* Toronto: University of Toronto Press 1975.

Kors, Alan C. *D'Holbach's Coterie: An Enlightenment in Paris.* Princeton: Princeton University Press 1976.

Kuhn, Thomas. *The Structure of Scientific Revolutions.* 2nd ed. Chicago: University of Chicago Press 1970.

Kula, Witold. *Measures and Men.* Princeton: Princeton University Press 1986.

Lacuée, Jean-Gérard. *Conseil des Anciens. Opinion de Lacuée sur la résolution relative à l'impôt sur le sel 1 ventôse VII.* Paris: Imprimerie nationale an VII.
- *Conseil des Anciens. Opinion sur la résolution relative au commerce des bleds 3 floréal V.* Paris: Imprimerie nationale an V.

Lafitau, Joseph-François. *Customs of the American Indians compared with the Customs of Primitive Times.* [1724]. Ed. William N. Fenton and Elizabeth L. Moore. Toronto: Champlain Society 1974.

Laguérenne, Claude de, and Jean-Pierre Kernéis. "French Interest in the Australian Aborigines in the Nineteenth Century." In John Hardy and Alan Frost, eds. *European Voyaging towards Australia* Canberra: Australian Academy of the Humanities, 1989. 147–48.

Lakanal, Joseph. *Exposé des travaux de Joseph Lakanal.* Paris: Firmin Didot 1838.

Lancelin, P.-F. *Introduction à l'analyse des sciences, ou de la génération, des fondemens, et des instrumens de nos connaissances.* 3 vols. Paris: Bossange, Masson, et Besson an IX–XI, 1801–3.

Landes, Joan B. *Women and the Public Sphere in the Age of the French Revolution.* Ithaca: Cornell University Press 1988.

Langlois, Claude, et al. "François Furet's Interpretation of the French Revolution." *French Historical Studies,* 16 (1990): 766–802.

La Pérouse, Jean-François de Galaup, Comte de. *Voyage de La Pérouse autour du monde pendant les années 1785, 1786, 1787, et 1788.* Ed. Milet-Mureau. 4 vols. Paris: Imprimerie de la Répulique an V-1797.

Laplace, Pierre-Simon de. *A Philosophical Essay on Probabilities.* [1814]. New York: Dover 1951.

Laqueur, Thomas. *Making Sex: Body and Gender from the Greeks to Freud.* Cambridge Mass.: Harvard University Press 1990.

La Revellière-Lépeaux, Louis-Marie. *Mémoires de La Revellière-Lépeaux.* 2 vols. Paris: E. Plon, Nourrit 1895.

– *Réflexions sur le culte, sur les cérémonies civiles, et sur les fêtes nationales.* Paris: H.J. Jansen an V.

Laromiguière, Pierre. *Leçons de philosophie, ou essai sur les facultés de l'âme.* 2 vols. Paris: Brunot-Labbe 1815. 2nd ed. Paris 1820. 3rd ed. 1823.

– *Paradoxes de Condillac.* 2nd ed. Paris: Brunot-Labbe 1825.

Larrère, Catherine. *L'Invention de l'économie au XVIIIe siècle: Du droit naturel à la Physiocratie.* Paris: Presses universitaires de France 1992.

Lavoisier, Antoine-Laurent. *Traité élémentaire de chimie.* 2 vols. Paris: Cuchet 1789.

Lécuyer, Bernard-Pierre. "Démographie statistique et hygiène publique sous la monarchie censitaire." *Annales de démographie historique,* 1977: 215–45.

Lefebvre, Georges. *The French Revolution from 1793 to 1799.* Vol.2. New York: Columbia University Press 1964.

Legrand d'Aussy, Abbé Pierre-Jean-Baptiste. *Contes dévots, fabliaux, et romans.* Paris: E. Onfroy 1781. Vol.4 of *Fabliaux.*

– *Fabliaux ou contes du XIIe et du XIIIe siècles.* 3 vols. Paris: E. Onfroy 1779–81.

– *Histoire de la vie privée des Français depuis l'origine de la nation jusqu'à nos jours.* 3 vols. Paris: P.D. Pierre 1782.

Leith, James A. *The Idea of Art as Propaganda in France, 1750–1799: A Study in the History of Ideas.* Toronto: University of Toronto Press 1965.

– *Media and Revolution.* Toronto: CBC Publications 1968.

– *Space and Revolution: Projects for Monuments, Squares, and Public Buildings in France, 1789–1799.* Montreal: McGill-Queen's University Press 1991.

Lejeune, Dominique. "La 'Société de Géographie' de Paris: Un aspect de l'histoire sociale française." *Revue d'histoire moderne et contemporaine,* 29 (1982): 141–63.

- *Les Sociétés de géographie en France et l'expansion coloniale au XIXe siècle* Paris: Albin Michel 1993.

Le Roy, Georges. *La Psychologie de Condillac.* Paris: Boivin 1937.

Leterrier, Sophie-Anne. "Les sciences morales et politiques à l'Institut de France 1795–1850." Thèse de l'Université Paris-I 1992. I have not had access to this work, which devotes 5 of 16 chapters to the period 1795–1803.

Leuliette, J.-J. *Discours qui a eu la mention honorable ... influence de la Réformation de Luther ...* Paris: Dentu an XII-1804.

Lévesque, Pierre-Charles. *La France sous les cinq premiers Valois.* 4 vols. Paris: de Bure l'aîné 1788.

- *L'Homme moral, ou les principes des devoirs.* 2nd ed. Paris: de Bure 1784.

L'Histoire au XVIIIe siècle: Colloque d'Aix-en-Provence, 1er, 2, et 3 mai 1975. Aix-en-Provence: Edisud 1980.

Lipset, Seymour, and Asoke Basu. "Des types d'intellectuels et de leurs rôles politiques." *Sociologie et sociétés,* 7 (1975): 51–90. Also in Lewis Coser, Ed. *The Idea of Social Structures.* New York: Harcourt Brace 1975.

Lively, Jack, Ed. *The Enlightenment.* New York: Barnes and Noble 1966.

Livingstone, David. *The Geographical Tradition.* Oxford: Blackwell 1992.

Locré, J.-G., ed. *La Législation civile, commerciale, et criminelle de la France.* 31 vols. Paris: Treuttel et Wurtz 1827–32.

- ed. *Procès-verbaux du Conseil d'État contenant la discussion du Code civil.* 5 vols. Paris: Imprimerie de la République an XII-1803–4.

Lough, John. *The Philosophes and Post-Revolutionary France.* Oxford: Oxford University Press 1982.

Luppé, Robert de. *Les Idées littéraires de Madame de Staël et l'héritage des lumières (1795–1800).* Paris: J. Vrin 1969.

Lyon-Caen, Charles. *Notice sur l'Académie des sciences morales et politiques 1795–1803, 1832–1932.* In *Institut de France. Académie des Sciences morales et politiques, séance commémorative du centenaire de son rétablissement.* Paris: Firmin-Didot 1932.

Lyons, Martyn. *France under the Directory.* Cambridge: Cambridge University Press 1975.

McClellan III, James E. "The Académie Royale des Sciences, 1699–1793: A Statistical Portrait." *Isis,* 72 (1981): 541–67.

MacIntyre, Alasdair. *After Virtue: A Study in Moral Theory.* London: Duckworth 1981.

McManners, John. *The French Revolution and the Church.* New York: Harper and Row 1969.

Madinier, Gabriel. *Conscience et mouvement, Étude sur la philosophie française de Condillac à Bergson.* Paris: Félix Alcan 1938.

Maine de Biran, François-Pierre Gontier. *Œuvres complètes.* Ed. Pierre Tisserand. Vols.1, 6. Paris: Félix Alcan 1922–30.

- *Œuvres, tome 2. Influence de l'habitude sur la faculté de penser.* Ed. Gilbert Romeyer-Dherbey. Paris: Vrin 1987.

– *Œuvres, tome 3. Mémoire sur la décomposition de la pensée.* Ed. François Azouvi. Paris: Vrin 1988.

Malandain, Pierre. *Delisle de Sales, philosophe de la nature, 1741–1816.* 2 vols. In *Studies on Voltaire and the Eighteenth Century.* Oxford: Voltaire Foundation 1982. 203–4.

Marat, Jean-Paul. *Plan de législation criminelle.* [1780]. Paris: Rochette 1790.

Margerison, Kenneth. "History, Representative Institutions, and Political Rights in the French Pre-Revolution 1787–89." *French Historical Studies,* 15 (1987): 68–98.

– *P.-L. Roederer: Political Thought and Practice in the French Revolution.* Philadelphia: American Philosophical Society 1983.

– "P.-L. Roederer, the Industrial Capitalist as Revolutionary." *Eighteenth-Century Studies,* 11 (1978): 473–88.

Marion, Marcel. *Histoire financière de la France depuis 1715.* 6 vols. Paris: A. Rousseau 1914–31.

Martin, Xavier. "Aux sources thermidoriennes du Code Civil: Contribution à l'histoire politique du droit privé." *Droits,* 6 (1987): 107–16.

Martin-Allanic, Jean-Étienne. *Bougainville navigateur et les découvertes de son temps.* 2 vols. Paris: Presses universitaires de France 1964.

Masseau, Didier. *L'Invention de l'intellectuel dans l'Europe du XVIIIᵉ siècle.* Paris: Presses universitaires de France 1994.

Mathiez, Albert. *La Théophilanthropie et le culte décadaire 1796–1801.* Paris: Félix Alcan 1903.

Matucci, Mario, Ed. *Gli "idéologues" e la rivoluzione.* Pisa: Pacini, 1991.

Maury, L.-F. Alfred. *Les Académies d'autrefois. L'ancienne Académie des Inscriptions et Belles-Lettres.* 2nd ed. Paris: Didier 1864.

Mauzi, Robert. *L'Idée du bonheur dans la littérature et la pensée françaises au XVIIIᵉ siècle.* Paris: Albin Michel 1960.

Meek, Ronald L. *The Economics of Physiocracy: Essays and Translations.* London: George Allen and Unwin 1962.

– *Social Science and the Ignoble Savage.* Cambridge: Cambridge University Press 1976.

Mellon, Stanley. *The Political Uses of History.* Stanford: Stanford University Press 1958.

Mémoires de l'Académie royale des Inscriptions. Vol.9. Paris: Imprimerie royale, 1831.

Mémoires de l'Institut national des Sciences et Arts. Sciences morales et politiques. An IV–an XI. 5 vols. Paris: Baudouin an VI–an XII.

Mentelle, Edme. *Cours d'histoire, 2ᵉ année.* Paris: l'auteur an X.

Mercier, Louis-Sébastien. *L'An 2440, rêve s'il en fut jamais.* [1770]. Ed. Alain Pons. Paris: France Adel 1977.

Merlin [de Douai], Philippe-Antoine. *Rapport et projet de code des délits et des peines présentés autour de la Commission des Onze, 10 vendémiaire IV.* Paris: Imprimerie nationale an IV.

Mirabeau, Honoré-Gabriel de Riqueti, Comte de. *Travail sur l'éducation publique, trouvé dans les papiers de Mirabeau l'aîné par P.-J.-G. Cabanis.* Paris: Imprimerie nationale 1791.

Mitchell, Harvey. "Tocqueville's Mirage or Reality? Political Freedom from Old Regime to Revolution." *Journal of Modern History*, 60 (1988): 28–54.

Montesquieu, Charles-Louis de Secondat, Baron de la Brède et de. *Œuvres complètes.* Ed. Daniel Oster. Paris: Le Seuil 1964.

Moore, F.C.T. *The Psychology of Maine de Biran.* Oxford: Oxford University Press 1970.

Moravia, Sergio. "The Enlightenment and the Sciences of Man." *History of Science*, 18 (1980): 247–68.

– *Il pensiero degli Idéologues: Scienza e filosofia in Francia, 1780–1815.* Florence: La Nuova Italia 1974.

– "Philosophie et géographie à la fin du XVIIIe siècle." *Studies on Voltaire and the Eighteenth Century*, 57 (1967): 937–1011.

– "Philosophie et médecine en France à la fin du XVIIIe siècle." *Studies on Voltaire and the Eighteenth Century*, 89 (1972): 1089–1151.

– *La Scienza dell'uomo nel settecento.* Bari: Laterza 1970.

– *Il tramonto dell'illuminismo: Filosofia e politica nella società francese (1770–1810).* Bari: Laterza 1968.

Morellet, André. *Du projet annoncé par l'Institut national de continuer le Dictionnaire de l'Académie française.* Paris: Migneret an IX-1801.

– *Mémoires (inédits) de l'Abbé Morellet.* 2 vols. Paris: Baudouin 1823.

Mortier, Roland. *Le "Tableau littéraire de la France au XVIIIe siècle", un épisode de la "guerre philosophique" à l'Académie française sous l'Empire (1804–1810).* Bruxelles: Palais des Académies 1972.

Naigeon, Jacques-André. *Philosophie ancienne et moderne.* 3 vols. Paris: Panckoucke 1791–94. In *Encyclopédie méthodique.*

Nathans, Benjamin. "Habermas's 'Public Sphere' in the Era of the French Revolution." *French Historical Studies*, 16 (1990): 620–44.

Necheles, Ruth. *The Abbé Grégoire, 1787–1831: The Odyssey of an Egalitarian.* Westport: Greenwood Press 1971.

Nelson, Robert H. "The Economics Profession and the Making of Public Policy." *Journal of Economic Literature*, 25 (1987):49–91.

Nougarède, André-Jean-Simon. *Essai sur l'histoire de la puissance paternelle.* Paris: Le Normant an IX-1801.

Novick, Peter. *That Noble Dream: The "Objectivity Question" and the American Historical Profession.* Cambridge: Cambridge University Press 1988.

Olsen, Mark. "A Failure of Enlightened Politics in the French Revolution: The Société de 1789." *French History*, 6 (1992): 303–34.

Olson, Richard. *The Emergence of the Social Sciences, 1642–1792.* New York: Twayne 1993.

Ouasti, Boussif. "La description de l'Égypte." *Dix-huitième siècle*, 22 (1990): 73–82.

Outram, Dorinda. *The Body and the French Revolution: Sex, Class, and Political Culture.* New Haven: Yale University Press 1989.

– "The Ordeal of Vocation: The Paris Academy of Sciences and the Terror, 1793–95." *History of Science,* 21 (1983): 251–73.

Ozouf, Mona. *Festivals in the French Revolution.* (1976). Cambridge Mass.: Harvard University Press 1988.

– "L'invention de l'ethnographie française: Le questionnaire de l'Académie celtique." *Annales: Économies, sociétés, civilisations,* 36 (1981): 210–30.

Paganini, Gianni. "Psychologie et physiologie de l'entendement chez Condillac." *Dix-huitième siècle,* 24 (1992):165–78.

Pagden, Anthony. *European Encounters with the New World.* New Haven: Yale University Press 1993.

Palmer, Robert R. *The Improvement of Humanity: Education and the French Revolution.* Princeton: Princeton University Press 1985.

– ed. *The School of the French Revolution.* Princeton: Princeton University Press 1975.

Papon, Jean-Pierre. *Histoire de la Révolution de France, mai 1789–novembre 1799.* 6 vols. Paris: Poulet 1815.

– *Histoire générale de Provence.* 4 vols. Paris: Moutard 1776–86.

Park, Mungo. *Voyages dans l'intérieur de l'Afrique, faits en 1795, 1796, et 1797 …* Trans. Jean Castéra. 2 vols. Paris: Dentu an VIII.

Parker, Harold T. *The Cult of Antiquity and the French Revolutionaries.* Chicago: University of Chicago Press 1937.

Pasquino, Pasquale. "Emmanuel Sieyès, Benjamin Constant et le 'gouvernement des modernes.'" *Revue française de science politique,* 37 (1987): 214–29.

Pastoret, Claude-Emmanuel-Joseph-Pierre de. *Histoire de la législation des peuples.* 11 vols. Paris: Didot l'aîné, Treuttel et Wurtz 1817–37.

Patrick, Alison. *The Men of the First French Republic.* Baltimore: The Johns Hopkins University Press 1972.

Pelosse, Valentin. "Imaginaire social et protection de l'animal: Des amis des bêtes de l'an X aux législations de 1850." *L'Homme,* 21 (1981): 5–33 and 22 (1982): 33–51.

Péron, François, and Louis-Claude de Freycinet. *Voyage de découvertes aux terres australes.* 3 vols. Paris: Imprimerie impériale et royale, 1807–16.

Perrot, Georges. "Notice sur la vie et les travaux de M. Bon-Joseph Dacier." *Institut de France. Académie des Inscriptions et Belles-Lettres. Séance publique annuelle 15 novembre 1912.* Paris: Firmin-Didot 1912.

Perrot, Jean-Claude. *L'Âge d'or de la statistique régionale française.* [An IV-1804]. Paris: Société des Études robespierristes 1977.

– "Condorcet: De l'économie politique aux sciences de la société." *Revue de synthèse, IVe série,* 1 (1988): 13–37.

– *Une Histoire intellectuelle de l'économie politique (XVIIe–XVIIIe siècle).* Paris: Éditions de l'École des hautes Études en Sciences sociales 1992.

– and Stuart J. Woolf. *State and Statistics in France 1789–1815.* Chur, Switz.: Harwood Academic Publishers 1984.

Petitain, Germain. *Question proposée ... L'Émulation ...* Paris: Renouard an IX.

Physiocrates. Ed. Eugène Daire. Paris: Guillaumin 1846.

Picavet, François. *Les Idéologues.* Paris: F. Alcan 1891.

Pocock, J.G.A. *Virtue, Commerce, and History.* Cambridge: Cambridge University Press 1985.

Polowetzky, Michael. *A Bond Never Broken: The Relations between Napoleon and the Authors of France.* Rutherford: Fairleigh Dickinson University Press 1993.

Ponce, Nicolas. *Discours qui a remporté le prix ... Par quelles causes l'esprit de liberté s'est-il développé en France, depuis François Ier jusqu'en 1789?* Paris: Baudouin an IX.

– *Essai historique sur cette question ... l'Influence de la Réformation de Luther.* Paris: Dentu, an XII-1804.

Popkin, Jeremy. "Conservatism under Napoleon: The Political Career of Joseph Fiévée." *History of European Ideas,* 5 (1984): 385–400.

– "The Press and the French Revolution after Two Hundred Years." *French Historical Studies,* 16 (1990): 664–83.

– *Revolutionary News: The Press in France, 1789–1799.* Durham, N.C.: Duke University Press 1990.

– *The Right-Wing Press in France, 1792–1800.* Chapel Hill: University of North Carolina Press 1980.

Porset, Charles. "Maçonnerie et idéologie: Le précédent de la Loge des Neuf Sœurs." In *Les Idéologues: Initiateurs de la République?* Lyon: Presses universitaires de Lyon 1990. 9–15.

Portalis, Jean-Étienne-Marie. *Discours, rapports et travaux inédits sur le Concordat de 1801.* Ed. F. Portalis. Paris: Joubert 1845.

Porter, Roy. *The Enlightenment.* Atlantic Highlands: Prentice-Hall 1990.

Powell, Judith. "The History and Influence of the Athénée de Paris." MA thesis. University College of Wales Aberystwyth, 1979.

Prévost, Pierre. *Des signes envisagés relativement à leur influence sur la formation des idées.* Paris: Baudouin an VIII.

Quesnay's Tableau Économique. Ed. Marguerite Kuczynski and Ronald Meek. London: Macmillan 1972.

Rabinow, Paul, ed. *The Foucault Reader.* London: Penguin 1991.

Racault, Jean-Michel. "Paul et Virginie et l'utopie." *Studies on Voltaire and the Eighteenth Century,* 242 (1986): 419–71.

Ramage, Edwin S., ed. *Atlantis: Fact or Fiction?* Bloomington, Ind.: Indiana University Press 1978.

Ramond de Carbonnières, Louis-François-Élisabeth. *Opinion annoncée à la Société de 1789 sur les loix constitutionnelles.* Paris: Belin 1791.

Ramsey, Matthew. *Professional and Popular Medicine in France, 1770–1830.* Cambridge: Cambridge University Press 1988.

Raymond, G.-M. *Essai sur l'émulation dans l'ordre social.* Geneva: J.J. Paschoud an X-1802.

Recueil de lois et règlements concernant l'instruction publique. 2 vols. Paris 1814.

Régaldo, Marc. *Un Milieu intellectuel: La Décade philosophique (1794–1807).* Thèse Paris-IV. 5 vols. Paris and Lille: Atelier Reproduction des thèses, Université de Lille III 1976.

Roche, Daniel. "Sciences et pouvoirs dans la France du XVIIIe siècle (1666–1803)." *Annales: Économies, sociétés, civilisations,* 29 (1974): 738–48.

– *Le Siècle des lumières en province: Académies et académiciens provinciaux 1680–1789.* 2 vols. Paris and The Hague: Mouton 1978.

Roederer, Pierre-Louis. *Des institutions funéraires convenables à une République qui permet tous les cultes, et n'en adopte aucun.* Paris: Mathey an IV.

– *Œuvres du Comte P.-L. Roederer.* Ed. A.-M. Roederer. 8 vols. Paris: Firmin Didot frères 1853–59.

Roger-Martin. *Conseil des cinq-cents. Rapport général fait … sur l'organisation de l'instruction publique.* 19 brumaire VII, Paris: Imprimerie nationale an VII.

Romeyer-Dherbey, G. "Maine de Biran et les signes." *Revue de métaphysique et de morale,* 88 (1983): 514–41.

– *Maine de Biran, ou le penseur de l'immanence radicale.* Paris: Seghers 1981.

Rosanvallon, Pierre. *Le Moment Guizot.* Paris: Gallimard 1985.

Ross, Dorothy. *The Origins of American Social Science.* Cambridge: Cambridge University Press 1992.

Rousseau, Jean-Jacques. *The First and Second Discourses.* Ed. Roger Masters. New York: St. Martin's Press 1964.

Rousseau, Nicolas. *Connaissance et langage chez Condillac.* Geneva: Droz 1986.

Roussel, Jean, ed. *L'Héritage des lumières: Volney et les idéologues.* Angers: Presses universitaires d'Angers 1988.

Roussel, Pierre. *Système physique et moral de la femme, ou tableau philosophique de la constitution, de l'état organique, du tempérament, des mœurs, et des fonctions propres au sexe.* Paris: Vincent 1775.

Rupp-Eisenreich, Britta. "Des choses occultes en histoire des sciences humaines: Le destin de la 'science nouvelle' de Christoph Meiners." *L'Ethnographie,* 79 (1983): 131–83.

– ed. *Histoires de l'anthropologie: XVI–XIXe siècles.* Paris: Klincksieck 1984.

– "The 'Société des Observateurs de l'Homme' and German Ethno-Anthropology at the End of the 18th Century." *History of Anthropology Newsletter,* 10 (1983): 5–11.

Sagnac, Philippe. *La Législation civile de la Révolution française (1789–1804)*. 3rd ed. Paris: Hachette 1898.

Said, Edward. *Representations of the Intellectual*. New York: Pantheon 1994.

Saricks, Ambrose. *Pierre-Samuel Du Pont de Nemours*. Lawrence, Kan.: University of Kansas Press 1965.

Say, Jean-Baptiste. *Olbie, ou essai sur les moyens de réformer les mœurs d'une nation*. Paris: Deterville an VIII.

– *A Treatise on Political Economy*. [Philadelphia, 1880, based on Paris 1826]. New York: Augustus M. Kelley 1971.

Séances des écoles normales recueillies par des sténographes et revues par les professeurs … Leçons … Débats. 13 vols. 2nd ed. Paris: Imprimerie du cercle social an IX [1801].

Searle, J.R. "How to Derive 'Ought' from 'Is.'" In Philippa Foot, ed. *Theories of Ethics*. New York: Oxford University Press 1967. 101–14.

Semple, Janet. *Bentham's Prison: A Study of the Panopticon Penitentiary*. Oxford: Oxford University Press 1993.

Serre, Pierre. *Nouvelle théorie des facultés de l'âme*. Paris: Henrichs an XII-1804.

Servet, J.-M., ed. *Idées économiques sous la Révolution, 1789–1794*. Lyon: Presses Universitaires de Lyon 1989.

Sewell, William. *A Rhetoric of Bourgeois Revolution: The Abbé Sieyes and "What Is the Third Estate?"* Durham, N.C.: Duke University Press 1994.

Sèze, Paul-Victor de. *Recherches phisiologiques et philosophiques sur la sensibilité ou la vie animale*. Paris: Prault 1786.

Sgard, Jean, ed. *Condillac et les problèmes du langage*. Geneva and Paris: Slatkine 1982.

– ed. *L'Écrivain devant la Révolution*. Grenoble: Université Stendhal de Grenoble 1990.

Shackleton, Robert. "The Evolution of Montesquieu's Theory of Climate." *Revue internationale de philosophie*, 9 (1955): 317–29.

– *Montesquieu: A Critical Biography*. London: Oxford University Press 1961.

Sieyès, Emmanuel-Joseph. *Écrits politiques*. Ed. Roberto Zapperi. Paris: Éditions des Archives contemporaines 1985.

– *Opinion de Sieyès sur plusieurs articles des titres IV et V du projet de constitution, 2 thermidor an III*. Paris: Imprimerie nationale an III.

– *Préliminaire de la constitution: Reconnaissance et exposition raisonnée des droits de l'homme et du citoyen*. Paris: Baudouin 1789.

– *Qu'est-ce que le tiers état?* Ed. Roberto Zapperi. Geneva: Droz 1970.

– *Sur les attributs du jury constitutionnaire, 18 thermidor III*. Paris: Imprimerie de la République an III.

Silvera, Alain, "The Origins of the French Expedition to Egypt in 1798." *Islamic Quarterly* 18 (1974): 21–30.

Silvestre, A.-F. de. *Notice biographique sur Coquebert de Montbret*. Paris: Mme. Huzard 1832.

Silvestre de Sacy, Antoine-Isaac. *Notice sur B.-J. Dacier*. Paris: Firmin Didot 1834.

Simon, Jules. *Une Académie sous le Directoire*. Paris: Calmann Lévy 1885.

Skinner, Andrew B. *A System of Social Science: Papers Relating to Adam Smith*. Oxford: Oxford University Press 1979.

Smith, Adam. *An Inquiry into the Nature and Causes of the Wealth of Nations*. [1776]. Ed. R.H. Campbell and A.S. Skinner. 2 vols. Oxford: Oxford University Press 1976.

– *Recherches sur la nature et les causes de la richesse des nations*. Trans. Germain Garnier. 5 vols. Paris: H. Agasse an X-1802.

Smith, Agnes. "François-Emmanuel Toulongeon: Contemporaneous Historian of the French Revolution." In Morris Slavin and Agnes Smith, eds. *Bourgeois, Sans-Culottes, and Other Frenchmen*. Waterloo, Ont.: Wilfrid Laurier Press 1981. 97–111.

Smith, Bernard. *European Vision and the South Pacific, 1768–1850*. Oxford: Oxford University Press 1960.

Solé, Jacques. "L'image de la Révolution française dans le 'Nouveau Paris' de Louis-Sébastien Mercier." In Michel Vovelle, ed. *L'Image de la Révolution française*, 3 (1989): 1899–903.

Souriau, Maurice. *Bernardin de Saint-Pierre d'après ses manuscrits*. Paris: Société française d'Imprimerie et de Librairie 1905.

Staum, Martin S. *Cabanis: Enlightenment and Medical Philosophy in the French Revolution*. Princeton: Princeton University Press 1980.

– "The Class of Moral and Political Sciences, 1795–1803." *French Historical Studies*, 11 (1980): 371–97.

– "The Enlightenment Transformed: The Institute Prize Contests." *Eighteenth-Century Studies*, 19 (1985–86): 153–79.

– "Human, not Secular Sciences: Ideology in the Central Schools." *Historical Reflections/Réflexions historiques*, 12 (1985): 49–76.

– "Images of Paternal Power: Intellectuals and Social Change in the French National Institute." *Canadian Journal of History*, 17 (1982): 425–45.

– "Physiognomy and Phrenology at the Paris Athénée." *Journal of the History of Ideas*, 56 (1995): 443–62.

Stewart, John Hall, ed. *A Documentary Survey of the French Revolution*. New York: Macmillan 1951.

Stocking, George, ed. *Bones, Bodies, and Behavior: Essays in Biological Anthropology*. Madison: University of Wisconsin Press 1988.

– *Race, Culture, and Evolution*. New York: Free Press 1968.

Stock-Morton, Phyllis. *Moral Education for a Secular Society: The Development of Morale Laïque in Nineteenth Century France*. Albany: State University Press of New York 1988.

Sutherland, D.M.G. *France, 1789–1815, Revolution and Counter-Revolution.* London: Fontana 1985.

Taillandier, Alphonse-Honoré. *Documents biographiques sur P.-C.-F. Daunou.* 2nd ed. Paris: Firmin Didot frères 1847.

Talleyrand-Périgord, Charles-Maurice de. *Rapport sur l'instruction publique.* Paris: Imprimerie nationale 1791.

Teysseire, Daniel. "Fonctionnalisme sexuel et privatisation de la femme chez Cabanis et … quelques autres." In *Les Femmes et la Révolution française.* 2 vols. Toulouse: Presses universitaires du Mirail 1989.

– "Lien social et ordre politique chez Cabanis." *Studies on Voltaire and the Eighteenth Century*, 267 (1989): 353–400.

Thiry, Jean. *Bonaparte en Égypte.* Paris: Berger-Levrault 1973.

Thomson, Herbert. "Adam Smith's Philosophy of Science." *Quarterly Journal of Economics*, 79 (1965): 212–23.

Thuillier, Guy. "Aux origines de l'enseignement des sciences politiques: De l'éducation civile de Jean-Jacques Garnier." *La Revue administrative*, 40 (1987): 434–40.

– "Les idées monétaires de Nicolas-François Canard en l'an x." *Revue de l'Institut Napoléon*, 151 (1988): 47–56.

– "Les projets d'Écoles des sciences politiques sous la Révolution et l'Empire." *La Revue administrative*, 36 (1983): 124–32.

Toulongeon, François-Emmanuel. *De l'esprit public.* Paris: Imprimerie Du Pont an x.

– *Histoire de France depuis la Révolution de 1789.* 7 vols. Paris: Treuttel et Wurtz 1801–10.

Trigg, Roger. *Understanding Social Science.* Oxford: Blackwell 1985.

Turgot, Anne-Robert-Jacques. *Œuvres de Turgot et documents le concernant.* Ed. Gustave Schelle. 5 vols. Paris: F. Alcan 1913–23.

– *Turgot on Progress, Sociology, and Economics.* Ed. R.L. Meek. Cambridge: Cambridge University Press 1973.

Vaggi, Gianni. "The Role of Profit in Physiocratic Economics." *History of Political Economy*, 17 (1985): 367–84.

Van Kley, Dale K. "New Wine in Old Wineskins: Continuity and Rupture in the Pamphlet Debate of the French Prerevolution, 1787–1789." *French Historical Studies*, 17 (1991): 447–65.

Ventre-Denis, Madeleine. "Sciences sociales et université au xixe siècle." *Revue historique*, 256 (1976): 321–42.

Véron de Forbonnais, François. *Analyse des principes sur la circulation des denrées, et de l'influence du numéraire sur cette circulation.* Paris an viii.

– *Principes et observations économiques.* 2 vols. Amsterdam: M.M. Rey 1767.

Villefosse, Louis, and Janine Bouissonouse. *L'Opposition à Napoléon.* Paris: Flammarion 1969.

Villers, Charles. *Essai sur l'esprit et l'influence de la Réformation de Luther.* Paris: Henrichs an XII-1804. 2nd ed. Paris: Didot 1808.

Villeterque, Alexandre. *Les Veillées philosophiques, ou essais sur la morale expérimentale st sur la physique systématique.* 2 vols. Paris: Fuchs an III.

Volney, Constantin-François. *La Loi naturelle/Leçons d'histoire.* [1793; 1795]. Ed. Jean Gaulmier. Paris: Garnier Frères 1980.

– *Œuvres complètes.* Ed. A. Bossange. 8 vols. Paris: Bosssange frères 1820–22.

– *Questions de statistique à l'usage des voyageurs.* Paris: Veuve Courcier 1813.

– *A View of the Soil and Climate of the United States of America.* [1804]. Ed. G.W. White. New York: Hafner 1968.

– *Voyage en Égypte et en Syrie.* [1787]. Ed. Jean Gaulmier. Paris: Mouton 1959.

Voutsinas, Dimitri. *La Psychologie de Maine de Biran.* Paris: SIPE 1964.

Vovelle, Michel, ed. *1793: La Révolution contre l'Église: De la raison à l'être suprême.* Brussels: Éditions Complexes 1988.

– *L'Image de la Révolution française. Congrès mondial pour le bicentenaire de la Révolution.* 4 vols. Paris: Pergamon Press 1989.

Waddicor, Mark. *Montesquieu and the Philosophy of Natural Law.* The Hague: Martinus Nijhoff 1970.

Wagner, Henry R. *The Life and Writings of Bartolomé de las Casas.* Albuquerque: University of New Mexico Press 1967.

Walch, Jean. *Les Maîtres de l'histoire 1815–1850. Augustin Thierry, Mignet, Guizot, Thiers, Michelet, Edgard Quinet.* Paris: Champion 1986.

Warnock, G.J. *The Object of Morality.* London: Methuen 1971.

Welch, Cheryl. *Liberty and Utility: The French Idéologues and the Transformation of Liberalism.* New York: Columbia University Press 1984.

Welschinger, Henri. *Chateaubriand: Le Génie du christianisme et le discours de réception à l'Académie française.* Amiens: Delattre-Lenoël 1889.

Weulersse, Georges. *La Physiocratie à l'aube de la Révolution 1781–1792.* Ed. Corinne Beutler. Paris: Éditions de l'École des hautes Études en Sciences sociales 1985.

Williams, Elizabeth A. *The Physical and the Moral: Anthropology, Physiology, and Philosophical Medicine in France, 1750–1850.* Cambridge: Cambridge University Press 1994.

– "The Science of Man: Anthropological Thought and Institutions in Nineteenth-Century France." PH.D. dissertation, University of Indiana 1983.

Winch, Peter. *The Idea of a Social Science and its Relation to Philosophy.* London: Routledge and Kegan Paul 1958.

Woloch, Isser. "'Le Palladium de la Liberté'? Vicissitudes du juré criminel." In Michel Vovelle, ed. *L'Image de la Révolution française.* Paris: Pergamon, 1989, 2: 983–9.

Zeldin, Theodore. *France, 1848–1945. III. Intellect and Pride.* Oxford: Oxford University Press 1980.

Index

Academies, Ancien
Régime, 3, 5, 45; pro-
vincial, 12, 64–6; sup-
pression of, 12–13
Académie française, 10–
11, 13, 35, 64–5,
223–5; dictionary,
88–90; eloquence,
79; re-creation of,
86–8
Académie royale des
Inscriptions et Belles-
Lettres, 12, 35, 39,
41–2, 65, 136, 141,
212, 225
Académie royale des
Sciences, 11–12, 30,
40–2, 47, 64, 154,
170–1
Academy of Moral and
Political Sciences, 115,
171, 226–8
Aguesseau, Henri Cardin
Jean-Baptiste de
Fresnes, Marquis d', 87
Ampère, André-Marie, 115
Andrieux, François-
Stanislas, 39, 88–9, 94,
120
Animals, cruelty to, 130–1

Anquetil, Louis-Pierre,
38, 42; career, 48, 141;
histories, 142–3; reli-
gion and royalism,
138, 144–5, 147–8, 150
Arnault, Antoine-Vincent,
87
Australia, 57, 63–4, 155,
165–9, 213. *See also*
Baudin, Nicolas
Auteuil circle, 39–40, 189

Babeuf, François-Noël,
148, 178
Barrot, Odilon, 226
Barruel, Abbé Augustin,
148
Barthélemy, François, 38,
41–2, 47, 83–4
Bastiat, Frédéric, 208
Baudeau, Abbé Nicolas,
24
Baudin, Nicolas, 54, 63–
4, 82, 155, 165–9, 213
Baudin des Ardennes,
Pierre-Charles-Louis,
47, 59, 68, 71; politi-
cal science and elec-
tions, 177–8, 183, 220
Beccaria, Cesare, 24

Bentham, Jeremy, 17,
174, 182–3
Bergson, Henri, 110
Bernardin de Saint-Pierre,
Jacques-Henri: anti-
academies, 36; anti-
Idéologue, 53–4, 87,
216; anti-Newtonian-
ism, 79; and Institute,
51, 82; moral philoso-
phy, 69, 128–9, 132–4,
218; and Rousseauism,
91–2
Berthollet, Claude-Louis,
61
Bichat, Xavier-François,
108, 127
Bigot de Préameneu,
Félix-Julien-Jean, 72–3,
76, 181, 185, 214
Bitaubé, Paul-Jérémie, 42
Bodin, Jean, 22
Boissy d'Anglas, François-
Antoine, 57, 177
Bonald, Louis de, 172
Bonaparte, Lucien, 68,
86–7, 213
Bonaparte, Napoleon:
and Chateaubriand,
225; and Church, 69,

152; Consul and Emperor, 48–9, 54, 56, 72, 74, 90–1, 149, 182, 204, 208–10; coups and constitution, 10, 85, 179–80, 220; and Delisle de Sales, 88, 147; and education, 58–9, 64; and elections, 176, 183, 187–8; and expeditions to Egypt and Australia, 61–3; and Idéologues, 181, 187, 189, 215, 222–3; and Institute, 14, 77, 80, 87, 185, 223; and slavery, 194–5; and statistics, 159, 198–9

Borda, Jean-Charles de, 30, 41, 187–8

Bordeu, Théophile de, 100

Bossuet, Jacques-Bénigne, 137

Bouchaud, Mathieu-Antoine, 52, 225

Boufflers, Stanislas-Jean, 87

Bougainville, Louis-Antoine de: on Americas and Tahiti, 160–2, 169–71; career and royalism, 42, 47–8; on colonies and Australia, 60, 63; on Northwest Passage, 82; on race and environment, 154–6

Boulainvilliers, Henri de, 145

Boulay de la Meurthe, Antoine-Jacques-Claude-Joseph, 180

Bourgeoisie: ideology of, 173, 185–7

Bourguignon, Claude-Sébastien, 73

Brissot, Jacques-Pierre, 10, 12, 64

Broca, Paul, 171

Broglie, Victor de, 226

Broussais, François-Joseph-Victor, 115, 217

Buache de la Neuville, Jean-Nicolas, 40–1, 63, 82, 162

Burke, Edmund, 162

Cabanis, Pierre-Jean-Georges: career, 4, 13, 30, 40, 47, 51, 89, 165, 180, 185, 220; and climate, 22, 157; on Condillacian empiricism and language theory, 27–8, 96–9, 102–3; and Institute, 39, 81, 93; and materialism, 53; on morality, 121–2, 124, 127–8, 218; and physiology, 109, 112, 116, 133, 224; on politics, 13, 21, 172, 183; on public assistance, 59; on "science of man," 95, 185; and Sieyès, 107–8; on society, 131, 186, 220; on temperament and hygiene, 61, 96–9, 130, 167, 217; on women, 101. See also Idéologues; Ideology

Caffarelli du Falga, Louis-Marie-Joseph-Maximilien, 41, 61

Cambacérès, Jean-Jacques Régis de: antimaterialist, 52; and Civil Code, 76, 185; Consul, 181; opportunist, 55, 214; and prize contests, 67, 71–3; on social science, 22, 176, 208

Camper, Peter, 156

Canard, Nicolas, 75, 111–12, 188, 200, 209

Cantillon, Richard, 201

Carnot, Lazare, 41, 47, 83–5

Carrel, Armand, 221

Causal explanation in history, 139–41

Cavaignac, Eugène, 228

Central schools (Directory secondary schools), 22, 27, 57–9

Chabrol de Volvic, Gaspard-Antoine, 62

Chamfort, Nicolas, 12

Champagne, Jean-François, 43, 52, 71, 186

Chaptal, Jean-Antoine: Interior minister, 58, 64; and reform of Institute, 88, 90–1, 150, 222–5

Chateaubriand, François-René, 79, 92, 155, 168, 215, 225

Chénier, Marie-Joseph, 39, 72, 222, 225

Chenot, Bernard, 228

Church and clergy: in Class of Moral and Political Sciences, 16, 43–4, 65; Concordat with Napoleon Bonaparte, 75–7, 126, 134, 152; and Idéologues, 95, 118, 120; and morality, 218; and Revolution, 120–1

Civil Code, Napoleonic, 67, 71–2, 76, 216

Climate, theories of: and culture of people, 160–2, 219; and temperament, 4, 21–2, 123, 141–2, 156–8

Colbert, Jean-Baptiste, 11

Collin d'Harleville, Jean-François, 85, 87, 212

Commerson, Philippe de, 161

Comte, Auguste, 115, 123, 134, 173, 187, 226

Comte, Charles, 183, 226–7

Condillac, Étienne Bonnot de: and analysis of sensations and ideas, 27–9; economist, 25, 191; and empiricism,

52, 59, 97; and habit, 110–13; and Idéologues, 95, 214; influence, 81; and Kant, 113–17; on learning and motivation, 69, 126; on transformed sensations, 27, 96, 105–9, 217; on well-made language, 28, 96–7, 102–5, 220

Condorcet, Marie-Jean-Antoine-Nicolas Caritat, Marquis de: on democracy and equality, 139, 174, 195, 198; on moral and political sciences, 21, 24; on philosophical history, 137, 140, 143, 151, 218; planning Institute, 30, 34–5, 37; on social mathematics, 20, 29–31, 156, 173, 187–9, 210; on social science, 22, 185

Condorcet, Sophie de Grouchy, Madame, 39

Constant, Benjamin, 72, 184, 226

Constituent Assembly, 24, 33–4, 193, 203

Consulate, government of, 4–5, 81, 214; and Council of State, 72–3, 76, 90, 223; and coup of Brumaire, 179; and education, 58–9, 223; and Fructidor exiles, 93; and Legislative Body, 223; and Senate, 51, 180, 182; and statistics, 159, 180–1; and Tribunate, 72–3, 146, 180, 222

Continuities, from Ancien Régime academies to Institute, 5, 33, 44–6, 211–3

Convention, National, 3, 13, 36–7, 47, 69; and constitution of 1795,

176–7; and festivals, 126; and price maximum, 200; and school of political sciences, 257n6

Cook, James, 82, 161

Coquebert de Montbret, Charles-Étienne, 41, 48, 159, 169, 171, 199, 214

Cousin, Victor, 107, 115, 134, 226–8

Creuzé-Latouche, Jacques-Antoine, 47, 177, 200–1, 205

Cuvier, Georges, 63, 85, 156, 165, 168–9, 171

Dacier, Bon-Joseph, 42, 47, 49, 54, 87, 149–50, 222

Damiron, Jean-Philibert, 115

Daunou, Pierre-Claude-François, 13, 39, 43, 47; and coups d'état, 84, 180; and education, 57–8; on elections, 188; and empiricism, 52; and Encyclopedism, 81; and foundation of Institute, 36–7; and history, 150–1; on individual rights and guarantees, 172, 175, 177, 181, 183–5, 187, 220; on intellectuals and power, 56, 214; on juries, 72–3; and liberalism, 221; and prize contests, 49, 67, 69, 71–2, 132; on separation of powers, 21; and Tribunate, 222

David, Jacques-Louis, 13, 110

De-Christianization, 6, 120–1. See also Idéologues on religion

Decomposition of mind: and Condillac's transformed sensations, 19–

20, 27, 96, 105–9. See also Maine de Biran

Deductive methods, 15, 23–5, 199. See also Physiocratic economists; political economy

Degérando, Joseph-Marie: and antimaterialism, 53; and Institute, 109, 227; and Interior ministry, 214; on Kant and eclectics, 113–16; and observing "savages," 93, 155, 161, 165–7, 169, 171, 218; and perfect language, 104–5, 116, 223; and prize contests, 28, 40; and royalism, 47; and transformed sensations, 107; and "wild child," 81

Delalot, Charles, 76

Deleyre, Alexandre, 47

Delille, Jacques, 86

Delisle de Sales, Jean-Baptiste-Claude Izouard, 38, 42, 91; and Académie française, 87–8, 224; anti-Idéologue, 53–4, 126, 216; and Napoleon Bonaparte, 215; and Fructidor exiles, 84–5, 179; and history, 140, 142, 144; and Institute, 51, 79, 150, 222; and moral philosophy, 120–1, 127–9, 131, 133, 138; and social hierarchy, 220; and Revolution, 145, 148; and royalism, 47–8, 78, 147, 213

Descartes, René, 27, 52

Destutt de Tracy, Antoine-Louis-Claude: career of, 40–1, 44, 47, 49, 165; and Condillac, 27, 96–7, 218; and economics, 26, 192, 195, 200–10, 221; and education, 58–9, 223; and elections, 188; and expertise, 220; on habit and festivals, 111, 134; on history, 137, 143, 151–2, 218; and Ideology, 95; on individual rights, 187, 220; and Institute, 39, 81, 93; and Kant, 114–16; and language, 103–5; and liberalism, 221; and materialism, 53, 217–18; and political science of Montesquieu, 21, 25, 172, 181, 183–6; and public morality, 67, 121, 124, 127–8, 179; on social mobility, 133–4, 181, 186; on transformed sensations, 106–7; on women, 101–2. *See also* Idéologues; Ideology

Devaisnes, Jean, 87

Diannyère, Antoine, 195, 198–200, 205, 210

Diderot, Denis, 10, 35, 52, 120, 124, 132, 161

Dilthey, Wilhelm, 15

Directory, 3, 5; and Council of Five Hundred, 51, 57; and coup of Floréal, 83–4, 178; and coup of Fructidor, 38, 44, 47–8, 77–8, 83–6, 93, 149, 178–9, 213–14, 225; and education, 58–9; and Institute, 13–14, 38, 42, 213; Interior minister, 57, 212; and political problems, 178–9, 189; and statistics, 159

Domergue, Urbain, 89

Droz, Joseph, 228

Ducis, Jean-François, 87

Dumont d'Urville, Jules-César, 170

Dunoyer, Charles, 183, 208; and "industrialism," 226–8

Duperrey, Louis-Isidore, 170

Du Pont de Nemours, Pierre-Samuel: career of, 30; and deductive method, 199; and education, 81; and Institute, 38, 41, 80, 210; and Physiocratic economics, 24, 192–7, 208, 210; and prize contests, 67; and royalism, 147; and stages of progress, 26; and theism, 124

Dupuis, Charles, 42

Durkheim, Émile, 135

Dussaulx, Jean, 42, 83

Duvillard de Durand, Emmanuel-Étienne, 74, 198–9, 207–8, 210, 214

École normale (of 1795), 107, 136, 157, 159, 267n35

Education policy: and Council of Public Instruction, 57–9, 213, 222–3

Egalitarianism, 6; anti-egalitarianism and stages of history, 140, 145–6. *See also* Duvillard; stages of historical progress

Egypt, 61–3. *See also* geography and colonial expeditions

Empiricism, 15–16, 28, 52, 54, 58, 195. *See also* Condillac; Idéologues

Emulation, 132–3

Encyclopedism, 27, 33–6, 78–9, 88, 212, 233

Enlightenment: deism, 52–4, 118–19; models of social sciences, 7, 19–32, 211, 215–16; natural morality, 120

Entrecasteaux, Antoine-Raymond-Joseph de Bruni, Chevalier d', 82

Ethics prize contest, 67–70

Eurocentrism, 19, 60–3, 139, 155, 160–71. *See also* geography and colonial expeditions; Talleyrand

Fabre, Auguste, 221

Fabre, Victorin, 221

Fénelon, François de Solignac de la Mothe, 126

Ferguson, Adam, 156

Feuillet, Laurent-François, 132–3

Fichte, Johann Gottlieb, 108, 114

Fiévée, Joseph, 84, 93, 222

Fleurieu, Charles-Pierre d'Eveux Claret de, 40–2, 48, 68, 169–70, 214; on Americas, 82; on Nicolas Baudin, 63; and colonies, 60; on Egypt, 61; on funerals, 68; on Marchand expedition to Pacific, 163–7

Fontanes, Louis, 84–5, 92, 107

Forbonnais, François Véron de, 198, 201, 203, 206, 208

Foucault, Michel, 17–18, 97, 105, 217, 229–30

Fourcroy, Antoine-François, 36, 41, 48, 58, 64, 85–6

Fourier, Jean-Baptiste-Joseph, 61

François de Neufchâteau, Nicolas, 58

Franck, Adolphe, 228

Frankfurt Institute of Social Research, 15

Freycinet, Louis de, 171

Funerals, 68–9, 142–3, 213

Gaillard, Gabriel-Henri, 48

Gall, Franz-Joseph, 115

Garat, Dominique-Joseph: in Auteuil circle, 39; career and politics of, 40, 47, 51, 90, 121; on education, 58; on language, 96, 102–3; on social science, 22; on transformed sensations, 105–7, 116
Garnier, Germain, 25; on loans, 206; on luxury, 205; on Physiocrats and Smith, 201, 208–9; on social mobility, 220; on taxation, 202–3
Garnier, Jean-Jacques, 38, 42, 48, 138; on Collège royal, 298n25; on history, 141; on Institute, 149–50; and royalism, 213
Garran-Coulon, Jean-Philippe, 47, 177
Gaudin, Jacques-Maurice, 43
Gautier de Sibert, Edme, 143–5
Geoffroy Saint-Hilaire, Étienne, 61, 156
Geography and colonial expeditions: Australia, 63–4; Egypt, 60–3, 213; and public sessions, 82–3
Geography, human, 16, 154–71
Ginguené, Pierre-Louis, 36, 39–40, 51, 222; and education, 58; and Institute, 49, 89; and prize contests, 70, 72, 74, 131, 179; and public sessions, 87
Girard, Pierre-Simon, 62
Girondins, 47, 92
Gossellin, Paschal-François-Joseph, 170, 225
Gramsci, Antonio, 65
Grégoire, Henri: on Africans and slavery, 126, 214; on Jews, 125; on

Kant, 114; on political science and separation of powers, 21, 43, 47, 53, 57, 86, 162; on science and freedom, 172–3; on theism and morality, 124, 129, 133
Grouvelle, Philippe-Antoine, 21, 30, 39, 174, 186
Grub Street, 6, 65
Gudin de la Brenellerie, Paul-Philippe, 48, 145, 149
Guizot, François, 151–2, 190, 219, 226–7

Habermas, Jürgen, 11, 214
Habit, power of, 28, 69–70, 110–13, 176, 269n4. See also Condillac; Idéologues; Maine de Biran; Roederer; Rousseau
Hallé, Jean-Noël, 22, 68, 85, 157, 167
Hegel, Georg Wilhelm Friedrich, 115
Helvétius, Anne-Catherine, Comtesse de Ligniville d'Autricourt, 39, 89, 102
Helvétius, Claude-Adrien: career of, 39, 52; on materialism, 224; on moral science, 119, 121, 123–4, 127–8; on government, 158; on psychology, 28, 156
Herder, Johann Gottfried, 15–16, 142
Hippocratic medical tradition, 19, 22; and temperament, 96, 99, 109, 154, 157, 195, 198
History, philosophical, 4, 136–53; and causal explanation, 151; and scepticism, 139–41; scope of, 141–2
Hobbes, Thomas, 28, 119

Holbach, Paul Thiry, Baron d', 10; on loans, 74; on natural morality and utilitarianism, 58, 69, 119–20; on sociability, 123–4
Houard, David, 42
Humboldt, Alexander von, 155, 169–71, 219
Hume, David, 74, 134, 174

Idéologues: and Académie française, 86; and anti-Idéologues, 49–55, 91–2, 113–14, 118, 126, 181, 216; definition of, 39, 41–2; on education, 58–9; on empiricism, 28, 116–17; on Encyclopedism, 79; on Kant, 114; on moralists and power, 4, 10; on political science, 47, 123; on religion, 38, 75, 95, 121; on social stability, 37. See also Cabanis; Destutt de Tracy; Roederer; Sieyès; Volney
Ideology, 80, 95; and Napoleon Bonaparte, 222–3; and the bourgeoisie, 186–7; and Condillac, 214; and history, 136, 146, 152; and individual rights, 134; and influence on liberalism and positivism, 173, 221; and Institute re-organization, 150; and moral science, 118, 128, 135, 149; Physiological, 109; and political science, 180–5; Rational, 106; and Revolutionary politics, 179; and social mathematics, 189; and work ethic, 131. See also Cabanis;

Condillac; Destutt de
Tracy; Sieyès; Volney
Institute of Sciences and
Arts, National: budget
of, 269n35; Class of
French Language and
Literature, 67, 215,
225; Class of History
and Ancient Literature,
49, 75, 150, 170, 188,
210, 224–5; Class of
Literature and Fine
Arts, 13, 35–6, 80, 86,
88; Class of Mathemat-
ical and Physical Sci-
ences, 13, 36, 188;
Class of Moral and
Political Sciences and
social origins and
careers, 43–6; elec-
tions, 38–9; foundation
of, 3, 13–14; reorgani-
zation (1803) of, 150
Institute of Sciences and
Arts of Egypt, 61
Intellectuals: advice to
governments by, 56–
64; autonomy of, 213;
foundation of Institute
and, 13–14; and
power, 7, 173, 215
Lipset-Basu model for
roles of, 8–9, 12, 38,
185; conservatives,
9, 18; gatekeepers
and moralists, 8–9,
215; protectors and
power, 7, 173, 215

Jacotin, Pierre, 62
Jacquemont, Frédéric-
François-Venceslas, 38,
43, 58
Janet, Paul, 134–5
Jansenism, 6
Jauffret, Louis-François,
165, 285n48
Jefferson, Thomas, 181
Joan of Arc, 144
Jomard, Edme, 62
Jouffroy, Théodore, 115
Juries, 72–4, 216

Kames, Henry Home,
Lord, 156
Kant, Immanuel, 54, 97,
107–8, 113–15, 129,
134–5
Koch, Christoph-Wilhelm,
48, 143
Kuhn, Thomas, 16

Lacepède, Bernard-
Germain-Étienne de la
Ville-sur-Illon, Comte
de, 41, 85
Lacretelle, Pierre-Louis,
22
Lacuée, Jean-Gérard, 41,
59–60, 74, 201, 214
Lacurne de Sainte-Palaye,
Jean-Baptiste de, 142
Laharpe, Jean-François,
86
Lakanal, Joseph, 36–8,
41, 43, 47, 102
Lalande, Jérôme, 40–1,
215
La Mettrie, Julien Offray
de, 53, 114, 120
Lancelin, Pierre-François,
103, 116
Lancret, M.-A., 62
Landed wealth and
mobile wealth, 201–3
Language: Académie
française dictionary
and, 89–90; Pasigra-
phy and, 103–4; Revo-
lution and, 79; use of,
4; well-made, 28, 96,
102–5. See also Condil-
lac; Degérando; Garat;
Laromiguière
Lapérouse, Jean-François
de Galaup, Comte de,
82
Laplace, Pierre-Simon,
Marquis de, 29, 85,
188–9
La Revellière-Lépeaux,
Louis-Marie, 47; on
coups d'état, 83–4,
178; on cults, 52, 126;
on deism, 218; on

middle classes, 186; on
natural rights, 177
Laromiguière, Pierre, 28,
43, 49; and Auteuil cir-
cle, 39; on Condillac
and language, 96–7,
102; and drift from
Idéologues, 53, 81; on
ideas, 81; on Kant and
eclectics, 113, 115–16;
on transformed sensa-
tions, 103, 106–7; and
Tribunate, 232
Lavoisier, Antoine-
Laurent, 19, 29, 102–
4, 198, 200
Le Breton, Joachim, 39,
49, 58, 189, 200
Lebrun, Charles-François,
47, 87, 214
Leclerc de Montlinot,
Charles-Antoine, 59
Lefebvre de La Roche,
Martin, 89
Legouvé, Gabriel-Marie-
Jean-Baptiste, 85
Legrand d'Aussy, Pierre-
Jean-Baptiste, 139,
142–3, 151
Leibniz, Gottfried
Wilhelm, 126
Le Mercier de la Rivière,
Pierre-Paul, 24, 193
Lenoir, Alexandre, 143
Lescallier, Daniel, 41, 82
Letourneur, Emmanuel-
Pierre, 13
Lévesque, Pierre-Charles,
42, 54; and antidemo-
cratic interpretation of
history, 145–6, 151; on
archaeology, 143; on
empiricism, 52; on
Enlightenment, 138,
144; on human pas-
sions, 140; on Revolu-
tion, 149; on
scepticism, 141, 144;
on stages of history,
139, 142, 219
Liberge de Granchain,
Guillaume-Jacques-

Constant de, 41–2, 44, 47–8
Locke, John, 52, 92, 107; and Condillac, 27; and Delisle de Sales, 126; and individual rights, 21, 25, 173–4; on labour theory of value, 201; and Mercier, 113; on pleasure and pain, 28, 119
Luther, Martin, 76
Luxury, 26, 205–6
Lycée: Bonaparte's secondary schools, 223–4; Daunou's proposed higher education institute, 35, 58; national, 34
adult education private forum: as Athénée royal, 226, 299n43; for Condorcet, 29; for Coquebert, 159; for Degérando, 107; for Garat, 51; for Roederer, 106–10, 202–4

Mably, Gabriel Bonnot de, 145
Machiavelli, Niccolò, 110, 220
Maimieux, Joseph de, 103–4
Maine de Biran, François-Pierre Gontier, 97; break with Condillac, 217; on decomposition of thought, 109–10; on fantasy, 117; on habit, 112–13; and Société de Philosophie, 115
Maistre, Joseph de, 152, 219
Malte-Brun, Conrad, 62
Marat, Jean-Paul, 10, 12, 64
Marmontel, Jean-François, 86
Marx, Karl, 105, 185–6
Masonic lodges, 6, 11, 40

Maugras, Jean-Baptiste, 109
Maury, Jean-Sifrein, Abbé, 87
Mentelle, Edme, 62, 155, 159–60
Mercantilism, 191. See also Forbonnais
Mercier, Louis-Sébastien, 51, 92, 97, 133; anti-Idéologue, 53–4; anti-Newtonian science, 79; and censorship, 130; and Kant, 113–15; on moral philosophy, 119, 129, 216, 218; at public session, 89
Merlin de Douai, Philippe-Antoine, 47, 78, 84, 177, 179, 214
Middle classes, 146. See also Bourgeoisie, ideology of
Mignet, François, 152, 219, 228
Millot, Claude-François, Abbé, 147
Minerva, head of, 4, 222
Mirabeau, Honoré-Gabriel-Riqueti de, 33–4, 111
Mirabeau, Victor Riqueti, Marquis de, 23, 191
Monge, Gaspard, 41, 61
Mongez, Antoine, 42
Montesquieu, Charles-Louis de Secondat, Baron de: and Baudin des Ardennes, 178; and Destutt de Tracy, 181, 183–6; environmental imperative and climate, 30–1, 156–7, 219; and geography, 168–9; and Grouvelle, 174; and history, 152; and juries, 73; and paternal power, 71; and public loans, 74; and Revolution, 146; science of government, 19–22, 172, 189,

220; and general spirit, 132, 153; and separation of powers, 184–5
Moral and political sciences: origin of term, 24
Morality and history, 138–9
Moral science, 118–35; and sympathy, 278
Morellet, André, 10, 53, 78; and Académie française, 87–9; and eloquence, 90–1, 94, 212, 224; and royalism, 79
Mullot, Charles, 112
Musée de Paris, 11

Naigeon, Jacques-André, 68, 124, 127
Native Americans, 160–2, 167–8, 170. See also Bougainville; Volney
Natural law, 16, 118; and history, 151; and Volney, 122–3, 218
Natural rights: and Declaration of Rights and Duties (of 1795), 176–8; and Delisle de Sales, 147; and Physiocrats, 25; and utilitarianism, 173–4, 180–5, 221
Necker, Jacques, 199
Neo-Jacobins, 178–9
Newton, Isaac, 19; and method, 31, 119; opposition to, 53–4, 92, 106
Nobility in Class of Moral and Political Sciences, 44
Nougarède, André-Jean-Simon, 71–2

Palissot, Charles, 89
Papon, Jean-Pierre, 47–8; on fanaticism, 144; and Genoese trade, 82; on geography in historical

writing, 141; and
morality, 138–9; on
plots and Revolution,
145, 148–9
Pascal, Blaise, 126
Pastoret, Charles-
Emmanuel-Joseph-
Pierre, Marquis de:
and Class of History
and Ancient Literature,
85, 225; and Council
of Five Hundred, 57;
and coups d'état, 38,
42, 84, 179; and royal-
ism, 47, 147–8
Paternal power, 70–2,
216
Patronage: in Enlighten-
ment, 9–10; in Insti-
tute, 38–41, 215,
257n9
Pauw, Cornelis de, 158,
169–70
Péron, François, 63,
166–70
Perrault, Charles, 34
Petitain, Louis-Germain,
70–1, 131, 179
Physiocratic economists,
19, 183, 191–5, 199,
201–5, 208–10, 221;
and Morellet, 89; and
proprietors, 32; and
public loans, 74; and
single land tax, 24,
67; and social science,
23–7, 185, 190; and
stages of history, 26.
See also political
economy
Pinel, Philippe, 103
Political economy, 23–7,
67, 191–210; division
of labour, 175; and
loans, 74; and luxury,
205–6; and morality,
131; and sources of
wealth, 201–3; and
taxes, 74–5, 203–5.
See also Physiocratic
economists; Smith; sta-
tistics

Political science, 20–2,
172–90. See also
Baudin des Ardennes;
Montesquieu; Sieyès
Polynesians, 161, 163–7.
See also Bougainville;
Fleurieu
Ponce, Nicolas, 140
Portalis, Jean-Étienne-
Marie, 75, 87, 224
Press: Ami des Lois, 85,
179; Annales catho-
liques, 84; audience
and circulation, 79,
265n2; Clef du cabinet
des souverains, 61, 81;
Décade philosophique,
86–7, 100, 192;
Gazette de France, 10,
85–6, 93, 224; Globe,
115; Grub Street, 6,
10; Journal de Paris,
10, 61, 83, 88, 222;
Journal des Débats, 85–
7, 89, 224; Journal des
Économistes, 228;
Journal des hommes
libres, 79; Le Mémo-
rial, 84; Mercure, 86,
88, 100, 224; Nou-
velles politiques, 61;
Le Publiciste, 81, 86
Prévost, Pierre, 40
Prize contests: and Acad-
emy membership,
263n31; in Ancien
Régime, 5, 12; in
Class of Moral and
Political Sciences, 64–
77, 216
Prony, Gaspard-Riche de,
41
Public assistance, 59–60
Public sessions of Insti-
tute, 13, 79–83, 212

Quesnay, François: eco-
nomic system, 23–4,
191–2, 194; and lux-
ury, 205; and stages of
history, 26, 156; and
taxation, 203

Race: and Bougainville,
154–6; and Cuvier,
156; and Grégoire,
125; and Humboldt,
170
Raimond, Julien, 289n33
Ramond de Carbon-
nières, Louis-François-
Élisabeth, 30, 47, 147,
175
Raynal, Guillaume-
Thomas, 170
Reid, Thomas, 107, 115
Reinhard, Carl-Friedrich,
41, 214
Restoration liberals, 226
Revolution, historical
interpretation in Insti-
tute of French, 144–9
Rey, Joseph, 126
Richelieu, Armand-Jean
du Plessis, Cardinal de,
11–12
Robertson, William, 156,
158, 168, 170
Robespierre, Maximilien:
and de-Christianiza-
tion, 121; and deism,
95, 122; and habits,
117; and poverty, 124;
and price maximum,
175; and prize con-
tests, 64–5
Roederer, Pierre-Louis,
41, 56; and Académie
française, 87, 90; and
Academy of Moral and
Political Sciences, 227;
and education, 57–8,
64, 223, 225; and Fruc-
tidor coup exiles, 84–
5; and Institute mem-
oirs, 50, 68; and
Lavoisier, 198; and
Lycée lectures on eco-
nomics, 110–11, 203–
9, 221; and middle
classes, 186; and oppor-
tunism, 51, 55, 58,
181, 185, 214; and
political science, 172,
175–7; and press, 81;

and prize contest commissions, 49, 67, 69–70, 74, 76, 129, 131, 134; and social mobility, 133, 179, 202, 220; and social science, 22, 223; and Société de 1789, 30; and transformed sensations, 106; and Volney, 121

Rohan, Louis-René-Édouard, Cardinal de, 87

Romme, Nicolas-Charles, 41

Rorty, Richard, 230

Rosetta Stone, 262n24

Rousseau, Jean-Jacques, 9, 13, 54; on animals, 80; on censorship, 101, 116, 130; on civil rights, 21; deism, 119–20; on emulation, 132; on general will, 29, 173; influence of, 91, 93, 111, 146, 167; on representation, 175; on "savages" and progress, 26, 155, 158, 160, 163; on women, 99

Roussel, Pierre, 39, 96, 100–1

Royalism in Class of Moral and Political Sciences, 47–8, 144–5. See also Directory, and coup of Fructidor

Royer-Collard, Pierre-Paul, 107, 115

Sabatier, Raphaël-Bienvenu, 85

Sade, Donatien-Alphonse-François, Marquis de, 15, 123, 224

Saint-Lambert, Jean-François de, 58, 69, 86–7

Saint-Simon, Claude-Henri, Comte de, 115, 173, 187, 221, 226–7

Sans-culottes, 3, 6, 121, 221

"Savages" and progress, 155, 165–70, 218; and Degérando, 165–6; in Marquesas, 163; in Queen Charlottes, 161–4; in Tahiti, 161–4

Say, Jean-Baptiste: on debt and luxury, 203, 205–7; and morality, 129–30; and political economy, 131–2, 192, 195, 208–10, 221; and social mobility, 133; and statistics, 200

Senebier, Jean, 43

Sèze, Victor de, 39, 127

Sicard, Roch-Ambroise, 84–5, 102, 165

Sieyès, Emmanuel-Joseph: and Condillac's transformed sensations, 107–9, 112, 116; and economics, 74, 201, 203, 207; and education, 57; and individual rights, 25, 172–5, 182; and Kant, 114; as patron, 39; political career, 41, 43, 47, 83–4, 97, 102, 178–9, 208, 214; political theory of, 7, 20, 180–1, 183, 185–6, 219; on representation and sovereignty, 176–7, 220; on social science, 22, 176

Silvestre de Sacy, Antoine-Isaac, 150

Slavery, 26, 125–6, 194–5, 214, 219

Smith, Adam: and division of labour, 113; and loans, 74; method, 25–6, 31–2; and moral sympathy, 128; and political economy, 131–2, 190–2, 195, 199–200, 205–9, 221; and sources of wealth, 201–

3; and stages of history, 26, 28, 156; and taxation, 204

Social hierarchy, 131. See also Delisle de Sales; Petitain; Toulongeon

Social sciences: definitions and origins, 22, 153; Enlightenment models, 19–32; laws and method in, 14–16

Social stability and the French Revolution, 4, 14, 134, 216–17

Société de 1789, 30

Société de Géographie (Paris), 171

Société des Observateurs de l'Homme, 63, 165–8, 170

Société ethnologique de Paris, 287n74

Spurzheim, Johann Caspar, 115

Staël, Anne-Louise-Germaine Necker, Madame de, 92

Stages of historical progress, 19, 26–7, 32, 139, 151–2, 162–70, 175, 219–20

Statistics, 31, 159, 195, 198–201, 283n17

Stewart, Dugald, 115

Suard, Jean-Baptiste, 9, 86–7, 90

Talleyrand, Charles-Maurice, 35, 37, 41, 43–4; and colonies, 82, 87, 155; and coup of Brumaire, 179; and Egypt, 57, 60–1, 64; and planning of Institute, 33

Target, Guy-Jean-Baptiste, 87

Terror, 7, 36–7, 132, 149, 174, 176, 216; and academies, 13; and Class of Moral and Political Sciences,

46–7, 92; and de-
Christianization, 120;
and Delisle de Sales,
128; and Lévesque,
145; and meaning of
Revolution, 220; and
virtue, 123
Theophilanthropy, 121,
126, 129
Thierry, Augustin, 151,
219
Thiers, Adolphe, 151–2
Thouret, Michel-
Augustin, 59–60
Thurot, François, 115
Toulongeon, François-
Emmanuel, Vicomte
de, 41–2, 47; on causal
explanation, 140, 141,
148; on hierarchy, 131;
on history and ideol-
ogy, 80–1; and moral-
ity, 138; and royalism,
81, 146–8
Turgot, Anne-Robert-
Jacques, Baron de: as
controller-general, 194;
as economist, 23, 25,
89, 191, 198, 202–3,

207–8; and prize con-
tests, 67; and stages of
history, 26, 156; and
theory of probability,
29

Verdun de la Crenne,
Jean-René-Antoine,
Marquis de, 41–2, 47–8
Vico, Giambattista, 142
Vicq d'Azyr, Félix, 102
Vidal de la Blache, Paul,
171, 219
Villeneuve-Bargemont,
Jean-Paul-Alban,
Vicomte de, 228
Villermé, Louis-René,
199, 217
Villers, Charles, 75–6,
114
Villeterque, Alexandre-
Louis de, 41
Volney, Constantin-
François, Chassebeuf
de, 47; and Académie
française, 87; career
of, 40, 165; on Ameri-
cans and French Cana-
dians, 158; and climate

theory, 22, 141, 156–
7, 219; and Egypt, 61–
2, 64; and geography,
154–5, 164, 282n4; on
individual rights and
political science, 172,
174, 219; and moral
catechism, 121–4, 127,
129, 133, 135; on
native Americans and
geography, 168–71;
and philosophical his-
tory, 137, 140, 143,
150–2, 218; on statis-
tics, 159, 166
Voltaire, François-Marie
Arouet de: and Enlight-
enment spirit, 6–9, 54,
91; and deism, 95,
132; and history, 137,
144, 160; and Revolu-
tion, 146

Weber, Max, 15
Women, temperament of,
99–102, 217
Work ethic, 131

Zola, Émile, 8–9